A·N·N·U·A·L E·D·I·T·I·O·N·S

Business Ethics   *05/06*

Seventeenth Edition

EDITOR

John E. Richardson

Pepperdine University

Dr. John E. Richardson is a professor of marketing in the George L. Graziadio School of Business and Management at Pepperdine University. He is president of his own consulting firm and has consulted with organizations such as Bell and Howell, Dayton-Hudson, Epson, and the U.S. Navy, as well as with various service, nonprofit, and franchise organizations. Dr. Richardson is a member of the American Management Association, the American Marketing Association, the Society for Business Ethics, and Beta Gamma Sigma honorary business fraternity.

McGraw-Hill/Dushkin

2460 Kerper Blvd., Dubuque, Iowa 52001

Visit us on the Internet
http://www.dushkin.com

Credits

1. **Ethics, Values, and Social Responsibility in Business**
   Unit photo—© Getty Images/PhotoLink
2. **Ethical Issues and Dilemmas in the Workplace**
   Unit photo—© Getty Images/PhotoLink/Jack Starr
3. **Business and Society: Contemporary Ethical, Social, and Environmental Issues**
   Unit photo—© Getty Images/PhotoLink/Ryan McVay
4. **Ethics and Social Responsibility in the Marketplace**
   Unit photo—© Getty Images/Javier Pierini
5. **Developing the Future Ethos and Social Responsibility of Business**
   Unit photo—© Getty Images/Keith Brofsky

Copyright

Cataloging in Publication Data
Main entry under title: Annual Editions: Business Ethics. 2005/2006.
1. Business Ethics—Periodicals. I. Richardson, John, *comp*. II. Title: Business Ethics.
ISBN 0–07–310196–6   658'.05   ISSN 1055–5455

Seventeenth Edition

Cover image © Photos.com
Printed in the United States of America   1234567890QPDQPD987654   Printed on Recycled Paper

Editors/Advisory Board

Members of the Advisory Board are instrumental in the final selection of articles for each edition of ANNUAL EDITIONS. Their review of articles for content, level, currency, and appropriateness provides critical direction to the editor and staff. We think that you will find their careful consideration well reflected in this volume.

Preface

In publishing ANNUAL EDITIONS we recognize the enormous role played by the magazines, newspapers, and journals of the public press in providing current, first-rate educational information in a broad spectrum of interest areas. Many of these articles are appropriate for students, researchers, and professionals seeking accurate, current material to help bridge the gap between principles and theories and the real world. These articles, however, become more useful for study when those of lasting value are carefully collected, organized, indexed, and reproduced in a low-cost format, which provides easy and permanent access when the material is needed. That is the role played by ANNUAL EDITIONS.

Recent events have brought ethics to the forefront as a topic of discussion throughout our nation. And, undoubtedly, the area of society that is getting the closest scrutiny regarding its ethical practices is the business sector. Both the print and broadcast media have offered a constant stream of facts and opinions concerning recent unethical goings-on in the business world. Insider trading scandals on Wall Street, the marketing of unsafe products, money laundering, and questionable contracting practices are just a few examples of events that have recently tarnished the image of business.

As corporate America struggles to find its ethical identity in a business environment that grows increasingly complex, managers are confronted with some poignant questions that have definite ethical ramifications. Does a company have any obligation to help solve social problems such a poverty, pollution, and urban decay? What ethical responsibilities should a multinational corporation assume in foreign countries? What obligation does a manufacturer have to the consumer with respect to product defects and safety?

These are just a few of the issues that make the study of business ethics important and challenging. A significant goal of *Annual Editions: Business Ethics 05/06* is to present some different perspectives on understanding basic concepts and concerns of business ethics and to provide ideas on how to incorporate these concepts into the policies and decision-making processes of businesses. The articles reprinted in this publication have been care-fully chosen from a variety of public press sources to furnish current information on business ethics.

This volume contains a number of features designed to make it useful for students, researchers, and professionals. These include the *table of contents* with summaries of each article and key concepts in italics, a *topic guide* for locating articles on specific subjects related to business ethics, and a comprehensive *index*.

Also, included in this edition are selected *World Wide Web* sites that can be used to further explore article topics.

The articles are organized into five units. Selections that focus on similar issues are concentrated into subsections within the broader units. Each unit is preceded by an overview which provides background for informed reading of the articles, emphasizes critical issues, and presents key points to consider that focus on major themes running through the selections.

Your comments, opinions, and recommendations about *Annual Editions: Business Ethics 05/06* will be greatly appreciated and will help shape future editions. Please take a moment to complete and return the postage-paid *article rating form* on the last page of this book. Any book can be improved, and with your help this one will continue to be.

John E. Richardson

John E. Richardson
Editor

Contents

UNIT 1
Ethics, Values, and Social Responsibility in Business

UNIT 2
Ethical Issues and Dilemmas in the Workplace

The concepts in bold italics are developed in the article. For further expansion, please refer to the Topic Guide and the Index.

The concepts in bold italics are developed in the article. For further expansion, please refer to the Topic Guide and the Index.

UNIT 3
Business and Society: Contemporary Ethical, Social, and Environmental Issues

The concepts in bold italics are developed in the article. For further expansion, please refer to the Topic Guide and the Index.

UNIT 4
Ethics and Social Responsibility in the Marketplace

The concepts in bold italics are developed in the article. For further expansion, please refer to the Topic Guide and the Index.

UNIT 5
Developing the Future Ethos and Social Responsibility of Business

The concepts in bold italics are developed in the article. For further expansion, please refer to the Topic Guide and the Index.

The concepts in bold italics are developed in the article. For further expansion, please refer to the Topic Guide and the Index.

Topic Guide

This topic guide suggests how the selections in this book relate to the subjects covered in your course. You may want to use the topics listed on these pages to search the Web more easily.

On the following pages a number of Web sites have been gathered specifically for this book. They are arranged to reflect the units of this *Annual Edition.* You can link to these sites by going to the DUSHKIN ONLINE support site at *http://www.dushkin.com/online/.*

ALL THE ARTICLES THAT RELATE TO EACH TOPIC ARE LISTED BELOW THE BOLD-FACED TERM.

Auditing
9. Corruption: Causes and Cures
20. Between Right and Right
21. The Padding That Hurts

Brands
25. Does It Pay To Be Good?
26. Trust in the Marketplace
30. A Dose of Denial
35. Diversity Training Ups Saks' Sales
39. Using Conversation to Change the World

Business and government
17. A Hero—and a Smoking-Gun Letter
30. A Dose of Denial

Business and law
17. A Hero—and a Smoking-Gun Letter

Business environment
17. A Hero—and a Smoking-Gun Letter

Business ethics
3. Ethics Can Be Gauged By Three Key Rules
4. Why Good Leaders Do Bad Things
34. A Matter of Trust
40. Business Ethics in the Current Environment of Fraud and Corruption
43. Are You Serious About Ethics?
46. Ensuring Ethical Effectiveness

Code of ethics
5. Best Resources for Corporate Social Responsibility
24. Ethical Compass
31. Values in Tension: Ethics Away From Home
34. A Matter of Trust
37. Managing for Organizational Integrity
43. Are You Serious About Ethics?
44. "See No Evil, Hear No Evil, Speak No Evil"—Leaders Must Respond to Employee Concerns About Wrongdoing
45. Why Corporations Can't Control Chicanery

Conflicts of interest
9. Corruption: Causes and Cures
10. Crony Capitalism
16. Into Thin Air
18. Hall Monitors in the Workplace: Encouraging Employee Whistleblowers
19. Academic Values and the Lure of Profit
20. Between Right and Right
21. The Padding That Hurts
22. Costco's Dilemma: Be Kind to Its Workers, or Wall Street?
23. The Parable of the Sadhu
25. Does It Pay To Be Good?
26. Trust in the Marketplace
30. A Dose of Denial
40. Business Ethics in the Current Environment of Fraud and Corruption
41. Ethics for a Post-Enron America

45. Why Corporations Can't Control Chicanery

Consumer protection
18. Hall Monitors in the Workplace: Encouraging Employee Whistleblowers
21. The Padding That Hurts
22. Costco's Dilemma: Be Kind to Its Workers, or Wall Street?
29. Privacy in the Age of Transparency
30. A Dose of Denial
33. The Perils of Doing the Right Thing

Discrimination
6. You've Got Mail…And The Boss Knows
7. Up Against Wal-Mart
11. Sexual Harassment and Retaliation: A Double-Edged Sword
13. Attitudes Toward Affirmative Action
14. Where Are the Women?
15. "Rife with Discrimination"
26. Trust in the Marketplace
27. Glass Breakers
32. Mideast Businesswomen Fight for Respect
35. Diversity Training Ups Saks' Sales
36. Surviving in the Age of Rage
45. Why Corporations Can't Control Chicanery

Diversity
13. Attitudes Toward Affirmative Action
15. "Rife with Discrimination"
27. Glass Breakers
28. Change of Heart
35. Diversity Training Ups Saks' Sales
39. Using Conversation to Change the World

Downsizing
16. Into Thin Air
20. Between Right and Right
43. Are You Serious About Ethics?

Economic environment
7. Up Against Wal-Mart
22. Costco's Dilemma: Be Kind to Its Workers, or Wall Street?
25. Does It Pay To Be Good?
32. Mideast Businesswomen Fight for Respect

Employee compensation
7. Up Against Wal-Mart
22. Costco's Dilemma: Be Kind to Its Workers, or Wall Street?

Employee responsibility
36. Surviving in the Age of Rage

Employee rights
1. Thinking Ethically: A Framework for Moral Decision Making
5. Best Resources for Corporate Social Responsibility
6. You've Got Mail…And The Boss Knows
7. Up Against Wal-Mart
15. "Rife with Discrimination"
29. Privacy in the Age of Transparency
32. Mideast Businesswomen Fight for Respect

World Wide Web Sites

The following World Wide Web sites have been carefully researched and selected to support the articles found in this reader. The easiest way to access these selected sites is to go to our DUSHKIN ONLINE support site at *http://www.dushkin.com/online/*.

AE: Business Ethics 05/06

The following sites were available at the time of publication. Visit our Web site—we update DUSHKIN ONLINE regularly to reflect any changes.

General Sources

American Civil Liberties Union (ACLU)
http://www.aclu.org/issues/worker/campaign.html

The ACLU provides this page in its "Campaign for Fairness in the Workplace." Papers cover such privacy issues as lifestyle discrimination, drug testing, and electronic monitoring.

CBSR (Canadian Business for Social Responsibility)
http://www.cbsr.bc.ca

CBSR says this is a "one-stop shop" for information on corporate social responsibility in Canada. You'll find news articles, member news, best practices, and resources.

Center for the Study of Ethics in the Professions
http://www.iit.edu/departments/csep/

Sponsored by the Illinois Institute of Technology, this site links to a number of world business ethics centers.

GreenMoney Journal
http://www.greenmoneyjournal.com

The editorial vision of this publication proposes that consumer spending and investment dollars can bring about positive social and environmental change. On this Web site, they'll tell you how.

Harvard Business School (HBS)
http://www.hbs.edu/educators.html

Surf through the many valuable links attached to this Educators and Research News site to preview upcoming issues of the *Harvard Business Review*.

Markkula Center
http://www.scu.edu/SCU/Centers/Ethics/

Santa Clara University's Markkula Center strives to heighten ethical awareness and to improve ethical decision making on campus and within the community. A list of published resources, links to ethical issues sites, and other data are provided.

Stockholm University
http://www.psychology.su.se/units/ao/ao.html

Explore topics related to job design and other business organizational concerns through this site presented by the Division of Work and Organizational Psychology.

U.S. Department of Labor
http://www.dol.gov

Browsing through this site will lead to a vast array of labor-related data and discussions of issues affecting employees and managers, such as the minimum wage.

U.S. Equal Employment Opportunity Commission (EEOC)
http://www.eeoc.gov

The EEOC's mission "is to ensure equality of opportunity by vigorously enforcing federal legislation prohibiting discrimination in employment." Consult this site for facts about employment discrimination, enforcement, and litigation.

Wharton Ethics Program
http://ethics.wharton.upenn.edu/

The Wharton School of the University of Pennsylvania provides an independently managed site that offers links to research, cases, and other business ethics centers.

UNIT 1: Ethics, Values, and Social Responsibility in Business

Association for Moral Education (AME)
http://www.amenetwork.org/

AME is dedicated to fostering communication, cooperation, training, and research that links moral theory with educational practices. From here it is possible to connect to several sites of relevance in the study of business ethics.

Business for Social Responsibility (BSR)
http://www.bsr.org/

Core topic areas covered by BSR are listed on this page. They include Corporate Social Responsibility; Business Ethics; Community Investment; the Environment; Governance and Accountability; Human Rights; Marketplace; Mission, Vision, Values; and finally Workplace. New information is added on a regular basis. For each topic or subtopic there is an introduction, examples of large and small company leadership practices, sample company policies, links to helping resources, and other information.

Business Policy and Strategy
http://www.aom.pace.edu/bps/bps.html

This site of the Business Policy and Strategy Division of the Academy of Management is full of information about various topics in business theory and practice.

Enron Online
http://www.enron.com/corp/

Explore the Enron Web site to find information about Enron's history, products, and services. Go to the "Press Room" section for Enron's spin on the current investigation.

Ethics Updates/Lawrence Hinman
http://ethics.sandiego.edu/index.html

This site provides both simple concept definitions and complex analysis of ethics, original treatises, and sophisticated search engine capability. Subject matter covers the gamut, from ethical theory to applied ethical venues.

Institute for Business and Professional Ethics
http://commerce.depaul.edu/ethics/

This site is interested in research in the field of business and professional ethics. It is still under construction, so check in from time to time.

National Center for Policy Analysis
http://www.ncpa.org

This organization's archive links lead you to interesting materials on a variety of topics that affect managers, from immigration issues, to affirmative action, to regulatory policy.

Open Directory Project
http://dmoz.org/Business/Management/Ethics

As part of the Open Directory Project, this page provides a database of Web sites that address numerous topics on ethics in business.

Working Definitions
http://www.workingdefinitions.co.uk/index.html

This is a British, magazine-style site devoted to discussion and comment on organizations in the wider social context and to supporting and developing people's management skills.

UNIT 2: Ethical Issues and Dilemmas in the Workplace

American Psychological Association
http://www.apa.org/homepage.html

Search this site to find references and discussion of important ethics issues for the workplace of the 1990s, including the impact of restructuring and revitalization of businesses.

International Labour Organization (ILO)
http://www.ilo.org

ILO's home page leads you to links that describe the goals of the organization and summarizes international labor standards and human rights. Its official UN Web site locator can point you to many other useful resources.

What You Can Do in Your Workplace
http://www.connectforkids.org/info-url1564/info-url_list.htm?section=Workplace

Browse here for useful hints and guidelines about how employees, employees' families, management, and society can help a company become more family-friendly.

UNIT 3: Business and Society: Contemporary Ethical, Social, and Environmental Issues

CIBERWeb
http://ciber.centers.purdue.edu

This site of the Centers for International Business Education and Research is useful for exploring issues related to business ethics in the international marketplace.

National Immigrant Forum
http://www.immigrationforum.org

The pro-immigrant organization offers this page to examine the effects of immigration on the U.S. economy and society. Click on the links to underground and immigrant economies.

Sympatico: Workplace
http://sympatico.workopolis.com

This Canadian site provides an electronic network with a GripeVine for complaining about work and finding solutions to everyday work problems.

United Nations Environment Programme (UNEP)
http://www.unep.ch

Consult this UNEP site for links to topics such as the impact of trade on the environment. It will direct you to useful databases and global resource information.

United States Trade Representative (USTR)
http://www.ustr.gov

This home page of the U.S. Trade Representative provides links to many U.S. government resources for those interested in ethics in international business.

UNIT 4: Ethics and Social Responsibility in the Marketplace

Business for Social Responsibility (BSR)
http://www.bsr.org/

BSR is a global organization that seeks to help companies "achieve success in ways that respect ethical values, people, communities, and the environment." Links to Services, Resources, and Forum are available.

Total Quality Management Sites
http://www.nku.edu/~lindsay/qualhttp.html

This site points to a variety of interesting Internet sources to aid in the study and application of Total Quality Management principles.

U.S. Navy
http://www.navy.mil

Start at this U.S. Navy page for access to a plethora of interesting stories and analyses related to Total Quality Leadership. It addresses such concerns as how TQL can improve customer service and affect utilization of information technology.

UNIT 5: Developing the Future Ethos and Social Responsibility of Business

Brazil's Instituto Ethos
http://www.ethos.org.br/docs/ingles/index.shtml

Ethos Institute for Corporate Social Responsibility provides this bulletin as an update of its activities and Brazil's progress in developing corporate social responsibility. Click on Vision, Activities, Ethos Indicators, and Guidelines for Social Reporting for an example of a program to encourage corporate social responsibility.

International Business Ethics Institute (IBEI)
http://www.business-ethics.org/index.asp

The goal of this educational organization is to promote business ethics and corporate responsibility in response to the growing need for transnationalism in the field of business ethics.

UNU/IAS Project on Global Ethos
http://www.ias.unu.edu/research/globalethos.cfm

The United Nations University Institute of Advanced Studies (UNU/IAS) has issued this project abstract, which concerns governance and multilateralism. The main aim of the project is to initiate a process by which to generate jointly, with the involvement of factors from both state- and nonstate institutions in developed and developing countries, a global ethos that could provide or support a set of guiding principles for the emerging global community.

We highly recommend that you review our Web site for expanded information and our other product lines. We are continually updating and adding links to our Web site in order to offer you the most usable and useful information that will support and expand the value of your Annual Editions. You can reach us at: *http://www.dushkin.com/annualeditions/.*

UNIT 1

Ethics, Values, and Social Responsibility in Business

Unit Selections

1. **Thinking Ethically: A Framework for Moral Decision Making**, Manuel Velasquez, Claire Andre, Thomas Shanks, and Michael J. Meyer
2. **Ethics: Time to Revisit the Basics**, Gregory D. Foster
3. **Ethics Can Be Gauged By Three Key Rules**, Dillard B. Tinsley
4. **Why Good Leaders Do Bad Things**, Charles D. Kerns
5. **Best Resources for Corporate Social Responsibility**, Karen McNichol

Key Points to Consider

- Do you believe that corporations are more socially responsible today than they were 10 years ago? Why or why not?

- In what specific ways do you see companies practicing social responsibility? Do you think most companies are overt or covert in their social responsibility activities? Explain your answer.

- What are the economic and social implications of "management accountability" as part of the decision-making process? Does a company have any obligation to help remedy social problems, such as poverty, urban decay, and pollution? Defend your response.

- Using the recent examples of stock, financial, and accounting debacles, discuss the flaws in America's financial system that allow companies to disregard ethics, values, and social responsibility in business.

 **Links: www.dushkin.com/online/**
These sites are annotated in the World Wide Web pages.

Association for Moral Education (AME)
http://www.amenetwork.org/

Business for Social Responsibility (BSR)
http://www.bsr.org/

Business Policy and Strategy
http://www.aom.pace.edu/bps/bps.html

Enron Online
http://www.enron.com/corp/

Ethics Updates/Lawrence Hinman
http://ethics.sandiego.edu/index.html

Institute for Business and Professional Ethics
http://commerce.depaul.edu/ethics/

National Center for Policy Analysis
http://www.ncpa.org

Open Directory Project
http://dmoz.org/Business/Management/Ethics

Working Definitions
http://www.workingdefinitions.co.uk/index.html

Ethical decision making in an organization does not occur in a vacuum. As individuals and as managers, we formulate our ethics (that is, the standards of "right" and "wrong" behavior that we set for ourselves) based upon family, peer, and religious influences, our past experiences, and our own unique value systems. When we make ethical decisions within the organizational context, many times there are situational factors and potential conflicts of interest that further complicate the process.

Decisions do not only have personal ramifications—they also have social consequences. Social responsibility is really ethics at the organizational level, since it refers to the obligation that an organization has to make choices and to take actions that will contribute to the good of society as well as the good of the organization. Authentic social responsibility is not initiated because of forced compliance to specific laws and regulations. In contrast to legal responsibility, social responsibility involves a voluntary response from an organization that is above and beyond what is specified by the law.

The selections in this unit provide an overview of the interrelationships of ethics, values, and social responsibility in business. The essays in this unit offer practical and insightful principles and suggestions to managers, enabling them to approach the subject of business ethics with more confidence. They also point out the complexity and the significance of making ethical decisions.

thinking ethically

A FRAMEWORK FOR MORAL DECISION MAKING

DEVELOPED BY MANUEL VELASQUEZ, CLAIRE ANDRE, THOMAS SHANKS, S.J., AND MICHAEL J. MEYER

Moral issues greet us each morning in the newspaper, confront us in the memos on our desks, nag us from our children's soccer fields, and bid us good night on the evening news. We are bombarded daily with questions about the justice of our foreign policy, the morality of medical technologies that can prolong our lives, the rights of the homeless, the fairness of our children's teachers to the diverse students in their classrooms.

Dealing with these moral issues is often perplexing. How, exactly, should we think through an ethical issue? What questions should we ask? What factors should we consider?

The first step in analyzing moral issues is obvious but not always easy: Get the facts.

The first step in analyzing moral issues is obvious but not always easy: Get the facts. Some moral issues create controversies simply because we do not bother to check the facts. This first step, although obvious, is also among the most important and the most frequently overlooked.

But having the facts is not enough. Facts by themselves only tell us what *is;* they do not tell us what *ought* to be. In addition to getting the facts, resolving an ethical issue also requires an appeal to values. Philosophers have developed five different approaches to values to deal with moral issues.

The Utilitarian Approach

Utilitarianism was conceived in the 19th century by Jeremy Bentham and John Stuart Mill to help legislators determine which laws were morally best. Both Bentham and Mill suggested that ethical actions are those that provide the greatest balance of good over evil.

To analyze an issue using the utilitarian approach, we first identify the various courses of action available to us. Second, we ask who will be affected by each action and what benefits or harms will be derived from each. And third, we choose the action that will produce the greatest benefits and the least harm. The ethical action is the one that provides the greatest good for the greatest number.

The Rights Approach

The second important approach to ethics has its roots in the philosophy of the 18th-century thinker Immanuel Kant and others like him, who focused on the individual's right to choose for herself or himself. According to these philosophers, what makes human beings different from mere things is that people have dignity based on their ability to choose freely what they will do with their lives, and they have a fundamental moral right to have these choices respected. People are not objects to be manipulated; it is a violation of human dignity to use people in ways they do not freely choose.

Of course, many different, but related, rights exist besides this basic one. These other rights (an incomplete list below) can be thought of as different aspects of the basic right to be treated as we choose.

- *The right to the truth*: We have a right to be told the truth and to be informed about matters that significantly affect our choices.
- *The right of privacy*: We have the right to do, believe, and say whatever we choose in our personal lives so long as we do not violate the rights of others.

the case of
maria elena

Maria Elena has cleaned your house each week for more than a year. You agree with your friend who recommended her that she does an excellent job and is well worth the $30 cash you pay her for three hours' work. You've also come to like her, and you think she likes you, especially as her English has become better and you've been able to have some pleasant conversations.

Over the past three weeks, however, you've noticed Maria Elena becoming more and more distracted. One day, you ask her if something is wrong, and she tells you she really needs to make additional money. She hastens to say she is not asking you for a raise, becomes upset, and begins to cry. When she calms down a little, she tells you her story:

She came to the United States six years ago from Mexico with her child, Miguel, who is now 7 years old. They entered the country on a visitor's visa that has expired, and Maria Elena now uses a Social Security number she made up.

Her common-law husband, Luis, came to the United States first. He entered the country illegally, after paying smugglers $500 to hide him under piles of grass cuttings for a six-hour truck ride across the border. When he had made enough money from low-paying day jobs, he sent for Maria Elena. Using a false green card, Luis now works as a busboy for a restaurant, which withholds part of his salary for taxes. When Maria Elena comes to work at your house, she takes the bus and Luis baby-sits.

In Mexico, Maria Elena and Luis lived in a small village where it was impossible to earn more than $3 a day. Both had sixth-grade educations, common in their village. Life was difficult, but they did not decide to leave until they realized the future would be bleak for their child and for the other children they wanted to have. Luis had a cousin in San Jose who visited and told Luis and Maria Elena how well his life was going.

After his visit, Luis and Maria Elena decided to come to the United States.

Luis quickly discovered, as did Maria Elena, that life in San Jose was not the way they had heard. The cousin did not tell them they would be able to afford to live only in a run-down three-room apartment with two other couples and their children. He did not tell them they would always live in fear of INS raids.

After they entered the United States, Maria Elena and Luis had a second child, Jose, who is 5 years old. The birth was difficult because she didn't use the health-care system or welfare for fear of being discovered as undocumented. But, she tells you, she is willing to put up with anything so that her children can have a better life. "All the money we make is for Miguel and Jose," she tells you. "We work hard for their education and their future."

Now, however, her mother in Mexico is dying, and Maria Elena must return home, leaving Luis and the children. She does not want to leave them because she might not be able to get back into the United States, but she is pretty sure she can find a way to return if she has enough money. That is her problem: She doesn't have enough money to make certain she can get back.

After she tells you her story, she becomes too distraught to continue talking. You now know she is an undocumented immigrant, working in your home. What is the ethical thing for you to do?

This case was developed by Tom Shanks, S.J., director of the Markkula Center for Applied Ethics. Maria Elena is a composite drawn from several real people, and her story represents some of the ethical dilemmas behind the immigration issue.

This case can be accessed through the Ethics Center home page on the World Wide Web: http://www.scu.edu/Ethics/. You can also contact us by e-mail, ethics@scu.edu, or regular mail: Markkula Center for Applied Ethics, Santa Clara University, Santa Clara, CA 95053. Our voice mail number is (408) 554-7898. We have also posted on our homepage a new case involving managed health care.

- *The right not to be injured*: We have the right not to be harmed or injured unless we freely and knowingly do something to deserve punishment or we freely and knowingly choose to risk such injuries.

- *The right to what is agreed*: We have a right to what has been promised by those with whom we have freely entered into a contract or agreement.

In deciding whether an action is moral or immoral using this second approach, then, we must ask, Does the action respect the moral rights of everyone? Actions are wrong to the extent that they violate the rights of individuals; the more serious the violation, the more wrongful the action.

The Fairness or Justice Approach

The fairness or justice approach to ethics has its roots in the teachings of the ancient Greek philosopher Aristotle, who said that "equals should be treated equally and unequals unequally." The basic moral question in this approach is: How fair is an action? Does it treat everyone in the same way, or does it show favoritism and discrimination?

Favoritism gives benefits to some people without a justifiable reason for singling them out; discrimination imposes burdens on people who are no different from those on whom burdens are not imposed. Both favoritism and discrimination are unjust and wrong.

The Common-Good Approach

This approach to ethics presents a vision of society as a community whose members are joined in the shared pursuit of values and goals they hold in common. This community comprises individuals whose own good is inextricably bound to the good of the whole.

The common good is a notion that originated more than 2,000 years ago in the writings of Plato, Aristotle, and Cicero. More recently, contemporary ethicist John Rawls defined the common good as "certain general conditions that are… equally to everyone's advantage."

In this approach, we focus on ensuring that the social policies, social systems, institutions, and environments on which we depend are beneficial to all. Examples of goods common to all include affordable health care, effective public safety, peace among nations, a just legal system, and an unpolluted environment.

Appeals to the common good urge us to view ourselves as members of the same community, reflecting on broad questions concerning the kind of society we want to become and how we are to achieve that society. While respecting and valuing the freedom of individuals to pursue their own goals, the common-good approach challenges us also to recognize and further those goals we share in common.

The Virtue Approach

The virtue approach to ethics assumes that there are certain ideals toward which we should strive, which provide for the full development of our humanity. These ideals are discovered through thoughtful reflection on what kind of people we have the potential to become.

Virtues are attitudes or character traits that enable us to be and to act in ways that develop our highest potential. They enable us to pursue the ideals we have adopted.

Honesty, courage, compassion, generosity, fidelity, integrity, fairness, self-control, and prudence are all examples of virtues.

Virtues are like habits; that is, once acquired, they become characteristic of a person. Moreover, a person who has developed virtues will be naturally disposed to act in ways consistent with moral principles. The virtuous person is the ethical person.

In dealing with an ethical problem using the virtue approach, we might ask, What kind of person should I be? What will promote the development of character within myself and my community?

Ethical Problem Solving

These five approaches suggest that once we have ascertained the facts, we should ask ourselves five questions when trying to resolve a moral issue:

- What benefits and what harms will each course of action produce, and which alternative will lead to the best overall consequences?
- What moral rights do the affected parties have, and which course of action best respects those rights?
- Which course of action treats everyone the same, except where there is a morally justifiable reason not to, and does not show favoritism or discrimination?
- Which course of action advances the common good?
- Which course of action develops moral virtues?

This method, of course, does not provide an automatic solution to moral problems. It is not meant to. The method is merely meant to help identify most of the important ethical considerations. In the end, we must deliberate on moral issues for ourselves, keeping a careful eye on both the facts and on the ethical considerations involved.

FOR FURTHER READING

Frankena, William. *Ethics*, 2nd ed. (Englewood Cliffs, N.J.: Prentice Hall, 1973).

Halberstam, Joshua. *Everyday Ethics: Inspired Solutions to Real Life Dilemmas* (New York: Penguin Books, 1993).

Martin, Michael. *Everyday Morality* (Belmont, Calif: Wadsworth, 1995).

Rachels, James. *The Elements of Moral Philosophy*, 2nd ed. (New York: McGraw-Hill, 1993).

Velasquez, Manuel. *Business Ethics: Concepts and Cases*, 3rd ed. (Englewood Cliffs, N.J.: Prentice Hall, 1992) 2–110.

This article updates several previous pieces from Issues in Ethics *by Manuel Velasquez—Dirksen Professor of Business Ethics at SCU and former Center director—and Claire Andre, associate Center director. "Thinking Ethically" is based on a framework developed by the authors in collaboration with Center Director Thomas Shanks, S.J., Presidential Professor of Ethics and the Common Good Michael J. Meyer, and others. The framework is used as the basis for many Center programs and presentations.*

Ethics:
time to revisit the basics

by gregory d. foster

ethics could be said to be very much like the weather in the sense that everybody talks about it but nobody does much about it.

Nearly all of us acknowledge the importance of ethics. Most of us hope for and expect ethical behavior and treatment from particular segments of society. Some of us pay close attention to the subject and seek to engage others in discussing (and practicing) it. But regrettably few of us really understand ethics as well as we think we do or as well as we should.

When people discuss ethics, there is a widespread tendency to gloss over the fundamental nature of the subject—as if it is so widely and well understood as to obviate the need for frustrating, time-consuming exegesis. The thinking is that it is better to immerse ourselves in real-world applications. After all, hasn't all that can be said on the subject already been said?

Yet, as with so many ostensibly well-understood concepts that provide continuing sources of disagreement, too much is left to assumption. Otherwise why do so many of us hedge our bets in daily discourse by consistently invoking the semantic couplet of "ethics and morality," much as we do in referring to "training and education" or "order and stability"? We aren't sure if there is a meaningful distinction between the two terms, but we don't want to sound stupid if there is, so we rarely mention the one without the other.

Why, similarly, do we so frequently conflate ethics and the law or morality and religion? Is complying with the law necessarily ethical and breaking the law unethical? Can a person be morally upright only by conforming to the dictates of religion? Conversely, does religiosity equate with ethical conduct?

And why, if we understand ethics so well, can't we reach readier agreement on what issues are ethical ones and thereby deserve to be treated as such? Pick an issue; the possibilities are endless: abortion; globalization; capital punishment; defense spending; gun control; genetic engineering; church-state relations; drugs; foreign aid; poverty, economic inequality, and welfare; intelligence gathering; affirmative action; covert operations; corporate performance and responsibility; democracy; military intervention; environmental degradation; government secrecy; privacy and transparency; health care; campaign financing; law enforcement and criminal justice; literacy and education; trade; immigration; propaganda; unemployment; homeland security.

> Ethics can be meaningfully discussed and applied only when it is fully understood. Such understanding requires that we periodically revisit the basics.

Such matters, even if they are predominantly political, economic, social, or military in nature, nonetheless have demonstrable ethical dimensions or ramifications. If we fail to recognize this fact, if we fail more fundamentally to understand ethics itself, we do the issues and those affected by them a serious disservice.

Ethics can't be dealt with as Justice Potter Stewart famously dealt with the inherent complexity of pornography. We can't, in other words, avoid defining pornography and say we know it when we see it because it isn't clear that we do. Ethics can be meaningfully discussed and applied only when it is fully understood. Such understanding requires that we periodically revisit the basics.

What Ethics is About

So for starters, what is ethics actually all about? Ethics is about right and wrong:

"No man is prejudiced in favor of a thing knowing it to be wrong. He is attached to it on the belief of its being right."—Thomas Paine, *The Rights of Man*.

"We do not call anything wrong, unless we mean to imply that a person ought to be punished in some way or other for doing it; if not by law, by the opinion of his fellow creatures; if not by opinion, by the reproaches of his own conscience. This seems the real turning point of the distinction between morality and simple expediency."—John Stuart Mill, *Utilitarianism*.

Ethics is about good and bad, or good and evil.

"Things then are good or evil, only in reference to pleasure and pain. That we call good, which is apt to cause or increase pleasure, or diminish pain in us; or else to procure or preserve us the possession of any other good or absence of any evil. And, on the contrary, we name that evil which is apt to produce or increase any pain, or diminish any pleasure in us: or else to procure us any evil, or deprive us of any good."—John Locke, *Concerning Human Understanding*.

"Moral philosophy is nothing else but the science of what is good and evil in the conversation and society of mankind. *Good* and *evil* are names that signify our appetites and aversions, which in different tempers, customs, and doctrines of men are different: and diverse men differ not only in their judgment on the senses of what is pleasant and unpleasant to the taste, smell, hearing, touch, and sight; but also of what is conformable or disagreeable to reason in the actions of common life.... So long as a man is in the condition of mere nature, which is a condition of war, private appetite is the measure of good and evil: and consequently all men agree on this, that peace is good, and therefore also the way or means of peace, which… are *justice, gratitude, modesty, equity, mercy*, and the rest of the laws of nature, are good; that is to say, moral virtues; and their contrary vices, evil."—Thomas Hobbes, *Leviathan*.

Ethics is about virtue and vice.

"It seems to me that virtue is something other and nobler than the inclinations toward goodness that are born in us. Souls naturally regulated and well-born follow the same path, and show the same countenance in their actions, as virtuous ones. But virtue means something greater and more active than letting oneself, by a happy disposition, be led gently and peacefully in the footsteps of reason. He who through a natural mildness and easygoingness should despise injuries received would do a very fine and praiseworthy thing; but he who, outraged and stung to the quick by an injury, should arm himself with the arms of reason against this furious appetite for vengeance, and after a great conflict should finally master it, would without doubt do much more. The former would do well, and the other virtuously; one action might be called goodness, the other virtue. For it seems that the name of virtue presupposes difficulty and contrast, and that it cannot be exercised without opposition."—Michel de Montaigne, *Essays* .

"Vice, the opposite of virtue, shows us more clearly what virtue is. Justice becomes more obvious when we have injustice to compare it to. Many such things are proved by their contraries."—Quintilian, *Institutio Oratoria*.

Ethics is about benefit and harm.

"A man can confer the greatest of benefits by a right use of [such things as strength, health, wealth, generalship] and inflict the greatest of injuries by using them wrongly."—Aristotle, *Rhetoric*.

"The two essential ingredients in the sentiment of justice are the desire to punish a person who has done harm, and the knowledge or belief that there is some definite individual or individuals to whom harm has been done."—John Stuart Mill, *Utilitarianism*.

Ethics is about propriety and impropriety.

"*Socrates*. And will not the temperate man do what is proper, both in relation to the gods and to men—for he would not be temperate if he did not? Certainly he will do what is proper. In his relation to other men he will do what is just; and in his relation to the gods he will do what is holy."—Plato, *Gorgias*.

"Without an acquaintance with the rules of propriety, it is impossible for the character to be established."—Confucius, *The Analects*.

But **ethics** isn't simply about all these things—right and wrong, good and bad, virtue and vice, benefit and harm, propriety and impropriety.

But ethics isn't simply about all these things—right and wrong, good and bad, virtue and vice, benefit and harm, propriety and impropriety. So too is it about principle—fixed, universal rules of right conduct that are contingent on neither time nor culture nor circumstance:

"If habit is not a result of resolute and firm principles ever more and more purified, then, like any other mechanism of technically practical reason, it is neither armed for all eventualities nor adequately secured against changes that may be brought about by new allurements."—Immanuel Kant, *Introduction to the Metaphysical Elements of Ethics*.

So too is it about character—the traits, qualities, and established reputation that define who one is and what one stands for in the eyes of others.

"Nothing can possibly be conceived in the world, or even out of it, which can be called good, without qualification, except a good will. Intelligence, wit, judgment, and the other *talents* of the mind, however they may be named, or courage, resolution, perseverance, as qualities of temperament, are undoubtedly good and desirable in many respects; but these gifts of nature may also become extremely bad and mischievous if the will which is to make use of them, and which, therefore, constitutes what is called *character*, is not good."—Immanuel Kant, *Fundamental Principles of the Metaphysics of Morals.*

So too is it about example—an established pattern of conduct worthy of emulation.

"When thou wishest to delight thyself, think of the virtues of those who live with thee; for instance, the activity of one, and the modesty of another, and the liberality of a third, and some other good quality of a fourth. For nothing delights so much as the examples of the virtues, when they are exhibited in the morals of those who live with us and present themselves in abundance, as far as is possible. Wherefore we must keep them before us."—Marcus Aurelius, *Meditations.*

And so too is it about conscience—"the voice of the soul," "the pulse of reason," "that inner tribunal," "the muzzle of the will," "the compass of the unknown," "a thousand witnesses".

How we **think** may not guarantee a right or best answer but it dramatically improves the prospects of finding one in sound, defensible fashion.

"The moral sense follows, firstly, from the enduring and ever-present nature of the social instincts; secondly, from man's appreciation of the approbation and disapprobation of his fellows; and thirdly, from the high activity of his mental faculties, with past impressions extremely vivid; and in these latter respects he differs from the lower animals. Owing to this condition of mind, man cannot avoid looking both backwards and forwards, and comparing past impressions. Hence after some temporary desire or passion has mastered his social instincts, he reflects and compares the now weakened impression of such past impulses with the ever-present social instincts; and he then feels that sense of dissatisfaction which all unsatisfied instincts leave behind them, he therefore resolves to act differently for the future—and this is conscience."—Charles Darwin, *Descent of Man.*

What Ethics Involves

There is more to ethics, of course, than just knowing what it is about. As important to understanding its nature is what it involves. Is there something about the process of ethical reflection and choice that distinguishes it from other modes of thought? Some years ago Clarence Walton, former president of Catholic University, suggested the following: "Ethics involves critical analysis of human acts to determine their rightness or wrongness in terms of two major criteria: truth and justice."

Walton would have us understand, first, that ethics has virtually everything to do with the quality—even more than the content—of our thinking. How we think may not guarantee a right or best answer but it dramatically improves the prospects of finding one in sound, defensible fashion. As Pascal observed: "All our dignity consists… in thought…. Let us strive then to think well; that is the foundation of all morality."

To think well is to think critically. Critical thinking—the conscious use of reason—stands clearly apart from other ways of grasping truth or confronting choice: impulse, habit, faith, and intuition.

Impulse is nothing more than unreflective spontaneity—the sudden whim of a mind on cruise control or autopilot. Given the magnifying and accelerating effects of the media, impulsiveness is much more likely than deliberation in characterizing the response of today's policy practitioners to the manifold crises that define contemporary political affairs.

Habit is programmed repetition, the routinization of thought by which we remove presumably mundane matters to our subconscious so they can be dealt with more efficiently or conveniently without the attendant need to constantly revisit first principles. For example this is what we do when we standardize, generalize, or stereotype.

Faith, in the words of Walter Kaufman, "means intense, usually confident, belief that is not based on evidence sufficient to command assent from every reasonable person." Intensity of feeling and insufficiency of evidence are the operative features here. The dictionary might tell us that faith is belief—in an idea, a person, an institution—without need of certain proof. For the true believer, though, it isn't just the certainty of proof that is unnecessary; evidence itself is superfluous, especially evidence that contradicts an established belief system, worldview, or doctrine. This is what cognitive dissonance is all about—the prevalent human tendency to ignore or reject events or data that run counter to one's preconceptions or predispositions. Though faith and trust may go hand in hand, blind faith typifies a deadening of the intellect that may just as readily produce intolerance, disrespect, and distrust. The nineteenth-century Swiss philosopher Henri Frederic Amiel noted: "Action and faith enslave thought, both of them in order not to be troubled or inconvenienced by reflection, criticism and doubt."

Intuition is what we colloquially refer to as gut feeling or sixth sense—a way of speculative "knowing" based more on experience (lived or vicarious) than on reason, more on our overall sensory apparatus than on the workings of the mind. It is in this sense that a superficial impression of what appears to be—traits, behaviors, tendencies—so often gives birth to deep-seated pseudo-knowledge of what is. Intuition is neither entirely conscious nor entirely rational. In the words of George Santayana: "Intuition represents the free life of the mind, the poetry native to it…; but this is the subjective or ideal element in thought which we must discount if we are anxious to possess true knowledge."

What distinguishes these various forms of "unreason" from critical thinking is the systematic, investigative nature of the latter. "If you wish to strive for peace of soul and pleasure," said Heinrich Heine, "then believe; if you wish to be a devotee of truth, then enquire." Thinking critically is a disciplined pattern of thought or mode of inquiry that requires three things: first, questioning—assertions, opinions, and givens—rather than accepting them at face value; second, seeking and weighing evidence on all sides of an issue, not just evidence that affirms one's beliefs; and third, employing rigorous logic to reach defensible conclusions.

> The object of **critical thinking** is to achieve a measure of objectivity to counteract or diminish the subjective bias that experience and socialization bestow on us all.

The object of critical thinking is to achieve a measure of objectivity to counteract or diminish the subjective bias that experience and socialization bestow on us all. Why should this be necessary? Because when we are dealing with matters of ethical concern, the well-being of someone or something beyond ourselves is always at stake. In the extreme, the lives of others may literally depend on the choices we make or don't make—whether we are jurors in a court of law judging the guilt or innocence of an accused, or policy-makers committing the blood and treasure of society to a foreign venture. The quality of our thinking, then, is a measure of the investment we are willing to make in an issue or situation. As Spinoza said, "If we live according to the guidance of reason, we shall desire for others the good which we seek for ourselves."

What is it, then, that we should think critically about? Human acts, suggests Walton—human rather than nonhuman—rather than thoughts. We focus on things human for two reasons. First, humans presumably possess abilities—predominantly intellectual—that other living species do not: the ability to make moral judgments, to deal with abstract concepts, to extrapolate from one set of circumstances to another, to exercise free will that surpasses conditioned response. "It is characteristic of man," said Aristotle, "that he alone has any sense of good and evil, of just and unjust, and the like."

Accordingly, a second reason we focus on humans is that we expect more of them than we do of other species. We don't expect the dog or cat, or even the dolphin or chimpanzee, to contemplate the propriety of its actions, to refrain from harming others, or to display empathy. We do expect such things from humans. But we also have grown to expect humanity's imperfections to outweigh its potential with disturbing frequency. Thus Mark Twain was moved to observe, with cynical accu-

racy: "The fact that man knows right from wrong proves his *intellectual* superiority to other creatures; but the fact that he can *do* wrong proves his *moral* inferiority to any creature that cannot."

We focus on human acts because acts have demonstrable effects on others. "The great end of life," said T. H. Huxley, "is not knowledge but action." To know is merely to possess the truth. To act is to do, to make something happen, to get something done. Thoughts, in and of themselves, have tangible effects only if they are translated into acts. This assumes that thoughts and actions are separable, that one can act without thinking or think without acting, that it is possible to harbor hatred or prejudice, understanding or good will, in one's heart (or mind or soul) without actually putting such feelings into effect. It isn't always clear, of course, what constitutes action, and therein lies much moral ambiguity. Is speech an act? If I say I am homosexual, call someone a disparaging name, or advocate the overthrow of government, am I acting? Should I be held responsible for such thoughts? By the same token, is inaction action? If I do nothing—like possessing (but not using) nuclear weapons, ignoring genocide, or declining to pay United Nations dues—am I actually doing something?

Why do we critically analyze human acts? To determine their rightness or wrongness. There are any number of bases for making such determinations.

We might rely on some principle, precept, or rule: a law, executive order, or regulation, for example, that mandates or prohibits something (such as full financial disclosure or political assassination or the mishandling of classified information); or more abstract guidelines for behavior, such as the Golden Rule, the Ten Commandments, or an honor code that proscribes lying, cheating, and stealing.

We might be guided by the anticipated consequences or effects of our actions. Who benefits, and who is harmed? Who benefits most or what is the greatest benefit? Who is harmed least or what is the least harm? What consequences matter—physical ones only or also psychological and emotional ones? Temporally and spatially proximate ones only or also more distant ones?

We might concern ourselves with the intentions or motives behind one's acts. Does it matter why we do (or fail to do) something—or are results all that count? Do intentions outweigh effects or not? If I unintentionally inflict harm (or do good), should I be held culpable (or receive credit)?

We might focus on the rights of those involved in, affected by, or having a stake in our choices. Who deserves or doesn't deserve what—conditionally or unconditionally? Are there fundamental, natural rights that all persons deserve to enjoy merely by virtue of being human? Do rights reflect underlying needs that all humans recognizably have? Whose rights and which rights take precedence over others?

Conversely, we might emphasize obligations, the flip side of rights. Do those with a stake in our choices bear certain obligations toward others? Do the powerful or those in authority have special obligations, for example? Does the possession of rights impose attendant obligations?

The most nettlesome and difficult moral dilemmas we face often revolve around **value conflicts** in which two or more positive values are at stake in a given situation.

Or we might be guided by values—traits, behaviors, or qualities to which we ascribe some worth or importance. The question in every case, of course, is which values—which normative values (or virtues)—should we seek, and which should we consider more important than others. Zeno, the Greek Stoic philosopher, spoke of wisdom, courage, justice, and temperance as primary virtues. Aristotle spoke more expansively of justice, courage, temperance, magnificence, magnanimity, liberality, gentleness, prudence, and wisdom, in that order. But there are yet other salutary values that seem no less worthy of attention: compassion, competence, decisiveness, empathy, honesty, integrity, loyalty, reliability, tolerance, and vision—to name but a few. The most nettlesome and difficult moral dilemmas we face often revolve around value conflicts in which two or more positive values are at stake in a given situation: duty verses friendship, for example, or honesty verses compassion, or loyalty to subordinates verses loyalty to superiors.

When we seek to determine the rightness or wrongness of something, we should do so with two major criteria in mind: truth and justice. Ralph Waldo Emerson made the monumentally insightful observation that "truth is the summit of being; justice is the application of it [truth] to affairs." The two go hand in hand. Ethics—ethical reasoning, ethical choice, ethical conduct—requires that we seek the truth, the pinnacle of life, in order to have a proper basis—the only legitimate basis—for achieving justice. Justice served is ethics realized.

Truth is what *is*—conditions, occurrences, statements whose existence and nature are there to be confirmed or verified by observation or reason. To possess truth is to have knowledge, the expected outcome of critical reasoning. If we possessed the truth, we would know what is ethical. But therein lies the rub. Truth is inherently elusive, and our ability to grasp it is tenuous at best, even illusory. Take any truth claim that passes for a statement of fact by those who believe it. To cite just one example: in the matter of whether women should be permitted to serve in combat, these are among the commonly asserted "truths" that drive discussion of the issue and ultimately determine whether justice is served or denied:

- Women are incapable of performing in combat.
- Women are less aggressive and less courageous than men. Combat requires aggressiveness and courage.
- Women destroy unit cohesion.
- The presence of women creates sexual tensions that otherwise wouldn't exist.
- Women require more protection than men. Women bring out natural protective tendencies in men.

- A woman's place is in the home.
- A minimally qualified man is preferable to a better qualified woman.
- A woman has less of an obligation to serve than a man does.
- The American people deserve the best defense the military can provide them.

Such claims pass for self-evident truth among those who are already thus predisposed. But such so-called truths are rarely anything more conclusive and unequivocal than arguable propositions that cry out for supporting evidence.

Believing something intensely, even if that belief is shared by others, **doesn't** necessarily make it **true** in some objective sense.

There is an old saying: "A man with a watch knows what time it is; a man with two watches isn't so sure." This aphorism suggests a number of things about certainty and doubt, fact and opinion, objectivity and subjectivity, perception, bias, conviction, and socialization. Truth, like beauty, may lie as much in the eye of the beholder as in the thing observed; there may be multiple claimants, all more or less equal in standing, to the same truth; two or more parties can observe the same thing but see something completely different, or even that the same party can observe the same thing over time but see something different each time. Believing something intensely, even if that belief is shared by others, doesn't necessarily make it true in some objective sense.

Truth—perhaps precisely because it is so difficult to grasp or discern—is the essential precondition for justice. If justice is to be served, other than by accident, it must be predicated on the truth. Of course in any given situation there may be multiple truths that we would like to have—or that we knowingly or unknowingly need.

Let us say the question at hand is how to respond—justly and justifiably—to the September 11, 2001, terrorist attacks on the United States. We would like to have the truth of what actually happened (however seemingly self-evident). We would want to know the truth of who did it, how it happened, why it happened, what its effects have been, and what the effects of particular responses will be (for example, will punishment deter future such incidents and enhance U.S. credibility?).

Or take global warming. If we are to respond to it appropriately (in a timely, conclusive, affordable manner that doesn't create or exacerbate harm for those affected), we clearly want to know the truth of whether it actually exists; whether it is temporary or permanent, natural or human-made, recurrent or not, widespread or confined; and what its causes, effects, and implications are.

Justice is about receiving one's due or getting what one deserves—whether we are talking about one's standing or status, one's access to valuable resources, or one's treatment at the hands of others. This could mean obtaining a proper (fair) share of humanity's or society's goods (wealth, perquisites, esteem, and basic necessities), or receiving appropriate rewards or punishments for what one has or hasn't done (from bonuses or promotions to criminal conviction or military retaliation). Why would (or should) we care, for example, if 5 percent of the population controls 95 percent of society's wealth; if particular people are advantaged or disadvantaged because of their birth or personal attributes rather than because of their accomplishments; if a third-time minor drug offender is sentenced to a long prison term or a confessed murderer is set free on a legal technicality; if civilian noncombatants are subjected to the violence and destruction of war? Because in every case these are matters of justice and injustice.

Trust: The Bottom Line

Together, truth and justice constitute the basis for trust. Therein lies their ultimate importance in distinguishing what is ethical from what is not. As Sissela Bok observed in her thoughtful and perceptive 1978 book *Lying*: "Trust is a social good to be protected just as much as the air we breathe or the water we drink. When it is damaged, the community as a whole suffers; and when it is destroyed, societies falter and collapse.... Trust and integrity are precious resources, easily squandered, hard to regain."

Trust is social glue. It is what unites rather than divides, what turns a gaggle of individuals into a community with a sense of oneness. If I am sure I can count on you to tell me the truth, to seek the truth where I am concerned, to treat me fairly, to care whether I get what I deserve and deserve what I get, then our relationship is more likely than not to be defined by trust. Where such trust exists—thinking, not blind, trust; lasting, not momentary, trust—the prevalence of ethical conflict and the burden of ethical choice are materially diminished. Restoring trust thus is the great task of ethics, and understanding ethics accordingly is the great task before humanity today.

Gregory D. Foster is a professor at the Industrial College of the Armed Forces, National Defense University in Washington, D.C., where he previously has served as George C. Marshall professor and J. Carlton Ward distinguished professor and director of research.

Ethics can be gauged
by three key rules

By Dillard B. Tinsley

Because the Golden Rule appears in many different cultures, it provides a starting place for analyzing multicultural marketing ethics. Situational variables differ between target markets, but marketers may generally expect multicultural approval of ethical intentions to "do unto others as you would have them do unto you." The admonition is proactive—to do something good for others.

Marketers, target markets, regulatory agencies and other interested parties can agree that the Golden Rule has positive ethical implications. Marketers can apply the Golden Rule to their customers as they seek to beat competitors in satisfying customers' needs, which in essence means: Seek to do good unto customers better than can competitors. For effective use, however, marketers need to understand that different people may understand the Golden Rule in different ways.

One difference is the obvious insight that the other person may be different from you and does not want to be treated as you want to be treated. Marketers have long recognized this insight in their use of market segmentation, where a segment's members have common needs that differ from the needs of other segments. The Golden Rule, therefore, is a reminder to do enough marketing research so that the marketing concept can be implemented in an ethical manner. Marketers who start with the Golden Rule should immediately extend attention to ascertaining the needs of their targeted market segments.

Another difference arises because the exact statement of the Golden Rule varies between cultures. The most significant difference lies in statements in which the admonition focuses on merely not hurting others. The admonition to "not do anything that injures someone else" is sometimes called the Silver Rule. It falls short of the Golden Rule's impetus to actively seek to do something good for others.

The Silver Rule, however, is a useful reminder for marketers to fulfill the relevant laws and regulations. This is an obvious need, but implementation can be chal-lenging, especially when social responsibility requirements vary between multicultural target markets. Even within a single target market, injury may be defined differently by different parties. For example, Northfield, Ill.-based Kraft Foods Inc. is reducing portion sizes because of obesity concerns in the United States. Kraft is also reducing marketing in schools because children are a controversial target market—just as other market segments, such as low-income consumers, are controversial target markets with regard to other products. A particularly difficult example in multicultural marketing is injury through cultural pollution, which can be defined as imposing certain aspects of one culture on another culture in a manner that is perceived as detrimental. For example, France tries to prevent the French language from incorporating English words such as "e-mail." In addition, the rise of American-style coffeehouses in Paris is seen by some as a threat to traditional French cafes and coffee.

The Silver Rule reminds marketers of ethical concerns about injuries that go beyond legal baselines, including psychological injuries. The Golden Rule leads marketers toward the goal of satisfying customer needs in ways that better their competitors. This goal, however, involves difficulties that can be approached through the two objectives of marketing promotion—to inform and persuade.

Assuming that marketers offer a product that customers find fulfilling, how much information do customers need about this product? For example, informational food labeling in terms of serving characteristics is controversial for several reasons. A serving is not the same as a portion, but many foods are packaged such that one portion is more than one serving. As recently noted by *The Wall Street Journal*, one 20-ounce soda has 2.5 servings at 100 calories each; one muffin may be several servings; some products that are 100% fat may be legally labeled as fat-free; and one slice of cream pie is defined as one-tenth of that pie, but one slice of lemon meringue is defined as one-eighth of that pie. Just deciding which ingredients to include on labels is controversial, as seen in the new requirements for trans-fat labeling.

Informational labeling may or may not affect consumption, but one ethical justification given for market systems is that they leave final product selections to informed customers. Ethical concerns arise, however, as to how information is presented. What if information is expressed in a persuasive manner? There is no generally accepted theory of ethics with regard to marketing persuasion, and persuasion is endemic in marketing. Marketing persuasion pervades competition. In addition, marketers, as experts in their discipline, often know better what will fulfill customers' needs than do the customers. Do customers want to be persuaded by altruistic marketers when something is in their own best interest? Will customers think this ethical? Most people want to feel that their decisions are their own—with no undue influence from others.

Even if marketers fulfill the Golden Rule and offer a product that fulfills the best long-term needs of customers, ethical concerns arise with regard to marketing persuasion. Who determines that the product really is best? For which needs is it best, and how is it best? What about a product that is desired by customers, even though its effects on society are bad, such as SUVs that cause environmental pollution? How thoroughly must marketers understand customer needs in order to justify a claim of adhering to the Golden Rule?

To deal with the situational variables that will influence the answers to concerns about multicultural marketing ethics, marketers can apply the Open Forum Rule. This rule, popularly known as the Television Rule, cautions marketers not to do anything that they cannot explain satisfactorily on television to the concerned stakeholders.

After considering the ethical implications of the Golden Rule and the Silver Rule, marketers should check their programs with the Open Forum Rule. "Would I want to explain my actions on television to the concerned parties?" Such explanations must satisfy ethical requirements as seen by the concerned parties in each market. This means that marketers should know what the cultures in each market deem ethical—not just what the marketers see as ethical in their own culture. These three simple rules provide a basic approach or starting place for achieving adequate multicultural marketing ethics.

Dillard B. Tinsley is a professor of marketing at Stephen F. Austin State University in Nacogdoches, Texas.

Why Good Leaders Do Bad Things

Mental gymnastics behind unethical behavior

In making ethical decisions, let virtuous values guide your judgments
and beware of the mental games that can undermine ethical decision making.

Charles D. Kerns, Ph.D.

As the General Manager for an industrial distributor, you have recently learned that your consistently top performing purchasing manager has violated company policy by accepting an expensive gift from a supplier. Since you believe that this was likely a one-time lapse in judgment, what would you say or do? Your response could range from "looking the other way" to firing the manager.

In this situation, as in all ethical choices or dilemmas, the leader's thought pattern (cognitive process) will significantly influence what action he or she takes. People's patterns of thinking will be influenced by their values, what they say to themselves (self-talk), and what they imagine will happen in response to their actions. At its most basic level, ethical managerial leadership involves discerning right from wrong and acting in alignment with such judgment.

Leaders with strong virtuous values are more likely to act ethically than are leaders who are operating with a weak or non-existent value system. One set of values that seems to be universally accepted includes wisdom, self-control, justice, transcendence, kindness, and courage.[1] When faced with challenging decisions, leaders who have not internalized a value system that includes these values will probably respond with more variability than will one who has such a system. It is primarily in the situation in which the leader does not have an internalized value system that mental gymnastics or mind games may cause an otherwise good person to make unethical decisions.

In this article we will review mind games that leaders may play when they face difficult decisions and lack both a strong value system and a professional and ethical approach to management. These leaders tend to react to circumstances on a situational basis. Some suggestions on how managerial leaders can deal with challenging decisions are offered throughout the following discussion.

Mind Games

Decision making can often result in managerial missteps, even those decisions that involve ethical considerations. Many common themes emerge as we look at these problematic decisions. Most significantly, various cognitive processes that leaders often unwittingly employ and which may be called "mental gymnastics" or mind games may serve to support and sustain unethical behavior.

Mind Game #1: Quickly Simplify—"Satisficing"

When we are confronted with a complicated problem, most of us react by reducing the problem to understandable terms. We simplify. Notwithstanding the considerable power of our human intellect, we are often unable to cognitively process all of the information needed to reach an optimal decision. Instead, we tend to make quick decisions based on understandable and readily available elements related to the decision. We search for a solution that is both satisfactory and sufficient. Full rationality gives way to bounded rationality, which finds leaders considering the essential elements of a problem without taking into account all of its complexities. Unfortunately, this process, called "satisficing," can lead to solutions that are less than optimal or even ethically deficient.[2]

"Satisficing" leads the managerial leader to alternatives that tend to be easy to formulate, familiar, and close to the status quo. When one grapples with complex ethical considerations, this approach to decision making may not produce the best solutions. Ethical dilemmas can often benefit from creative thinking that explores ideas beyond the usual responses. If a decision maker uses satisficing when crafting a solution to an ethical problem, the best alternative may be overlooked. David Messick and Max Bazerman, researchers in decision making, tell us that when executives "satisfice," they often simplify, thereby overlooking low probability events, neglecting to consider some stakeholders, and failing to identify possible long-term consequences.[3]

One of the best ways to guard against oversimplifying and reaching less than optimal solutions to ethical challenges is to discuss the situation with other trusted colleagues. Have them play devil's advocate. Ask them to challenge your decision. The resulting dialogue can improve the quality of your ethical decision making.

Scholar and ethics consultant Laura Nash suggests twelve questions that can help leaders avoid the mind game of over simplifying.[4] The following questions may raise ethical issues not otherwise considered, or help generate a variety of "out of the box" alternatives. Before settling on a solution, ask yourself the following questions:

- Have I specified the problem accurately?
- How would I describe the problem if I were on the opposite side of the fence?
- How did this situation begin?
- To whom and to what do I give my loyalties as a person or group and as a member of the organization?
- What is my intention in making this decision?
- How does this intention compare with the likely results?
- Whom could my decision or action harm?
- Can I engage those involved in a discussion of the problem prior to making a decision?
- Am I confident that my position will be valid over the long term?
- Could I disclose without reservation my decision or action to my boss, our CEO, the Board of Directors, my family, or society as a whole?
- What is the symbolic impact of my action if it is understood?
- Under what conditions would I allow exceptions to my position?

These questions initiate a thought process that underscores the importance of problem identification and information gathering. Such a process can help leaders guard against over simplifying an otherwise complicated ethical decision.

Mind Game #2: The Need to Be Liked

Most people want to be liked. However, when this desire to be liked overpowers business objectivity, ethical lapses can occur. For instance, when managers witness ethical transgressions, the need to be liked may cause them to overlook these transgressions. Such a situation is particularly acute for those recently promoted into management from within the same organization. Because they want to be liked by their former peers, they may have a difficult time saying, "No." Dr. Albert Ellis, author of *A New Guide to Rational Living*,[5] notes that one of eleven irrational beliefs that some people hold is the belief that one can or should always be liked. He states that people who are affected by this need carry around in their heads statements such as, "I believe I must be approved by virtually everyone with whom I come in contact."

Such an overriding desire to be liked can ultimately adversely affect the ethics of people in an organization and thus can decrease the firm's bottom line. For instance, a retail store manager who wants her employees to like her may readily give them additional hours when they request them to enable employees to earn more money. However, in so doing, the manager contributes to the accumulation of too many hours of labor relative to sales volume. Over time, excessive labor costs can then begin to eat into profit margins.

After recognizing that she is playing this mind game, one way that the manager might stem this problem is to distance herself from her subordinates (e.g., reduce unnecessary socializing) until she can establish some objective boundaries. Another successful approach would be to respond warmly and assertively toward employees while still going forward with appropriate but possibly less popular decisions. (If necessary, the manager could even take assertiveness training.) Finally, in such situations, the newly appointed manager might want to read Alberti and Emmons' book, *Your Perfect Right*.[6] This book provides excellent advice on how to say "no" while preserving a quality relationship.

Mind Game #3: Dilute and Disguise

In trying to strike a diplomatic chord, leaders can disguise the offensiveness of unethical acts by using euphemisms or softened characterizations. Words or phrases such as "helped him make a career choice" are used to describe firing someone, or "inappropriate allocation of resources" is used to describe what everyone knows is stealing. Regardless of whether people want to be seen as kinder and gentler, or just politically correct, this process merely helps wrongdoers and those associated with them to get away with unethical behavior.

Such softened characterizations serve to reduce the anxiety of the leader, but these euphemisms are dishonest. They serve to dilute and disguise unethical behavior. This form of mental gymnastics defuses discomfort that may otherwise develop among those involved in unethical "mischief," but such an approach dilutes the necessary intensity of ethical constraints that should be brought to bear in the situation. The antidote is for leaders to talk straight and to avoid euphemistic labeling or re-characterizing unethical behavior.

Mind Game #4: "Making Positive"

The mental gymnastic of comparing one's own unethical behavior to more heinous behavior committed by others serves only to avoid self-degradation. For example, the salesperson who occasionally cheats when reporting his expenses may say to himself, "I do this only a few times a year, while Tom, Dick, and Harry do it all the time." Or, "If you think I disregard my colleagues' feelings, you ought to see Andy in action. He is a bona fide bully!" Unethical behavior appears more ethical by comparing it to worse behavior.

Such justifications for unethical behavior are not valid. The tendency to diminish misdeeds by making dishonest comparisons also contributes to sustaining unethical conduct. To avoid this mind game, ask three questions about the comparison:

- Am I comparing apples to oranges?
- How self-serving is this comparison?

- What would three objective observers say about me and my objectivity regarding this comparison?

While behavior may often legitimately be compared to that of others, when ethical transgressions are involved, relativity does not excuse ethical lapses.

Mind Game #5: Overconfidence

Overconfident managers tend to perceive their abilities to be greater than they actually are. Self-perception often does not match objective reality. By indulging in the mental gymnastics of overconfidence, such leaders can discount others' perceptions and thus easily overlook the insights and talents of other people. Without benefit of input from those around them, overconfident managerial leaders may be blind to the most appropriate ethical choices in given circumstances and may consider only their own ideas regarding the best course of action. Overconfident managers act as though they are "above it all," relegating their people, useful information, and learning opportunities to the sidelines while pursuing their own courses of action.

Overconfident decision makers deny themselves fresh perspectives and thus perhaps better solutions to ethical problems. The overconfident manager is typically perceived as arrogant. Research tells us that the manager labeled thusly is headed for career derailment.[7] Arrogant managerial leaders who have performance problems, which may include ignoring, overlooking, or causing ethical concern, are likely to receive less understanding and support from others in their time of trouble. Their air of overconfidence not only interferes with the practice of quality ethical decision making, but it can also virtually wreck their careers.

One tool to counterbalance this unproductive and potentially deadly tendency is for the overconfident managerial leader to catch himself or herself when preparing to make declarative, "This is the way it is" statements, and replace them with more open ended, "What do you think?" types of inquiries. If practiced conscientiously, this simple communication tool can help the overly confident manager begin to consider others' perspectives. Accepting input from other people will improve the manager's decision making ability generally, including those issues that involve ethical consideration. Applied broadly, this practice will positively impact the ethical problem solving climate within the entire organization.

These five mind games can influence an otherwise good leader to act unethically. Each of the mental maneuvers provides an easy way around difficult decisions, with the likely outcome that some of those decisions will result in unethical behavior. However, the intrinsic benefit of pursuing an ethical course will be a source of motivation for leaders to get on track ethically and stay there. By staying the course and behaving in a way that is consistent with his or her virtuous values and attitudes, the ethical managerial leader will have less need to play these types of mind games.

A Call to Action

Examine your thoughts when confronted with ethical choice points. In making ethical decisions, let virtuous values guide your judgments, and avoid playing mental games that undermine ethical behavior. If unchecked, indulging in these games can lead you to do bad things while feeling justified by your wrongdoing, at least temporarily. You are encouraged to heed the following suggestions that can help defend against participating in these mind games.

As you approach an ethical decision, to what extent do you do the following?

- Deliberate the obvious and not so obvious circumstances surrounding the issue.

- Decide objectively without regard to being liked.

- Talk about transgressions and ethical breaches using straightforward words.

- Make valid comparisons when discussing specific ethical behavior.

- Act with an appropriate level of confidence.

If you responded favorably to these questions, then perhaps these five mind games are not stumbling blocks for you. Less favorable or more uncertain responses may impel you to consider how your patterns of thinking may be adversely affecting your approach to ethical decision making.

Notes

1. Martin Seligman, *Authentic Happiness* (New York: Free Press, 2002). For definitions of these "virtuous values," and a discussion about their role in the business environment see Charles D. Kerns, "Creating and Sustaining an Ethical Workplace Culture," Graziadio Business Report, 6, Issue 3.

2. Stephen P. Robbins, *Essentials of Organizational Behavior,* 7th ed., New Jersey: Prentice-Hall (2003).

3. David M. Messick and M. H. Bazerman, "Ethical Leadership and the Psychology of Decision Making," *Sloan Management Review* 37 (Winter, 1996), p. 9.

4. Laura L. Nash, "Ethics Without the Sermon," in K. R. Andrews (ed.) *Ethics in Practice: Managing the Moral Corporation,* Boston: Harvard Business School Press, (1989), p. 243-257.

5. Albert Ellis and R. A. Harper, *A New Guide To Rational Living*, 3rd ed., 1997, (North Hollywood, CA: Wilshire).

6. Robert Alberti and M. L. Emmons, *Your Perfect Right: A Guide to Assertive Living,* 7th ed. (San Luis Obispo, CA: Impact, 1995).

7. Morgan W. McCall, *High Flyers: Developing the Next Generation of Leaders,* (Boston: Harvard Business School Press, 1998).

Best Resources for Corporate Social Responsibility

RESEARCH BY KAREN McNICHOL

W hat most of us lack these days isn't data but time. The World Wide Web is a marvelous research tool, but the sheer amount of information available can be overwhelming. How do you weed through it to find the very best sites, where someone has already synthesized masses of material for you? Well, consider the offerings below a garden without the weeds: a selection of the best of the best sites in corporate social responsibility (CSR).

1. Best Practices and Company Profiles

www.bsr.org—This may well be the best CSR site of all. Run by the business membership organization Business for Social Responsibility, its focus is on giving business hands-on guidance in setting up social programs, but data is useful to researchers as well, particularly because of "best practice" examples. Topics include social auditing, community involvement, business ethics, governance, the environment, employee relations, and corporate citizenship. New topics are being researched all the time. One recent report, for example, looked at companies linking executive pay to social performance, while others have looked at how to implement flexible scheduling, or become an "employer of choice." Visitors can create their own printer-friendly custom report on each topic, selecting from sections like Business Importance, Recent Developments, Implementation Steps, Best Practices, and Links to Helping Resources. To receive notices about updates, plus other CSR news, subscribe to BSR Resource Center Newsletter by sending a message to centerupdates@bsr.org with "subscribe" in the subject line.

www.ebnsc.org—You might call this the BSR site from Europe. It is sponsored by Corporate Social Responsibility Europe, whose mission is to help put CSR into the mainstream of business. This site includes a databank of best practices from all over Europe on topics like human rights, cause-related marketing, ethical principles, and community involvement. To give just one example of the site's capability, a search on the topic "reporting on CSR" came up with a dozen news articles available in full, plus a case study, and a list of 20 books and reports on the topic. One unique feature is the "CSR Matrix," which allows visitors to call up a complete social report on companies like IBM, Levi Strauss, or Procter & Gamble. The "matrix" is a grid, where the visitor clicks on one box to view the company's code of conduct, another box to see how the company interacts with public stakeholders, a third box to access the company's sustainability report, and so forth.

www.worldcsr.com is a World CSR portal offering one-stop access to the leading business-led organizations on corporate social responsibility in Europe and the U.S., including the two sites mentioned above. Another site on the portal—www.businessimpact.org—offers a useful databank of links to related organizations, such as the Global Reporting Initiative, Institute for Global Ethics, and World Business Council for Sustainable Development. Readers can also subscribe to the Business Impact News e-mail newsletter.

www.responsibleshopper.org For individuals wishing to shop with or research responsible companies, Responsible Shopper from Co-op America offers in-depth social profiles on countless companies. A report on IBM, for example, looks at everything from Superfund sites, toxic emissions, and worker benefits to laudatory activities. Different brand names for each company are listed, and social performance is summarized in letter ratings—as with IBM, which got an "A" in Disclosure, and a "B" in the Environment.

www.worldcsr.com offers one-stop access to the leading business-led organizations on corporate social responsibility in Europe and the U.S.

2. Social Investing

www.socialfunds.com—Run by SRI World Group, Social Funds is the best social investing site on the web. A staff of reporters researchers breaking news and posts it without charge. For socially responsible mutual funds, the site offers performance statistics plus fund descriptions. There's an investing center where you can build your own basket of social companies, plus a community banking center with information on savings accounts and money market funds with responsible banking organizations. A shareholder activism section offers a status report on social resolutions and is searchable by topic (equality, tobacco, militarism, etc.). Also available is a free weekly e-mail newsletter, SRI News Alert—which goes beyond social investing. One recent issue, for example, looked at new labeling programs for clean-air office construction, an Arctic Wildlife Refuge resolution against BP Amoco, and why greener multinationals have higher market value. A new service from SRI World Group, offered jointly with Innovest Strategic Advisors, offers subscribers ($100 annually) ratings of companies in various industries, based on environmental and financial performance.

www.socialinvest.org—This is the site of the nonprofit professional membership association, the Social Investment Forum, and is a useful pair to the above site. One unique feature is the collection of Moskowitz Prize-winning papers on research in social investing. The 2000 winner, for example, was "Pure Profit: The Financial Implications of Environmental Performance." Also available is a directory to help visitors find a financial adviser anywhere in the country; a mutual funds chart; a guide to community investing (showing resources by state and by type); and materials on SIF's campaign to end predatory

lending. You can also access the Shareholder Action Network-which shows how to submit shareholder resolutions, and offers information on both current campaigns and past successes.

www.goodmoney.com.—Offering some unique investing features of its own is the Good Money site, which showcases the Good Money Industrial Average: a screened index which outperformed the Dow in 2000. Also available are social profiles and performance data for a variety of public companies—including the 400 companies in the Domini Social Index, companies with the best diversity record, the Council on Economic Priorities "honor roll" list, and signers of the CERES Principles (a voluntary environmental code of conduct). Another section on Eco Travel has dozens of links and articles.

3. Corporate Watchdogs

www.corpwatch.org—For activists, this may be the best site of all. Calling itself "The Watchdog on the Web," Corp-Watch offers news you may not find elsewhere on human rights abuses abroad, public policy; and environmental news—plus on-site reporting of protests. Its director Josh Karliner was nominated by Alternet.org (an alternative news service) as a Media Hero 2000, for using the web to fight the excesses of corporate globalization. CorpWatch puts out the bimonthly Greenwash Awards, and runs a Climate Justice Initiative, as well as the Alliance for a Corporate-Free UN. An Issue Library covers topics like the WTO and sweatshops, while the Hands-on Guide to On-line Corporate Research is useful for research ideas. A free twice-monthly e-mail newsletter updates readers on recent Corp-Watch headlines. One recent issue of "What's New on Corp-Watch" looked at topics like the World Bank's record, the

For activists, www.corpwatch.org may be the best site of all.

protests at the World Economic Forum, California's deregulation troubles, plus the regular "Take Action" feature urging readers to send e-mails or faxes on a specific issue. To subscribe to the e-letter, send blank message to corp-watchers-subscribe@igc.topica.com.

www.corporatepredators.org—Featuring Russell Mokhiber, editor of the weekly newsletter *Corporate Crime Reporter*, this site offers a compilation of weekly e-mail columns called "Focus on the Corporation," written by Mokhiber and Robert Weissman. They offer a valuable, quirky voice in corporate responsibility. Taking on topics not covered elsewhere, the columns have looked at how the chemical industry responded to Bill Moyers TV program on industry coverup, how little academic research focuses on corporate crime, and why it's inappropriate to legally view corporations as "persons." At this site (which also features the book *Corporate Predators* by Mokhiber and Weissman), readers can access weekly columns back through 1998. Subscribe free to the column by sending an e-mail message to corp-focus-request@lists.essential.org with the text "subscribe."

4. Labor and Human Rights

http://oracle02.ilo.org/vpi/welcome—Sponsored by the International Labor Organization, this web site offers a new Business and Social Initiatives Database, compiling Internet sources on employment and labor issues. It covers topics like child labor, living wage, dismissal, investment screens, monitoring, international labor standards, glass ceilings, safe work, and so forth. It features information on corporate policies and reports, codes of conduct, certification criteria, labeling and other programs. A search feature allows visitors to retrieve information on specific companies, regions, and business sectors. This is one of the most comprehensive labor sites out there.

www.summersault.com/~agj/clr/—Sponsored by the Campaign for Labor Rights, this site keeps activists up to date on anti-sweatshop struggles and other pro-labor activities around the world. Particularly useful is the free e-mail newsletter Labor Alerts, which updates readers on recent news about trade treaties, plant shutdowns, labor organizing, job postings, upcoming protests, recent books, and so forth. One recent issue contained a "webliography" of sites about the pending creation of the Free

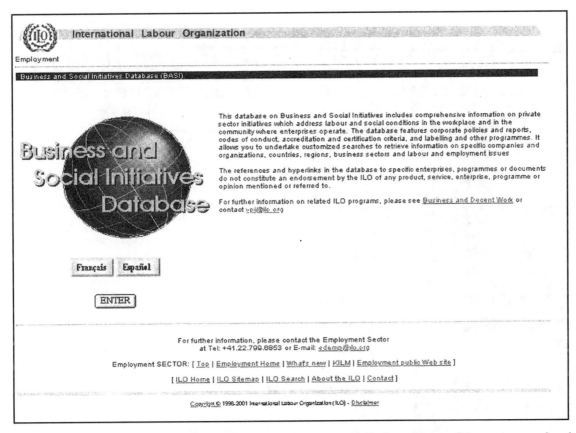

The Business and Social Initiatives Database (http://oracle02.ilo.org/vpi/welcome) is one of the most comprehensive labor compilations out there.

Trade Area of the Americas (FTAA). To subscribe contact clr-main@afgj.org.

5. Progressive Economics

www.epn.org—For the best thinking in progressive economic policy, this site managed by *The American Prospect* magazine is a one-stop source. It's the Electronic Policy Network, an on-line consortium of over 100 progressive policy centers nationwide, like the Center for Public Integrity, the Brookings Institution, the Financial Markets Center, and many more. (The focus of member groups is heavily though not exclusively economic.) A feature called Idea Central offers on-line bibliographies on topics like globalization, poverty, and livable cities. Certain topics get "Issues in Depth" treatment: One, for example, looks at campaign finance reform—including history, alternatives, and legal background, with numerous links to sites like a database of soft-money contribution, research from the Center for Responsive Politics, ACLU fact-sheets, and more. Another feature, "What's New," looks at recent reports and research papers by member policy centers—like a recent report from the Economic Policy Institute on privatization, or a report on state initiatives for children from the National Center for Children in Poverty. Readers can receive summaries of new research reports by subscribing to the e-mail EPN News; send an e-mail to majordomo@epn.org with "subscribe epnnews" in the message body.

www.neweconomics.org—This valuable site is run by The New Economics Foundation (NEF), a UK nonprofit think tank created in 1986 to focus on "constructing a new economy centered on people and the environment." Different areas on the site focus on powerful tools for economic change, like alternative currencies, social investment, indicators for sustainability, and social accounting. A monthly web-based newsletter reports on topics like Jubilee 2000 (the movement to cancel the debt of developing nations), May Day plans, an "indicator of the month," and more. A new bimonthly e-briefing is called "mergerwatch," which looks at the hidden costs behind mergers, and who pays the price. Its first issue in April 2001 reported, for example, that a 1999 KPMG study showed 53 percent of mergers destroy shareholder value, and a further 30 percent bring no measurable benefit.

6. Employee Ownership

http://cog.kent.edu—For researchers in employee ownership, the Capital Ownership Group site is indispensable. COG is a virtual think tank of individuals—including academics, employee ownership specialists, and business leaders worldwide—who aim to promote broadened ownership of productive capital. The site's library allows visitors to browse ongoing discussions, on topics like promoting employee ownership globally, getting economists more involved in issues of capital ownership, the role of labor in employee ownership, and more. The library of-

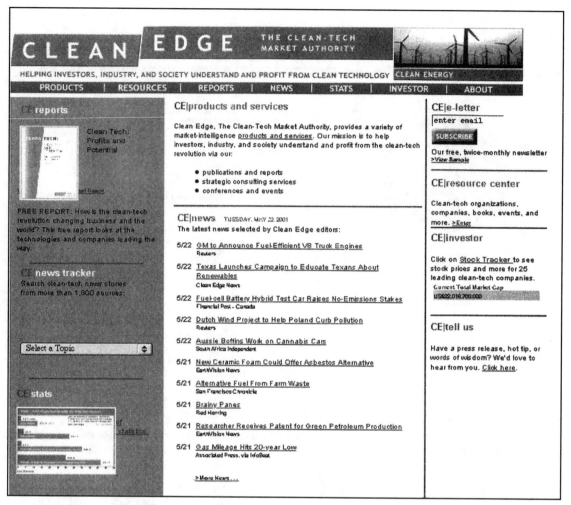

www.cleanedge.com **offers news from 1,800 sources, stock trading information on 25 companies, plus lists of conferences, trade associations and research centers.**

fers hundreds of papers and research reports, on topics like labor-sponsored venture capital, employee governance, case studies, and much more.

www.nceo.org—This is the site of the National Center for Employee Ownership, a nonprofit research and membership organization that is one of the best sources for employee ownership information. Its web library features a valuable introduction to the history of Employee Stock Ownership Plans (ESOPs), plus information on open book management, stock options, and alternatives to ESOPs. An "Interactive Introduction to ESOPs" lets visitors "chat" with an expert in the same way as if they spent fifteen minutes on the phone with a lawyer. Also available are a wealth of links to related sites, plus news and statistics on employee ownership.

www.fed.org—The sponsor of this site is the Foundation for Enterprise Development—a nonprofit started by Robert Beyster, founder of employee-owned SAIC—which is an organization that aims to promote employee ownership. Its focus is not ESOPs but stock options and other forms of equity ownership. A monthly online magazine features profiles of employee ownership at specific companies, articles on developing an owner-

ship culture, plus news. An e-mail service updates readers on headlines.

www.the-esop-emplowner.org—From the ESOP Association—a membership and lobbying organization—this site offers a resource library, news of events, reports on legislative victories, and information on legislative initiatives. The site also offers information on the ESOP Association's political action committee, which since 1988 has helped candidates for federal office who support ESOPs and ESOP law.

7. Sustainability

www.GreenBiz.com—Run by Joel Makower, editor of *The Green Business Letter*, Green Biz is the best site on progressive environmental business activities. It enables visitors to discover what companies are doing, and to access citations of countless web resources and reports, on topics like sustainable management, green auditing, EPA programs, pending legislation, clean technologies, recycling, and all things green. A new service features free job listing for environmental professionals. Get regular updates from a free e-mail newsletter, GreenBiz, published every other week.

www.rprogress.org—Run by the nonprofit Redefining Progress—which produces the Genuine Progress Indicator (as a counterpoint to GDP)—this site offers news on topics like climate change, forest-land protection, tax reform, and congressional influence peddling. Recent stories featured a proposal to promote market-based policies for reducing sprawl, a better way to return the government surplus, plus a look at Living Planet 2000—calculating the ecological footprints of the world's largest 150 countries. Numerous studies on environmental justice, tax fairness, and community indicators are available, plus links to other climate change sites.

www.sustainablebusienss.com—The monthly on-line magazine Sustainable Business offers news on the "green economy," covering recycling, product take-back, legislative developments, and so forth. Other features are a database of "Green Dream Job" openings; plus a section to help green businesses find venture capital. A library features web sites, reports, and books.

www.cleanedge.com—The new organization Clean Edge focuses on helping investors, industry, and society understand and profit from clean technology, like wind, solar, energy efficiency, and alternative fuels. The site offers news from 1,800 sources, stock trading information on 25 companies, plus lists of conferences, trade associations and research centers. The group's premier publication, "Clean Tech: Profits and Potential," reports that clean energy technologies will grow from less than $7 billion today to $82 billion by 2010.

8. Ethics

www.depaul.edu/ethics—Sponsored by the Institute for Business and Professional Ethics at DePaul University, this site offers a large compilation of ethics resources on the web, categorized by topic; educational resources for teachers and trainers, including syllabi; faculty position announcements; calls for papers; a calendar of events; a list of other ethics institutes, and much more.

www.ethics.ubc.ca—From the Center for Applied Ethics at the University of British Columbia in Canada, this site offers a particularly valuable compilation about ethics codes—featuring sample codes, guidance on writing a code, plus books and articles on the topic. Other features are links to ethics institutes, consultants, course materials, publications, and collections of articles.

www.ethics.org/businessethics.html—Sponsored by the **Ethics Resource Center**, this site features valuable data from several business ethics surveys 1994–2000, information on character education for youth, a compendium of codes (coming soon), plus links to many ethics centers and organizations. A research bibliography covers topics like measuring success in an ethics program, or ethics in a global economy. And a provocative "Ethics Quick Test" can be taken on-line, with results available by e-mail.

UNIT 2

Ethical Issues and Dilemmas in the Workplace

Unit Selections

Key Points to Consider

- What ethical dilemmas do *managers* face most frequently? What ethical dilemmas do *employees* face most often?

- What forms of gender and minority discrimination are most prevalent in today's workplace? In what particular job situations or occupations is discrimination more widespread and conspicuous? Why?

- Whistle-blowing occurs when an employee discloses illegal, immoral, or illegitimate organizational practices or activities. Under what circumstances do you believe whistle-blowing is appropriate? Why?

- Given the complexities of an organization, where an ethical dilemma often cannot be optimally resolved by one person alone, how can an individual secure the support of the group and help it to reach a consensus as to the appropriate resolution of the dilemma?

 **Links: www.dushkin.com/online/**
These sites are annotated in the World Wide Web pages.

American Psychological Association
http://www.apa.org/homepage.html

International Labour Organization (ILO)
http://www.ilo.org

What You Can Do in Your Workplace
http://www.connectforkids.org/info-url1564/info-url_list.htm?section=Workplace

LaRue Tone Hosmer, in *The Ethics of Management*, lucidly states that ethical problems in business are truly managerial dilemmas because they represent a conflict, or at least the possibility of a conflict, between the *economic performance* of an organization and its *social performance*. Whereas the economic performance is measured by revenues, costs, and profits, the social performance is judged by the fulfillment of obligations to persons both within and outside the organization.

Units 2 to 4 discuss some of the critical ethical dilemmas that management faces in making decisions in the workplace, in the marketplace, and within the global society. This unit focuses on the relationships and obligations of employers and employees to each other as well as to those they serve.

Organizational decision makers are ethical when they act with equity, fairness, and impartiality, treating with respect the rights of their employees. An organization's hiring and firing practices, treatment of women and minorities, tolerance of employees' privacy, and wages and working conditions are areas in which it has ethical responsibilities.

The employee also has ethical obligations in his or her relationship to the employer. A conflict of interest can occur when an employee allows a gratuity or favor to sway him or her in selecting a contract or purchasing a piece of equipment, making a choice that may not be in the best interests of the organization. Other possible ethical dilemmas for employees include espionage and the betrayal of secrets (especially to competitors), the theft of equipment, and the abuse of expense accounts.

The articles in this unit are broken down into sections representing various types of ethical dilemmas in the workplace. The initial article in this first section describes why monitoring employees is a commonplace practice in the work arena. "Up Against Wal-Mart" discloses how workers are fighting back at Wal-Mart because of alleged illegal business practices such as low wages, unpaid overtime, and union busting.

In the subsection entitled *Organizational Misconduct and Crime*, articles explore the costs of organizational dishonesty, ways auditors can help deter bribery and kickbacks, and methods whereby some executives are still practicing old-fashioned corporate cronyism.

The two selections under *Sexual Treatment of Employees* take a close look at how women are treated in the workplace and how recent court decisions are attempting to clarify sexual harassment.

The readings in the *Discriminatory and Prejudicial Practices* section scrutinize why opinions vary widely on affirmative action, why there are still so few women in top organizational positions, and the sex-discrimination lawsuit against Wal-Mart.

The next subsection, *Downsizing of the Workforce*, examines why many high-tech workers have lost jobs to low-wage countries because of outsourcing.

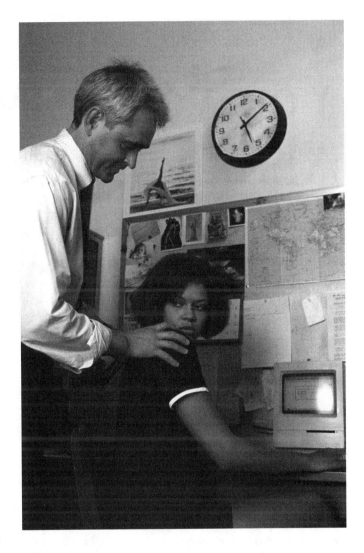

The first selection included under the heading *Whistle-Blowing in the Organization* analyzes the ethical dilemma and possible ramifications of whistle-blowing. The second article describes how whistle-blowing can help a company resolve problems before they become national news headlines.

The article "Between Right and Right," in the last subsection of *Handling Ethical Dilemmas at Work*, summarizes three specific ethical dilemmas that have been provoked by recent events. Another article covers Costco's dilemma of catering to its workers, or satisfying shareholders and Wall Street. "The Parable of the Sadhu" presents a real-world ethical dilemma for the reader to ponder.

You've Got Mail ... And the Boss Knows:

A Survey by the Center for Business Ethics of Companies' Email and Internet Monitoring

W. MICHAEL HOFFMAN, LAURA P. HARTMAN, AND MARK ROWE

The use of email, the Internet, and corporate databases by individuals and companies is increasing exponentially, and has probably affected business more profoundly during the last few years than any other single phenomenon. [1] More than 50 million Americans connect to the Internet and use email at work. A U.S. Department of Commerce survey,[2] published in February 2002, shows that the proportion of employed persons aged 25 and over who use the Internet and/or email at work increased in just one year from 26.1 percent in August 2000 to 41.7 percent in September 2001. Whether they realize it or not, more and more of these employees are liable to have their Internet and email activities monitored by their employers. The Center for Business Ethics (CBE) at Bentley College, Waltham, MA, has conducted a survey of corporations that are Sponsoring Partners of the Ethics Officer Association (EOA). The survey was designed to discover the extent to which companies monitor their employees' use of the Internet and email, their reasons for doing so, and the means by which they go about it.

We have found that monitoring is commonplace, with nine out of every ten companies checking up on their employees' online activities while at work. Given the sensitive and somewhat controversial nature of the practice, it was surprising to discover how many companies monitor all the time, not just when something gives cause for concern. For the same reason, we were surprised at the nature of ethics officer involvement in the process. The majority of companies that responded to our survey seem to aspire to a system of responsible, sensitive, and appropriate monitoring. Nevertheless, we believe the survey has highlighted some issues that companies might want to revisit in the quest for best practices in this area.

BACKGROUND

Does New Technology Mean New Value Judgments? Employers have always gathered information about their employees. For instance, in the early 1900s Milton Hershey, of Hershey's Chocolate, used to tour Hershey, Pennsylvania, to see how well his employees maintained their homes. He hired detectives to spy on Hershey Park dwellers in order to learn who threw trash on its lawns. Henry Ford used to condition wages on his employees' good behavior *outside* the factory, maintaining a Sociological Department of 150 inspectors to keep tabs on them.

As the business world has become increasingly complex, and American society ever more litigious, employers have tended to regard employees as one of many potential sources of risk—at least, those employees whose conduct departs from the norm. This trend was intensified by the introduction, in 1991, of the Federal Sentencing Guidelines for Organizations (FSGOs).[3] Imposing a mandatory system of heavy fines and rigorous probation conditions for organizations convicted of federal offences, the FSGOs caused employers to scrutinize employee activity closer than ever before.

Advances in technology have been dramatic, and have facilitated information gathering in ways that Hershey and Ford could never have imagined possible. From an ethical perspective, this does not mean that technology has created new value judgments; simply new ways to gather the information on which to base them. The manner in which employers collect information about employees may have changed far more than the values underlying the decision to do so, but there are some challenging issues that now confront us. In conducting our survey, we had in mind a number of issues, including the following:

- Managing employee and employer expectations.
- Distinguishing between work use and personal use of technology.
- Managing and measuring employee productivity and performance.
- Optimizing work/life balance.
- Balancing privacy interests.
- Managing risk and liability issues.
- Maintaining a virtual workplace.
- Responding to accessibility issues related to the "digital divide."
- Protecting proprietary information.
- Operating flex-time.

In this article, we examine corporate monitoring of employees' email and Internet usage in the context of some of these issues.

How Does Monitoring Work? Technological advances in information gathering have allowed monitoring that was never before possible. Worldwide sales of monitoring technology are estimated at $140 million annually.[4] One example of new technology is Raytheon's *SilentRunner*, which allows firms to track everything that occurs on a network, including not only emails but also instant messaging—one of the new ways in which employees thought they had foiled email monitoring.[5]

The most prevalent Internet monitoring product in the United States is *Websense*, with 8.25 million users worldwide. While *Websense* merely blocks certain websites, *Websense Reporter,* an add-on, records all web accesses (not only attempted accesses blocked by *Websense,* but also all non-prohibited web surfing). Seventy percent of *Websense* customers install *Reporter.* *MIMEsweeper* is the most used email monitoring system in the United States with 6,000 corporate customers and over 6 million ultimate users worldwide. In a less publicized form of monitoring, SWS Security offers a product that allows managers to track the messages a worker receives on a portable paging device so that one could track whether the employee is being distracted by outside messages.

Why Monitor Email and Internet Usage? There are numerous arguments that support the choice of a firm to monitor. Since the current research surveyed members of the Ethics Officer Association, we sought to determine attitudes and practices related to monitoring at those firms in particular that may be more acutely aware of the ethical challenges to monitoring. Recent research has found that monitoring serves a number of purposes for a firm. Consider the following:

h) Managing the workplace.
- Ensuring compliance with affirmative action.
- Administering workplace benefits.
- Placing workers in appropriate positions.

i) Ensuring effective, productive performance.
- Preventing loss of productivity to inappropriate technology use. Calculations have been made as to the cost of productivity lost as a result of employees spending work time on the Internet for non-business reasons. One study calculates that if 50 users spend 3 hours per week on recreational surfing during work hours, the cost to the organization is $3,322.50 per week in lost salary expenses; this is $172,770 per year.[6]
- 13 percent of employees spend over two hours a day surfing non-business sites.[7]
- A recent survey in the U.K. reports that, of the workers surveyed:
  – 53 percent behave "immorally" in email.
  – 38 percent have used email in the pursuit of political gain within their company, at the expense of others.
  – 30 percent admit to having sent racist, pornographic, sexist, or otherwise discriminatory emails while at work.[8]

j) Protecting information and guarding against theft.
k) Protecting investment in equipment and bandwidth.
l) Protecting against legal liability, including possible
- perceptions of hostile environments;
- violations of software licensing laws;
- violations regarding proprietary information or trade secrets;
- inappropriate gathering of competitive intelligence;
- financial fraud;
- theft;
- defamation/libel;
- discrimination.

m) Maintaining corporate records (including email, voice-mail, etc.).
n) Investigating *some* personal areas—consider Infoseek executive Patrick Naughton's pursuit of a tryst with an FBI agent posing as a 13-year-old girl in a chat room.

These purposes do not appear unreasonable. Nevertheless, there may be a number of reasons to limit monitoring and we will explore these arguments below.

How Far Should Monitoring Go?

Notwithstanding a number of persuasive justifications for monitoring in the workplace, there remain several reasons to limit monitoring. Below, we set out a number of them.

- Monitoring may create a suspicious and hostile workplace.
- Monitoring constrains effective performance (employees claim that lack of privacy may prevent "flow").
- It may be important to conduct *some* personal business at the office, when necessary.
- Monitoring causes increased workplace stress and pressure, negatively affecting individual and, by extension, company performance.
- Employees claim that monitoring is inherently an invasion of privacy.
- Monitoring does not always allow for workers to review and correct misinformation in collected data.
- Monitoring constrains the right to autonomy and freedom of expression.

• Monitoring intrudes upon one's right to privacy of thought (*"I use a company pen; does that mean the firm has a right to read my letter to my spouse?"*)

There is some force in these arguments, yet some counterarguments might also be made.

For instance, it is arguable that monitoring is less likely to be a cause than a symptom of a suspicious and hostile work environment. We have anecdotal evidence of monitoring that is carried out without breeding suspicion and hostility. If the management of a company is respectful of the employees, manages their expectations realistically, and is frank about the company's objectives, it is more likely to cultivate an atmosphere of trust and transparency. Then, the employees are more likely to view the monitoring process as serving a business need than as a sinister intrusion. A 2001 survey found that 75 percent of employees thought it was acceptable for companies to implement email and Internet monitoring if the employees were notified in advance. [9]

Secondly, it is clear from our interviews that many companies recognize that changing work patterns and lifestyles make it not only appropriate but also necessary for some personal affairs to be dealt with from the workplace. It is incumbent upon employers to let employees know that this is acknowledged, at the same time giving the best indication of what is, and is not, acceptable.

In the American Management Association's 2001 survey, more than two-thirds reported that they engaged in monitoring as a result of their concerns for legal liability. Given the courts' focus in many cases on employer response to claims of sexual harassment or unethical behavior, among other complaints, firms believe that they need a way to uncover these inappropriate activities. More than 10 percent of firms have reported receiving a subpoena for employee email and one-third of the largest firms report firing employees for inappropriate email. [10] Without monitoring, how would they know what occurs? Moreover, as courts maintain in many cases the standard of whether the employer "knew or should have known" of wrongdoing, the state of the art definition of "should have known" becomes all the more vital. If most firms use monitoring technology to uncover this wrongdoing, the definition of *"should have* known" will begin to include an expectation of monitoring.

Survey Methodology

The survey was conducted over the spring and summer of 2002. It was designed in two parts. The first part sought quantitative data and involved a questionnaire with 18 questions submitted to 192 corporations that are EOA sponsoring partners. The second part of the survey was qualitative in nature and necessitated telephone interviews with a sample of corporate ethics officers and senior managers.

The first four questions in the questionnaire were concerned with the existence and communication of any policies that companies might have adopted in relation to the monitoring of email and Internet usage. Questions 5–7 were designed to investigate the degree of permissibility of personal usage by employees of compa-

nies' electronic systems. The final 11 questions dealt with the motives and methods of corporate monitoring, and the responsibilities and safeguards attaching to such activity. In answering some questions, respondents were invited to indicate more than one category (if appropriate) and this should be borne in mind when viewing some of the figures. The survey was emailed to the chief ethics officer of each sponsoring partner company in spring 2002. Respondents were given the option of completing and returning the questionnaire electronically or, alternatively, printing out and mailing back a hard copy. The response rate was 54 percent, with all data received back by July 2002.

Ten interviewees were selected for follow-up questions in order to provide data of a more qualitative nature. Selections were made on the basis of interviewees' reputations and experience, and in such a way that a variety of industries were represented. In July 2002 we spoke to ethics officers and senior managers employed in the following sectors: accounting; aviation; defense; energy; insurance; paper; and telecommunications. Interviewees were asked seven pro forma questions to elicit detailed comments on specific areas of particular interest or concern.

SURVEY FINDINGS

Monitoring Policy

Unsurprisingly, all of the 103 companies responding to the survey provide their employees with access to email, the Internet, or other communication technology. Monitoring employees' usage of such technology is widespread, with 92 percent of companies that responded to the survey confirming that they do monitor use of email, Internet, and other technology.[*] All of the firms surveyed who engage in monitoring maintain a policy in this regard. Only one company responding to the survey does not tell employees that their use of email, the Internet, or other technology is subject to scrutiny.

Companies use various communications tools, often in combination, to notify employees of the monitoring policy. Incorporating a clause in the company's code of ethics/business conduct is the route most frequently taken, although almost as many companies publish a separate manual containing details of the policy. Other methods adopted by respondents include notifying employees of the monitoring policy while they are actually using the technology—for example, by means of "popups" that appear on the screen—or in the course of orientation or ongoing training programs. Figure 1 shows the prevalence among survey respondents of various means of communicating the company policy on monitoring. The question asked was, "How does your company communicate the email, Internet monitoring or technology usage policy to employees? (Check all that apply)."

---

*It is possible that the percentage of companies that engage in monitoring is even higher than 92 percent. In their responses to our question on frequency of monitoring (see following section "How Often Do Companies Monitor?"), only 2 out of 102 companies said they "never monitor." This may be a discrepancy explained by a few inconsistent answers but we felt it worthy of mention.

Figure 1
Notification of Monitoring Policy to Employees

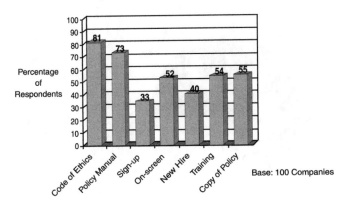

Base: 100 Companies

Figure 2
What Is Considered "Reasonable Use"?

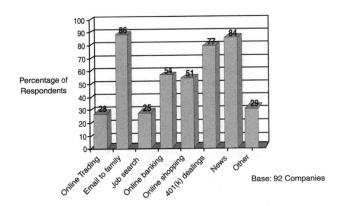

Base: 92 Companies

Should Email and the Internet Be Treated Differently? The survey explored whether companies draw a distinction between monitoring employee email and monitoring Internet usage. The majority of those company executives whom we interviewed made no such distinction. One vice president explained his company's rationale: "We tell employees up front that our systems and our hardware are proprietary. There's no expectation of privacy and, depending on the situation, we will monitor activity and take action." Although seeing no ethical distinction in principle between monitoring email and Internet usage, one manager told us that her firm was sensitive to the fact that employees have less control over what types of electronic mail they receive than over the websites they access. She did see an ethical issue if "reading" email content is included in the monitoring of emails, saying, "Our corporate policy on access to this information is rather strict and requires a real business need to obtain such information [the content of emails]."

Some companies do, however, see a difference in principle between monitoring employee email and monitoring their use of the Internet. The director of legal compliance and business ethics at one corporation observed, "The monitoring of employee email has a greater propensity to surface employee concerns regarding privacy. Email, like the telephone, is a tool that is used for both business and personal reasons. Unlike the Internet, email affords the user the ability to communicate with others on matters that are personal and private. The Internet is simply an information gathering tool." However, this approach appears not to take into account problems that might arise as a result of employees joining Internet chat rooms or engaging in instant messaging while at work.

"Reasonable" Personal Usage The same percentage of respondent companies that engages in monitoring (92 percent) also allows "reasonable" personal usage of their electronic systems. Of course, this begs the question as to what reasonable use is. Only 42 percent of responding companies define "reasonable personal usage" in their policies, which means a majority of companies offer employees no guidance. One company takes away the problem entirely, at least where email is concerned, since it stip-

ulates to employees that email is to be used only for company business. Figure 2 shows a range of employee activities permitted by those companies that do attempt to define reasonable email and Internet usage. There is consensus in several areas, with similar percentages of respondents (around 80 percent) giving approval to email contact with family, keeping abreast of news, and dealing with 401(k) matters. Some companies do not even mind usage such as research and communications as part of a job search, although three-quarters of our respondents do not think that this is a reasonable use of company facilities.

However companies define reasonable usage of email and the Internet, many draw an analogy with personal telephone calls. "For email," one manager commented, "usage would be comparable to personal telephone usage. That's to say a quick call to a family member or friend, some personal business needs, a call to your insurance agency or telephone company." Her company's policy on Internet usage is similar, allowing "incidental and occasional" usage.

A recurring theme in responses to the survey was that an employee's use of email and the Internet should never compromise his or her ability to do their job, nor conflict with any of their employer's business activities. The survey suggests, therefore, that the key criteria for determining reasonableness of personal use of email and the Internet are individual performance, productivity, and the safeguarding of company interests. In the section "Monitoring and Discipline" we will look at attitudes and practices in situations where performance or conflict issues do arise, and the employer considers it appropriate to take action.

Monitoring Methods

Monitoring in the workplace can take several forms and occurs for numerous reasons. Privacy scholar Colin Bennett identifies several types of surveillance that can specifically impact workers.[11] The first is surveillance by "glitch," where information is uncovered by mistake. In the workplace, a glitch could occur when a technician checks to see if a computer's hard drive has been erased by the previous users for use by someone else. That technician might notice inappropriate content on that hard

Figure 3
Which Methods Are Used?

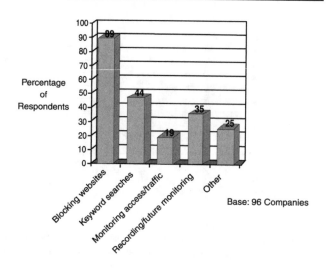

Base: 96 Companies

Figure 4
Frequency of Monitoring

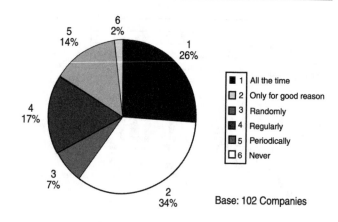

Base: 102 Companies

drive. In another example of a glitch or mistake, an employee's salacious email could, through inattention to predictive text in the address box, be sent to an unintended recipient who reports the matter. These glitches may uncover violations of a usage policy even when no systematic monitoring is being conducted.

Bennett's second form of surveillance is "surveillance by default." This is where the default setting is to monitor, where all information that is sent through a system is caught and catalogued. In the context of this survey, surveillance by default occurs when all employees' email and Internet usage is monitored all of the time, whether there is a good reason or particular purpose or not. The American Management Association reports that 75 percent of firms surveyed in 2001 regularly record their employees' email transmissions as a default setting.[12]

A third form of monitoring is "surveillance by design," where the entire purpose of the technology is to collect information, and, generally, the user is aware of this purpose. One means of surveillance by design is when firms conduct either random or periodic keyword searches of email or other transmissions. One-quarter of firms surveyed by the American Management Association reported that they performed keyword searches, generally seeking sexual or scatological language to protect themselves from later liability.[13] This illustrates the point made earlier about companies viewing employees, in one sense, as a risk element in their business.

Much of the monitoring that occurs today in American firms is surveillance by *design* or *default*. For instance, an email program that systematically sorts and saves all email that uses certain terms (such as those used in a job search or those terms that might be considered sexual harassment) would constitute surveillance by default. Some programs are designed to record email and Internet traffic for later monitoring as necessary. A monitoring program that tracks Internet accesses and blocks inappropriate websites would be surveillance by design. Figure 3 shows the relative usages of different monitoring techniques by

How Often Do Companies Monitor? In our interviews the overwhelming majority of executives said that monitoring was conducted in their companies in response to particular concerns or allegations that came to management's attention. However, this is not in line with the survey results. Instead, 64 percent of companies responding report that they either monitor all of the time (26 percent), or utilize "random," "regular," or "periodic" monitoring (38 percent). Thirty-four percent of companies monitor "only for good reason." The latter figure is surprisingly low when compared to the interview responses. The breakdown is shown in Figure 4.

Monitoring for Due Cause If a company has adopted a policy of monitoring where it considers there is good reason to do so, how does it decide when and whom to monitor? According to the survey respondents, the decision might be taken by a variety of individuals or departments, but most commonly it is the ethics officer, the general counsel, or a senior member of the human resources department who will sanction the monitoring (see Figure 5).

As we have observed, monitoring is often undertaken to address a particular problem or complaint that has come to management's attention. The treatment of email and the Internet may, however, be different. One company's chief ethics officer describes a procedure that is fairly typical in relation to email monitoring: "Upon receipt of an allegation of misconduct, the receiving party (Legal Compliance and Business Ethics, management, HR, corporate security, etc.) evaluates the information provided, to determine if there is enough substance to warrant an investigation or monitoring. Once the decision is made to move forward, the employee is informed of the allegation and that their email account will be searched."

The same executive says of Internet monitoring: "Employee use of the Internet is tracked regularly in terms of sites visited and the time a particular site was accessed. Additionally, by means of a firewall, sites deemed inappropriate by the company (e.g., sexually explicit content, games, gambling sites) are filtered and access is denied."

Figure 5
Who Determines There Is Good Reason for Monitoring?

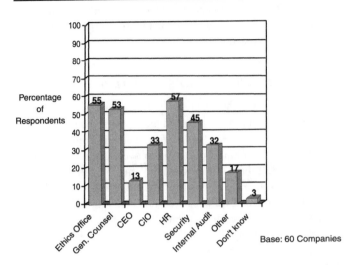

Base: 60 Companies

Figure 6
Who Is Responsible for Monitoring?

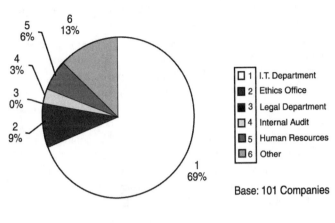

1	I.T. Department
2	Ethics Office
3	Legal Department
4	Internal Audit
5	Human Resources
6	Other

Base: 101 Companies

Figure 7
Who Has Access to Information Collected Through Monitoring?

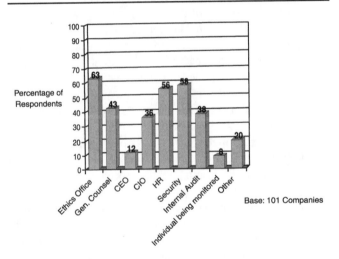

Base: 101 Companies

Referring to his company's practice of monitoring employees' Internet usage on a random basis, a vice president of ethics and compliance explains, "We look at the top ten sites at a [company] location, and when we see something unusual popping up, or something that has a lot of usage but doesn't have a clear business purpose, the people doing the monitoring would go in and take a look at it."

Responsibility for Monitoring So who actually does the work of checking on their co-workers' email and Internet usage? In the overwhelming majority of companies that responded to our survey, this is the responsibility of the IT department. Figure 6 demonstrates that respondent companies delegate this responsibility in different ways and, interestingly, the ethics office is responsible in only 9 percent of cases. That is not to say that the ethics officers do not become involved in the monitoring process. In the following sections we explore the extent to which this happens.

Monitoring the Monitors: How Is the Process Overseen? We have already alluded to the fact that monitoring employees' email and Internet usage necessarily involves an impingement on employees' privacy, to a greater or lesser degree. Even if employees accept that monitoring is necessary, it is critical that the process is carried out in a responsible and professional manner, and that information about employees does not fall into the wrong hands. In addition to the privacy issue, the fact that monitoring can lead to disciplinary action, including dismissal, would lead one to expect universal acceptance of the need for oversight and guidance of the monitoring process to prevent abuses. To our surprise, this appears not to be the case, as 25 percent of companies surveyed do not have in place procedures to ensure that the monitoring process is not subject to abuse. Furthermore, only 57 percent of companies responding to the survey have written guidelines, policies, or procedures to direct the monitoring process.

Given the potentially sensitive nature of the information collected about employees, it is perhaps also surprising that only 36 percent of companies in the survey require the monitoring department or person to sign a confidentiality agreement.

An essential requirement of any effective monitoring process is that relevant information needs to reach those people in the company who have a legitimate need to know it. As one might expect, different companies have different "need to know" criteria and they disseminate information gathered through monitoring to various individuals and corporate functions. It is perhaps not surprising that the largest consumers of such information are ethics officers, with 63 percent of companies allowing their ethics office access to the monitoring data. Security and human resources departments are not far behind, followed by legal departments (see Figure 7).

Ethics Office Involvement An organization's greatest source of knowledge about the ethical implications of monitoring is usually its ethics office (if it has one), and one would therefore expect the ethics office to have significant involvement in the monitoring process. Our survey sought to discover the extent to which this is true in practice.

We asked each company whether the monitoring process and the information thereby collected are overseen, implemented, and reviewed by its ethics office. The results were surprising. Only 43 out of 98 companies responding to this question (44 percent) involved their ethics offices in this way. We sought to clarify the situation in our interviews. When asked whether his company's ethics officer was involved in overseeing the monitoring of employee email and Internet usage, one corporate director of ethics and compliance was quite categorical, responding, "Frankly, no. It's more of an IT or Security responsibility." When asked whether he thought his office *should* be involved, he said, "I get involved where there are complaints that come to our ethics [help] line." Two other interviewees took a similar line, explaining that they became involved only if contacted directly with a complaint or allegation that warranted investigation. It appeared they did not otherwise see a role for the ethics office in the monitoring process.

At other companies, the degree of involvement of the ethics office appears to be greater. One director of ethics and compliance said, "I'm not part of the initial group that would be notified personally. That would be legal and HR. But those [ethics] incidents are reported in our working group, where Legal, HR and I meet on a monthly basis; I chair the group. In some cases, where an incident is reported through the helpline, of course I'm notified then."

While not getting involved in specific cases, a vice president to whom we spoke said that the ethics office at his company was involved in setting up the procedure for oversight of monitoring and determining the checkpoints along the way. He elaborated: "We were involved in setting up the procedures so that all the right people [are involved] before they go in specifically to open up an employee's file and look at all of their data and systems and email and Internet usage. There are several people who have to be involved: an attorney, someone from Human Resources, someone from the management team. And if they follow that protocol, then we're sure that we're treating people properly. And then … I oversee every disciplinary action."

Monitoring and Discipline The executives and managers interviewed were asked about their respective company's experience of email and Internet monitoring leading to disciplinary action against employees. The ten interviewees all knew of instances where this had happened, with employees being subject to a range of sanctions, from verbal warning to termination, depending on the circumstances. In all cases, employees were left in no doubt that abuse of company email, Internet, and other technology was viewed very seriously.

In most cases we found that discipline is handled by the human resources department in conjunction with line management. In the majority of cases, ethics office involvement is in an advisory capacity only. None of our interviewees had figures for disciplinary action in relation to email and Internet abuses.

Is Monitoring Ethical?

Our survey asked companies whether they believe it is ethical for them to monitor, read, or review employee email and/or Internet usage. Unsurprisingly, none thought monitoring was unethical. Fifty-seven percent gave an unqualified "yes" while the remaining 43 percent were prepared to support monitoring "only for good reason."

Changing Times, Changing Expectations

Several of the company representatives we interviewed had interesting observations on how changes in working practices and the work environment had affected their companies' approaches to the monitoring of employee email and Internet usage. One felt that "our previous policies, which did not contemplate reasonable personal use, and which were written at different times and in different styles, and not comprising a unified policy framework, really were not serving us well…. So this move [policy change] by us is a recognition that we want to create our policy in a manner that is aligned with the behavior that we are prepared to tolerate … and to make sure that some important values that we believe in are fully carried out with this policy."

Commenting on his company's change of policy to allow certain personal usage of company email and the Internet, another executive explained that it formally recognized what was happening anyway, but also acknowledged that as working hours had increased it was only reasonable to allow employees to take care of certain personal affairs such as online banking and bill-paying.

One manager of a global corporation highlighted geographical limitations on their monitoring policy, explaining that, in Europe, European Union regulations prevented the corporation from filtering and monitoring email and Internet usage to the full extent permissible in the United States. This is evidence of the difference between European and American attitudes to employee monitoring of technology use.

Summary of Survey Findings

A general sense that email and Internet monitoring is extremely widespread in corporate America has been affirmed by the finding that it is carried out by 92 percent of the corporations responding to our survey. Only one of these companies does not notify its employees that their use of email, the Internet, and other electronic media may be monitored. We can envisage no ethical justification for such a policy. About 4 out of every 5 companies that do notify their employees of the possibility of monitoring commonly publicize the fact in their ethics code and/or other manuals. It surprises us that only half of our respondents consider this an issue to be covered in training sessions.

Although all of our respondent corporations had adopted some kind of monitoring policy, it is worth noting one commentator's observation that despite—or possibly because of—the rapid expansion in the use of email and the Internet, most companies have not addressed the associated legal issues in a formal policy statement.[14] Note that, although we asked corporations about their adoption of monitoring policies, it was not our aim in this survey to examine the details of such policies.

Only one out of the ten executives we interviewed made an ethical distinction between monitoring employees' email usage and monitoring Internet usage. His distinction was based on his view that monitoring email is more likely to raise employee privacy concerns. We believe such concerns are legitimate and important, recognizing the controversial nature of the privacy issue and the case for limits on monitoring.

Almost all companies participating in the survey (92 percent) allow their employees reasonable personal usage of their electronic systems, yet fewer than half actually define what they consider reasonable. More than three-quarters of those companies that do attempt such a definition have no difficulty with emails to family members, occasional visits to news websites, and attending to retirement plan issues. Other activities are also permissible at some firms, albeit at only half or less of the respondent firms. Our interview questions elicited a recurring analogy with personal telephone calls. As with use of the telephone, employers do not want work patterns, productivity, or performance to be disrupted; and where that starts to happen is the point at which most employers draw the line on personal usage. Another major consideration for employers, apart from misuse of company time, is the protection of corporate interests. By certain kinds of personal usage of email and the Internet, employees can put themselves into conflict with the legitimate interests of their employers. Our interviews revealed that employers' greatest concerns in this area pertain to minimizing corporate risk exposure.

Some might find it surprising, if not alarming, that two-thirds of companies in our survey that monitor employees' email and Internet usage do not characterize their monitoring activities as "only for good reason." This is not to suggest that they do not have legitimate concerns that they are addressing, but it does seem to imply that the majority of companies do not consider it necessary to have suspicions, allegations, or complaints before monitoring.

Perhaps the most surprising discoveries of our survey were in the area of monitoring oversight. In the face of what is evidently an emotive issue, having ramifications in such sensitive areas as privacy, discipline, fiduciary relationships, and career progression—and having the potential to affect livelihoods very significantly—one might expect that great care is being taken by employers to prevent abuses and errors. In very many corporations we are sure that this is the case. Nevertheless, attention should be paid to the following statistics:

- A quarter of the companies in our survey admitted that they do not have in place any procedures or safeguards to ensure that the monitoring process is not abused.
- Nearly half do not have written guidelines, policies, or procedures by way of monitoring guidance.
- Two-thirds of respondents do not require the monitoring department or person to sign a confidentiality agreement.

Another surprising revelation was that less than half (44 percent) of the companies we surveyed involved their ethics office

as a matter of course in the monitoring process, by way of oversight, implementation, or case review. When we sought clarification, we found that several ethics officers among our interviewees regarded their involvement as being restricted to cases in which an allegation or complaint is made to them directly. Other companies appear to retain ethics officers in more of a consultative or advisory capacity; for example, in helping an HR manager to determine appropriate disciplinary action. It seems rare, however, for companies to involve their ethics officer throughout the monitoring process. Like many aspects of business practice, email and Internet monitoring appears to be evolving. There was recognition of this by a number of our interviewees who explained that their respective companies had reviewed their monitoring policies and revised them. Their concern was to ensure that the policies are aligned with altered perceptions and expectations concerning acceptable conduct by employees.

CONCLUSION

Perhaps the most effective means by which to achieve legitimate objectives of monitoring, while remaining sensitive to the valid concerns of employees, is to strive toward a balance that is respectful of both purposes. This balance would safeguard individual dignity and also hold individuals accountable for the satisfaction of their particular roles in the organization. Notwithstanding the impact on personal rights, as well as management objectives, the achievement of this balance is not without significant rewards for the organization as a whole. The Centre for Innovation in Management (CIM), in conjunction with the Schulich School of Business, has recently published the results of a research project examining the link between high trust stakeholder relationships and business value creation.[15] Ann Svendsen, CIM executive director, concludes that "trust, a cooperative spirit and shared understanding between a company and its stakeholders create greater coherence of action, better knowledge sharing, lower transaction costs, lower turnover rates and organizational stability. In the bigger picture, social capital appears to minimize shareholder risk, promote innovation, enhance reputation and deepen brand loyalty."

A monitoring program developed according to the mission and values of the organization (i.e., with integrity), then implemented in a manner that remains accountable to the affected employees, approaches that balance. In line with other survey findings, critical program elements would include adequate notice of the intent to monitor, including the form of monitoring, its frequency, and the purpose of the monitoring. Additionally, in order to be respectful of the balance between personal and professional interests, the employer should offer a means by which the employee can control the monitoring in order to create personal boundaries. Finally, monitoring should be connected to some specific legitimate business purpose, which will help the organization to create the most effective and least impactful program possible.

The survey evidences the broad impact of monitoring technology on our workplace decisions and environment. However, it also presents some relatively distressing data surrounding the responsibility for the implementation of monitoring—25 percent are lacking in policies designed to prevent abuse and almost 50 percent fail to have in place relevant policies and procedures. Where advances in technology allow us the ability to explore new activities of any type, it is critical that we also explore the ethical implications of, and accountability for, "pushing the envelope." Technological growth is only responsible where we also continue to maintain and develop our ethical awareness and we respect underlying organizational values. Therefore, when faced with innovative technology in the workplace, perhaps the response with the most integrity is the one that preserves appropriate traditional values while remaining open to exploring new ones.

NOTES

1. David Farrington, Foreword to *Employee Use of the Internet and EMail: A Model Corporate Policy*, ed. David M. Doubilet and Vincent I. Polley (American Bar Association, 2002).

2. U.S. Department of Commerce, Economics and Statistics Administration and National Telecommunications and Information Administration, "A Nation Online: How Americans Are Expanding Their Use of the Internet" (February 2002).

3. United States Sentencing Commission, *Guidelines Manual*, Chapter 8 (Washington, D.C., 1991).

4. Andrew Schulman, "One-third of U.S. Online Workforce under Internet/Email Surveillance," *Workforce Surveillance Project* (Privacy Foundation, July 9, 2001). http://www.privacyfoundation.org/workplace/ business/biz_show.asp?id=70&ac.

5. Jeffrey Brenner, "Privacy at Work? Be Serious," *Wired Magazine*. http://www.wired.com/news/business/0,1367, 42029,00.html (accessed 2/26/02).

6. Elron Software, "Guide to Internet Usage and Policy," p. 12 (2003). http://www.elronsoftware.com/pdf/IUP_Guide.pdf (accessed 5/20/03).

7. Alan Cohen, "Worker Watchers," *Fortune/CNET Technology Review* (summer 2001), 70, 76.

8. Institute for Global Ethics, "U.K. survey finds many workers are misusing email," *Newsline* 5(10) (3/11/02).

9. Elron Software, "The Year 2001 Corporate Web and Email Usage Study," p. 8. http://www.elronsoftware.com/pdf/ NFOReport.pdf (accessed 5/ 21/03).

10. Dana Hawkins, "Lawsuits Spur Rise in Employee Monitoring," *U.S. News & World Reports*, August 13, 2001.

11. Colin Bennett, "Cookies, Web bugs, Webcams and Cue Cats: Patterns of Surveillance on the World Wide Web," *Ethics and Information Technology* 3 (2001), 197–210.

12. Hawkins, *Lawsuits Spur Rise.*

13. Ibid.

14. Farrington, "Foreword."

15. Ann C. Svendsen, Robert G. Boutilier, Robert M. Abbott, and David Wheeler, *Measuring the Business Value of Stakeholder Relationships*, Part 1 (Toronto: Canadian Institute of Chartered Accountants, 2001).

Michael Hoffman is executive director of the Center for Business Ethics at Bentley College, Waltham, MA. Laura P. Hartman is Associate Vice President, Academic Affairs and Professor of Business Ethics at DePaul University, and a research fellow at the Center for Business Ethics. Mark Rowe is the senior research associate at the Center for Business Ethics.

The authors wish to pay grateful tribute to the valuable research and interviewing assistance provided by Yasam Tandogdu and Larissa Wilner, both graduate assistants at the Center for Business Ethics.

The Center for Business Ethics is also grateful for the support of the Ethics Officer Association and would like to thank its Sponsoring Partner corporations (and their interviewed representatives) for making this survey possible.

UP AGAINST WAL-MART

At the world's largest and most profitable retailer, low wages, unpaid overtime, and union busting are a way of life. Now Wal-Mart workers are fighting back.

BY KAREN OLSSON

JENNIFER MCLAUGHLIN IS 22, has a baby, drives a truck, wears wide-leg jeans and spiky plastic chokers, dyes her hair dark red, and works at Wal-Mart. The store in Paris, Texas—Wal-Mart Supercenter #148—is just down the road from the modest apartment complex where McLaughlin lives with her boyfriend and her one-year-old son; five days a week she drives to the store, puts on a blue vest with "How May I Help You?" emblazoned across the back, and clocks in. Some days she works in the Garden Center and some days in the toy department. The pace is frenetic, even by the normally fast-paced standards of retailing; often, it seems, there simply aren't enough people around to get the job done. On a given shift McLaughlin might man a register, hop on a mechanical lift to retrieve something from a high shelf, catch fish from a tank, run over to another department to help locate an item, restock the shelves, dust off the bike racks, or field questions about potting soil and lawn mowers. "It's stressful," she says. "They push you to the limit. They just want to see how much they can get away with without having to hire someone else."

Then there's the matter of her pay. After three years with the company, McLaughlin earns only $16,800 a year. "And I'm considered high-paid," she says. "The way they pay you, you cannot make it by yourself without having a second job or someone to help you, unless you've been

there for 20 years or you're a manager." Because health insurance on the Wal-Mart plan would deduct up to $85 from her biweekly paycheck of $550, she goes without, and relies on Medicaid to cover her son, Gage.

Complaints about understaffing and low pay are not uncommon among retail workers—but Wal-Mart is no mere peddler of saucepans and boom boxes. The company is the world's largest retailer, with $220 billion in sales, and the nation's largest private employer, with 3,372 stores and more than 1 million hourly workers. Its annual revenues account for 2 percent of America's entire domestic product. Even as the economy has slowed, the company has continued to metastasize, with plans to add 800,000 more jobs worldwide by 2007.

Given its staggering size and rapid expansion, Wal-Mart increasingly sets the standard for wages and benefits throughout the U.S. economy. "Americans can't live on a Wal-Mart paycheck," says Greg Denier, communications director for the United Food and Commercial Workers International Union (UFCW). "Yet it's the dominant employer, and what they pay will be the future of working America." The average hourly worker at Wal-Mart earns barely $18,000 a year at a company that pocketed $6.6 billion in profits last year. Forty percent of employees opt not to receive coverage under the company's medical plan, which costs up to $2,844 a year, plus a deductible.

As Jennifer McLaughlin puts it, "They're on top of the Fortune 500, and I can't get health insurance for my kid."

Angered by the disparity between profits and wages, thousands of former and current employees like McLaughlin have started to fight the company on a variety of fronts. Workers in 27 states are suing Wal-Mart for violating wage-and-hour laws; in the first of the cases to go to trial, an Oregon jury found the company guilty in December of systematically forcing employees to work overtime without pay. The retailer also faces a sex-discrimination lawsuit that accuses it of wrongly denying promotions and equal pay to 700,000 women. And across the country, workers have launched a massive drive to organize a union at Wal-Mart, demanding better wages and working conditions. Employees at more than 100 stores in 25 states—including Supercenter 4-148 in Paris—are currently trying to unionize the company, and in July the UFCW launched an organizing blitz in the Midwest, hoping to mobilize nearly 120,000 workers in Michigan, Kentucky, Ohio, and Indiana.

Wal-Mart has responded to the union drive by trying to stop workers from organizing—sometimes in violation of federal labor law. In 10 separate cases, the National Labor Relations Board has ruled that Wal-Mart repeatedly broke the law by interrogating workers, confiscating union literature, and firing union supporters. At the first sign of organizing in a store, Wal-Mart dispatches a team of union busters from its headquarters in Bentonville, Arkansas, sometimes setting up surveillance cameras to monitor workers. "In my 35 years in labor relations, I've never seen a company that will go to the lengths that Wal-Mart goes to, to avoid a union," says Martin Levitt, a management consultant who helped the company develop its anti-union tactics before writing a book called Confessions of a Union Buster. "They have zero tolerance."

The retaliation can be extreme. In February 2000, the meat-cutting department at a Wal-Mart in Jacksonville, Texas, voted to join the UFCW—the only Wal-Mart in the nation where workers successfully organized a union. Two weeks after the vote, the company announced it was eliminating its meat-cutting departments in all of its stores nationwide. It also fired four workers who voted for the union. "They held a meeting and said there was nothing we could do," recalls Dotty Jones, a former meat cutter in Jacksonville. "No matter which way the election went, they would hold it up in court until we were old and gray."

IF YOU'VE SEEN ONE WAL-MART, you've seen the Paris store, more or less: a gray cinder-block warehouse of a building, with a red stripe across the front, flags on the roof, WAL*MART spelled in large capitals in the center, and the company credos ("We Sell for Less" and "Everyday Low Prices") to the left and the right. Inside, the cavernous store is bathed in a dim fluorescent light that makes the white walls and linoleum look dingy, and on a

Friday shortly before Christmas, the merchandise is everywhere: not only in bins and on shelves, but in boxes waiting to be unloaded, or just stationed in some odd corner, like the pine gun cabinets ($169.87) lined up by the rest rooms. Television monitors advertise thermometers and compact discs, Christmas carols play over the audio system, and yet there's a kind of silence to the place, a suspension of ordinary life, as shoppers in their trances drift through the store and fill carts with tubs of popcorn, a microwave, a chess set, dog biscuits. Here Protestant thrift and consumer wants are reconciled, for the moment anyway, in carts brimming with bargains.

The only way to advance, says one former manager, is to work off the clock: "Working unpaid overtime equaled saving your job."

Wal-Mart's success story was scripted by its founder, Sam Walton, whose genius was not so much for innovation as for picking which of his competitors' innovations to copy in his own stores. In 1945, Walton bought a franchise variety store in Newport, Arkansas. The most successful retailers, he noticed, were chains like Sears and A&P, which distributed goods to stores most efficiently, lowered prices to generate a larger volume of sales, and in the process generated a lot of cash to finance further expansion. These, in turn, would serve as basic principles of Walton's business. As he explains in his autobiography, Sam Walton, Made in America, he drove long distances to buy ladies' panties at lower prices, recognizing that selling more pairs at four for a dollar would bring greater profits than selling fewer pairs at three for a dollar. The women of northeastern Arkansas were soon awash in underwear, and a discounter was born. Walton opened his first Wal-Mart Discount City in 1962 and gradually expanded out from his Arkansas base. By 1970 Wal-Mart owned 32 outlets; by 1980 there were 276; by 1990, 1,528 in 29 states.

The company grew, in no small part, by dint of its legendary frugality—a habit that started with Sam Walton himself, who drove an old pickup truck and shared hotel rooms on company trips and insisted on keeping the headquarters in Arkansas as plain as possible. Payroll, of course, tends to be a rather larger expense than hotel rooms, and Walton kept that as low as he could, too. He paid his first clerks 50 to 60 cents an hour—substantially below minimum wage at the time—by taking questionable advantage of a small-business exemption to the Fair Labor Standards Act. In 1970, Walton fended off an organizing push by the Retail Clerks Union in two small Missouri towns by hiring a professional union buster, John Tate, to lecture workers on the negative aspects of unions. On Tate's advice, he also took steps to win his workers over, encouraging them to air concerns with managers and implementing a profit-sharing program.

A few years later, Wal-Mart hired a consulting firm named Alpha Associates to develop a "union avoidance program." Martin Levitt, the consultant who worked on the program, says that Wal-Mart does "whatever it takes to wear people down and destroy their spirit." Each manager, he says, is taught to take union organizing personally: "Anyone supporting a union is slapping that supervisor in the face." The company also encouraged employees to believe in the good intentions of "Mr. Sam," who peppered his autobiography with tributes to his "associates": "If you want to take care of the customers you have to make sure you're taking care of the people in the stores."

Yet many Wal-Mart workers allege that the company Walton left behind when he died in 1992 is anything but a benevolent caretaker. "We're underpaid, and I'm worried about my retirement," says an overnight stocker in Minnesota who asked not to be identified. "I imagine I'll be working until I'm 90." Her daughter works as a stocker, too, but after nine years she doesn't make enough to support her children. "She's had to go down to the food bank, and I've sent stuff over for them," her mother says. "They just can't do it." On the job, she adds, workers are forced to scramble to make up for understaffing. "We're short—we have a skimpy crew at night. We've got pallets stacked over our heads, and we can't get caught up with all of it."

A quick look around at the store in Paris makes clear what an employee is up against: thousands of items (90,000 in a typical Wal-Mart) that customers are constantly removing from the shelves and not putting back, or putting back in the wrong place, or dropping on the floor—the store a kind of Augean stable, with a corps of blue-vested Herculeses trying to keep things clean. (When I mention this to Jennifer McLaughlin, she tells me that's why no one likes to work the 2 a.m. to 11 a.m. shift, because "all it is, is putting stuff back.") To get the job done, according to the dozens of employee lawsuits filed against the company, Wal-Mart routinely forces employees to work overtime without pay. In the Oregon wage-and-hour case, a former personnel manager named Carolyn Thiebes testified that supervisors, pressured by company headquarters to keep payroll low, regularly deleted hours from time records and reprimanded employees who claimed overtime. In 2000, Wal-Mart settled similar lawsuits involving 67,000 workers in New Mexico and Colorado, reportedly paying more than $50 million.

Wal-Mart blames unpaid overtime on individual department managers, insisting that such practices violate company policy. "We rely on our associates," says spokesman Bill Wertz. "It makes no business sense whatsoever to mistreat them." But Russell Lloyd, an attorney representing Wal-Mart employees in Texas, says the company "has a pattern throughout all stores of treating their workers the same way." Corporate headquarters collects reams of data on every store and every employee, he says, and uses sales figures to calculate how many hours of labor it wants to allot to each store. Store managers are then required to schedule fewer hours than the number allotted, and their performance is monitored in daily reports back to Bentonville. To meet the goals, supervisors pressure employees to work extra hours without pay.

"I was asked to work off the clock, sometimes by the store manager, sometimes by the assistant manager," says Liberty Morales Serna, a former employee in Houston. "They would know you'd clocked out already, and they'd say, 'Do me a favor. I don't have anyone coming in—could you stay here?' It would be like four or five hours. They were understaffed, and they expected you to work these hours."

Wal-Mart has made clear that keeping its stores union-free is as much a part of its culture as door greeters and blue aprons.

When Judy Danneman, a widow raising three children, went to work as an hourly department manager in West Palm Beach, Florida, she quickly realized that she would have to climb the management ladder in order to survive—because, as she puts it, "my kids had this bad habit of eating." The only way to do that, she says, was to work off the clock: "Working unpaid overtime equaled saving your job." When she finally became an assistant manager, Danneman knew she had to enforce the same policy: "I knew for my department managers to get their work done, they had to work off the clock. It was an unwritten rule. The majority of them were single mothers raising children, or else married women with children. It was sad, and it was totally demanding and very draining and very stressful."

In fact, more than two-thirds of all Wal-Mart employees are women—yet women make up less than 10 percent of top store managers. Back when she was first lady of Arkansas, Hillary Clinton became the first woman appointed to the Wal-Mart board, and tried to get the company to hire more women managers, but that effort apparently went the way of national health insurance. Wal-Mart today has the same percentage of women in management that the average company had in 1975.

Attorneys representing workers contend that Wal-Mart is too tightly controlled from headquarters in Arkansas to claim ignorance of what's happening in its stores. "In Bentonville they control the air conditioning, the music, and the freezer temperature for each store," says Brad Seligman, a lawyer with the Impact Fund, a nonprofit legal organization in Berkeley. "Most companies divide stores into regions, and then you have a home office of senior management. At Wal-Mart, the regional managers are based in Bentonville; they're on the road

Sunday to Wednesday, and then back meeting with management Thursday to Saturday. They're the ones who make the fundamental employee decisions—and the home office knows exactly what they are doing."

The company insists it adequately trains and promotes female managers. But in 2001, a Wal-Mart executive conducted an internal study that showed the company pays female store managers less than men in the same position. "Their focus at Wal-Mart has always relentlessly been on the bottom line and on cost cutting," says Seligman. "Virtually every other consideration is secondary—or third or fourth or fifth."

To PROTECT THE BOTTOM LINE Wal-Mart is as aggressive at fighting off unions as it is at cutting costs. Employees approached by co-workers about joining a union are "scared to even talk," says Ricky Braswell, a "greeter" at the store in Paris. "They're afraid they'll lose their jobs."

In Paris, it was Jennifer McLaughlin's boyfriend, 21-year-old Eric Jackson, who first started talking about a union. Raised by a mother who works in a factory, Jackson always assumed he would find a job after high school rather than go on to college. But the few factory jobs in Paris are highly sought after, so Jackson wound up at Wal-Mart, which employs 350 people out of a local workforce of only 22,000. "People ain't got no other place to go," he says. "There's no other jobs to be had."

Jackson started as an evening cashier earning $5.75 an hour, and it wasn't long before he was regularly asked to perform the duties of a customer service manager, supervising the other cashiers and scheduling their breaks. He asked for a promotion, but three months later he was still doing the extra work for no extra pay. "I took it because I wanted more money, but I never got the raise," Jackson says. "They knew they could do it to me." He fought for the promotion and eventually won, but by then he had already contacted a local union office about organizing the store.

"When Eric first suggested it, I looked at him like he was on crack," says McLaughlin. "I said, 'You can't take down a company like Wal-Mart with a union.'" Nevertheless, Jackson arranged for a UFCW organizer to come to Paris and meet with a small group of workers one June afternoon at the Pizza Inn. But the company soon caught wind of the organizing effort. As one worker left an early meeting of union supporters, he spotted a Wal-Mart manager in the parking lot. From then on, workers seen as pro-union were watched closely by management.

"By the time we had our first meeting, they were holding their first anti-union meeting," says McLaughlin. The response came straight from the company's union-avoidance playbook: Troops from the Bentonville "People Division" were flown in, and employees were required to attend hour-long meetings, where they were shown anti-labor videos and warned about unions. "They tend to treat you like you're simple, and they use real bad scare

tactics," says McLaughlin. Those who supported the union, she says, were told, "Some people just don't belong at Wal-Mart."

McLaughlin isn't shy about speaking her mind, and in the meeting she confronted one of the men from the People Division. "Let me tell you, I used to have epilepsy," she told him. "My dad was in a union, and we had health insurance, and I got better. I don't have health insurance. If my child got epilepsy, what would I do? Doesn't a union help you to get company-paid insurance?" The man, she recalls, became flustered. "Jennifer, I don't have an answer about that," he said. "I'll have to get back with you."

The meetings were just the beginning. "The videos and group meetings are the surface cosmetics," says Levitt, the former consultant. "Where Wal-Mart beats the union is through a one-on-one process implemented from Bentonville. They carefully instruct management to individually work over each employee who might be a union sympathizer." In Paris, Eric Jackson was called into a back room by five managers and made to watch an anti-union video and participate in a role-playing exercise. "I was supposed to be a manager, and one of them was the associate who came to me with a question about a union," says Jackson. "So I quoted the video. I said, 'We do not believe we need a union at Wal-Mart,' and they were like, 'Good, good!' and then I said, 'We're not anti-union— we're pro-associate,' just like I'm supposed to say."

Before the onslaught by the company, says McLaughlin, she talked to more than 70 workers at the Paris store who were prepared to sign cards calling for a vote on union representation, but that number quickly dwindled. Those who'd signed cards felt they were being watched. "All of a sudden the cameras start going up," says Chris Bills, who works in the receiving area. "Now there's three in receiving. This one manager took up smoking so he could sit with us on our breaks." Other hourly employees learned for the first time that they were actually counted as managers. "They said we were considered management, so we shouldn't get involved with the union stuff," says Dianne Smallwood, a former customer service manager who worked at the store seven years. Employees opposed to the union were given "pro-associate" buttons to wear, while managers amended the dress code to exclude T-shirts with any kind of writing on them, apparently to prevent workers from wearing union shirts.

Wal-Mart declined to let *Mother Jones* interview store managers or representatives from the People Division in Bentonville, but says it sends out people from corporate headquarters "to answer questions associates may have and to make sure that all store personnel are aware of their legal requirements and meet those requirements exactly." But the company has also made clear that keeping its stores union-free is as much a part of Wal-Mart culture as door greeters and blue aprons. "Union representation may work well for others," says Cynthia Illick, a company spokeswoman. "However, it is not a fit for Wal-Mart."

With the company so determined to ward off unions, the prospects of employees in towns like Paris, Texas, winning significant improvements in wages and working conditions seem awfully slim. "It's a long process," Jennifer McLaughlin concedes. "I wish it could be done in the next year, but people come and go, and for every one union card you get signed, two other ones who signed cards have gotten fired or left. It's real frustrating, and a lot of times I don't want to do it no more. But I'm not going to give up until I end up leaving the store."

In the end, the success of the organizing drives may depend on labor's ability to mobilize more than just store employees. "We'll never bring Wal-Mart to the table store by store," says Bernie Hesse, an organizer for UFCW Local 789 in Minneapolis. "I can get all the cards signed I want, and they'll still crash us. They'll close the frigging store, I'm convinced. We've got to do it in conjunction with the community." That means going to small businesses and religious leaders and local officials, he says, and convincing them that it's in their interest to stand up to Wal-Mart. "As a community we've got to say, 'All right, if you want to come here and do business, here's what you've got to do—you've got to pay a living wage, you've got to provide affordable health insurance.'"

Putting together such a broad initiative can be "like pulling teeth," Hesse says, but the stakes are high. If employees succeed in improving wages and working conditions at the country's largest employer, they could effectively set a new benchmark for service-sector jobs throughout the economy. Some 27 million Americans currently make $8.70 an hour or less—and by the end of the decade, Hesse notes, nearly 2 million people worldwide will work at Wal-Mart.

"These are the jobs our kids are going to have," he says.

Karen Olsson, a former editor for the *Texas Observer*, writes primarily about labor and politics for such publications as *Texas Monthly, The Nation*, and the *Washington Post*.

The Hidden Costs of Organizational Dishonesty

Companies that engage in unethical practices face consequences far more harmful than is traditionally recognized. The resulting damage can easily outweigh the short-term gains.

By Robert B. Cialdini, Petia K. Petrova and Noah J. Goldstein

A brief scanning of *The Wall Street Journal*—or, tellingly, almost any other newspaper in the country—reveals the alarming prevalence and far-reaching impact of organizational dishonesty. Reports of malfeasance or criminal conduct in corporate governance, accounting practices, regulatory evasions, securities transactions, advertising misrepresentations and so on have become all too commonplace. It's no wonder that business schools across the country have been rushing to design and introduce courses that emphasize a subject traditionally given short shrift: ethics.[1]

This is not to say that, as a group, business people are inherently unethical. All other things being equal, most executives would unhesitatingly choose the high road. Except in hypothetical situations, however, all other things are never equal. In any organization, people are motivated by myriad factors—sales quotas, corporate economic health and survival, competitive concerns, career advancement and so forth—which can easily override their moral compasses. Indeed, in spite of the assortment of arguments contending that "ethics pays,"[2] the number and extent of the recent transgressions suggest that a significant portion of the business world has yet to be persuaded.

Of course, companies should always adhere to universal ethical principles because, after all, that's the right thing to do. But one additional reason for businesses to engage in honest practices is that the consequences of failing to do so may be much more harmful to the bottom line than has traditionally been recognized. Companies that deploy dishonest tactics typically do so as a means of increasing their short-term profits, and in that regard they might succeed. But the misconduct is likely to fuel a set of social psychological processes with the potential for ruinous fiscal outcomes that can easily outweigh any short-term gains. In other words, organizations that behave unethically will find themselves heading down a slippery and dangerous fiscal path.

In this article we chart that path, providing details of the extent of the damage and its insidious nature. Our formulation begins with a fundamental assertion: An organization that regularly teaches, encourages, condones or allows the use of dishonest tactics in its external dealings (that is, toward customers, clients, stockholders, suppliers, distributors, regulators and so on) will experience a set of internal consequences. These outcomes, which we call malignancies, are likely to be surprisingly costly and particularly damaging for two reasons. First, they will be like tumors—growing, spreading and eating progressively at the organization's health and vigor. Second, they will be difficult to trace and identify via typical accounting methods as the true causes of poor productivity and profitability. Thus, they might easily lead to expensive misguided efforts that fail to target the genuine culprits of the dysfunction. The malignancies can be categorized into three types, according to the processes involved (see "The Consequences of Organizational Dishonesty").

Malignancy #1: Reputation Degradation

Perhaps the most obvious consequence of systematic organizational dishonesty is that a company will develop a poor reputation among current and prospective clients and business partners. To be clear, we are not referring to small-scale, localized or infrequent ethical infractions but rather to an organizational culture in which employees are socialized into an environment that either implicitly condones or, worse, explicitly teaches dishonest business practices. When anyone outside the company (such as customers, partners, suppliers, regulators or the media) uncovers the improper tactics, the fallout can be swift and devastating. As Edson W. Spencer, the former chairman of Honeywell Inc., once stated, "The businessman who straddles a fine line between what is right and what is expedient should remember that it takes years to build a good business reputation, but one false move can destroy that reputation overnight."[3]

For one thing, the damage to the firm's opportunities for new and repeat business can be considerable. According to a recent survey of the general public conducted by Wirthlin Worldwide of Reston, Virginia, 80% of respondents stated that their perception of the ethicality of a particular company's business practices has had a direct effect on their decisions to purchase

The Consequences of Organizational Dishonesty

A company with dishonest business practices toward customers, vendors, distributors and other outsiders might achieve higher short-term profits, but it would incur various costs from three types of malignancy.

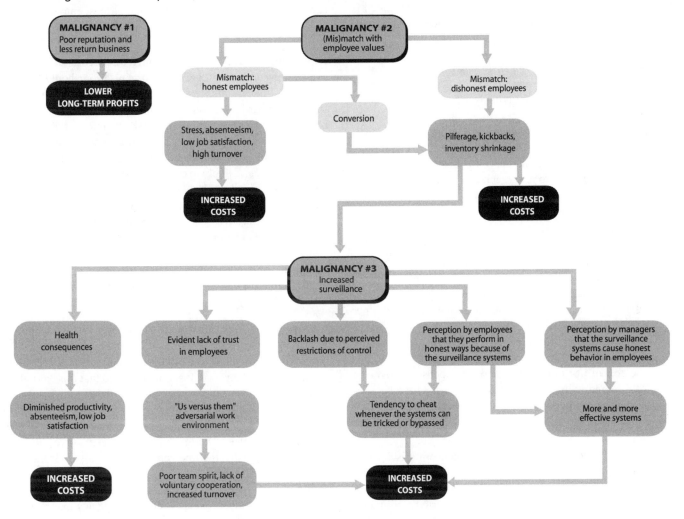

goods or services from that firm.[4] And the financial damage could extend further. According to the Wirthlin survey, 74% of the respondents asserted that their perceptions of the honesty of a corporation's behavior had also influenced their decisions about whether to buy that company's stock.[5]

More importantly, the damage could be irreparable. An organization that has historically been successful but is currently suffering from inefficient operations, a lack of creativity or even incompetence still has the ability to regain people's confidence by demonstrating the early stages of a turnaround (for example, by hiring a well-respected consulting group, by developing an alliance with a highly regarded organization or by impressing industry insiders with an innovative new product line). But companies that are perceived to be corrupt will find it much more difficult, if not impossible, to shed themselves of that stigma. Past research has found that, by nature, people react more adversely to deceitfulness than to any other attribute.[6] And even if only one branch of a company is caught in the wrongdoing, the whole organization might suffer because dishonesty is a trait that, when discovered in one domain, is immediately perceived to be underlying the behaviors across other domains.[7]

Dishonesty is a trait that, when discovered in one branch of a company, is immediately perceived to be underlying the behaviors across other domains.

Consequently, once outsiders perceive that dishonest policies and practices have become central to the way a company does business, that organization will face a long, uphill battle. Research suggests that a disreputable company attempting to recover lost trust needs to demonstrate its newfound integrity consistently on numerous occasions (many more than the number taken to display its dishonesty in the first place) to stand even a chance of convincing wary others that it has changed for the better.[8] During the recovery process, which could easily take years, customers and clients who have defected are likely to commit themselves to another, more respectable, organization. To speed its rehabilitation, a company may need to replace top management quickly in an effort to convince others of its sincerity and eagerness to attack the root cause of the dishonesty.

Malignancy #2: (Mis)matches Between Values of Employee and Organization

The extent to which the values of an organization coincide with those of its employees is another issue. Whether that match is good or not, companies with dishonest practices are likely to incur substantial costs.

A Poor Fit for Organizational Dishonesty An organization that encourages deceptive business practices by rewarding the use of duplicity with outside contacts is likely to be met with moral opposition by a number of employees whose values do not comport with those espoused by the company. Many of these individuals will find their moral standards continually clashing with workplace expectations, leading to constant stress from the ever-present conflict.[9] The resulting costs to the organization can be considerable: greater instances of illness and absenteeism,[10] lower job satisfaction,[11] decreased productivity and higher turnover.

Increased absenteeism. Corporate expenditures on illness and absenteeism amount to far more than the costs of "get well" cards and Mylar balloons. A recent survey on unscheduled absences in the workplace revealed an all-time high of $789 per employee annually, which amounts to more than $3.6 million in yearly losses for larger corporations. This number reflects only the direct payroll costs for the absent employees. It does not include the cost of lost productivity and the expense of covering for the absent individuals, including overtime pay for other employees and the hiring of temporary workers.[12]

Lower job satisfaction. An even greater concern arises when the mismatch between the moral standards of some employees and the unethical practices of a company leads to lower job satisfaction among those individuals. From a strictly utilitarian perspective, an organization should be concerned about worker job satisfaction only to the extent that it affects employee productivity and turnover. Clear evidence has existed for the latter (to be discussed shortly) but not for the former until relatively recently. Specifically, traditional studies on the relationship between job satisfaction and productivity suggested only a weak connection between the two.[13] But subsequent research has qualified this finding, revealing that the correlation between job satisfaction and performance is rather weak only for workers with low skill levels, presumably because those individuals do not have the capability to produce high-quality work even when they are quite content with their jobs.[14] But for employees who are highly skilled, job satisfaction actually makes a substantial difference: Those who were satisfied with their jobs outperformed those who were not by a margin of 25%.

These findings have serious implications. When moral employees are required to engage in immoral behaviors, the productivity of the most competent and proficient workers will suffer most. This outcome should be extremely troubling to many organizations for two reasons. First, companies generally earn a sizable portion of their revenues (and enhance their reputations) based on the highest efforts of their ablest workers. If those individuals aren't motivated, revenues (and reputation) could easily suffer. Second, because the most capable workers are usually the ones better able to find other jobs, dishonest companies bear a large risk of losing their best employees.

Higher turnover. Because of the high direct costs of recruiting and training new employees, any organization should be concerned if it has trouble retaining people. Dishonest companies should take particular note, though, because their turnover will be selective in nature. Research has shown that workers who do not share the values of their organizations tend to be less satisfied with their jobs, less committed to their organizations and significantly more likely to quit.[15] Thus, over time, an unethical corporation is likely to have employees who are disproportionately dishonest. Moreover, policies that promote dishonest business practices are likely to drive the most productive workers into the offices of more honest competitors, where those individuals can find greater job satisfaction and be more at ease with their work environments. In other words, once a dishonest organization has unwittingly thrown out the baby, all that will be left is the dirty bath water.

A Good Fit for Organizational Dishonesty We have already discussed how honest workers select themselves out of dishonest firms by leaving to work for companies with values more consistent with their own. It should be noted that this "moral dilution" also occurs at an earlier point in the employment process. Specifically, job seekers tend to be attracted to organizations with attributes that are congruent with their own personality profiles.[16] For example, in a recent survey, 76% of respondents said that their perceptions of a company's integrity would influence their decision about accepting a job there.[17] Of course, selection through the filter of value congruency also occurs on the employer's side. That is, companies that regularly require their workers to engage in unethical practices tend to seek people who are willing (if not eager) to play ball in that system. As these various forces attract unethical prospects and repel ethical employees, the low standards of a dishonest organization can be self-reinforced in perpetuity.

Unethical corporations do not merely select and retain dishonest employees; they create them as well. Honest employees can be converted into wrongdoers in various ways, but the process often begins with peer pressure or a supervisor's direct request.[18] After transgressors have had the opportunity to reflect on their recent misconduct, the incongruity between their values and behavior will strongly motivate them to rationalize their actions. (Otherwise, they would need to change their views of themselves in light of what they've just done.) Counterintuitive as it may sound, many of these individuals will continue to engage in dishonest business practices in an attempt to bring a sense of legitimacy to their original offenses. These workers are likely to find further comfort in the vast system of justifications embedded in the corrupt ideology of the organizational culture.[19] As the practice of rationalizing their misdeeds becomes routine, the employees gradually adopt that ideology for themselves.[20]

Regardless of whether a company's dishonest workforce comes primarily from turnover, recruitment or conversion, an organization that consists of dishonest workers is certain to suffer from various internal consequences, such as employee theft, fraud and delinquency. After all, if workers are cheating customers and others outside the company, why shouldn't they also be bilking their employer?

Consider the experiences of a former employee of a consulting firm whose manager suggested that she withhold information from a client. "I was constantly on guard to what I was 'supposed' to tell them," says the former employee. "I felt dishonest." Later, the employee found herself regularly cheating on her travel expenses. "We were allotted a set amount of money per day that was the maximum we would be reimbursed for," she recalls. "I began charging this amount to my expenses each day, regardless of my actual expenses. This was the accepted practice for most people on the project, but it was unethical." Since leaving the firm, the employee has had some time to reflect on her actions. "Looking back," she says, "I have to wonder if the dishonesty that I felt at the client site as a firm representative had anything to do with the ease with which I was able to be dishonest with the firm in another way."

When moral employees are required to engage in immoral behaviors, the productivity of the most competent and proficient workers will suffer most.

According to a recent survey, fraud perpetrated by employees is the most common type of fraud that afflicts companies. In fact, it is nearly twice as widespread as consumer fraud, the next most prevalent type.[21] The financial burdens of internal fraud, including employee theft, are mind-boggling. According to the Association of Certified Fraud Examiners, U.S. companies lose roughly $400 billion dollars a year to internal fraud.[22] Years ago, a government legislative committee noted that nearly one-third of all business losses in the United States were the result of internal larceny.[23] More recently, in 2003 nearly two-thirds of corporations surveyed reported they had suffered from employee fraud, and the trends suggest that the situation is likely to worsen.[24] For example, compared with data from half a decade ago, theft of company assets has more than doubled, expense-account abuse has nearly tripled and fraud through collusion between employees and third-parties is also on the rise.[25]

In response to this growing problem, many organizations have overlooked any role that their own dishonest policies and practices might have played. Instead, they have focused on the symptoms of the problem, implementing a host of specific preemptive and reactive measures. Of these, the use of stronger internal controls, such as increased security and more sophisticated surveillance systems, is growing at the fastest pace.[26] But the unintended consequences of such countermeasures can sometimes be nearly as deleterious as the problems they are aimed at solving in the first place.

Malignancy #3: Increased Surveillance

The direct expenses associated with the installation of surveillance systems are staggering. Between 1990 and 1992, for example, more than 70,000 U.S. corporations spent over half a billion dollars on surveillance software.[27] But the indirect costs—degradation of the work environment that leads to adversarial relations between employer and workers, diminished productivity and other dysfunctions—can also be considerable.

Health Consequences Employee monitoring is associated with a host of mental health problems,[28] including high levels of tension, severe anxiety and depression.[29] Employees are also more likely to experience physical disorders, such as carpal tunnel syndrome, when they perceive their organization's surveillance system as encroaching on their privacy.[30] These types of psychological and physical ailments are linked directly to increased absenteeism and diminished productivity.

Lack of Trust in Employees Workers often perceive the installation of surveillance software and other devices as clear indications that their organization doesn't trust them. This perception eventually harms any existing companywide esprit de corps, often creating an atmosphere of antagonism between employees and management.[31] In addition, workers who feel insulted that their integrity is being questioned are more likely to quit or retaliate with a variety of counterproductive behaviors, ranging from the simple withholding of voluntary support to outright acts of revenge and sabotage.[32] This type of dysfunctional environment has been described by a former manager of a company that was trying to curtail inventory shrinkage due to employee theft: "Senior management brainstormed the best way to solve the issue and came up with the use of expensive video surveillance equipment in the stockrooms to monitor employees leaving and also the process of opening new shipments. This implementation did not decrease shrinkage, but did have a negative impact on employee turnover."

Honest and dishonest workers alike may assume that monitoring reflects the corrupt dispositions of fellow employees and the large rewards of cheating.

Backlash to Perceived Restrictions of Control People who feel that their sense of freedom is being threatened will often try to reassert some control over their environment.[33] In the workplace, employees might attempt to empower themselves through both corrective and retributive means—that is, by trying to regain the control that was previously taken away and by committing deliberately hostile actions to retaliate.[34] Consequently, in an organization with excessive control systems, some employees might be more motivated to steal from the company.[35] Of course, employee theft and other dishonest behaviors are only likely to motivate management to procure even higher levels of surveillance technology, further perpetuating the vicious cycle.

Undermining of Positive Behavior Another potential consequence of surveillance equipment is that many employees might come to believe that the systems are warranted even when they're not. That is, honest and dishonest workers alike might assume that the monitoring must reflect both the corrupt dispositions of fellow employees and the large rewards of cheating. Unfortunately for the company, actions that convey expectations of wrongdoing (either implicitly or explicitly) may in fact lead to a rise in misconduct for both honest and dishonest workers by creating self-fulfilling prophesies for the former[36] and self-perpetuating ones for the latter.[37]

Surveillance technology can also undermine employee behavior in subtler ways. Specifically, when individuals are being monitored closely, they might begin to attribute any of their honest behavior not to their own natural predisposition but rather to the coercive forces of the controls. Eventually, they might view their actions as being directed less by their own moral standards and more by the prying eyes of management.[38] When that happens, they might lower their ethical standards and be more inclined to try to outwit or elude the surveillance system and engage in misconduct when they aren't being monitored.[39] This, too, will spur supervisors to find more effective (and more expensive) control systems.

Overestimated Influence of Monitoring Management, too, can begin to overestimate the power of surveillance systems. That is, people who are responsible for the implementation, maintenance and strengthening of control systems are likely to assume that the desirable conduct of the monitored workers is primarily a result of the surveillance equipment even when that behavior would have occurred without the use of such systems.[40] This misconception may help explain why internal controls continue to rise in popularity in corporate America despite the dramatic increases in supervisors' workloads when new systems are first established.[41] After these systems are in place, management may come to see them as more effective and more vital than they truly are. And once again such mistaken assumptions might lead to greater expenditures to purchase even more sophisticated systems.

Toward the Honest Organization

Beyond moral grounds, we have discussed sound utilitarian reasons for organizations to conduct themselves ethically. We focused primarily on what the costs might be for those businesses otherwise tempted to teach, condone or merely allow the systematic use of dishonest practices with external contacts.

Although many of the effects of organizational dishonesty are difficult to trace, the damage done is no less real. Consider the following account of how the unprincipled practices of a company helped cost it nearly $1 billion in losses. According to a former employee, "The CEO … abused ethical principles on a regular basis…. People believed him in the short run, but as the truth would leak out, the company's reputation deteriorated. Few companies are willing to do business with him now—those that do will only do so on onerous terms."

Eventually, that culture of dishonesty had permeated the entire organization. "The marketing department was coerced to exaggerate the truth," says the former employee. "The PR department wrote mostly false press releases, and salespeople coerced customers." Moreover, the misconduct was directed internally as well as externally. "Taking a cue from the executives, employees would steal from the company whenever they could, usually via travel and expense reports. Some would cut side deals with suppliers," recalls the employee.

To make matters worse, a security force was hired to roam the building routinely, ostensibly to protect employees, but many workers instead felt that they were being spied on. That suspicion only intensified when reports of even minor infractions, such as people taking long smoking breaks, were sent to the CEO. Not surprisingly, job satisfaction at the company was bad, morale terrible and turnover high. "People were attracted to the company by high salaries, which the CEO saw as justification for treating employees poorly, but left as soon as they could find work elsewhere," recalls the former employee.

The various costs of organizational dishonesty—decreased repeat business, low job satisfaction and performance, high worker turnover, employee theft, expensive surveillance mechanisms and an atmosphere of distrust—have often been cited as severe business problems. But many organizations have failed in their efforts to address those issues, often because they are unaware of a root cause: their own tendencies to conduct business with customers and others unscrupulously. So, instead, corporations often launch wrongheaded efforts to control one fiscal hemorrhage (for example, losses from employee theft) by creating another (namely, investments in increasingly expensive security systems).

The more effective solution is to staunch the wound at its self-inflicted site, with an unblinking examination of corporate dishonesty and a true commitment to end it. But achieving ethical standards requires more than just implementing institutional codes of conduct[42] or more effective security systems because increased control often leads only to even more negative outcomes. Instead, the effort must begin at the top, with senior executives setting the right example and then implementing policies to encourage the same behavior from employees in their dealings with clients, customers, vendors and distributors as well as with other employees. For example, top managers should incorporate customers' ratings of the ethicality of specific employees into the incentive structures of those individuals. Also, the ethical reputation of the organization as a whole should be measured regularly and included in the annual assessments of the company's performance. With such policies in place, companies can maintain high standards of conduct and attract (and retain) honest employees, and by doing so they can avoid the various hidden costs of organizational dishonesty.

REFERENCES

1. A. Sachdev, "Ethics Moves to Head of Class," Chicago Tribune, Friday, Feb. 14, 2003, Business Section, p. 1.

2. For a discussion of the history of "ethics as enlightened self-interest" arguments, see A. Stark, "What's the Matter With Business Ethics?" Harvard Business Review 71 (May–June 1993): 38–48.

3. F.W. Steckmest, "Corporate Performance: The Key to Public Trust" (New York: McGraw-Hill, 1982), 73.

4. D.E. Lewis, "Corporate Trust a Matter of Opinion," Boston Globe, Sunday, Nov. 23, 2003, p. G2.

5. Ibid.

6. N. Anderson, "Likeableness Ratings of 555 Personality-Trait Words," Journal of Personality and Social Psychology 9, no. 3 (1968): 272–279; and D. Barrett, "The Persistent Undermining Effects of Source Dishonesty on Persuasion" (Ph.D. diss., Arizona State University, 2002).

7. D. Trafimow, "The Effects of Trait Type and Situation Type on the Generalization of Trait Expectancies Across Situations," Personality and Social Psychology Bulletin 27, no. 11 (2001): 1463–1468.

8. M. Rothbart and B. Park, "On the Confirmability and Disconfirmability of Trait Concepts," Personality and Social Psychology Bulletin 50, no. 1 (1986): 131–142.

9. P. Dewe, "Measuring Primary Appraisal: Scale Construction and Directions for Future Research," Journal of Social Behavior and Personality 8, no. 4 (1993): 673–685.

10. S. Cohen, D.A.J. Tyrrell and A.P. Smith, "Psychological Stress and Susceptibility to the Common Cold," New England Journal of Medicine 325, no. 9 (1991): 606–612.

11. R.C. Barnett, N.L. Marshall, S.W. Raudenbush and R.T. Brennen, "Gender and the Relationship Between Job Experiences and Psychological Distress," Journal of Personality and Social Psychology 64, no. 5 (1993): 794–806.

12. "2002 CCH Unscheduled Absence Survey" (Riverwoods, Illinois: CCH Inc., 2002).

13. M.T. Iaffaldano and G.H. Muchinsky, "Job Satisfaction and Job Performance: A Meta-Analysis," Psychological Bulletin 97, no. 2 (1985): 251–273.

14. P.E. Varca and M. James-Valutis, "The Relationship of Ability and Satisfaction to Job Performance," Applied Psychology: An International Review 42, no. 3 (1993): 265–275.

15. C.A. O'Reilly, J. Chatman and D.F. Caldwell, "People and Organizational Culture: A Profile Comparison Approach to Assessing Person-Organization Fit," Academy of Management Journal 34, no. 3 (1991): 487–516; and C.H. Schwepker, Jr., "The Relationship Between Ethical Conflict, Organizational Commitment and Turnover Intentions in the Salesforce," Journal of Personal Selling & Sales Management 19, no. 1 (1999): 43–49.

16. D.M. Cable and T.A. Judge, "Person Organization Fit, Job Choice Decisions, and Organizational Entry," Organizational Behavior and Human Decision Processes 67, no. 3 (1996): 294–311.

17. Lewis, "Corporate Trust a Matter of Opinion," Boston Globe.

18. A.P. Brief, R.T. Buttram and J.M. Dukerich, "Collective Corruption in the Corporate World: Toward a Process Model," in "Groups at Work: Advances in Theory and Research," ed. M.E. Turner (Hillsdale, New Jersey: Lawrence Erlbaum Associates Inc., 2000), 471–499.

19. Ibid.

20. B.E. Ashforth and V. Anand, "The Normalization of Corruption in Organizations," in "Research in Organizational Behavior, Vol. 25," eds. B.M. Staw and R.M. Kramer (Greenwich, Connecticut: JAI Press, 2003), 1–52.

21. "Fraud Survey 2003," available at http://www.us.kpmg.com/news/index.asp?cid=1493 (KPMG, 2003).

22. Cf. J. Greenberg, "Who Stole the Money, and When? Individual and Situational Determinants of Employee Theft," Organizational Behavior and Human Decision Processes 89, no. 1 (2002): 985–1003.

23. B. Young, R. Mountjoy and M. Roos, "Employee Theft" (Sacramento, California: Assembly of the State of California Publications Office, 1981).

24. "Fraud Survey 2003," available at http://www.us.kpmg.com/news/index.asp?cid=1493 (KPMG, 2003).

25. Ibid.

26. Ibid.

27. D. Kipnis, "Trust and Technology," in "Trust in Organizations: Frontiers of Theory and Research," eds. R.M. Kramer and T.R. Tyler (Thousand Oaks, California: Sage Publications, 1996), 39–49.

28. K. Martin and R.E. Freeman, "Some Problems with Employee Monitoring," Journal of Business Ethics 43, no. 4 (2003): 353–361.

29. L.P. Hartman, "The Rights and Wrongs of Workplace Snooping," Journal of Business Strategy 19 (May–June 1998): 16–19.

30. "Employee Monitoring: Is There Privacy in the Workplace?" available at http://www.privacyrights.org/FS/fs7-work.htm (San Diego, California: Privacy Rights Clearinghouse).

31. E.L. Deci, J.P. Connell and P.M. Ryan, "Self-Determination in a Work Organization," Journal of Applied Psychology 74, no. 4 (1989): 580–590.

32. R.J. Bies and T.M. Tripp, "Beyond Distrust: 'Getting Even' and the Need for Revenge," in "Trust and Organizations," eds. R.M. Kramer and T. Tyler (Thousand Oaks, California: Sage Publications, 1996), 216–245.

33. J.W. Brehm, "A Theory of Psychological Reactance" (New York: Academic Press, 1966).

34. R.J. Bennett, "Perceived Powerlessness as a Cause of Deviant Employee Behavior," in "Dysfunctional Behavior in Organizations, Vol. 1," eds. R. Griffin, A. O'Leary-Kelly and J. Collins (Greenwich, Connecticut: JAI Press, 1998), 231–238; and A.W. Kruglanski, "Attributing Trustworthiness in Worker-Supervisor Relations," Journal of Experimental Social Psychology 6, no. 2 (1970): 214–232.

35. J. Greenberg and K.S. Scott, "Why Do Workers Bite the Hands That Feed Them? Employee Theft as a Social Exchange Process," in "Research in Organizational Behavior, Vol. 18," eds. B.M. Staw and L.L. Cummings (Greenwich, Connecticut: JAI Press, 1996), 111–155.

36. M.J. Harris, R. Milch, E.M. Corbitt, D.W. Hoover and M. Brady, "Self-Fulfilling Effects of Stigmatizing Information on Children's Social Interactions," Journal of Personality and Social Psychology 63, no. 3 (1992): 41–50.

37. L. Jussim, "Social Perception and Social Reality: A Reflection-Construction Model," Psychological Review 98, no. 1 (1991): 54–73.

38. For a review, see E.L. Deci and R.M. Ryan, "The Support of Autonomy and the Control of Behavior," Journal of Personality and Social Psychology 53, no. 6 (1987): 1024–1037.

39. L.M. Van Swol, "The Effects of Regulation on Trust," Basic and Applied Social Psychology 25, no. 3 (2003): 221–233.

40. A.W. Kruglanski, "Attributing Trustworthiness in Worker-Supervisor Relations," Journal of Experimental Social Psychology 6, no. 2 (1970): 214–232.

41. J. Chalykoff and T.A. Kochan, "Computer-Aided Monitoring: Its Influence on Employee Satisfaction and Turnover," Personnel Psychology 40, no. 3 (1989): 807–834.

42. J. Finegan and C. Theriault, "The Relationship between Personal Values and the Perception of the Corporation's Code of Ethics," Journal of Applied Social Psychology 27, no. 8 (1997): 708–724.

Robert B. Cialdini is the Regents' professor of psychology at the Department of Psychology at Arizona State University. **Petia K. Petrova** and **Noah J. Goldstein** are doctoral students in psychology at ASU. Contact them at robert.cialdini@asu.edu, petia.petrova@asu.edu and noah.goldstein@asu.edu.

Reprinted from *MIT Sloan Management Review*, Vol. 45, No. 3, Spring 2004, pp. 67–73, by permission of publisher. Copyright © 2004 by Massachusetts Institute of Technology. All rights reserved.

Corruption: Causes and Cures

Auditors can help detect and deter bribery and kickbacks.

By Joseph T. Wells

"You'll never catch Burgin," television investigative reporter Marsha Halford said to me during an off-camera interview regarding rumors of bribery in the Mississippi senate. "He is the smartest and most corrupt politician in the state."

The Federal Bureau of Investigation had Senator William G. Burgin Jr., chairman of the Mississippi State Senate Appropriations Committee, under scrutiny. As the agent in charge of the case, I wasn't allowed to answer her. But I knew something that Halford and even Burgin didn't know: We'd just about nailed him, and he wasn't very smart after all.

Within a month of that interview, Burgin was indicted for pocketing at least $83,000 in bribes. He later was convicted and served three years in federal prison. The Burgin investigation illustrates a checklist of classic lessons that CPAs can apply when confronted with allegations or suspicions of bribery.

RUMORS OFTEN ARE TRUE

Those who accept illegal payments usually have a motive for doing so. For most people, it is debt; but once they pay their debts, they end up spending the rest of the loot. Co-workers often notice extravagances and report them; CPAs should be alert to rumors or complaints about employees who seem to live beyond their means.

Burgin's lifestyle. For years Burgin—a part-time legislator—had one of the most successful solo law practices in Mississippi and lived the life of a wealthy plantation owner. Because of his visibility as a politician, people noticed his ostentatious wealth, and it was one of them who tipped the FBI off to his illegal scheme. Evidence later showed that one of the principal reasons for his "success" was that his firm served as a conduit for the lucre of corruption.

LOOK TO THE TOP

At some point, regardless of internal controls or safeguards, a person at the top of an organization has the ultimate authority to decide how it spends its money;

lower-level employees must contend with restrictions. This means that within an entity the chief purchasing agent or similar officer would be the most likely suspect for corruption. CPAs therefore should satisfy themselves that controls over purchasing managers are adequate and are not being overridden.

Burgin's opportunity. As chairman of the Mississippi Senate Appropriations Committee, Burgin was the state's chief purchasing agent of sorts. The state neatly divided its finances according to revenue and appropriations. While the Senate Revenue Committee raised money to fund state programs, Burgin's committee was in charge of spending it. Every check the state wrote was within his powerful domain. There were controls, of course—but none the enterprising politician couldn't bypass.

THE "SNIFF TEST"

In theory, any employee authorized to spend an organization's money is a possible candidate for corruption. Those paying the bribes tend to be commissioned salespeople or intermediaries for outside vendors. The following players usually are present in a corruption scheme.

The gift bearer. Illegal inducements often begin when a businessperson routinely offers inappropriate gifts or provides lavish entertainment to an employee with purchasing authority or otherwise tries to ingratiate himself or herself for the purpose of influencing those in charge.

The odd couple. When a purchasing agent becomes the "friend" of an outside vendor, beware. A key technique bribe-givers use is to befriend their targets. They go to lunch together, take trips and engage in other social outings. But often the pair has nothing in common except for an illegal scheme.

The too-successful bidder. A supplier who consistently wins business without any apparent competitive advantage might be providing under-the-table incentives to obtain the work. Be alert to sole-source contracts and to bidders who nearly always win, who win by thin margins and who bid last. These are indicators someone at the company is supplying the winning bidder inside information.

The one-person operator. Some suppliers, rather than directly engage in payoffs, hire someone—called a bagman—to do the dirty work. Be alert to independent sales representatives, consultants or other middlemen, as they are favored conduits for funneling and concealing illegal payments.

Once an employee crosses the line and accepts kickbacks, he or she hardly is in a position to complain to the vendor about goods or services. The vendor knows this and often reacts by supplying items of poor quality and raising prices for purchases.

When a corrupt employee takes bribes, the underlying business arrangement usually is flawed. For instance, the products or services the dishonest worker contracted for, besides being substandard, are often unneeded, purchased from remote or vague sources, bought at odd times or from odd places or make little economic sense. To help uncover fraudulent transactions, CPAs should employ skepticism when examining the rationale for material purchases by the company.

Burgin's scheme. My investigation of Bill Burgin had commenced a year earlier when a confidential banking source alerted me to a contract between the state of Mississippi and Learning Development Corp. (LDC). Because the document was public record, I went down to the secretary of state's office to take a look.

I discovered there were two contracts under which the state would pay LDC a total of $860,000, purportedly to provide "educational services for disadvantaged youths in the state of Mississippi." In examining the details of the agreements, three items jumped out at me. First, they were sole-source contracts—ones with no competitive bids. The second oddity: LDC was headquartered in Nashville. With the pressure on politicians to create jobs in their own states, I wondered why the contracts didn't go to a Mississippi service provider. And there was one other thing—it was hard to decipher what the contract said and what LDC actually had to do for its money.

UNDER-THE-TABLE PAYMENTS

Being the conduit or bagman for bribe money is a profession of sorts; learning to pass bribes and get away with it takes experience and know-how. This particular profession tends to attract a small cadre of sleazy people. They typically are one-person operations and pass bribes for a variety of "clients." For example, during the Pentagon procurement scandals of the 1980s, just one bagman represented some of America's largest defense contractors. And when I investigated corruption in the private sector, I found the same trend. CPAs therefore should be alert to shadowy "consultants" on the payroll.

Burgin's "consultant." Burgin's bagman was D. Flavous Lambert, a lobbyist and former politician with a questionable reputation. On the surface the two men seemed to have little in common. I theorized that if Burgin's job was to see that the state approved the LDC con-

tract, Lambert's task was to work with LDC to ensure the twosome got their take.

Since the contracts didn't pass the sniff test, I decided to take the investigation to the next level by examining LDC's books. The odor got worse. In tracing the corporation's receipts and disbursements, a pattern emerged. LDC received its state payments in monthly installments of $65,000 Each time LDC deposited a state check, it would immediately disburse $32,500—exactly half of the deposit amount—to Developmental Associates, a Georgia concern. The disbursement code identified it as a "finder's fee." Development Associates turned out to be nothing more than a bank account in Atlanta with only one name on the signature card: D. Flavous Lambert. The following business day, Lambert would send a share of the money to the bank account of Burgin's law firm. Believe it: Burgin was accepting bribes by check. The only reason I could figure for his flagrancy was that he had been corrupt for so long that he felt immune to discovery.

THE BRIBE-TAKER GETS INVOLVED

Anyone who takes a bribe makes a pact with the devil. Since the employee is committing a crime, he or she will go to extreme lengths to avoid discovery; that means keeping the bribe-giver happy. Corrupt employees must frequently intercede to resolve problems for the vendor, such as demanding that payments be expedited or requesting that substandard work be accepted. CPAs should look for these anomalies.

Burgin's downfall. No physical evidence linked Burgin to the crime until he interceded directly for LDC. In fact, Burgin didn't even sign the contract between the state of Mississippi and LDC. Instead, welfare commissioner Fred St. Clair signed it. Later, before a federal grand jury, St. Clair admitted he had been pressured by Burgin to approve the deal. St. Clair also told the grand jury that problems with LDC led to the checks from the state being delayed. But shortly before the holidays, Burgin showed up at the welfare commissioner's office demanding he be given LDC's overdue $65,000 check at once. Otherwise, the senator lamented, "Employees of LDC are not going to have a Christmas." It was obvious to St. Clair that LDC or Lambert had pressured the senator to intercede. Burgin, on the other hand, denied the incident ever occurred. Evidence to incriminate Burgin would be so important that, wearing surgical gloves in order not to contaminate any fingerprints on the check, I spent two days in the bowels of the dusty state archives examining canceled checks. Once I located the "Christmas check" the FBI lab found Burgin's thumbprint right in the middle of it. Sure enough, the check had been deposited to the LDC bank account.

BOOK 'EM, DAN-O

As corruption schemes progress, conspirators usually get careless.

Auditing Vendors

If an employee in your company is taking bribes, the illegal payment will not be reflected in your client's books, but rather it will be in those of the bribe-giver. The payments often are disguised in the vendor's records as consulting or finder's fees, commissions or similar expenses.

To help keep your vendors honest, you should insist that major suppliers agree to let you audit their books if necessary. Here is a sample of the way such an agreement could be worded.

"Vendor grants to purchaser the right to audit vendor's books and records, and to make copies and extracts, to the extent the books or records relate to the performance of this contract."

Frauds—including bribes and kickbacks—normally are not onetime events, but continuous crimes that occur over extended time periods. The Association of Certified Fraud Examiners' 2002 *Report to the Nation: Occupational Fraud and Abuse* concluded the average fraud lasted about 17 months and corruption schemes typically took about two years to be discovered.

The perpetrator's modus operandi tends to change over time. Initially, the crooked employee carefully covers his or her tracks. But as the crime progresses without being uncovered, perpetrators look for ways to accomplish the same illegal goals with less hassle. In the beginning the suspect may make sure all of the documents appear in order. Later, he or she may not even bother with any phony paperwork.

CPAs should consider major deficiencies in contract documentation to be a significant red flag. Moreover, many fraudsters don't continue to conceal their ill-gotten gains very well. In short, they get sloppy. In fact, most of the time, the bribe-taker will deposit the illicit funds in his or her own bank account.

Burgin's last stand. Burgin's trial, held in Gulfport, Mississippi, lasted about two weeks. The government presented its case against the senator. In his defense Burgin took the stand and claimed he had no idea the money in his firm's bank account came from LDC. His story—and he stuck to it—was that he had represented Lambert in a legal matter 20 years ago and that Lambert finally was paying the bill.

During the dramatic closing of the trial, Burgin looked directly at the jury and said, "There is no way I would ever deprive the citizens of this great state of their hard-earned tax money." He then pulled a large red bandana from his breast pocket, dabbed his eyes and honked loudly into the handkerchief.

For the FBI agent in charge of the investigation, the scene was too much; without thinking, I burst out laughing. Then the jurors started guffawing. Burgin's defense lawyer was immediately on his feet shouting, "Mistrial!" The prosecutor glared at me. The trial recessed for about 15 minutes so the judge could chew me out. Then he sent the case to the jury.

In less than half a day, the jury convicted Burgin and Lambert. A reporter later asked one of the jurors about the strength of the government's evidence. In his soft Mississippi drawl, the juror said: "Well, when we saw the paper trail, we were convinced. The only way the case could have been stronger was if the checks to Burgin would've had the word *bribe* written on the description line."

JOSEPH T. WELLS, CPA, CFE, is founder and chairman of the Association of Certified Fraud Examiners and a professor of fraud examination at the University of Texas at Austin. Mr. Wells is a member of the AICPA Business and Industry Hall of Fame. He won the Lawler Award for the best *JofA* article in 2000. Mr. Wells' e-mail address is joe@cfenet.com.

Crony Capitalism

Are these people in the corner office tone-deaf? The public is clamoring for clean corporate governance, and here they are cutting themselves cute little side deals with shareholders' money.

By Elizabeth MacDonald

Lawmakers applauded when President George W. Bush signed the Sarbanes-Oxley bill into law on July 30, 2002, ushering in a postscandal crackdown aimed at curbing the kind of self-dealing and conflicts of interest that brought down Enron, WorldCom and other giants. One day earlier executives at Crescent Real Estate Equities of Fort Worth, Tex. were busy trying to blunt the impact of one part of the new law.

Sarbanes-Oxley, among other things, bans company loans to executives and extending the terms of existing loans. Crescent previously had lent $26 million to its chief executive, John Goff, and $9 million more to half a dozen insiders, to buy shares in Crescent. So Crescent, a real estate investment trust, extended the payback deadline by ten years. Myriad companies made similar moves in the weeks before the signing ceremony. Electronic Arts gave a $4 million loan to Warren Jenson, its chief financial officer, admitting in a filing it was doing so a month prior to "the prohibition on loans to executive officers." Reebok International gave a $300,000 relocation loan to then-executive Martin Coles. Wyeth, the drugmaker, handed a $250,000 relocation loan to a division president, Ulf Wiinberg.

As a form of fringe benefit, most corporate loans like these are petty change, really. After all, you expect the boss to be paid a few million dollars. So what's wrong with them? Just that they are in bad taste. Despite all the furor about bad governance, despite the bad name that miscreants at Tyco and Enron gave to capitalism, some executives are still practicing old-fashioned corporate cronyism. Some 75% of companies still engage in related-party deals, says the Corporate Library, a research group in Portland, Me. that studied 2,000 publicly held firms. That means the companies have to make embarrassing disclosures in their proxy statements about nepotism, property leased from the boss, corporate-owned apartments and other forms of insiderism that ought to be passé. What's the matter with these guys?

With help from the Corporate Library and a review of 520 company reports, we went trolling for mischief in the executive suite. What follows is a summary of the more outlandish moves. Please note that none of them is illegal (although new corporate loans would be) and a lot are a continuation of arrangements in place before the congressional crackdown on self-dealing. But self-dealing is bad for the corporate image. Directors should give serious thought to just giving the boss a pay raise, if he's really hard up, and knocking off the monkeyshines.

◆BACK-SCRATCH BUDDIES

Crescent, a publicly held REIT that owns 75 commercial properties primarily in the Southwest, has been involved in at least 70 related-party deals totaling $1.6 billion since 1997, according to its own related-party disclosures. The deals entail investments in or loans to companies in which Crescent insiders own a stake. Crescent has booked at least $279 million in related writedowns for these deals since 1999.

"Crescent engages in way more related-party deals than the majority of other REITs; it has a lot of conflicts of interest," says Jon A. Fosheim, cofounder of Green Street Advisers, a research boutique that studies REITs. Crescent officials counter that the filings create a misleading picture. They argue the $1.6 billion figure is overstated by as much as $200 million by dint of double counting. They say deals with insiders the company can trust are sometimes better for shareholders than deals with strangers. And numerous deals, Crescent argues in an e-mail, are due to arcane tax rules that "place very strict limits on the amount of operating and inventory revenue a company can earn without losing its REIT status." To get around this Crescent created separate units, typically owning 90% or more, and gave 1% stakes—and all voting control—to a Crescent insider. Once the old rules were reformed in 2001, the REIT retook control of the units,

Crescent says. A spokeswoman says the REIT "takes very seriously its responsibility of full and complete disclosure" of these deals and that its independent directors approved them.

One insider deal was particularly ugly for Crescent, which was formed in 1994 by Goff and billionaire Richard Rainwater, now chairman. In 1997 Rainwater got Crescent to pay Magellan Health Services $387 million for a chain of psychiatric hospitals. Crescent and Magellan then each took a 50% stake in the chain's holding company, Charter Behavioral Health Systems. Rainwater held a 19% stake in Magellan, and his wife, Darla Moore, was a director. Goff, for his part, had 28,500 warrants to buy Magellan stock, along with 57,000 shares; disclosures are unclear as to whether Goff cashed out his stake.

In 2000 Charter filed for bankruptcy protection, months after *60 Minutes II* reported on allegations of mistreatment at the Charter chain. Crescent eventually booked $170 million in writedowns to cut the value of its stake. Crescent insists the price it paid for the hospitals was fair; it says a committee of independent directors, along with advisers at Merrill Lynch, concurred.

Crescent also used shareholder capital to buy a house in 2002 from its chief investment officer, Kenneth Moczulski, paying him $2.7 million. And though its specialty is real estate, a year later it effectively admitted it overpaid and took a charge of $900,000 on the deal. Since Sarbanes-Oxley became law, Crescent's related-party disclosures indicate that it has had related-party deals totaling $72 million.

◆FRIENDS AND FAMILY

American Financial Group's 84-year-old chief executive, Carl H. Lindner, has controlled the big Cincinnati insurer and its predecessors for 26 years. And though it went public in 1995, he still runs it as if it were his own personal fief; he owns a 14% stake and his family owns another 27%. Since 1997 American Financial has done at least $60 million in business with companies owned by his brothers or by Lindner himself.

"I'm surprised at the amount of insider dealmaking still going on—and the number of executives who are in on it."

An American unit in 1997 paid $4.9 million for a 49% stake in a private ethanol company, New Energy Corp. of South Bend, Ind., in which Lindner had invested $5.1 million for a 51% share. American Financial units then gave the ethanol company a $10 million credit line and a $4 million loan. When Lindner decided to buy out the American-held stake in 2000, instead of putting up his own money he had the American unit accept a $19 million IOU, a subordinated debenture, from New Energy in exchange for the 49% interest. The ethanol company also paid the American unit $7.5 million in cash. The $19 million subordinated debt

and the $4 million loan were repaid in 2003; New Energy still has access to the $10 million credit line.

Lindner family members also own 24% of Provident Financial Group (American owns 15%), a publicly traded state bank that paid American $3.3 million in 2003 to rent its main banking and corporate offices, situated in the same buildings as American's headquarters. American says the rent is at market rates. During 2003 American Financial's units invested $20 million in a separate, undisclosed "unrelated party," which then used those funds to repay $3.4 million in loans and fees it owed to Provident.

American also owned 49% of American Heritage Homes, a home builder in Orlando, Fla. 51%-owned by Lindner's brothers. American paid $3.6 million for its stake in 1995. In 1998 American loaned $8 million to the home builder, which repaid the loan when American sold its stake in 2002. American says it netted $9.3 million on the sale; it's unclear what the brothers earned. Investing in home builders "is not something we generally do, I can tell you that," concedes spokeswoman Anne Watson. Then why do it at all? "We didn't do it in a large way here."

UICI, a North Richland Hills, Tex. insurer, has done tens of millions of dollars in business with its executives, as well as with companies that are partly owned by UICI's founder and chairman, Ronald Jensen, 73, and his family. Jensen and his adult children owned 59% of a long-distance company that billed UICI $5 million for calls from 2001 through the first half of 2003. The phone company typically charged 7 cents a minute for long distance, higher than IDT's 5 cents and AT&T's 6 cents. UICI says it put this contract out for a competitive bid.

And Jensen's children, through their company, also got a put option to sell 369,200 of their UICI shares back to UICI for $11.9 million, or $32.25 a share, in 2002—even though the stock at the time had never traded higher than $20. UICI's general counsel, Glenn Reed, says that, in hindsight, "the facts proved our deal was not a good one." UICI says all of these deals were fair and were approved by a majority of its board, and that Jensen didn't vote on them. But it refuses to identify how many directors voted against the deals. UICI also gave $3.7 million in loans to Gregory Mutz, who stepped down as chief executive on June 30, 2003. UICI forgave $1.5 million of the loans, and by 2003 Mutz paid off the rest in cash by selling back to UICI shares that the company had given him.

UICI's conflicts have spilled over into suits alleging UICI is concealing its "incestuous relationship" with a nonprofit that it uses to sell insurance. The suits say that though the National Association for the Self-Employed purports to be an independent nonprofit, it really is run by Jensen's children and his former business partner in order to sell UICI's insurance. UICI settled the suits in May; it has set up a $25 million reserve to handle any payouts. "We disagree with the allegations in the complaints," says Reed. "The lawsuits did not have merit."

Nice Deals If You Can Get Them

As corporate executives line their pockets via insider deals, investors are often left clueless as to just how they're making these moves. Here are the most common actions, ranked by frequency. Find them in the related-party-transaction section of a company's proxies and annual filings with the Securities & Exchange Commission. The numbers don't add up to 100%, as companies typically engage in more than one type of insider deal. —*E.M.*

47% Purchases or sales of insiders' products or services.
39% Loans to executives.
35% Directors who sell legal or banking services to company.
21% Buying, selling, lending to or investing in companies insiders own.
14% Hiring relatives.
11% Director consulting arrangements.
10% Leasing, selling or buying airplanes to or from insiders.
6% Company borrowing from insider or insider's company.

Source: The Corporate Library.

Anam Semiconductor and Amkor Technology operate a world apart, but they enjoy a rather cozy relationship. Anam, in Seoul, South Korea, makes microchips. Amkor, of West Chester, Pa., packaged and sold them, hawking $874 million worth of Anam chips in three years, from 2000 to 2002, or 17% of Amkor's total sales in the period. Amkor, in the same time, paid $58 million to Anam for financial services, construction services, materials and equipment, which included assistance in building factories in the Philippines. Amkor's chief executive: James Kim, 68. Anam's founder: Kim's father, H.S. Kim.

Amkor held a 42% stake in Anam, which it acquired for $501 million in 1999 and 2000. But it took a $172.5 million charge on its Anam holdings in 2002 when Anam got hit by the downturn that swept the semiconductor industry. It has since pared its holdings to 4%, losing $275 million in the process. In February 2003 the son's Amkor sold its chip-packaging business to the father's Anam for $62 million. The company admits in filings that investors "could have had different conclusions as to fair value" of such deals when viewed on a "stand-alone basis."

Elsewhere in the chip business Alliance Semiconductor Chief N. Damodar Reddy, 65, has committed $20 million of his company's cash to Solar Ventures, a venture capital company run by his brother C.N. Reddy. Other unnamed insiders bought undisclosed stakes in Solar, but Alliance won't disclose who they are, and it won't say whether its chief executive is one of them. To date it has

invested $12.5 million. "The question is, is Reddy using shareholder capital just to keep afloat his brother's fund and the insiders' investment?" says Beth M. Young, senior research associate at the Corporate Library.

Despite the bad name that miscreants at Tyco and Enron gave to capitalism, some executives are still practicing old-fashioned corporate cronyism.

◆PLAY BALL

On the board of FedEx Corp. is sports fan J.R. Hyde III, who with his wife owns 13% of the NBA Memphis Grizzlies basketball team. FedEx paid the team $90 million for a multiyear deal to name the new arena in Memphis, Tenn. the FedExForum. FedEx also bought $2 million in municipal bonds to help finance it.

FedEx boss Frederick W. Smith owns a 10% stake in the Washington Redskins, which sold a 27-year, arena-naming license to FedEx for $205 million. He presumably isn't getting rich off the arrangement since he bought the Redskins stake long after the license deal was signed.

Micky M. Arison, 54, is chief executive of Carnival, the big cruise line. He's also chief executive and an owner of the Miami Heat basketball team. Carnival paid the Heat $675,000 in fiscal 2002 and 2003 for sponsorship and advertising as well as season tickets. That's a small sum given Carnival's $2.2 billion in earnings for the period. "But would Carnival be spending that shareholder money on something else if it wasn't for Arison's stake?" asks Young. Both companies say these are just good marketing moves.

◆COME FLY WITH ME

Young says 200 companies have leased or bought airplanes from insiders. Among them is Pilgrim's Pride of Pittsburg, Tex., a chicken processor with $2.6 billion in annual sales. It has leased an airplane from its chief executive and founder, Lonnie Pilgrim, since 1985. The chief made $656,000 in fiscal 2003 from this deal, on top of his $1.7 million compensation. The company defends the pact as cost-efficient since it's in a small town. Pilgrim also provides some bookkeeping services for his personal businesses but won't give details.

That any company would shield any information in this pious, postscandal era surprises even veteran regulators. Says Lynn Turner, former chief accountant for the Securities & Exchange Commission: "I'm surprised at the amount of insider dealmaking still going on—and the number of executives who are in on it."

Sexual Harassment and Retaliation: A Double-Edged Sword

Ann C. Wendt
Raj Soin College of Business, Wright State University

William M. Slonaker
Raj Soin College of Business, Wright State University

Introduction

"She was just so thrilled they believed her," said the plaintiff's attorney following a $2 million jury verdict for a woman who experienced retaliation after complaining about sexual harassment (Cruz, 2001, p. 1D). The plaintiff had been fired and escorted off the employer's premises within two hours after reporting sexual harassment to her boss. If harassment *displays* power over another, then retaliation *flaunts* power. Its origin is Title VII, which provides for separate relief if an adverse action ("retaliation") is taken against a complainant "because he has opposed any practice made an unlawful employment practice… " (Title VII, 1964). Retaliation is an attorney's "gotcha." That is, even if a woman would have lost her original sexual harassment claim for lack of proof, she will win if she can prove that she experienced retaliation for having complained about sexual harassment (*Morris v. Oldham County Fiscal Court*, 2000).

Aggrieved employees claiming retaliation under Title VII must prove that they engaged in a protected activity, that the employer took an adverse action against them, and that there was a causal connection between the protected activity and the adverse action (*Burger v. Central Apartment Management Inc.*, 1999). Implicit in these requirements is that the employer knew of the employee's participation in a protected activity, and that the adverse action follows sufficiently close in time to justify an inference of retaliatory motivation (*Wille v. Hunkar Laboratories, Inc.*, 1998).

Retaliation for complaining about sexual harassment can be expensive. Over the last five years, employers have lost a higher percentage of retaliation lawsuits than suits for age, disability, race, or sex discrimination (Oppel, 1999, p. C8). Consider recent examples:

- A jury award of $152,500 was upheld by a U.S. Court of Appeals for a woman who was fired after complaining to police that her supervisor had grabbed her breast (*Worth v. Tyler, et. al.*, 2001).

- A New Jersey jury awarded $1.5 million to a female police officer who was demoted after she took legal action for being sexually harassed (*Mancini v. Teaneck*, 2000).

- A U.S. Court of Appeals upheld a $410,156 judgment in favor of a female employee who lost her office and her secretary, and who was demoted from her six-figure job following harassment that included sexual harassment (*Durham Life Insurance Co. v. Evans*, 1999).

Retaliation is becoming *the* form of employment discrimination of the new decade. Retaliation for all forms of employment discrimination (not just sexual harassment) is increasing. In 1992, the Equal Employment Opportunity Commission (EEOC) reported that 14.5% of claims filed included a claim of Title VII retaliation. By 1998, the percentage had increased to 21.7% (U.S. EEOC, 2001), and by 2000, it was 25% (The Bureau of National Affairs, 2001, p. 1324).

Claimants may identify more than one basis (race, age, *etc.*) when filing a claim. EEOC's data include all bases that each claimant used, without distinguishing a primary basis. Thus, EEOC's data on the bases on which claims are filed totals more than 100%. For example, for 1998 claims, the data total 144.4%. However, the authors' database prioritizes each claimant's bases, enabling analyses based on 100% of the bases on which the claimants filed. Using this approach, in 1992, 10.1% of the claims were for retaliation. By 1998, the percentage was 21.9%, having more than doubled. Regardless of the counting method, retaliation claims are rising.

Brief Review of Sexual Harassment

"Sex" under Title VII includes two types of harassment. The first, *quid pro quo*, occurs when an employee is pressed to exchange "this for that," e.g., a promotion for sexual favors. The second type is where discriminatory actions have created a hostile or abusive working environment (*Meritor Sav. Bank, FSB v. Vinson*, 1986). "For [hostile environment] sexual harassment to be actionable, it must be sufficiently severe or persuasive to alter the conditions of employment and create an abusive working environment" (*Meritor*, p. 2405). Whether a working environment rises to this level is determined on a case-by-case basis, by looking at all the circumstances. "These may include the frequency of the discriminatory conduct; its severity; whether it is physically threatening or humiliating, or a mere offensive utterance; and whether it unreasonably interferes with an employee's performance" (*Harris v. Forklift Sys., Inc.*, pp. 20–1).

There are two possible sources of the sexual harassment: nonsupervisors, e.g., co-workers, customers, others; or, supervisors, immediate or higher level. Courts have held that employers will not be liable for harassment by nonsupervisory personnel if employers implement effective policies and promptly take action to rectify any harassment. The question has been more difficult, however, when the source of the harassment is a supervisor. Supervisors are agents for employers. Thus, when a supervisor is the source, it is as though the employer itself was the harasser ("vicarious liability"), even though harassment is not a typical job duty.

The U.S. Supreme Court recently (*Burlington Industries, Inc. v. Ellerth*, 1998; and, *Faragher v. City of Boca Raton*, 1998) reconciled the two types of sexual harassment, clarified when employers would be vicariously liable for their supervisors' behavior, and recognized an affirmative defense for employers in certain situations. First, the Court clarified that *quid pro quo* includes situations where a supervisor's threat is carried out, while "hostile environment" includes both situations where there is an unfulfilled threat or offensive conduct with no threat. Second, the Court rejected the notion that employers are vicariously liable for supervisors' behavior only in *quid pro quo* situations. Employers also will be liable for hostile environments created by supervisors with immediate- or higher-level authority over the victim. Finally, in cases where an employee suffered no adverse tangible employment action (such as discharge, demotion, etc.), the employer may have an affirmative defense to their supervisor's harassing behavior if two conditions are met. First, the employer must have "exercised reasonable care to prevent and correct promptly any sexually harassing behavior" (including having a policy); and second, that the employee must have "unreasonably failed to take advantage of any preventive or corrective opportunities provided by the employer or to avoid harm otherwise" (including failing to follow policy procedures) (*Burlington*, p. 2264).

The Claim Process

The EEOC is the primary federal agency charged with enforcing the federal anti-discrimination laws. However, it has delegated much of its responsibilities to state agencies, called "706 agencies," or "deferral agencies." It is within the state agencies that most formal claims are filed,

investigated, and resolved. As a practical matter, this is as far as most formal claims are pursued. An employee needs only go to an office and complete a form, under oath and with agency assistance, describing the essential facts.

The agency will conduct investigations as it deems appropriate. Some are limited to requests for documents concerning the allegations. Others include documents, on-site investigations, and interviews with the parties and witnesses. Usually, the agency will then attempt to help the parties resolve the claim. If conciliation fails, then the agency will refer the claim to EEOC, which may further attempt to resolve the dispute. Ultimately, if the dispute is not resolved, and regardless of whether the state agency found that there was "probable cause" that discrimination occurred, the claimant is entitled to a "right to sue" letter. The letter is necessary if the claimant wishes to file a lawsuit in the courts.

In 1998, 23,735 employment discrimination cases were filed in federal courts. Thirty-nine percent were settled, 14% were dismissed voluntarily, 5% went to trial, and the remainders were pending at the end of 1998. Most (78%) of the cases that went to trial were heard by juries. Of the cases that went to trial, plaintiffs won 36%, with $137,000 being the median award. However, the verdicts in 11% of the cases were $10 million or more (The Bureau of National Affairs, 2000, p. 62). These statistics reflect only employment discrimination cases filed in federal courts. Increasingly, plaintiffs are filing in state courts.

Sample and Methodology

To better understand the current level and characteristics of employment discrimination, the authors have been conducting a longitudinal study, *The Ohio Employment Discrimination Studies*. To date, they have examined 7,072 claims of employment discrimination closed by the Ohio Civil Rights Commission (OCRC) from 1985 through 1999. The claims were randomly drawn as a stratified random sample (8.7%) from the 81,355 cases closed during that time. The authors used a content analysis research method to analyze the variables (discussed in this article) within each claim. The claims were filed under federal (85%) and state (15%) laws, against all types of employers, whose sizes ranged from micro-businesses to Fortune 500 firms.

Based on a comparison of sample claimants to the workforces of both Ohio and the U.S., the findings of this research are generalizable to those workforce populations. Women compose 46% of the Ohio and the U.S. workforces. Ohio is seventh in the country for gross state product (Ohio Bureau of Employment Services, 1998, p. 1–2) (U.S. Department of Labor, 2000, Table A-1). Ohio's goods producing industries are slightly higher (at 25%), and service producing industries slightly lower (at 75%) than those of the U.S. (20% goods and 80% service). For Ohio, local and state government employment is about 12.5%, while nationally it averages about 13.5% of total employment (Ohio Bureau of Employment Services, 1998, Table 2; U.S. Department of Labor, 2000, Table B-1).

Of the 7,072 claims in the authors' database, women filed 3,760 (53%). Of these, 515 (14%) were based on retaliation for having previously complained of employment discrimination. Of the 515 claims, 35 did not identify the basis of their original complaint, leaving 480 claims where the original basis was identified. Cumulatively for the 15 years of the authors' study, retaliation-based claims ranked third in frequency of all bases for women's claims, following only race (30%) and sex-based (29%) claims. Of the women's retaliation claims, 129 (25% of the 515 claims) identified sexual harassment as the original basis, and these are analyzed in this paper. The authors' analyses included only claims of sexual harassment of a woman by a man.

Outcomes

For the 129 retaliation claims made by the sexually harassed women, the outcomes were as follows:

- "no probable cause" was found in 50% of the claims;

- employers settled 27% of the claims;

- women withdrew their claims in 17% of the cases (mostly to proceed directly to court);

- "probable cause" was found in just 4% of the claims; and,

- no jurisdiction occurred in 2% of the claims.

"No probable cause" (50%) means that there was not sufficient evidence to prove the claim, while "probable cause" (4%) means there was sufficient evidence. These outcomes are typical. In Ohio, for all employment discrimination claims, "no probable cause" was found in 58% of the claims, while "probable cause" was found in only 6% (OCRC, 1992–1999). An immediate question might be why employers and managers should worry about any form of employment discrimination, including retaliation against women for complaining about sexual harassment. When asked this question, LeAnn Dickerson, Western Region Director of Human Resources for Delta Air Lines said that "such an employer or manager would send two harmful messages: first, to employees not to bother reporting discrimination, with the result that management does not learn about serious problems; and second, a message to perpetrators of discrimination that it is 'OK,' only encouraging them to continue. At Delta, we take every employee's concerns very seriously."

The authors also believe that to conclude that employers and managers need not worry about discrimination is erroneous. First, the authors' primary explanation for the low percentage of "probable cause" findings is that employment discrimination claims are very difficult to prove. Specifically, retaliation complainants must demonstrate, by a preponderance of the evidence, that reporting sexual harassment motivated the employer's adverse

action, i.e., the retaliation (*McNairn v. Sullivan*, 1991). In 57% of the women's retaliation claims, their employers gave reasons for their allegedly retaliatory actions. The most common reason was that the complainant engaged in an improper work behavior, such as absenteeism, insubordination, or interpersonal conflicts. The next most common reason was simply inadequate performance. Thus, in at least 57% of the retaliation claims, the agency is faced with evaluating the alleged retaliation versus the employers' alleged legitimate reasons for their actions. Further, proof almost always is complicated by a lack of "smoking guns." Based on analyses of more than 7,000 employment discrimination claims spanning 15 years, the authors believe that in recent years, employers, managers, and supervisors who discriminate, or who will not take action against those who do, have become much more subtle. Additionally, state agencies (such as the OCRC) and the EEOC have limited budgets for investigations. By necessity, many are phone or paper investigations, without the benefit of personal visits to the workplaces. Also, with rare exception, employees who file complaints with these agencies do not have legal counsel. They have stated their claims as best they can and rely on the agencies to investigate.

A second reason why employers and managers should be concerned about every discrimination claim is that 90% of employees who perceive that they are experiencing discrimination will not complain to anyone in authority within the organization (Samborn, 1990, p. 1; Dubois, Faley, Kustis and Knapp, 1999, p. 202). Thus, on average, for every reported instance of discriminatory retaliation, there are nine possible complaints lurking in the wings.

Finally, a third reason that employers and managers to be concerned is the inherent cost. Employees who believe they are the victims of discrimination will not be as productive or loyal to their organizations. Their decreased morale can infect co-workers. A national study by the Families and Work Institute found that, "The *perception* of discrimination, or unequal opportunity in one's work place seems to exact a toll on workers' attitudes and behavior—*whether or not their perceptions would be found to have an objective basis* [emphasis added]" (Galinsky, Bond, and Friedman, 1993, p. 31). Because no employer would rationally allow its employees to be surveyed regarding sexual harassment experiences, it is virtually impossible to impute actual monetary costs to discrimination. However, a former EEOC investigator, Susan Crawford, estimates that sexual harassment costs the 500 largest companies $3.4 billion (average $6.7 million each) annually due to absenteeism, low productivity, and turnover (Feminist Majority Foundation, 2001).

Thus, the focus should not be on what percentage wins or loses formal discrimination complaints. Rather, employers and managers should consider unreported claims and the inherent costs of discrimination. They should take steps, such as training, to prevent both perceptions and actual discrimination.

Table 1 *General Characteristics of the Sexual Harassment Retaliation Claimants (n=129)*

To Whom The Women First Complained	Percentage	Quickness to File	Percentage
Immediate Supervisor	21	Same Day	2
Higher Manager	13	1st Week	13
Human Resources	13	2nd Week	11
Other Company Rep.	35	3rd & 4th Week	20
State 706 Agency	13	2nd Month	13
Other*	5	3rd Month	28
		4th + Month	13
Total	100	Total	100

* For example a union representative

Table 2 *General Characteristics Continued (n=129)*

Terms of Employment	Percentage	Jobs Held by Claimants	Percentage
1 Year	43	Managerial/Executive	12
2 to 5 Years	33	Professional Specialties	5
6 to 10 Years	10	Technicians	5
11 to 15 Years	4	Sales	9
16 to 20 Years	2	Clerical	20
21 to 30 Years	2	Service	20
Not Identified	6	Production	13
		Transportation/Labor	12
		Miscellaneous	4
Total	100	Total	100

Regarding the other outcomes, for the 27% of claims that settled, terms varied from as little as an apology to $21,800. The average financial settlement was $4,498. Overwhelmingly, these retaliation complainants did not have legal counsel, but the authors believe settlement costs would have been higher if lawyers had been involved. Additional settlement terms varied, including: firing or disciplining the harasser, rehiring the complainant, neutral letters of reference, and instituting new anti-discrimination policies and training programs. For the 17% of women who withdrew their claims, most did so to proceed directly to court. These complainants had legal counsel.

General Characteristics of Sexual Harassment Retaliation Complaints

Table 1 shows that most women (82%) complained to someone within the employer's organization: their boss (21%); a higher-level manager (13%); human resources (13%); or another company representative (35%). Only 13% went outside of the organization and filed a formal complaint with Ohio's 706 agencies. The other 87% of the claimants gave their employers an opportunity to manage the alleged sexual harassment complaint in-house.

Ultimately, these employers lost this opportunity when the female complainants perceived that they were experiencing retaliation for complaining and then filed with the state 706 agency.

Table 1 shows the women's quickness to file. While only 2% file the same day, and another 13% file within the first week, a total of 39% will file within the first four weeks following the retaliation. Thus, if employers needed an additional reason to promptly respond to initial complaints of sexual harassment, they have it. Some suggestions for managing sexual harassment to avoid complaints include: having a written anti-harassment policy; communicating the policy to all employees; training supervisors and employees; investigating all allegations promptly; and, remediating the problem when allegations are found to be true (Bland and Stalcup, 2001).

A rapid response to a complaint of sexual harassment must include a message to all involved that there must be no retaliation. Suggestions for avoiding retaliation claims include: have a separate anti-retaliation policy; encouraging complainants to come forward without fear of retaliation; and, not treating complainants differently than they otherwise would have been treated (Kandel, 1999).

Table 3 *Women's Retaliation Claims By Original Bases Compared to Nonretaliation Claims Filed During 1985 through 1999*

Basis	Retaliation Claims	Nonretaliation Claims	Percentage
Race	158	1,114	14
Sex-Gender	77	543	14
Sex-Pregnancy	4	255	2
Sex-Harassment	129	275	47
Disability	56	453	12
Age	43	345	12
National Origin	7	48	15
Religion	6	37	16
Not Identified*	35	0	N/A
No Basis**	0	175	N/A
Total	515	3,245	N/A

*Original basis not identified
**Claimants failed to state a prima facie case.

Nearly half (43%) of the female complainants had been employed for one year or less (with the employer against whom they filed their retaliation claim) when they first experienced the sexual harassment and the retaliation (see Table 2). Another 33% were employed for two to five years. Thus, it appears that if sexual harassment and retaliation are going to occur, it does so relatively soon after they are hired.

Most women (40%) who complained of retaliation for reporting sexual harassment worked in either clerical (administrative support) or service jobs (Table 2). Both types of jobs have traditionally been filled by women and often serve as entry-level jobs. However, sexual harassment can occur at the highest levels of the organization. For example, in one complaint within the authors' database, the male chairman of the board literally chased the female president around her desk attempting to initiate sexual contact. Finally, claimants identified the persons who were the harassers (not shown on any Table). Thirty-seven percent identified immediate supervisors, while 20% identified higher managers. Overall, 57% were supervisors or managers, that is, agents of the employer. Under the most recent U.S. Supreme Court decisions discussed earlier, employers with supervisors and managers who engage in sexual harassment are risking financial liability.

Nearly One-half of Women Who Complain Can Expect Retaliation

As Table 2 reports, women who experience sexual harassment initially complain to a variety of authorities, and only a small percentage (13%) file a formal complaint

with a state 706 agency. Even for those who do initially file with a state agency, it is not feasible within the authors' database to track individual sexual harassment complainants to see if they subsequently report experiencing retaliation. However, to gain a better perspective on the significance of the women's 129 claims of retaliation where sexual harassment was identified as the original basis, the authors made some comparisons. They compared all retaliation claims filed by women (not just those related to sexual harassment) to all women's employment discrimination claims (claims not involving retaliation) filed during the same 15-year period. Table 3 reports the results.

Table 4 *Retaliatory Actions Identified by Claimants (n=129)*

	Percentage
Termination	61
Economic Loss	15
Aggression	13
Sexual Harassment	2
Miscellaneous Actions	9
Total	100

Retaliation claims based on sexual harassment compared with original sexual harassment claims occur substantially more frequently than any of the other retaliation claims compared with their respective original basis. From this comparison, the authors conclude that nearly half (47%) of all women who complain of sexual harassment can expect to experience retaliation.

What accounts for the high rate of retaliation? The authors believe that sexual harassment is fundamentally unlike any of the other forms of employment discrimination. The underlying purpose of a male sexually harassing a female is a display of power through sexual acceptance. When the victim complains or reports the perpetrator, she is rejecting his power and his implicit sexual advances. By comparison, the perpetrator in a race, pregnancy, gender, disability, age, or national origin situation is not seeking acceptance from the victim; to the contrary, he (or she) is expressing rejection of the victim. Conversely, when the victim of sexual harassment complains or reports the harasser's actions, she is rejecting the harasser. As a final display of power, and potentially to save face, the harasser "evens the score" by retaliating against (rejecting) the victim.

Forms of Retaliatory Actions

What were the retaliatory actions alleged by the complainants? The good news is that only 2% of the 129 retaliation claimants said that the sexual harassment continued. The bad news is what they allege as the retaliatory actions in the other 98% of the claims. Table 4 identifies the harmful retaliatory actions. Unfortunately, termination was the most frequently reported (61%) retaliatory action. In the workplace, discharge is the ultimate rejection. Not surprisingly, 27% of the terminations were "constructive discharges." This is when a woman resigns because the working conditions are "so difficult or unpleasant that a reasonable person in [the] employee's shoes would have felt compelled to resign" (*Chertkova v. Connecticut General Life Ins. Co.*, 1996).

The second most frequently identified retaliatory action, economic loss, included such actions as demotions, reduced wages or hours, and denial of training. These harmful actions were likely intended to force the complainants out of the organizations. While complainants can likely prove from employer records that they were terminated or experienced one or more of the economic actions, the following identified actions may be more difficult to prove as most complainants alleged that they were committed one-on-one by the perpetrators.

Most unexpected were retaliatory actions the authors categorized as "aggression." Such actions included: stalking, destruction of personal property, public humiliation, screaming, threats of physical violence, assaults, and others. These are dangerous conditions. "Physical aggression is almost always preceded by verbal aggression. Physical abuse does not just arise out of nowhere—it follows hostile, competitive verbal acts" (Wilmot and Hocker, 2001, p. 153).

Recommendations

Effective Supervisors and Managers
Three of the top five reasons that employees consider "very important" in deciding to accept a job with their current employer are open communications, management quality, and their supervisor (Galinsky, et al., p. 17). A woman needs these the most when she perceives that she is the victim of sexual harassment. As reported in Table 1, 21% of the claimants originally reported the sexual harassment to their immediate supervisor, and another 13% reported it to a higher manager. How might job satisfaction and motivation suffer when these very supervisors and managers fail to protect her from retaliation? Job satisfaction and performance are even more negatively affected when her supervisor (37%) or a higher manager (20%) is the source of the harassment, as reported by the claimants in the authors' study.

The authors recommend that organizations invest training dollars in frontline supervisors and managers. Traditionally, supervisors are selected because they have demonstrated task proficiency, and therefore, can supervise others performing the same tasks (Taylor, 1903, p. 1394). Organizations should also consider a candidate's people skills. For example, has the candidate demonstrated a willingness to stand up to discrimination in the workplace? Or, has the candidate participated in discriminatory remarks, jokes, harassment, assignments, hiring, or other discriminatory decisions? Will the candidate model the behaviors that will help to prevent sexual harassment, retaliation, and other forms of discrimination?

Policies and Procedures
"The court makes it clear that if employers have adopted clear policies regarding harassment and discrimination—if employers have clearly informed and trained employees and managers and has published clear policies—and if the employer can show it is taking clear and decisive action to address issues, then the employer is likely to be able to establish in many cases a sufficient affirmative defense to win on liability or to minimize or avoid punitive damages" (Pagano, 2000, p. 1230). Policies should tell potential complainants the procedure for reporting discrimination. There should be more than one person or office to whom a claimant can turn, in case the immediate supervisor is the cause. Next, all complaints of discrimination should be taken seriously and should be investigated by those with special training or experience. Colleen McHugh, a management attorney, suggests that an employer should investigate a complaint "with the assumption that a judge and a jury will be evaluating everything you have done" (Pagano, 2000, p. 1230).

Talk with Female Employees Who Report Sexual Harassment
Reassure a complainant there will be no retaliation for reporting sexual harassment and instruct her to report any

perceptions of retaliation. Periodically engage her in conversation to confirm that she is not experiencing anything out of the ordinary in her job. For example, following a report of sexual harassment, a waitress' table assignments were changed, she was required to work longer hours, and to regularly stay until closing (*Reed v. Cracker Barrel Old Country Stores, Inc.*, 2000). Talking with the waitress following her initial report might have alerted managers or human resources that adverse actions were occurring, giving them a chance to avoid the subsequent retaliation charge.

Prior Review of Discipline and Termination Decisions
Smart employers will have a procedure for rapid review of any disciplinary decisions concerning a sexual harassment claimant—before they are implemented. Additionally, the authors recommend that employers use an internal review procedure before any termination decision is made. So often top managers watch the "front door" to make sure that women are being recruited and hired but fail to monitor what occurs after they are hired, including terminations.

Plan for the Iceberg—Not Just the Tip
Sexual harassment is much more prevalent than reported incidents would indicate. A *New York Times* poll found 40% of women reported experiencing sexual harassment. The *National Law Journal* reported that 60% of female attorneys said they experienced sexual harassment. *Parade Magazine's* survey found that 70% of women who served in the military, and 50% of women who worked in congressional offices on Capitol Hill had been sexually harassed. Yet, only about 5% of sexual harassment in the workplace is ever reported (Bennett-Alexander and Hartman, 2001, p. 254). Fears of being sexually harassed (or being accused of sexual harassment) are among Americans' top fears (*USA Weekend*, 1997, p. 5). This perspective should motivate greater efforts to prevent both acts and perceptions of harassment and retaliation. (See Greenlaw and Kohl, 1996.)

Insurance
Recently, some insurers have offered Employment Practices Liability Insurance (EPLI). Typical coverage includes discrimination, wrongful discharge, harassment, negligent retention and supervision, and hiring. Some include retaliation and tort claims. There is no standard for EPLI policies, so employers must shop carefully. Further, some insurers have very specific requirements, such as the employer having anti-harassment policies and human resource professionals (Newhouse, 1999, pp. 14–16).

Conclusion

Nearly half (47%) of women who complain of sexual harassment report that they subsequently experience retaliation. We believe that sexual harassment claimants essentially want two things. First, they want to be "heard," meaning they want to be understood and valued (Edelman and Crain, 1993, p. 3). Second, if there is sexual harassment, they want it to stop. "Unfortunately, in the legal arena, there is no such thing as taking 'no action.' Doing nothing can have deep legal consequences." (McAfee, Deadrick, Kezman, 1999, p. 79) Victims are not looking for special treatment or money. As shown in Table 1, they do not want to file a formal complaint, and they do not want to go to court. Primarily, they want to do their job free of harassment.

The authors' 15-year study examined retaliation claims filed by 129 women who previously reported sexual harassment. Good news was that in 98% of the claims, sexual harassment ceased after the women reported it. The bad news was that in 98% of the claims, the women reported experiencing other forms of retaliatory adverse actions. A number of variables were examined and discussed, including the source of harassment, harmful retaliatory actions, and the quickness of women to file retaliation claims. While not all claims are meritorious, all are important symptoms of organizational ailments. They are real to the individual and have negative effects on that employee, co-workers, supervisors, and the employer—regardless of who ultimately prevails (Galinsky, et al., 1993, p. 31). These negative effects reduce job satisfaction, promote turnover, and ultimately increase costs. Only top executives, managers, and supervisors can create an environment free of sexual harassment and retaliation.

Acknowledgements
The authors gratefully acknowledge the cooperation and encouragement that they have received from the Ohio Civil Rights Commission, Pastor Aaron Wheeler, Sr., Chairman, G. Michael Payton, Executive Director, and Alan J. Clark, Director of IT and Workforce Design, and the assistance of Jennifer Davis, Graduate Research Assistant. This article is part of *The Ohio Employment Discrimination Studies* that have been supported by grants from Wright State University and the Raj Soin College of Business and created in partnership with the Ohio Civil Rights Commission. The authors are solely responsible for the contents.

REFERENCES
Bennett-Alexander, D. D., & Hartman, L. P. (2001). *Employment law for business* (3rd ed.). New York: Irwin McGraw-Hill.
Bland, T., & Stalcup, S. (2001, Spring). Managing harassment. *Human Resource Management*, 40 (1), 51–61.
Bureau of National Affairs, Inc. (2000, January 24). *Human Resources Report* (Washington, D.C.) 18 (3), 62.
Bureau of National Affairs, Inc. (2001, December 10). *Human Resources Report* (Washington, D.C.) 19 (48), 1324.
Burger v. Central Apartment Management Inc., 168 F.3d 875 (5th Cir. 1999).
Burlington Industries, Inc. v. Ellerth, 524 U.S. 742 (1998).
Chertkova v. Connecticut General Life Ins. Co., 92 F.3d 81, 89 (2d Cir. 1996).
Cruz, S. (2001, February 11). Jury awards ex-Seagate employee $2 million. *Star Tribune* (Minneapolis), p. 1D.

Dickerson, L. (2002, January 27). Western Region Director of Human Resources, Delta Air Lines, Inc. Personal communication.

Dubois, C., Faley, R., Kustis, G., & Knapp, D. (1999, Summer). Perceptions of organizational responses to formal sexual harassment complaints. *Journal of Managerial Issues, 11* (2), 202.

Durham Life Insurance Co. v. Evans. 166 F.3d 139 (3d Cir. 1999).

Edelman, J., & Crain, M. B. (1993). *The Tao of negotiation.* New York: Harper Collins Publishers.

Faragher v. City of Boca Raton, 118 S. Ct. 2275 (1998).

Feminist Majority Foundation. 911 for women: Sexual harassment resources. Retrieved May 3, 2001, from http://www.feminist.org/911/harasswhatdo.html.

Galinsky, E., Bond, J., & Friedman, D. (1993). *The national study of the changing workforce.* New York: Families and Work Institute.

Greenlaw, P., & Kohl, J. (1996, Winter). Creative thinking and sexual harassment. *Advanced Management Journal, 61* (1), 1–10.

Harris v. Forklift Sys., Inc., 510 U.S. 17, 20–1 (1993).

Kandel, W. L. (1999, Summer). Retaliation: Growing riskier than 'discrimination.' *Employee Relations Law Journal, 25* (1), 5–27.

McAfee, R. B., Deadrick, D. L., & Kezman, S. W. (1999, March–April). Workplace harassment: Employees v customers. *Business Horizons,* 79–84.

Mancini v. Teaneck, No. BER-L-5491-96 (N.J. Super. Ct. 2000).

McNairn v. Sullivan, 929 F.2d 974 (4th Cir. 1991).

Meritor Savings Bank, FSB v. Vinson, 477 US 57 (1986).

Morris v. Oldham County Fiscal Court, 201 F.3d 784 (6th Cir. 2000).

Newhouse, D. (1999, May/June). Are you covered? *Ohio Lawyer,* 14–16.

Ohio Bureau of Employment Services. (1998, November). Ohio job outlook to 2006, Labor Market Information Division (Columbus, Ohio).

Ohio Civil Rights Commission. Historical Data 1992–99 (Columbus, Ohio).

Oppel, Jr., R. (1999, September 29). Retaliation lawsuits: A treacherous slope. *The New York Times,* p. C8.

Pagano, S. (2000, November 13). Preventive policies, prompt investigations important to minimizing employers' liability. *Human Resources Report, 8* (44), 1230.

Reed v. Cracker Barrel Old Country Stores, Inc., No. 2-99-002 (M.D. Tenn. 2000).

Samborn, R. (1990, July). Many Americans find bias at work. *The National Law Journal,* 16.

Taylor, F. (1903). Shop management. *Transactions of the American Society of Mechanical Engineers, XXIV.* New York: Published by the Society.

Title VII of the Civil Rights Act of 1964, 42 U.S.C.A. Sec. 2000e *et seq.* (West 2000).

U.S. Department of Labor. (2000, December 8). News. Washington, D.C.: Bureau of Labor Statistics.

U.S. Equal Employment Opportunity Commission. (Charge statistics from the U.S. EEOC FY 1992 through 2000. Retrieved May 3, 2001 from http://www.eeoc.gov/stats/charges.html.

USA Weekend. (1997, August 22). Exclusive poll: What Americans fear, p. 5.

Wille v. Hunkar Laboratories, Inc., 132 Ohio App. 3d 92 (1998).

Wilmot, W., & Hocker, J. (2001). *Interpersonal conflict* (6th ed.). New York: McGraw-Hill.

Worth v. Tyler, et. al., No. 00-2414 (7th Cir. 2001)

Dr. Wendt, who teaches human resource courses, previously worked in the human resources area in the private sector. Dr. Slonaker, who teaches business law and human resource courses, formerly practiced law. The authors are co-developers of The Ohio Employment Discrimination Studies, *the most complete database of employment discrimination in the U.S.; both served as labor arbitrators for the Federal Mediation and Conciliation Service.*

Legal Intelligence

Harassment Grows More COMPLEX

BY CAROLE O'BLENES

Aside from gender, harassment claims are being asserted based on other protected characteristics, including race, religion, age, disability and national origin.

Sexual harassment complaints filed with the EEOC have more than doubled since 1991, and some recent Supreme Court decisions provide new guidance to employers.

In addition to damage awards, harassment complaints carry many intangible costs, such as adverse publicity and reduced morale. Retaliation claims also are a risk.

Develop a comprehensive policy that addresses all forms of unlawful harassment, outlines procedures for reporting and investigating complaints and prevents retaliation.

Awareness of sexual harassment in the workplace has reached unprecedented levels as President Clinton's sexual encounters—Monica Lewinsky, Paula Jones and others—have made sexual harassment a common topic in the news. For employers, this heightened awareness often results in additional sexual harassment complaints as employees develop higher expectations about what behavior is appropriate and conclude that their workplaces fall short of those expectations.

In 1998, more than 15,000 sexual harassment charges were filed with the U.S. Equal Employment Opportunity Commission (EEOC), up from about 6,900 in 1991. Amounts paid out by employers charged with sexual harassment in EEOC proceedings and actions alone exploded from $7.1 million in 1990 to $49.5 million in 1997.

But unlawful workplace harassment is not limited to sexual harassment of women by men. Men also can be (and are) sexually harassed. And harassment claims are being asserted based on protected characteristics other than gender, such as race, age, religion, disability and national origin. Such recent cases include a black Muslim correction officer who claimed he was subjected to racial and religious harassment by coworkers and supervisors; a disabled employee who asserted she was ridiculed about "the disability being in her mind only"; and an Italian-American who claimed he was subjected to racist comments, slurs and jokes based on his national origin. Lifestyle issues also can lead to harassment claims, as in the case of a gay employee offended by a "born-again Christian" coworker's views on homosexuality.

RISK REDUCTION

Every employee falls into at least one of the protected categories, and many belong to several. Therefore, it's essential to prevent incidents that might lead to harassment claims and respond effectively when they do arise. This will reduce your exposure to liability and maximize workplace productivity.

The litigation costs associated with the rise in harassment complaints are enormous and increasing. As a result of the Civil Rights Act of 1991, jury trials are now available in federal harassment cases, and the remedies available to plaintiffs in such cases have expanded to include not just equitable relief, such as reinstatement and back pay, but also compensatory and punitive damages.

Last year, a federal jury awarded nearly $5.7 million to the family of a former U.S. Postal Service engineer who complained of sexual harassment prior to committing suicide. A male dude ranch wrangler was awarded $300,000 by a federal jury based on his claim that he was sexually harassed by his female supervisor. In California, the average jury verdict in employment cases in 1998 was $2.5 million. Equally important are the intangible damages associated with harassment claims, such as absenteeism, employee turnover, low morale and low productivity.

WHAT IS UNLAWFUL HARASSMENT?

The concept of unlawful harassment grew out of sexual harassment claims, but it has been applied in cases involving other protected characteristics as well. The EEOC's "Guidelines on Discrimination Because of Sex" define sexual harassment as "unwelcome sexual advances, requests for sexual favors, and other verbal or physical conduct of a sexual nature." The EEOC, commentators and courts have identified two types of harassment: "quid pro quo" and "hostile environment."

Employees who are subjected to harassment tend to assume it's because of a protected characteristic.

In two cases last summer, *Faragher v. City of Boca Raton* and *Ellerth v. Burlington Indus.*, the Supreme Court clarified the definition of sexual harassment. The court explained that quid pro quo harassment occurs when a "tangible employment action," such as termination, demotion or a significant change in assignment or benefits, results from a refusal to submit to a supervisor's sexual demands. If there is no tangible employment action, an employee may still be a victim of sexual harassment if he or she is subjected to unwelcome sexual conduct that is sufficiently severe or pervasive to unreasonably interfere with his or her work performance or create an intimidating, hostile or offensive work environment.

Quid pro quo claims are limited to the sexual harassment context. Not so for the hostile work environment standard, which the courts have applied to other types of harassment claims. Regardless of the protected characteristic relied on by the plaintiff, in these cases the courts look to the severity and pervasiveness of the alleged harassment. To prevail on a hostile environment claim, the plaintiff must also show that he or she was subjected to severe and offensive conduct *because* of his or her protected characteristic.

When a company can show that the alleged harasser treated all employees in the same negative manner—sometimes referred to as an "equal opportunity harasser"—the harassment would not be unlawful because it is not related to the plaintiff's membership in a protected class. In *Pavone v. Brown*, for example, the court held that a disabled plaintiff could not prove unlawful harassment because other, nondisabled employees complained of the same mistreat-

BRIEF CASES

THE ADA AND CORRECTIVE DEVICES

Two cases currently before the Supreme Court will resolve a difference of opinion among the courts as to whether an individual can be considered "disabled," and thus protected by the Americans with Disabilities Act (ADA), if his or her medical condition is corrected with medication or assistive devices. The two cases involve employees who were denied jobs because of medical conditions—twin pilots who are nearsighted in *Sutton v. United Airlines*, and a truck mechanic with high blood pressure in *Murphy v. United Parcel Service*. In both cases, the 10th Circuit ruled that the employees were *not* disabled because their conditions were corrected with lenses and medication, respectively.

NEW GUIDANCE ON 'REASONABLE ACCOMMODATIONS'

The EEOC issued new Guidance in February that addresses some tough questions about the reasonable accommodation requirements of the ADA. Among those questions: When must you provide an accommodation? What type is required? Under what circumstances can you claim that a requested accommodation would impose an undue hardship? According to the EEOC, once an employee indicates that her medical condition is affecting some aspect of her work, the employer is obligated to clarify her needs and identify an appropriate accommodation. Reasonable accommodations may include restructurings of some job functions, leaves of absence, modified or part-time work schedules, modified workplace policies and job reassignments.

EEOC CHALLENGES AN ENGLISH-ONLY POLICY

A federal district court recently denied an employer's motion to dismiss a lawsuit filed by the EEOC that challenges the company's brief use of an English-only policy. The employer, Synchro-Start, had established a policy requiring employees to speak only English during work hours, allegedly in response to complaints that multilingual employees were harassing and insulting coworkers in their native tongues. It rescinded the policy within nine months. The EEOC suit claims the policy discriminates on the basis of national origin because it focuses on employees whose primary language is not English. EEOC Guidelines express a presumption that English-only rules create a discriminatory environment based on national origin.

ment by the plaintiff's supervisor. But companies need to be aware that employees who are subjected to verbal abuse and other harassment tend to assume that it is because of a protected characteristic. Thus, such behavior (particularly by supervisors) presents risks of claims, litigation costs and workplace disruption even if the employer may ultimately prevail on an "equal opportunity abuser" theory.

Proof that harassment was because of a protected characteristic was the pivotal issue in a case decided by the Supreme Court last year. In *Oncale v. Sundowner Offshore Services, Inc.*, the plaintiff, a male employee alleged, among other things, that he was grabbed by his male supervisor and a male coworker who physically abused him while threatening rape. The Supreme Court concluded that a heterosexual can state a viable claim of sexual harassment against another heterosexual of the same gender (i.e., same-sex harassment), but remanded the case to the lower court to determine whether Oncale was in fact harassed *because of his sex*.

EMPLOYER LIABILITY

The Supreme Court's recent decisions in *Ellerth* and *Faragher* also clarified the circumstances under which an employer can be held liable for harassment by a supervisor. When an immediate (or successively higher) supervisor's harassment culminates in a tangible employment action, such as discharge, demotion or undesirable reassignment, the employer will be liable for the supervisor's actions.

When the harassment does not result in a tangible employment action, the employer may raise an "affirmative defense" to liability or damages. This defense is made up of two parts: First, that the employer exercised reasonable care to prevent and correct promptly any harassing behavior. Second, that the plaintiff employee unreasonably failed to take advantage of any preventive or corrective opportunities provided by the employer or to avoid harm otherwise.

The reasonableness of an employer's response also determines liability in hostile environment cases involving harassment by a coworker, nonsupervisory employee or nonemployee (such as a vendor, customer, consultant or client). For example, a local Pizza Hut franchise was held liable for $200,000 in compensatory damages plus nearly $40,000 in attorney's fees and costs because it failed to prevent two of its customers from sexually harassing a waitress. In *Lockard v. Pizza Hut, Inc.*, the waitress claimed that her manager forced her to wait on two customers who pulled her hair and sexually assaulted her. The customers had engaged in other abusive conduct in prior visits and the plaintiff had complained to her manager. A federal appeals court upheld the verdict, observing that the manager had been given notice of the harassing conduct and had unreasonably failed to remedy or prevent the harassment.

• POINTS OF POLICY

Here are the hallmarks of an effective nondiscrimination and anti-harassment policy:
- Introductory statement that expresses a commitment to a work environment that is free of discrimination and harassment.
- Equal employment opportunity statement.
- Definitions of harassment, with examples of behaviors that may constitute harassment.
- Coverage extending to all applicants, employees and third parties, such as outside vendors, consultants or customers, and to all conduct in a work-related setting—including social occasions such as client lunches and holiday parties.
- Prohibition of retaliation, enforced through disciplinary action.
- Complaint procedure designating several different "avenues of complaint" and strongly urging the reporting of all incidents.
- Assurance of a prompt investigation of complaints.
- Confidentiality maintained to the extent consistent with adequate investigation and appropriate corrective action.
- Corrective action upon a finding of misconduct, with specific examples of possible actions.

—C.O.

In light of the Supreme Court's recent decisions, it is critical for employers to take affirmative steps to prevent and remedy harassment. At a minimum, they should:
- Develop a written nondiscrimination and anti-harassment policy (see box).
- Ensure that the policy provides employees with effective avenues to bring complaints forward (not just through their supervisor, who may in fact be the harasser).
- Include the policy in a prominent place in an employee handbook (if there is one).
- Widely disseminate the policy (independent of the handbook) throughout the workplace on a periodic basis to make sure all employees know of its existence and understand the complaint procedure.
- Train appropriate segments of the workforce, such as senior management, managers/supervisors and complaint-receivers, to understand and apply the policy.
- Promptly respond to complaints brought under the policy by thoroughly investigating them to determine if policy violations have occurred.
- Take prompt, effective remedial action to respond to violations.

PREVENTING RETALIATION

In addition to distributing an anti-harassment policy, companies need to develop policies and procedures to prevent retaliation against individuals who file complaints of harassment or discrimination or who participate in their investigation. Charges of retaliation are on the rise, with more than 19,000 claims filed with the EEOC in 1998 alone.

Retaliation is an independent basis for employer liability under the federal discrimination laws. All too often, companies are finding that even after a discrimination or harassment claim has been dismissed for lack of evidence, the courts are ordering them to proceed to trial on claims of unlawful retaliation. This is because adverse action taken against an employee who opposes unlawful practices (by filing or threatening to file a complaint) can be considered unlawful retaliation.

For example, a federal appellate court recently reinstated a retaliation claim filed against Wal-Mart, while affirming the dismissal of the plaintiff's claims of racial harassment and discrimination. The plaintiff had alleged that within the two months after she filed a discrimination complaint with the EEOC, she was listed as a "no-show" on a scheduled day off, twice reprimanded by her manager and then given a one-day suspension. In addition, she claimed, her manager began soliciting negative statements about her from coworkers. The court held that this conduct was sufficient to support a claim of retaliation, especially because the plaintiff had not received any reprimands in the 11 months before she filed her EEOC charge.

To minimize the risk of liability for such claims, employers need to incorporate a strong prohibition against retaliation in their anti-harassment policies. They also should advise employees at all levels that retaliation will not be tolerated and will result in disciplinary action up to and including termination. Then make sure the policies are fully enforced.

After filing a charge of harassment or discrimination, employees often perceive any adverse actions as related to their complaint. Therefore, a human resources officer or other appropriate manager should carefully monitor a complainant's work environment and work with his or her supervisor to avoid even the appearance of retaliation. Further, ensure that the complainant is not shunned by his or her coworkers, and counsel managers to make a conscious effort to include complainants in appropriate workplace meetings or events.

If a complainant is a candidate for discipline for performance-related reasons, his or her manager should consult with human resources before any discipline is imposed to verify that it is warranted and consistent with comparable situations. Similarly, decisions involving raises and promotional opportunities in the complainant's department should be discussed with HR to ensure the complainant received appropriate consideration and was treated even-handedly.

Carole O'Blenes, a partner in the New York office of Proskauer Rose LLP, has practiced labor and employment law since 1976. She has represented employers in collective bargaining, arbitration, administrative proceedings and employment litigation. She also provides advice and guidance to clients on a wide range of employment and labor law matters. E-mail: coblenes@proskauer.com. Tracey I. Levy, an associate at Proskauer Rose, also contributed to this article.

A CRITICAL LOOK AT AMERICAN NEWS

ATTITUDES TOWARD AFFIRMATIVE ACTION

Opinions vary widely, depending on how the issue is presented in poll questions

BY PAMELA PAUL

Affirmative action is such a hot-button subject that even its definition sets off debates. While some consider the policy a necessary remedy for past and current discrimination, and essential to or democracy, others see it as unconstitutional, un-American and intrinsically discriminatory against people of all racial and ethnic backgrounds.

Public opinions on the issue often depends on how the topic is worded and framed in poll questions. Affirmative action for minorities is sometimes lumped together with affirmative action for women, and education programs are sometimes grouped with hiring and employment policies. When asked whether they favor "affirmative action programs for women and minorities," a majority of Americans (58 percent) said they are in favor, according to a 2001 Gallup poll. (That approval rate increased only slightly from 55 percent in 1995.) But when a question is asked about affirmative action for minorities only, the approval rate tends to be lower.

The debate over affirmative action often revolves around the question of whether or not diversity of its own sake is valuable. According to a 1999 CNN/*USA Today*/Gallup poll, a majority of Americans agreed that diversity is a laudable goal, with 54 percent of whites and 90 percent of blacks saying more should be done to integrate schools. (The disparity between blacks' and whites' responses to this question is typical for affirmative action issues, which, not surprisingly, draw more support from blacks than whites.) Interestingly, however, most black parents say school districts that are mostly black should hire teachers regardless of race (77 percent), according to a 1998 Public Agenda poll. Though black and white Americans may agree on the benefits of diversity, they do not see eye to eye on other underlying issues: whether all races should have equal opportunities in education and the workplace, whether affirmative action itself is a "discriminatory" policy and whether people should be compensated for past and current discrimination.

THE LEGACY OF AFFIRMATIVE ACTION

A majority of Americans believe that affirmative action programs have improved conditions for black Americans in recent years. A poll conducted in 1999 for *Newsweek,* by Princeton Research Associates, found that 52 percent of the blacks and 51 percent of whites believe such programs have done "a lot" to help blacks in this country or have helped them "some." Only 32 percent of blacks and 36 percent of whites believe that the programs have done "little" or "nothing" to improve matters. (The remainder of the respondents said they "didn't know.") In one of its 2001 polls, the Gallup Organization found that, in response to a question worded differently, 58 percent of Americans think that affirmative action has been good for this country, up slightly from 54 percent in 1995.

If anything, the perceived need for affirmative action programs has increased in recent years, with 56 percent of Americans in the 2001 Gallup poll saying that they are necessary "to help women and minorities overcome discrimination," up from 49 percent who said so in 1995. Furthermore, 66 percent of Americans in the 2001 poll said they believe such programs will always be needed, compared with only 30 percent who said the day will come when they will no longer be necessary.

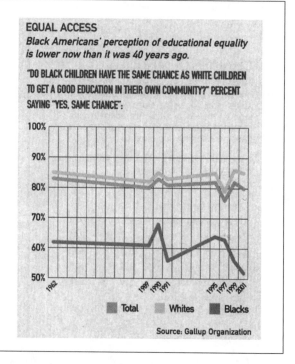

EQUAL ACCESS
Black Americans' perception of educational equality is lower now than it was 40 years ago.

"DO BLACK CHILDREN HAVE THE SAME CHANCE AS WHITE CHILDREN TO GET A GOOD EDUCATION IN THEIR OWN COMMUNITY?" PERCENT SAYING "YES, SAME CHANCE":

■ Total   ■ Whites   ■ Blacks

Source: Gallup Organization

BLACK ON BLACK

Most blacks continue to believe that affirmative action policies are needed in schools and the workplace. In a 1997 CBS News/New York Times poll, 77 percent of blacks said it was very important for companies to have a racially diverse workforce, compared with 32 percent of white Americans. Similarly, 76 percent of blacks said it was very important for colleges to have a racially diverse student body, versus 36 percent of whites.

In a 2001 National Urban League poll of 800 black adults, 87 percent of the respondents said that affirmative action in higher education and employment was still necessary, up from 83 percent in 2000. This result is not surprising, considering that 68 percent of those polled said affirmative action played a very or somewhat important role in their own education and employment. In this poll, the term "affirmative action" was not explained, and the incendiary word "quota" wasn't mentioned at all.

THE RIGHT TO LEARN

More than two-thirds of black Americans say affirmative action played an important role in their educational or employment experience.

	FAVOR	OPPOSE	DON'T KNOW
Do you favor or oppose permitting parents to choose which public school they send their children to?	82%	13%	5%

	BETTER	WORSE	SAME
Over the next 5 years, do you think the quality of public schools in your community will get better, get worse or stay about the same?	37%	25%	33%

	VERY IMPORTANT	SOMEWHAT IMPORTANT	NOT AT ALL IMPORTANT
How important a role did affirmative action play in your own educational or employment experience?	39%	29%	28%

	YES	NO	DON'T KNOW
Do you think there is still a need for affirmative action programs in higher education and places of employment?	87%	8%	5%

Source: National Urban League. 2001

THE BOTTOM LINE

- A majority of Americans seem to favor affirmative action, but more support is shown when poll questions are vaguely worded.
- When the words "preferences" or "quotas" are used, support for affirmative action falls dramatically. In a 2000 National Opinion Research Center poll, the following question was asked: "Some people say that because of past discrimination, blacks should be given preference in hiring and promotion. Others say that such preference in hiring and promotion of blacks is wrong because it discriminates against whites. What about your opinion—are you for or against preferential hiring and promotion of blacks?" Only 13 percent of whites and 43 percent of blacks said they were "for" it.
- Blacks continue to support affirmative action programs more strongly than do whites, seeing both a greater need and a larger role for such programs in the present as well as in the future.

A QUESTION OF QUOTAS

In general, using terms such as "affirmative action," "equal" and "opportunity" in survey questions yields more support for affirmative action policies, while the use of "special preferences," "preferential treatment" and "quotas" tends to lessen approval ratings. In addition, including "women" along with "minorities" tends to increase support.

A 1997 CBS News/*New York Times* survey highlights how differently phrased questions yield different responses. For example, when asked, "Do you favor or oppose programs which give preferential treatment to racial minorities?" 21 percent of white Americans said they were in favor (compared with 51 percent of black respondents). But when asked, "Do you favor or oppose programs which impose quotas for racial minorities?" only 15 percent of whites were in favor (versus 48 percent of blacks). The words "quota" and "impose" lowered approval rates. Yet when whites were asked, "What do you think should happen to affirmative action programs?" 80 percent said they should continue as is or be phased out over time until they are no longer necessary. Only 13 percent of whites opposing affirmative action on principle said that such practices should end now. (By contrast, no blacks said such programs should end at this time.)

Similarly, in an August 1995 poll by the Pew Research Center for the People and the Press, 58 percent of Americans approved of "affirmative action programs *designed to help* [*American Demographics'* emphasis] blacks, women and other minorities get better jobs and education." Only 46 percent approved of "affirmative action programs which give special preferences [*American Demographics'* emphasis] to qualified blacks, women and other minorities in hiring and education."

MOVING ON UP?

The gap between blacks' and whites' opinions on whether white people will be denied a job or promotion due to affirmative action has narrowed during the past 10 years.

WHAT DO YOU THINK THE CHANCES ARE THESE DAYS THAT A WHITE PERSON WON'T GET A JOB OR PROMOTION, WHILE AN EQUALLY OR LESS QUALIFIED BLACK PERSON GETS ONE INSTEAD?

1990	VERY LIKELY	SOMEWHAT LIKELY	NOT VERY LIKELY
Whites	28%	42%	30%
Blacks	8%	24%	68%

2000	VERY LIKELY	SOMEWHAT LIKELY	NOT VERY LIKELY
Whites	21%	48%	31%
Blacks	14%	30%	56%

Source: National Opinion Research Center

Where Are the Women?

Not in the corner office, even after all these years.
Not now. Maybe not ever. So what happened?

By Linda Tischler

Brenda Barnes knows what it takes to hold a top job in a highly competitive company. As president and chief executive of the North American arm of PepsiCo, a place famous for its driven culture, she set a fast pace. Rising at 3:30 a.m., she would blitz through a few hours of work before waking her three children at 7 a.m., then dash off to the office, where she'd grind through an 11- or 12-hour day crammed with meetings, conference calls, and strategy sessions. Then it was home for dinner and bedtime stories before finishing up with phone calls or email before falling into bed. Three nights a week, she was on the road. Seven times, she relocated when the company wanted her in another office. For eight years, she and her husband lived in separate cities, trying valiantly to juggle both job demands and those of marriage and family. And all the effort was paying off: Barnes was widely considered a real contender for the top job at PepsiCo when CEO Roger Enrico retired. But in September 1997, at 43, she suddenly stepped down when the toll of the job began, in her mind, to outstrip its rewards.

Unlike some women executives who have famously dropped out, Barnes did not go home to write her memoirs or devote herself to charity and her children's soccer schedules. She just chose what is for her, a less demanding path: She serves on the board of six major companies, among them Sears, Avon, and The New York Times; she's taught at the Kellogg School of Management, and stepped in as interim president of Starwood Hotels and Resorts in early 2000. Although she's had many offers for other enticing jobs, she's unwilling to consider another gig at the top. "When you talk about those big jobs, those CEO jobs, you just have to give them your life," she says. "You can't alter them to make them accommodate women any better than men. It's just the way it is."

Six years after the fact, Barnes is still happy with her decision. But she admits that despite her considerable post-PepsiCo accomplishments, she's been forever branded as The Woman Who Walked Away. Small wonder. In a workplace where women CEOs of major compa-

nies are so scarce that they can be identified, like rock stars, by first name only—Carly and Martha and Andrea and Oprah and Meg—it's shocking each time a contender to join their august ranks steps down.

It wasn't supposed to turn out this way. By 2004, after three decades of the women's movement, when business schools annually graduate thousands of qualified young women, when the managerial pipeline is stuffed with capable, talented female candidates for senior positions, why are there still so few women at the top?

In part, the answer probably still lies in lingering bias in the system. Most women interviewed for this story say that overt discrimination is rare; still, the executive suites of most major corporations remain largely boys' clubs. Catalyst, the women's business group, blames the gap on the fact that women often choose staff jobs, such as marketing and human resources, while senior executives are disproportionately plucked from the ranks of those with line jobs, where a manager can have critical profit-and-loss responsibility. Others fault the workplace itself, saying corporations don't do enough to accommodate women's often more-significant family responsibilities.

All those things are true. But there may be a simpler—and in many ways more disturbing—reason that women remain so underrepresented in the corner office: For the most part, men just compete harder than women. They put in more hours. They're more willing to relocate. They're more comfortable putting work ahead of personal commitments. And they just want the top job more.

Let's be clear: Many, many individual women work at least as hard as men. Many even harder. But in the aggregate, statistics show, they work less, and as long as that remains true, it means women's chances of reaching parity in the corner office will remain remote. Those top jobs have become all-consuming: In today's markets, being CEO is a global, 24-hour-a-day job. You have to, as Barnes says, give it your life. Since women tend to experience work-life conflicts more viscerally than their male peers, they're less likely to be willing to do that. And at the upper reaches of corporate hierarchy, where the pyramid narrows sharply and the game becomes winner-take-all, a moment's hesitation—one important stint in the Beijing office that a woman doesn't take because of a sick child or an unhappy husband—means the odds get a little worse for her and a little better for the guy down the hall.

And let's be clear, too, that we're not talking about women who simply opt out. They've been getting a lot of press and sparking a lot of controversy lately—those young women investment bankers and lawyers who are quitting to become stay-at-home moms (and, really, they're still using those MBA skills on the board of the PTA). That's still a fringe phenomenon affecting relatively few privileged women with high-earning husbands.

Many, many women work at least as hard as men. But the disturbing truth is that *most* women don't compete as hard as *most* men.

No, the women we're talking about here work, want to work, want to continue to work. But not the way you have to work in order to reach the top these days. That's the conclusion that Marta Cabrera finally came to four years ago. By 1999, Cabrera was a vice president at JP Morgan Chase, one of only two women on the emerging-markets trading desk. True, the demands were steep—12-hour days were the norm. But the rewards, at the peak of the boom, were pretty delicious, too: an apartment in Manhattan, a country home, and the chance for an artist husband to pursue his vocation.

Not only was Cabrera at the top of her game, but she had, by all measures, managed to pull off the career woman's trifecta—a great job, a happy marriage, and two beautiful, healthy little daughters—all by age 43. But in October of that year, as she watched her second-grader blow out the candles on her birthday cake, Cabrera had an unsettling realization: She didn't know her own child as well as most of the friends and family who had gathered to celebrate the big event. "I realized seven years had gone by, and I had only seen her and my five-year-old on weekends," she says. No first words. No school plays. No class trips. "I asked myself, 'What the hell am I doing?'" Then she thought about her job. To walk away would mean upheaval. Plus, there was a principal at stake: "I had the sense I was letting down my sex by leaving."

It took another seven months, and much soul-searching, to reach her decision, but in May of 2000, Cabrera quit. Like Barnes, she did not opt out. No 180-degree turn to a life of play dates or book groups. No reconnecting with her inner tennis-lady. Instead, she became executive director of EMPower, a microlender in developing countries. Facing a precipitous drop in income, she and her husband rented out their Manhattan place and moved to the country. Now she works from home three days a week, and is in the city the other two, an arrangement that lets her do rewarding work and still spend time with her kids.

And what did her experience at JP Morgan Chase teach her? "There's a different quality of what men give up versus what women give up" when they attempt to reconcile the demands of a senior job with those of family responsibilities. "The sacrifices for women are deeper, and you must weigh them very consciously if you want to continue," she says. "I didn't want to be the biggest, best, greatest. I didn't feel compelled to be number one."

She was doing what women often do: scaling back on work for the sake of family, with a clear-eyed realization that she was, simultaneously, torpedoing her chances for a climb up the ladder. What's more, she didn't care. It's a choice women often make, with no particular social sanctions. For some, it's even an easy and convenient way to escape an increasingly hostile and unfriendly work world, an out that men simply don't have. But it's also the reason women may continue to be stalled at the lower rungs in organizations and men may continue to rule.

Charles A. O'Reilly III, professor of organizational behavior at Stanford Graduate School of Business, has been particularly interested in women's career attainment and the problem of why, despite notable gains in education and experience, women are still so woefully underrepresented in the top ranks of American corporations. In 1986, he began following a group of University of California, Berkeley MBAs to see if he could isolate those qualities that led to a corner office. His conclusion is starkly simple: Success in a corporation is less a function of gender discrimination than of how hard a person chooses to compete. And the folks who tend to compete the hardest are generally the stereotypical manly men.

Think of careers as a tournament, he says. In the final rounds, players are usually matched pretty equally for ability. At that point, what differentiates winners from losers is effort—how many backhands a tennis player hits in practice, how many calls a sales rep is willing to make. "From an organization's perspective," he says, "those most likely to be promoted are those who both have the skills and are willing to put in the effort. Individuals who are more loyal, work longer hours, and are willing to sacrifice for the organization are the ones who will be rewarded."

Today's women, he says, are equal to their male counterparts in education, experience, and skill. But when it's a painful choice between the client crisis and the birthday party, the long road trip and the middle schooler who needs attention, the employee most likely to put company over family is the traditional, work-oriented male. Interestingly, the women in O'Reilly's study reported levels of career satisfaction equal to those of their more-driven male peers, even if they were not as outwardly successful. In other words, women may be happier not gunning for power positions if it means they can work less and have a life.

After seven years with the big computer leasing company Comdisco, Diane Brandt, for example, left to form a small investment banking firm with two male colleagues. She decided to leave that job, too, when the growing business's hours increased and the moment approached when her only son would leave for college. Recently, she launched a small company, Captio Corp., that offers budgeting and scheduling tools for college students. "I've made choices all through my career," she says from her home in Menlo Park, California, days before heading to Germany to visit her son, who's studying abroad. "I've not pursued promotions in the same way I might have had I not been trying to balance other things in my life. It's been important to me to be home and have dinner with my family. You can't do that and move up the ladder."

Beth Johnson, a banker in Chicago, describes herself as "very ambitious," and says she has always loved business: the deal making, the challenge, the money. But she still remembers when her son was a baby, calculating the percentage of his waking hours that she could, if all went well, actually be present. "I doubt that his father was doing the same," she says dryly.

Recently, when the fund she was managing fell victim to the stock market, she decided to take some time off to help her son negotiate his final precollege year. Her brief attempt to be a "golf lady" didn't pan out. "I just couldn't do it," she confesses. She's now mulling various job offers. While she will go back to work, she knows there are sacrifices she and most other women are less willing to make than men. "People may get mad if I describe women as a group," she says, "but we are relational family beings. We do not have a world that's structured to understand that, to know how to account for it, and I don't know that we ever will."

There's a scene near the end of the 1956 movie *The Man in the Gray Flannel Suit* in which Fredric March, who plays a work-obsessed network president, turns on Gregory Peck, who plays his conflicted speechwriter. "Big, successful companies just aren't built by men like you, nine-to-five and home and family," March says. "They're built by men like me, who give everything they've got to it, who live it body and soul." March, of course, has sacrificed his own happiness to the company, a choice that Peck is unwilling to make.

Not much has changed in 48 years, says David Nadler chairman of Mercer Delta Consulting. Nadler, who advises senior managers, says that because top jobs are typically crushing in their demands, they require a certain psychological type. "I've worked closely with 20 CEOs over the past two decades—both men and women," he says. "All of them are characterized by being driven. Something in them says, 'This is important enough for me to make the sacrifices that are inherent with the job.'"

Certainly, there are women willing and able to compete by those draconian rules. A 2003 Catalyst study found that more than half of the women not yet in senior

average hours worked per week

	Men	Women
Lawyers*	47.5	43.0
Management, business, and financial operations occupations*	46.1	40.4
Doctors (primary care physicians)**	50.0	45.0

Sources: *Bureau of Labor Statistics, Current Population Survey 1989 (lawyers), 2002 (business); ** *Medical Economics*, 2003

leadership positions within their companies aspired to be there (although 26% also said they weren't interested.) And some women want nothing less than a full-throttle engagement with work. "I don't seek balance. I want to work, work, work," Ann Livermore, executive vice president of Hewlett-Packard, told Karin Kauffmann and Peggy Baskin for their book, *Beyond Superwoman* (Carmel, 2003). Or as Kim Perdikou, CIO of Juniper Networks, told the author, "I'm wired 24 hours a day."

But such decisions continue to have consequences that thoughtful women are all too aware of. Asked what advice she would give to a daughter, M.R.C. Greenwood, chancellor of the University of California at Santa Cruz, warns, "Remember that the assumption that one's marriage will remain intact as she moves up is a false assumption. You really have to know yourself and know it will take a toll."

Conversely, there are plenty of men who would like the option to lead saner lives. A recent study of 101 senior human-resource managers found that men are also starting to leave big companies to try to improve the balance between their home lives and their worklives. Still, many more men than women seem to get an adrenaline rush from work that allows them to log long hours, zoom through time zones, and multitask savagely.

As a nation, we now clock more time on the job than any other worker on earth, some 500 hours a year more than the Germans, and 250 hours per year more than the British. But the true heavy lifters in the productivity parade are American men. According to the Bureau of Labor Statistics, men work longer hours in every industry, including those traditionally identified with women. In financial fields, for example, men worked an average of 43.8 hours per week compared with women's 38.7; in management, it was men 47.2, women 39.4; in educational services, men 39.2, women 36.0; in health services, men 43.1, women 36.4.

The same pattern holds true in professions whose elaborate hazing rituals are designed to separate potential chiefs from the rest of the tribe. Young associates at prestigious law firms, for example, often put in 60- to 70-hour weeks for long periods of time. "It's almost an intentional hurdle placed by the firms to weed out those who simply don't have the drive and ambition to do it," says Stanford

University economist Edward Lazear. "It may be excessive, but you select out a very elite few, and those are the ones who make it to partner and make very high salaries."

Women are as scarce in the upper reaches of the legal profession as they are in top-tier corporate offices. According to the National Directory of Legal Employers and Catalyst, women represented only 15.6% of law partners nationwide and 13.7% of the general counsels of Fortune 500 companies in 2000 (even though they have accounted for at least 40% of enrollments at top law schools since 1985 and nearly 50% since 2000). Women in these firms say personal or family responsibilities are the top barrier to advancement, with 71% of women in law firms reporting difficulty juggling work and family, and 66% of women in corporate legal departments citing the same struggle.

Depending on the specialty, medical practices can be similarly pitiless. Among doctors, women work 45 hours per week compared with men's 50. Male physicians also see 117 patients per week, compared with 97 for women. And, as with the law, the top rungs of the medical ladder are populated by men who are willing to put work ahead of family, with women doctors concentrated in lower-paying positions in hospitals, HMOs, and group practices.

Meanwhile, back in the executive suite, researchers at Catalyst say some progress has been made. Women made up 15.7% of corporate officers in the *Fortune* 500 in 2002, up from 8.7% in 1995. In 2003, they held 13.6% of board seats in the same companies, up from 12.4% in 2001. But their actual numbers, compared to the percentage of women in the workforce, are still minuscule. This has occasioned much hand-wringing among business organizations and women's advocacy groups. But maybe all that angst is misplaced.

"The higher up you go, jobs get greedier and greedier," says one researcher. "The idea that if only employers would reshape jobs they would be perfectly easy for women to do is just nonsense."

"When a woman gets near the top, she starts asking herself the most intelligent questions," says Warren Farrell, the San Diego-based author of *The Myth of Male Power* (Simon & Schuster, 1993). The fact that few women make it to the very top is a measure of women's power, not powerlessness, he maintains. "Women haven't learned to get their love by being president of a company," he says. "They've learned they can get respect and love in a variety of different ways—from being a good parent, from being a top executive, or a combination of both." Free of the ego needs driving male colleagues, they're likelier to weigh the trade-offs and opt for saner lives.

Mary Lou Quinlan has seen the view from the top and decided it's not worth the price. In 1998, she stepped down as CEO of the big advertising agency N.W. Ayer when she realized she was no longer enjoying a life that had no room for weekends, vacations, or, often, sleep. She went on to found Just Ask a Woman, a New York-based consulting firm that helps big companies build business with women. The decision wasn't driven by guilt over giving family responsibilities short shrift (Quinlan has no children); it was about calibrating the value of work in one's life. Quinlan thinks that calculation is different for women. "The reason a lot of women aren't shooting for the corner office is that they've seen it up close, and it's not a pretty scene," she says. "It's not about talent, dedication, experience, or the ability to take the heat. Women simply say, 'I just don't like that kitchen.'"

Catalyst and other groups have suggested that the heat can be turned down in that kitchen—that senior jobs can be changed to allow for more flexibility and balance, which will in turn help more women to the top of the heap. Catherine Hakim thinks that is bunk. Hakim, a sociologist at the London School of Economics, has been investigating the attitudes toward work among European men and women, and says reengineering jobs won't solve two fundamental problems: First, many women have decidedly mixed feelings about working, and second, top jobs by their very nature will remain relentlessly demanding. In surveys of 4,700 workers in Britain and Spain, she found that only 20% of women considered themselves "work-centered"—they made their careers a primary focus of their lives, and said they would work even if they didn't have to. By contrast, 55% of men said they focused primarily on work. Given those numbers, most top jobs will continue to go to men, she says, despite the equal-opportunity movement and the contraceptive revolution.

That's because work-centered employees are most likely to leap to the tasks that are most disruptive to life. "That's the bottom line, and it's not a sexist bottom line," Hakim says. "Of course, you could say jobs shouldn't be so greedy, but in practice, the higher up you go, by and large, jobs get greedier and greedier. The idea that some people have, that if only employers would reshape jobs they would be perfectly easy for women to do, is just nonsense."

Not surprisingly, the suggestion that the fault lies with women and not with the system drives many women nuts. Margaret Heffernan, the outspoken former CEO of the CMGI company iCast, for example, goes apoplectic at what she calls the perennial "little black dress stories"—tales of how various women have stepped down from their big jobs to spend more time with their families. Their implicit message, she says, is that women can't cut it and would prefer to be back in the kitchen. Indeed, she says, the conclusion we should be drawing is, "Another company just f****d up big time. Another company just trained somebody and made them incredibly skilled and still couldn't keep them."

Heffernan says the hordes of women refusing to play the career-advancement game aren't doing so because

percentage of workers in top jobs

	Men	Women
Lawyers (partner)*	84.4%	15.6%
Corporate officers in the *Fortune* 500**	84.3%	15.7%
Top-earning doctors**	93.4%	6.6%

Sources: *National Directory of Legal Employers, NALP 2000, and 2000 Catalyst Census of Women Corporate Officers and Top Earners; **2002 Catalyst; ***Medical Economics: cardiology, gastroenterology, and orthopedic surgery are top-earning specialities. Percentages of women in those fields calculated from data on doctors (by gender and specialty), from American Medical Association.

they can't hack it, but because they've lost faith in the institutions they've worked for and are tired of cultures driven by hairy-chested notions of how companies must function. Instead, they are founding businesses where they can use the experience in an environment they can better control. "They leave to create companies where they don't have to be the change agents, where they can start from scratch without the fights, without the baggage, and without the brawls," she says.

Stanford's Lazear so envisions a different scenario for women, one in which they wouldn't have to leave corporate America to get the jobs they want. Given the coming labor shortage, which the U.S. Department of Labor predicts will hit by 2010, companies maybe forced to redesign jobs to a talented workers. And that, combined with technology that will let people work from a variety of locations, he says, will make it possible for more women to reach the top. He predicts that 20% of CEOs in top organizations will be women in 15 to 20 years. But total parity? "I don't expect it ever to be equal—ever," he says.

Brenda Barnes thinks as today's business-school students gain power in companies, they will force changes that benefit men and women. When she taught at Kellogg, she asked her students to write a paper describing how they saw their careers playing out. "They were far more focused on having a life than my generation was," she says. "And it wasn't just a female thing. They grew up seeing their parents killing themselves and then being downsized despite their loyalty. How much this generation is willing to give to any enterprise is a totally different ballgame."

We can hope so. Unfortunately, her students' desire for more balance could be one more form of youthful idealism. As a 24-hour global economy makes it ever more difficult to turn off the office, it's hard to imagine a day when the promotions won't go to the worker who makes just a little more effort, who logs on just a little longer. Or to envision a day when there won't be plenty of contenders—maybe most of them men—who will be willing to do just that.

Linda Tischler (ltischler@fastcompany.com) is a FAST COMPANY senior writer.

'Rife with discrimination'

Plaintiffs describe their lives at Wal-Mart

By Stephanie Armour

The class-action sex-discrimination lawsuit against Wal-Mart Stores will force the retail giant to face claims that the company is rife with sexism, with women denied promotions, paid less and in some cases subjected to demeaning comments or sexist acts.

One woman claims she was taken to a strip club. Others say they were told to "doll up," called a "worthless broad" or asked to wear lower-cut shirts, and female employees were paid 5% to 15% less than men in similar jobs, according to the lawsuit. Knowledge of the discrimination stretched all the way to the top executives at Wal-Mart's corporate headquarters in Bentonville, Ark., lawyers say.

"It was known by the very top," says plaintiffs lawyer Brad Seligman in Berkeley, Calif. "Wal-Mart is rife with discrimination."

Wal-Mart declined to comment. On Tuesday, officials released a statement saying they "strongly disagree" with a federal judge's decision to certify a lawsuit by six current and former Wal-Mart employees as a class action.

The certification means more than 1.6 million women who worked at any of Wal-Mart's stores since Dec. 26, 1998, will be covered by the case. Wal-Mart plans to appeal.

Interviews with some of the plaintiffs, statistics compiled for their attorneys and sworn statements by current and former Wal-Mart employees depict a company where women are blocked from management jobs and subjected to demean-ing comments—a characterization that Wal-Mart has strongly denied.

Plaintiff Melissa Howard, 36, of Indianapolis quit her job as store manager in August 2000 after she says monthly sales meetings were held at a Hooters restaurant. And on a business trip to Arkansas, she says she was taken to a strip club and pressured to go inside.

She decided to join the lawsuit, she says, because she wanted to set a good example for her daughter, who is now 8.

"I had a little girl. I had to make a stand for her," Howard says. "It was belittling."

In an earlier interview with USA TODAY, class member Stephanie Odle says she learned a male manager with less experience than she had was earning $20,000 more a year. She says she complained but was told the man was a single father, that he had children and was the sole financial support for them.

"They have a blatant disregard," said Odle of Norman, Okla. "They can't continue to treat people that way."

Promotion policy questioned

Other women tell similar stories. Sandra Stevenson worked at the Gurnee, Ill., Sam's Club in different jobs from November 1996 to June 2000 and requested promotion to management. Instead, she said in a sworn statement, she wasn't given the staff she needed as an overnight supervisor and watched as less-experienced male employees were supported and groomed for management.

"My spirit was broken," she said in her statement. She now lives in Lake Villa, Ill.

Kim McLamb, who worked at Wal-Mart from 1991 to 2001 as an assistant manager at stores in Virginia, says she discovered men made more than women in the same jobs. She says she complained to three different managers. Each told her it was because the men "had families to support," according to her statement.

According to the federal judge's decision, one female employee was told by a male manager that "men are here to make a career and women aren't. Retail is for housewives who just need to earn extra money."

> According to the federal judge's decision, one female employee was told by a male manager that "men are here to make a career and women aren't. Retail is for housewives who just need to earn extra money."

Another woman who sought a transfer to the hardware department says she was told, "We need you in toys.... You're a girl, why do you want to be in hardware?" according to the decision. And another woman was told by a female manager that a sporting goods department manager job went to a man because they "needed a man for the job," according to the decision.

Number of declarants by state

States in which one or more declarants worked:

Alabama	8
Alaska	2
Arkansas	6
California	19
Colorado	3
Connecticut	1
Florida	16
Georgia	3
Idaho	2
Illinois	5
Indiana	1
Iowa	2
Kansas	3
Kentucky	3
Michigan	1
Minnesota	1
Mississippi	5
Missouri	9
Nebraska	1
Nevada	4
New Hampshire	1
New Mexico	3
New York	4
North Carolina	7
Ohio	4
Oklahoma	9
Pennsylvania	3
South Carolina	6
South Dakota	1
Tennessee	3
Texas	10
Utah	3
Virginia	4
Washington	2
Wisconsin	4

Source: walmartclass.com

Workers' statements

Summaries of some sworn statements taken from women who are current or former Wal-Mart employees:

☞ **Micki Earwood** of Springfield, Ohio, worked for Wal-Mart for 10 years as an associate, department manager, support manager and personnel manager. She says Wal-Mart denied her requests to be placed into a management-training program that would lead to a salaried position. She says she reported gender-based pay discrepancies to superiors and believes she was fired in September 2000 for her whistle-blowing activities.

☞ **Deborah Gunter** worked at three Wal-Mart stores in California from April 1996 through August 1999. Three times, she says, she was denied a job as support manager in favor of men who had less seniority or qualifications. She believes she was fired for complaining. "I want to change Wal-Mart's corporate culture and employment practices so that women have the same opportunity to advance with the company as men currently do," she says in her statement.

☞ **Gina Espinoza-Price**, who worked at Wal-Mart from 1990 through 1997, in the photo division. She says promotions went to men with less experience, and she says she was subjected to sexist and racist comments, including being called "the little Mexican princess." She says she was fired six weeks after complaining about sexual harassment. "I believe that I was terminated for complaining about sexual harassment and because I am a woman who wanted to be promoted within Wal-Mart," she says in her statement.

☞ **Vicki Thornton** was fired from Wal-Mart in 2001 after working at a store in Racine, Wis. She says she asked to be promoted to a management-training program but was told there were no openings, although men were put into the program. She says she was sexually harassed by managers, who made comments such as, "Can't you wear lower cut shirts?" She says she was told to "grin and bear it" after she complained to superiors. She says she was fired after contacting the lawyers in the sex-discrimination case against Wal-Mart.

fand, an employment lawyer in Houston.

The judge did note the women "present largely uncontested . . . statistics which show that women working at Wal-Mart stores are paid less than men in every region, that payment disparities exist in most job categories, that the salary gap widens over time, that women take longer to enter management positions and that the higher one looks in the organization the lower the percentage of women."

The ruling raises the legal stakes for Wal-Mart, and it casts new attention to the plaintiffs' claims and Wal-Mart's treatment of its female employees.

It took women, on average, about four years from date of hire to be promoted to assistant manager, while men took about three years, according to a statistician's analysis done for the plaintiffs. It took 10 years for women to reach store manager, compared with just under nine years for men.

But another expert argues that women have been selected for management jobs at a rate that's about equal to the rate at which they apply, according to the judge's decision.

Wal-Mart's new pay system

Wal-Mart officials have denied that there are any widespread problems and have said they can't comment on specifics in the lawsuit. In past interviews with USA TODAY, officials have said Wal-Mart is a great place for women to work and that any complaints are isolated.

In June the company unveiled a pay system designed to ensure equality. One thrust of the plan: Executive bonuses will be cut as much as 7.5% in this year and 15% in the next fiscal year if individual diversity goals aren't met. The company also has an office of diversity that was launched in November 2003 to ensure diversity in recruiting and other employment practices.

But plaintiffs lawyers say they are seeking more changes in how

"This is a companywide practice," says Jocelyn Larkin, litigation counsel for the Impact Fund, a Berkeley, Calif.-based non-profit that is the lead counsel for the women.

The decision to certify the lawsuit as a class action makes this the largest private civil rights case ever, but it does not mean that evidence shows Wal-Mart is guilty of discrimination. Rather, it means the claims are similar enough that they should be treated as a class action.

"The court isn't saying there's merit to the claims," says Bill Hel-

Wal-Mart operates, including a court-appointed monitor to oversee the 40-year-old chain's employment practices.

According to their lawsuit, there are problems in at least three major areas:

* **Women are denied equal promotions.** Lawyers say women receive fewer promotions and wait longer to get promoted. Roughly 65% of hourly employees are women, while about 33% of management employees are women, according to an analysis done for plaintiffs lawyers. Only 14% of store managers are women.

* **Women are paid less for the same jobs, even when they have more experience.** A labor economist for the plaintiffs performed a bench-marking study of 20 Wal-Mart competitors and found the chain promotes a lower percentage of women than its retail counterparts, according to the legal decision. He found a shortfall in female managers was present in nearly 80% of Wal-Mart stores.

While the in-store management workforce at other stores was about 57% female, it was 35% female at Wal-Mart.

Wal-Mart has argued that the analysis is flawed.

* **Women are subjected to sexist actions and gender stereotyping.** According to class members' statements, women claim they were subjected to various sexist acts. They say they had to train men for jobs they wanted, were told they shouldn't pursue certain positions because they were women and got no reaction after complaining to corporate headquarters.

Class member Christine Kwapnoski of Concord, Calif., who has held a variety of positions at Sam's Club since 1986, says she was told to "doll up" and "blow the cobwebs off her makeup."

Gretchen Adams of Florida, who quit her job in December 2001 with Wal-Mart, where she worked as an hourly employee, assistant manager and co-manager, says she was called a "worthless broad" by a male district manager.

INTO THIN AIR

THESE PEOPLE LOST HIGH-TECH JOBS TO LOW-WAGE COUNTRIES. TRY TELLING *THEM* THAT OFFSHORING IS A GOOD THING IN THE LONG RUN.

By Jennifer Reingold
with Jena McGregor, Fiona Haley, Michael Prospero, and Carleen Hawn

It was Saddam Hussein who broke the news to Myra Bronstein that her job was *gone forever*.

A 48-year-old senior engineer at WatchMark Corp., a Bellevue, Washington, software company, Bronstein had spent three years running tests and hunting for bugs in the company's software. She knew that things weren't going so well at work; she'd been asked to pull 12- to 18-hour shifts frequently, her boss reiterating that the company's success depended on her "hard work and efforts." So when Bronstein received a brusque email in March 2003 instructing her to come to a 10 a.m. meeting in the boardroom the next day, she began to worry. "No way can that be good," she thought.

Looking for guidance, Bronstein logged on to a Yahoo users' group for WatchMark employees. And there it was, in a post written by "Saddam Hussein": "Here's what's going to happen tomorrow," Bronstein remembers the post read. "For all the quality assurance engineers reading this, your jobs are gone." At that very moment, it said, their replacements were on their way here from India for training. It listed their names, then concluded with sadistic glee: "Make sure on Monday you

welcome your replacements with open arms, because your company has chosen them over you."

Bronstein says she felt an icy chill. "It's a feeling of horror and panic because there's nothing to be done," she says. "Saddam Hussein's" intelligence proved absolutely right. The next morning, a Friday, Bronstein and some 60 others were told that they were being terminated. Some left immediately; others, like Bronstein, were asked to stay on for several weeks to train the new folks. "Our severance and unemployment were contingent on training the replacements," she says. "It was quite explicit." WatchMark's new CEO, John Hansen, says an additional payment beyond the severance was offered to those who stayed on.

And so the next week, Bronstein walked into a room to find her old coworkers on one side and the new group from India on the other. "It was like a sock hop where everyone's lined up against the wall blinking at each other," she says. "People were trying not to cry." In an attempt to lighten the mood, her boss said she would like to introduce the old

staff to the new staff, while the VP of engineering chimed in with familiar words. "We're depending on you to help this company succeed," he said. Bronstein spent the next four weeks training her two replacements who then went back to India—two people whose lives were suddenly bettered in exchange for one whose life had taken an unexpected turn for the worse.

Since leaving WatchMark (now called WatchMark-Comnitel), Bronstein, who made $76,500 plus bonus, has been out of work, making ends meet with unemployment and by cashing out her 401(k). With both of those gone, she's turned to selling her collection of antique women's compacts on eBay. "It's the difference between hopeful and hopeless," she says. "If you're just laid off, you can tell yourself that the economy swings back and forth, but if it's outsourced offshore, it ain't coming back. It still exists, but it just exists in another place. The IT industry in the United States has gone from being a very high-level, well-paying industry to being very low-paying sweatshop labor, and that's an inexorable trend."

Bronstein's story is increasingly common in a global economy where labor is crossing borders almost as freely as capital. Starting decades ago with low-skilled manufacturing jobs in basic industries, followed by textiles, cars, semiconductors, and now, services, the nimbleness of the world's economy has allowed us to reduce costs by moving production to wherever it's least expensive. The benefits to our economy—in increased productivity, lower prices, and greater demand for American products—are touted by corporate America as the only way to remain competitive. "This is the next iteration of the global economy," says Atul Vashistha, CEO of neoIT, an offshore advisory firm. "The story is what would happen to these companies if they did not go offshore."

Whether you believe such dislocations are ultimately good or bad, they're here, they're real, and they're happening at speeds and levels unforeseen just a few years ago. In December 2003, IBM decided to move the jobs of nearly 5,000 programmers to India and China. GE has moved much of its research and development overseas. Microsoft, Dell, American Express, and virtually every major multinational from Accenture to Yahoo has already offshored work or is considering doing so, with 40% of the Fortune 500 expected to have done so by the end of this year, according to the research firm Gartner Inc. The savings are dramatic: Companies can cut 20% to 70% of their labor costs by moving jobs to low-wage nations—assuming that the work is of comparable quality.

Equally dramatic are the displacement, downward mobility, and suffering of the people left behind. So far, at least, that enhanced productivity hasn't translated into jobs at home. Offshoring is steadily eating its way into the educated classes, both in the United States and elsewhere, affecting jobs traditionally considered secure. People whose livelihoods could now be at risk include everyone from

Going, Going, GONE?

Offshoring jobs is an old story in the manufacturing sector. Now, service jobs once considered safe are being shipped overseas. Lawyers, accountants, journalists, engineers, take heed. "Any knowledge-worker job is at some risk," says Michael T. Robinson, president of Careerplanner.com. Working with his firm and our own research, we've come up with a list of jobs and their relative vulnerability.

EXTREME RISK Accountant • Industrial Engineer • Production Control Specialist • Quality Assurance Engineer • Call-Center Operator • Help-Desk Specialist • Telemarketer

HIGH OR MODERATE RISK Automotive Engineer • Computer Systems Analyst • Database Administrator • Software Developer • Customer-Service Representative • CAD Technician • Paralegal/Legal Assistant • Medical Trancriptionist • Copy Editor/Journalist • Film Editor • Insurance

LOW RISK Airplane Mechanic • Artist • Carpenter • Civil Engineer • Headhunter • Interior Designer

Data: Careerplanner.com, UC Berkeley Fisher Center for Real Estate and Urban Economics, FAST COMPANY

IT experts to accountants, medical transcriptionists to customer-service representatives. In IT alone, Gartner estimates that another 500,000 positions in the U.S. may leave by the end of this year; in one scenario, as many as 25% of all IT professional jobs could go overseas by 2008. If just 40% of those people never find another job in their field, that could be more than 1 million whose careers are altered forever.

The implications of this colossal transformation are only just beginning to be understood. This time around, these categories cover a much greater share of our economy; manufacturing accounts for just 14% of U.S. output, while services provide 60% and employ two-thirds of all workers. "It's happening much

faster [than in manufacturing]," says Cynthia Kroll, senior regional economist at UC Berkeley's Haas School of Business. "There are fewer capital investments required in outsourcing a services job." Kroll cowrote a recent study that pegged the current number of jobs vulnerable in some way to offshoring at a stunning 14 million.

Wait a second. Wasn't it this transition to a service economy that was supposed to give us a lasting edge over our global competition? And weren't technology jobs supposed to offer a secure refuge to other displaced workers? So far, things haven't worked out that way. There are now millions of trained and educated people abroad who can do many of our jobs at a fraction of the price. And this upheaval has many people worried. "Industrialization happened and people moved from farms to factories," says Marcus Courtney, president of the Washington Alliance of Technology Workers. "In this round of globalization, people aren't moving to anything. Skills do not grant one immunity." Some argue that the shift will free resources for the innovations that will create the next big boom; others see it as an admission that our competitive advantage is gone. "More than just outsourcing IT or anyone's job, we're outsourcing the American middle class," says Bronstein.

It's no surprise, then, that offshoring is suddenly one of the hottest topics around. Presidential hopefuls like John Kerry have waded into the debate, and the media have leaped on the subject. Even CNN's Lou Dobbs—hardly a bleeding heart—has jumped in with his "shame on you" list of companies that have moved jobs overseas. Blogs and Web sites such as YourjobisgoingtoIndia.com have sprung up to rail against evil corporate interests, and some antiforeigner groups have seized on this issue as a way to promote their beliefs. Offshoring has reenergized an ugly strain of nativism in the United States, with anti-immigration groups using it to argue against work visas. Other groups, often company-sponsored, use the dirty word "protectionist" against opponents. The din grows louder every day.

Yet much of this discussion is beside the point. Offshoring is here to stay (as long as the cost savings are for real) and there's little point in hand-wringing over whether it should or shouldn't take place. Equally useless—and disingenuous—are the bland, marginally empathetic statements of business leaders alluding to the "short-term pain" as if it were a stubbed toe or a nick from shaving. When contacted, some companies refused comment, while many confirmed that they had moved some jobs overseas or said some losses were simply the result of lay-offs. A Microsoft spokesperson, for example, disputed one person's claim to have been offshored, saying it was just "part of the ebb and flow of business." Drowned out in all the hype are the voices of those on the bleeding edge of the change—the real people caught in the crosswinds of this massive global shift. The macro outlook seems irrelevant when the goal is to pay the rent.

That's the challenge faced by both Rexanna Sieber and Doug Hill every day. They come from different backgrounds—Sieber, 58, was an $11-an-hour keyboarder in Villisca, Iowa, for a company that helped make textbooks, while Hill, 60, worked as a contractor in automotive design at Lear Seating in Dearborn, Michigan, and earned six figures. But both saw their jobs move overseas and neither has found permanent work since. Hill works part-time in the veterans' benefits office of American Indian Health and Family Services; Sieber is unemployed.

"I'm done," says Hill. "I know that. Who's going to hire me? I'm 60. I'm just living one day at a time, and I do a lot of praying." Both Hill and Sieber are philosophical about the offshoring trend, saying that's the way the world works, but they worry about the long-term impact on the middle class. "I believe in free enterprise," says Sieber, "but per-

sonally, I think that the government makes it too easy to do it."

Sieber's argument is gaining support among some politicians, who are writing legislation that may make offshoring more difficult. One bill that passed the Indiana Senate on February 2 by a vote of 39–10 would require that any state government work be performed in the U.S. The measure was a reaction to a contract—later canceled by the governor—that gave Tata America International Corp., an American subsidiary of the Indian multinational, $15 million for a computer upgrade of the unemployment insurance program, of all things. It's just one of several initiatives addressing offshoring. "It's a national crisis," says the bill's sponsor, Republican state senator Jeff Drozda.

Even some corporate leaders are looking to the government for guidance. "In the absence of a public policy that tells me what to do," former Intel CEO Andrew Grove told an audience last October, "I have no choice as corporate manager, nor do my colleagues . . . [but to make decisions] that very often involve moves of jobs into other countries."

But most companies see such laws as the worst kind of protectionism. Ultimately, these measures will lead to more job loss, not less, critics say. "A lot of times [offshored people] don't think about people that are still left here," says Hansen, WatchMark's CEO. "What about those companies that didn't survive?" In an economy where "There is no job that is America's God-given right anymore," in the words of Hewlett-Packard CEO Carly Fiorina, they believe that job security is up to the individual.

Fiorina probably never had the chance to meet Debi Null. A 49-year-old former system administrator at Agilent Technologies who worked for the company and its former parent, Hewlett-Packard, for more than 20 years, Null was laid off in January 2002, then was hired for less money as a contract employee to do the same job. When her contract ended

last year, Null got the news that her job was moving to Singapore. Although she says Agilent treated her with respect throughout the process, finding a new position in her field has proven impossible. In order to get by and pay her health insurance, which costs some $650 a month for treatment related to a liver transplant, she sold her two cars, cashed out her 401(k), and took on three jobs. One, at Foley's department store, pays $6.50 an hour; a second, as a real estate saleswoman, depends on commission. She has yet to sell a house.

To qualify for benefits, Null has also taken a job as a $12-an-hour call-center operator at T-Mobile. But with call centers one of the most commonly offshored jobs in the country, it's hardly a secure gig. "I'm part of history, I guess," she says resignedly. "I worked for high tech in the glory days, but I would not encourage my kids to go into [it]," she says. "Right now, my oldest son is a furniture salesman and my younger one is an apprentice plumber. I don't think they can send those things overseas yet."

It's easy to argue that people like Null should have seen it coming and ought to have constantly upgraded their skills. But as offshoring eats away at ever more sophisticated jobs, is it safe to assume that there is a skill level or point in the food chain at which jobs can no longer be outsourced? "No one's immune," says Frances Karamouzis, a research director at Gartner. "We as analysts have had internal discussions, [wondering] are we next?"

Job insecurity, of course, is hardly limited to victims of offshoring. And there is less sympathy for well-educated IT workers, many of whom benefited from a dramatic run-up in salaries during the bubble. "The cost of technology inside the U.S. and the salaries along with it are outrageous," says Michael Mullarkey, CEO of Workstream Inc., a Canadian-based tech company. "I'm paying $65,000 Canadian for developers that were making $147,000 [in California], and they're smiling ear to ear. People are a dime a dozen."

With that kind of pressure, even those who keep their jobs are feeling the squeeze: A January 2004 study by Foote Partners shows that IT compensation has fallen for four straight quarters in the areas most vulnerable to outsourcing, dropping an average of 7.6% in 2003 alone. "There's no way to stay competitive, no matter how hard you work, when you can get 8 to 16 heads for the price of one," says Bronstein.

So is there any such thing as a safe refuge? Melissa Charters was a data security administrator in Los Angeles with five kids and a freelancer husband. Her $70,000 job was first outsourced to a local company and then offshored to India in May 2003. It's an increasingly common pattern. Full-time jobs become contract work, without benefits, and then vanish overseas. Thanks to a state-funded program for displaced IT workers, Charters is going back to college—to learn to teach home economics. "I seriously considered going back to school to do data or network security," she says. "But then I thought, how could I invest my own money in a career to have it taken away again? I'm pretty sure teachers can't be offshored, but if I start seeing big-screen TVs in my classes, I am going to be worried."

Charters is lucky to have found some government help. While the Trade Adjustment Assistance Reform Act of 2002 provides federal aid for those whose jobs have moved overseas, it is aimed at manufacturing jobs; most software developers and other white-collar workers aren't eligible. In January, a group of former IBM programmers filed a class action suit against the U.S. government to change that.

Corporations bear some responsibility to the workers they leave behind, argues Ray Lane, the former COO and president of Oracle Corp. and currently a partner at Kleiner Perkins Caufield & Byers. "Take some of your expected profits from offshoring and make your severance

packages higher or retrain the employees … in known growth industries," he says. "But don't kid them. My cousin worked as a bartender for eight years while he waited for his $22-an-hour steel mill job to 'come back.' These jobs never come back."

In an August 2003 report entitled "Offshoring: Is It a Win-Win Game?" McKinsey Global Institute concludes with great specificity that every dollar of offshoring results in 58 cents of savings to the American economy. But even that report acknowledges that 31% of workers who lost their jobs in earlier waves were never fully reemployed, with 80% taking pay cuts. That's the reality for Clifford Paino, a systems analyst whose job moved to Ireland in December 2002. After six months, he found a new job as a contract worker for the same company—earning 40% less, with no job security. "They can tell me they can get rid of me tomorrow," he says.

The situation is particularly acute in certain cities—often the very ones that were a little slice of heaven in the 1990s. In the Colorado Springs area, a thriving IT industry was powered in part by Agilent, the company that was spun off from HP in 1999. The retrenchment that resulted from the decline of the Internet economy has led to the loss of thousands of jobs in the area, many of which went overseas. Agilent won kudos for handling the difficult process as gracefully as possible. Yet its status as part of the original HP—a place once famous for treating its workers with loyalty and respect and for fostering lifelong careers—makes the human impact all the more poignant.

"I walked to work when I was seven months' pregnant in a blizzard and stayed for three more shifts," says Joan Pounds, an IT representative at Agilent who lost her job in July 2003. "I did that because I cared about the company." Pounds wasn't surprised to get the bad news—she'd already survived seven layoffs—but she was surprised to learn that she had to train her replacements in India via teleconference.

One of the Indian replacement workers did, however, congratulate Pounds on her new job. "I said, 'I don't know where that is,' and he said that they had been told we were going on to much better positions," she remembers. "It was emotional on both sides." Shocked to learn that they were, in fact, putting Pounds out of work, both replacement workers tried to back out of the contract, Pounds says. But their employer, a contractor in India, told them they couldn't. As for Pounds, a single mother, she sent out 25 résumés a week with no luck before taking a 13-hour-a-week job as a senior-citizen caregiver. The pay: $7 an hour. She has no medical benefits and must pay the costs of treatment for a son with bipolar disorder. A few months ago, she sold her house at a loss just two days before it was scheduled to be foreclosed.

After his job on Agilent's Windows NT support team ended up in Singapore, William V. Grebenik decided to set up a company that would help smaller companies move offshore. He thought he could help clients with the cultural issues that often create problems, but he blew through his severance before the company could get any traction. "I'm living on one-fourth of what I was making," says Grebenik, who now runs a part-time technical training company. "I've got to make the rent in five days. I'm going to be borrowing it off somebody."

It took courage for people like Grebenik and Pounds to share their stories, because many others whom FAST COMPANY contacted refused, terrified that speaking out would further harm their chances of finding work. "People are really frightened about potential blacklisting," says Natasha Humphries, a former senior software engineer for Palm who was laid off last August. Humphries says she was sent to Bangalore to train some contractors, only to find out later that they were her group's replacements. (Palm disputes Humphries's account, saying her work was split between two local managers.) One man we contacted who had spoken to a local paper about being offshored was told he'd be fired from his new position if he was quoted elsewhere. His wife spoke to us instead.

Many U.S. companies are also doing their best to stay out of the spotlight on this issue—even as they rely increasingly on overseas workers. Rather than loudly proclaiming the benefits—or, alternatively, opting not to shift those jobs overseas—many are simply continuing their offshoring as quietly as possible. "Nobody wants to be the poster child for this," says Vashistha of neoIT, who says publicity-shy clients asked him to take their names down from his Web site. Even McKinsey, which extols offshoring's benefits publicly, didn't respond to a reporter's request to learn more about its own offshoring efforts.

For many multinationals, in fact, offshoring can be a public-relations nightmare at both ends of the pipeline. They fear being associated with the loss of U.S. jobs, of course—but they also worry about offending huge markets if they pull back from employing workers in places such as India, China, and Indonesia. Dell, for example, has tried hard to downplay its decision to bring back some of its call-center operations to the United States from India after criticism about the service quality. According

to Barry French, a Dell spokesman, it was "a lot of flurry over something reasonably insignificant. The climate is pretty intense, so what was a small action got blown out of proportion. We remain absolutely committed to India." And at Lehman Brothers, questions about a recent decision to bring back its help desk, which had been outsourced to Indian tech company Wipro Ltd. in January 2003, brought the following clipped response from a spokeswoman: "We're not getting into the details of it. We don't want to be quoted on this. It was a management decision."

The irony is that offshoring is not an American-only concern. In manufacturing, the jobs have trampolined from country to country. In a world where people are treated as any other factor of production, scapegoating one country is pointless. Already, jobs that just five years ago went to Ireland are now done in India; as wages rise there, new, cheaper sources of well-trained workers are springing up in such places as the Philippines and, of course, China. "People in India, of course they're happy, they're getting more money," says Andres Urv, whose job as a quality assurance engineer was offshored in 2003. "But when companies pull out and say, 'Thank you so much but we found someone cheaper,' will they be feeling like we do?"

Where will it all end? Some people believe that population trends make the whole debate a waste of time. Even if the worst-case scenario for offshoring comes true, they say, the departure of boomers from the workforce will create a demographic earthquake so severe that filling, not finding, jobs will pose the biggest challenge.

But other observers see a bleaker prospect ahead. "As centers of skilled high-tech professionals build up in other parts of the world, the U.S.... may no longer dominate the next wave of innovations," a fall 2003 Berkeley study on outsourcing reads. Or perhaps it doesn't matter. "Anyone who is looking at this current debate isn't looking down the road far enough," says Tim Chou, president of Oracle Outsourcing. "The future is HAL [the superintelligent computer in 2001: A Space Odyssey]—a computer sitting in a dark room spitting out money. It won't involve any people, because [computers] are way more repetitive, reliable, and much lower cost than any human."

Perhaps Pounds, formerly of Agilent, sums it up best: "We've had throwaway clothes, throwaway cars, and now we have throwaway people." Is that what globalization was supposed to be all about?

THE WHISTLE-BLOWER

A HERO—AND A SMOKING-GUN LETTER

Watkins' memo spoke volumes about Enron's behavior. So did higher-ups' tepid response

At last, someone in the sordid Enron Corp. scandal seems to have done the right thing. Thanks to whistle-blower Sherron S. Watkins, a no-nonsense Enron vice-president, the scope and audacity of the accounting mess is becoming all too clear. Her blunt Aug. 15 letter to Enron CEO Kenneth L. Lay warns that the company might "implode in a wave of accounting scandals." And now that her worst fears have been realized, it is also clear that Watkins' letter went far beyond highlighting a few accounting problems in a handful of off-balance-sheet partnerships. Watkins' letter lays bare for all to see the underbelly of Enron's get-rich-quick culture.

Watkins, 42, a former Arthur Andersen accountant who remains Enron's vice-president for corporate development, put her finger on the rot: top execs who, at best, appeared to close their eyes to questionable accounting maneuvers; a leadership that had lost sight of ordinary investors and the basic principles of accounting; and watchdogs—the outside auditors and lawyers whose own involvement may have left them too conflicted to query the nature of the deals. Perhaps the question shouldn't be how Enron collapsed so quickly—but why it didn't implode sooner.

Lay's response to Watkins' complaints is nearly as damning as her letter itself. Yes, he talked to her for an hour. And, yes, he ordered an outside investigation. But contrary to Watkins' advice, he appointed the company's longtime Houston law firm, Vinson & Elkins, despite the obvious conflict: V&E had worked on some of the partnerships. And Enron and V&E agreed there would be no "second-guessing" of Andersen's ac-

counting and no "detailed analysis" of each and every transaction, according to V&E's Oct. 15 report. The inquiry was to consider only if there was new factual information that warranted a broader investigation. V&E declined comment.

Surprise: V&E concluded that a widespread investigation wasn't warranted. It simply warned that there was a "serious risk of adverse publicity and litigation." And Watkins' letter reveals the inadequacy of Lay's response in the months following CEO Jeffrey K. Skilling's sudden Aug. 14 resignation for "personal reasons." His departure triggered the letter. Lay never fully disclosed the partnerships or explained their impact to investors, even as he vowed there were no accounting issues and "no other shoe to fall." Even after Enron revealed on Oct. 16 a $1.2 billion hit to shareholder equity related to the partnerships, Lay continued to express ignorance about details of these deals and support for Chief Financial Officer Andrew S. Fastow, who managed and had stakes in certain partnerships. But on Oct. 24, Fastow was removed from his job and promptly left the company.

Watkins, an eight-year Enron veteran, is not some disgruntled naysayer who is easy to dismiss. Her lawyer, Philip H. Hilder, says she became familiar with some of the partnership dealings when she worked in June and July in Fastow's finance group. Her position allowed her to review the valuation of certain assets being sold into the partnerships, and that's when she saw "computations that just didn't jibe," says Hilder.

Former executives say the Tomball (Tex.) native was tenacious and competent. "She wasn't really an alarmist," says one

> Skilling's abrupt departure will raise suspicions of accounting improprieties and valuation issues.

> I am incredibly nervous that we will implode in a wave of accounting scandals. My 8 years of

> I realize that we have had a lot of smart people looking at this and a lot of accountants including AA&Co. have blessed the accounting treatment. None of that will protect Enron if these transactions are ever disclosed in the bright light of day. (P... problems of Waste Manag...

former Enron employee. Her mother, Shirley Klein Harrington, a former high school accounting teacher, calls her daughter "a very independent, outspoken, good Christian girl, who's going to stand up for principle whenever she can." Watkins had previously worked at Andersen in Houston and New York and then for Germany's Metallgesellschaft AG.

At those companies, she befriended Jeffrey McMahon, whom she helped recruit. Now the CFO at Enron, McMahon "complained mightily" about the Fastow partnerships to Skilling, Watkins told Lay in the letter. "Employees question our accounting propriety consistently and constantly," she claimed. McMahon didn't return calls. Skilling has denied getting any warnings about accounting.

Watkins didn't stop there. Five days after she wrote to Lay, Watkins took her concerns directly to an Andersen audit partner, according to congressional investigators. He in turn relayed her questions to senior Andersen management on the Enron account. It's not known what, if any, action they took.

Of course, Skilling and Andersen execs shouldn't have needed a letter and a phone call from Watkins to figure out something was seriously amiss. Red flags abounded. And Wat-

kins, for one, had no trouble putting her finger on questionable accounting practices. She wondered if Enron was hiding losses in off-balance-sheet entities while booking large profits from the deals. At the same time, the outside partnerships were backed with Enron stock—a tactic sure to backfire when it was falling—and no outsiders seemed to have any capital at risk. Was Enron creating income essentially by doing deals with itself? "It sure looks to the layman on the street that we are hiding losses in a related company and will compensate that company with Enron stock in the future," she wrote.

In the end, Watkins grasped one thing that Enron's too-clever-by-half dealmakers didn't: Enron's maneuvering didn't pass the smell test. Even if Enron and its high-priced auditors and lawyers can ultimately show that they followed the letter of the law, it matters little. As Watkins herself wrote, if Enron collapses, "the business world will consider the past successes as nothing but an elaborate accounting hoax." And that seems destined to become Enron's epitaph.

By Wendy Zellner, with Stephanie Forest Anderson, in Dallas and with Laura Cohn in Washington

HALL MONITORS IN THE WORKPLACE

Encouraging Employee WHISTLEBLOWERS

Remember the teacher's pet in grade school? Everyone resented the kid who would tattletale on his or her peers. This might explain why we're uncomfortable with employee whistleblowers. Get over it.

BY SHARIE A. BROWN

It's actually in a company's best interests to encourage employee whistleblowers who can uncover problems before they become fodder for front-page news.

Creating an environment in which workers feel safe confiding in management about potential accounting errors, questionable business deals and government compliance oversights could save millions of dollars in the long run. It could even save the company.

In today's world of corporate mistrust, public companies may not realize that they really don't have a choice. With corporate financial and ethic scandals topping the news every day, you can rest assured that if an employee's complaints fall on deaf ears in the office, there will be a line of people on the outside willing to listen.

Government prosecutors are always willing to listen to articulate, disgruntled employees with documents to validate their claims of misconduct. And to make matters worse for misbehaving companies, whistleblowers are being paid huge sums from courts for uncovering problems. They're entitled to as much as one-third of the monetary damages they unearth.

EMPLOYEE HOTLINES

Smart companies know that they should clean their own houses in hopes of preventing Uncle Sam from being asked to do the job. Creating an effective *internal* whistleblower program is one of management's best tools for heading off possible government enforcement actions, unwanted media scrutiny, third-party legal measures and large pay-outs.

Some companies already have internal whistleblower programs of a sort in place—they just call them "employee hotlines" or "helplines." Many organizations even include information about them in mission statements or use employee handbooks to spell out procedures for reporting information.

Even with these existing programs, it is a tough challenge to create an *effective* internal whistleblower program. To begin with, some supervisors are uncomfortable with employees who report the misdeeds of others. They generally don't like their departments or personnel to be painted in a negative light to management.

Management must be willing to virtually guarantee employees that no retaliatory action will be taken against them for coming forward....

AN EFFECTIVE PROGRAM

As organizations begin to build suitable programs, they need to remember that it's no longer enough just to set up a system where employees can expose a problem to a supervisor. Employees have to understand that they won't be harmed because of their honesty. Management must be willing to virtually guarantee employees that no retaliatory action will be taken against them for coming forward—and employees have to believe management.

Once an infraction is reported, the company must also be committed to conducting internal reviews or investigations, taking appropriate actions to correct problems and disciplining the employees at fault. Companies may even decide to refer the offender to law enforcement or regulatory authorities.

Companies must walk the walk as well as talk the talk. Otherwise, employees will see no reason to step forward. Moreover, legal precedence shows that officers and directors who learn of misconduct but fail or refuse to take appropriate action can be held liable.

There's good news for companies that want to do the right thing but are not sure how to begin. There are guidelines that describe many of the attributes that an effective whistleblower program should have.

For instance, we know from sentencing guidelines that courts will consider a program successful if it has standards and procedures that are capable of reducing the prospect of criminal activity.

That's easier said than done. But, it is important to create an internal reporting system where employees feel able to report suspected misconduct without fear of reprisal and with the confidence that appropriate action will be taken. Intended or not,

many workers are intimidated and fear for their jobs if they rock the boat.

THE CORNERSTONE

Fostering comfort and confidence is a cornerstone of a strong internal system. Without those features, frustrated employees might be driven into the arms of eager journalists, government officials or private lawyers.

Another key attribute of a successful program is confidentiality. Your system should ensure that employees can maintain their anonymity and report in a confidential environment to someone other than a direct supervisor, who may be part of the problem. Usually, a worker should be able to report impropriety to senior management, someone from human resources, or counsel from the company's legal department.

And it has to be stressed again: management cannot be vindictive in any way toward the whistleblower—whether it is through a transfer, denial of a bonus, demotion in title or loss of a job.

Retaliation not only destroys trust within the internal program but also leads to criminal charges and jail time. Under the corporate responsibility bill authored by Senator Sarbanes and Congressman Oxley and recently passed by Congress, retaliatory measures can result in up to 10 years in prison for the responsible executives.

Companies can also prevent problems, based on sentencing guidelines, by having their whistleblower programs overseen by high-level personnel. Too often, lower-level personnel oversee these programs, while senior management remains disengaged and uninformed. Officers and directors can be caught off-guard when problems arise, but courts may still view them as being liable.

The helpful level of involvement comes if senior management goes the extra step and *encourages* watchdogs. Today, some companies are actually providing incentives and recognition for workers who catch problems before they get out of hand or become public knowledge.

A whistleblower program is useless without an effective communication and education policy that reaches all levels of employees.

In summary, a responsible company's job doesn't end by taking a whistleblower's report. That's just the first step.

To make sure your system can live up to the government's standards, ask yourself the following two key questions before the Department of Justice does:

1. Do you enforce compliance standards in a *consistent* manner, using appropriate disciplinary measures? There can be no exceptions; punishments must be consistent.

2. Upon detection of the violation, have you taken reasonable steps to respond and to prevent similar offenses in the future? The government and shareholders are quite unforgiving of repeat offenses.

EFFECTIVE COMMUNICATION AND EDUCATION

Now that your system is in place, it's time to tell all of your workers about it. A whistleblower program is useless without an effective communication and education policy that reaches all levels of employees. This is more than just an insert in the employee handbook. It means constant internal communications—tell them early, and tell them often.

When designed correctly, and when encouraged from the top, your employees can be your eyes and ears.

These modern-day hall monitors might not win any office popularity contests among wrongdoing colleagues, but in the long run, they could keep you out of big trouble. MW

Sharie A. Brown is a partner in the Litigation Department of the Washington, D.C., office of Foley & Lardner, where she counsels companies on corporate ethics and compliance. As a senior counsel in Mobil Oil Corporation's legal department, she helped build and oversee one of the nation's most successful internal whistleblower programs.

Academic Values and the Lure of Profit

By Derek Bok

JOHN LE CARRÉ'S LATEST NOVEL, *The Constant Gardener*, tells of the murder of a young woman in Africa and her husband's valiant efforts to avenge her death. It soon appears that these events all grow out of a major pharmaceutical company's campaign to develop a new drug for combating tuberculosis. Discovered in a Polish laboratory, the drug looks promising at first, raising hopes of earning hundreds of millions of dollars. As tests on human subjects begin in Kenya and other African countries, however, problems start to surface. There are side effects. Patients die.

One of the scientists who discovered the drug has second thoughts and threatens to go public. Frantic, the company tries to suppress the unfavorable evidence and to buy off or intimidate critics. To bolster its case, the company uses money to get help from universities. It contrives to have several well-known professors publish favorable reports about the drug in leading journals without disclosing that the reports were actually written by the company itself and that the purported authors are beneficiaries of lucrative research contracts from the same source. A distant medical school is persuaded to offer the disaffected discoverer of the drug an amply funded post where she can be watched and induced to keep silent. When she finally speaks out, she is quickly vilified and ostracized by colleagues at her university and its affiliated hospital, which just happen to have been promised large donations by… that's right, the drug's manufacturer.

Le Carré takes care to point out that his book is a work of imagination. He makes no claim that pharmaceutical companies resort to beatings and killings to get new drugs to the market. Still, the author does say that his account "draws on several cases, particularly in the North American continent, where highly qualified medical researchers have dared to disagree with their pharmaceutical paymasters and suffered vilification and persecution for their pains."

Is Le Carré correct? Just how far have industrial sponsors actually gone in seeking to use higher-education institutions and professors for their own commercial ends? How willing have universities been to accept money at the cost of compromising values central to the academic enterprise?

To understand what lies behind Le Carré's book, one must appreciate the predicament in which universities find themselves. Now more than ever, they have become the principal source of the three most important ingredients of progress in a modern, industrial society: expert knowledge, highly educated people, and scientific discoveries. At the same time—in a depressed economy, with the federal budget heavily in deficit and state governments cutting investments in higher education—campus officials are confronting a chronic shortage of money to satisfy the demands of students, faculty members, and other constituencies.

As a result, university administrators are under great pressure to become more entrepreneurial. They feel compelled to search more aggressively for novel ways of making profits that can help meet pressing campus needs. Increasingly, one reads of new lucrative ventures launched by one university or another: medical-school consortia to test drugs for pharmaceutical companies; highly advertised executive courses to earn a tidy surplus for their business-school sponsors; alliances with venture capitalists to launch for-profit companies producing Internet courses for far-flung audiences.

The "entrepreneurial university" is the subject of a growing body of scholarly literature and media commentary. Led by resourceful executives, these institutions are often portrayed in books and articles as constantly looking out for new and ingenious ways to serve society's needs while reaping profits with which to scale new pinnacles of excellence and prestige. Reading such accounts, skeptics are quick to assume that such institutions have turned their backs on their academic missions and to criticize them for attempting to bring such businesslike ways into the academy.

Yet profit seeking has undoubtedly helped in some instances to improve academic work and to enhance higher education's value to society. Before Congress made it easy for universities to patent government-financed scientific discoveries and license them to corporations, administrators made little effort to scour campus laboratories for advances that could be turned to practical use to benefit consumers. Today, several hundred institutions have active technology-transfer offices to perform that function, and the number of patents issued to universities has grown more than tenfold. The lure of profit has likewise brought about keener competition to produce more and better-quality training programs for business executives than would have existed otherwise. Similar incentives could conceivably spur a more rapid development of Internet courses that will allow universities to make excellent educational programs available to distant audiences.

But, in their pursuit of moneymaking ventures, universities also risk compromising their essential academic values. To earn a handsome profit from a company, business schools may divert assistant professors from their on-campus duties so that they can teach elementary material to entry-level executives. To win at football, colleges may admit students with grades and scores far below the normal requirements. To profit from the Internet, universities may offer gullible students overseas a chance to take inferior courses that will earn them a dubious certificate of business studies. Once such compromises are made, competitive pressures can cause the questionable practices to spread and eventually become so deeply rooted as to be well nigh irreversible. One can imagine a university of the future tenuring professors because they bring in large amounts of patent royalties, seeking commercial advertisers to sponsor courses on the Internet, and admitting undistinguished students on the quiet understanding that their parents will make substantial gifts.

To avoid those pitfalls, universities need to examine the process of commercialization with greater care than in the past. Otherwise, they may gradually alter their essential character in ways that could eventually forfeit the respect of students and faculty members, and erode the trust of the public.

History offers several lessons about commercialization that are well worth pondering. One conclusion that emerges repeatedly is that rewards from profit-seeking ventures seldom are as great as their university sponsors hoped at the beginning. High-profile athletics teams—the academy's first big commercial venture—have certainly produced revenues. But their costs have risen at least as rapidly, to the point where very few institutions consistently make money from their sports programs. Likewise, patent licensing has brought substantial revenues to a handful of universities, but most institutions do not earn

much more than the cost of operating their technology-transfer offices.

Internet courses have been recently touted as the latest El Dorado in the long history of commercial ventures. Not long ago, newspapers were filled with accounts of exciting new schemes offering large potential profits. In the last two years, however, New York and Temple Universities have both shut down for-profit Internet ventures, and Columbia University in January announced the demise of its widely publicized Fathom program after losing millions of dollars in the enterprise.

If disappointing profits were the only problem with moneymaking activities, there would be little reason to lose much sleep over growing commercialization. But profit seeking has already shown disturbing tendencies to get out of hand and threaten far more important matters than expected revenues. In high-profile sports, for example, the prior grades and test scores of freshman athletes and their subsequent academic performance in college have fallen further and further below the levels of their classmates, and scandals have continued to erupt periodically in one university after another.

Commercialization has already taken a toll on the quality of educational programs.

While athletics may be dismissed as an extracurricular activity peripheral to the main academic enterprise, other commercial ventures have begun to strike closer to the core of research and education. In their zeal to build financial support from industry, many universities have signed research agreements with companies that allow more secrecy than is needed to protect the legitimate interests of their sponsors. Many campuses have failed to impose strict conflict-of-interest rules to prevent their scientists from performing experiments on human subjects for companies to which they have significant financial ties. Echoing the events described by John Le Carré, some universities have failed to protect their scientists from corporate pressure to suppress unfavorable research findings. Thomas Bodenheimer, a clinical professor of family and community medicine at the University of California at San Francisco, has even reported that as many as 10 percent of published reports by university researchers on the efficacy of products manufactured by the commercial sponsors of the research are actually ghostwritten by company personnel. As practices of this kind become more widely known, the public's confidence in the credibility and objectivity of university research is bound to suffer.

Commercialization has also taken a toll on the quality of educational programs. Many institutions, seeking to profit from their continuing-education divisions, follow practices in those areas that they would never tolerate in their regular degree programs. They typically offer little or no financial aid, while paying salaries to instructors that are well below the normal university scale. As a result, access to such programs has suffered, along with the quality of teaching.

In medical schools, administrators hoping to extract a greater surplus from continuing-education programs accept substantial subsidies from pharmaceutical companies in exchange for agreeing to choose instructors from company-approved lists and allowing the sponsor to prepare the slides and teaching notes that are used in the lectures. Further harm could result from commercializing Internet programs if universities (and their venture-capital partners) try to maximize profits by attracting large audiences of unwary students with flashy lecture courses taught by famous professors who do not take full advantage of the (more expensive) interactive power that new technology allows to improve the effectiveness of teaching and learning.

HOW SIGNIFICANT are the questionable practices that many universities already tolerate? Because they involve values as well as money, the costs are impossible to quantify. But that does not mean they are unimportant. Far from it. It is vital to uphold admissions standards, preserve the integrity of evaluating faculty scholarship and student papers, maintain the openness and objectivity of scientific inquiry, and sustain other important academic values. These values are essential to maintaining the public's trust in student transcripts and published faculty research. They preserve professors' faith in the academic enterprise and help ensure that they will continue to regard their work as a calling rather than merely a way to make a living.

University officials may insist that they can keep commercial activity from getting out of hand. Yet the long, sorry history of intercollegiate sports clearly shows how far the erosion of values can proceed. Through a series of small steps, many prominent institutions have come to sacrifice the most basic academic standards in their quest for added athletics revenue and visibility. Left unchecked, the chronic need for money could drive universities to similar extremes in more-central programs of education and research.

What can universities do to protect themselves against that danger? Five steps seem especially important.

First, universities should not rely upon presidents alone to protect the institution and its values from the pitfalls of commercialization. Presidents are under enormous pressure to find the money not only to balance the budget but to improve financial aid, build new buildings and laboratories, increase faculty salaries, launch new programs, and hire star professors to enhance the institution's reputation. Trustees judge presidential performance in substantial part by the amount of money that the chief executive raises. Faculty members hold presi-

dents accountable for finding the means to fulfill intellectual ambitions. Students want better residence halls. Boosters insist on winning teams.

In the face of these pressures, if presidents are left by themselves to preserve academic values, questionable compromises are likely to occur. Though none may be glaring by itself, their accumulation will gradually threaten the integrity of the institution. The values of a college or university can be preserved only if boards of trustees make upholding academic standards an integral part of evaluating presidents—and insist on reviewing conflict-of-interest rules, admissions practices for athletes, and other standards that are at risk from commercialization.

The second principle to observe is not to consider commercial opportunities on a case-by-case basis. Rather, institutions should insist on promulgating general rules to govern matters such as secrecy provisions in corporate-research agreements, admissions standards for athletes, and conflicts of interest for scientists. Ad hoc decisions are bound to lead to a gradual erosion of academic values; the cards are almost always stacked in favor of allowing moneymaking schemes to proceed.

When such opportunities present themselves, interested faculty members and administrators are typically those with a stake in having the project move forward; the risks are usually too diffuse to generate opposition. The potential rewards seem tangible and very tempting at the outset, while the dangers will be speculative and hard to quantify. The hoped-for benefits are, for the most part, immediate, whereas the risks loom far in the future.

In addition, the benefits accrue to the institution and its members, but the costs often involve matters, such as a loss of trust in the objectivity of research, that are shared by all universities. Similarly, the blame for turning a project down falls squarely on identifiable university officials, but the responsibility for undermining academic standards and squandering public trust can never be traced to any specific decision or institution. Under such circumstances, in the absence of clear, well-publicized rules, the path of least resistance will almost always lie in approving the questionable project.

A third important principle is to involve the faculty in developing and enforcing all rules that protect academic values. Many administrators have a dangerous habit of regarding the faculty as an irritating obstruction to discussions of commercial ventures. The entrepreneurial university, it is said, must be able to move quickly. It cannot wait for windy faculty debates to run their course lest valuable opportunities be lost in the fast-moving corporate world in which we live.

In fact, there is remarkably little evidence to support this view. Looking back over the checkered history of commercial activity on campuses, one can much more easily point to examples of costly unilateral decisions by impatient administrators, such as ill-advised Internet ventures or grandiose athletics projects, than to valuable opportunities lost through inordinate faculty delays.

That is not to say that existing processes of faculty governance are perfect, or even nearly so. New and streamlined procedures may be needed, with smaller committees staffed by carefully chosen, well-respected, highly knowledgeable professors, in order to deal with conflicts of interest, secrecy, and other complex issues created by emerging commercial opportunities. Still, the essential fact remains that faculty members have the greatest stake in preserving academic values—and hence have a critical role to play in making sure that the quest for revenue does not impair the basic intellectual standards of the institution.

Universities should ponder the sorry history of intercollegiate athletics.

A fourth useful step in safeguarding academic standards is to look for opportunities for universities to agree among themselves on basic rules governing matters such as conflicts of interest in research, the length of time that results can be kept secret under commercially sponsored research agreements, or conference-wide rules protecting academic standards in athletics. The Ivy League agreement setting minimum admissions requirements for athletes is a case in point.

Without such agreements, competition works to erode academic standards. In the struggle for revenue or competitive advantage, a few institutions are bound to succumb to the temptation to undertake highly questionable commercial ventures. Once a few agree, competitive pressures on other universities will cause them to do likewise. Before long, what began as suspect behavior will become accepted practice. Uniform rules, by agreement or by legislation, are often the only defense against such corrosive pressures (although universities need to take pains to avoid the sort of restrictive agreements without a redeeming public purpose that could run afoul of antitrust laws).

Finally, reasonably stable government support is the ultimate guarantee of high academic standards. Faced with a choice between sacrificing academic values and enduring serious cuts in programs, most universities will find a way to choose the former. Fortunately, government support for higher education has been relatively generous over the years. That is one important reason why American universities have achieved such a place of eminence in the world. My point is not to complain or to urge massive increases in public support for higher education. I simply want to make clear that sudden, major cuts, or steady erosion of support over an extended period of time, will put intolerable pressure on universities to sacrifice important academic standards in the hope of gaining badly needed revenue through dubious commercial ventures.

Above all, university leaders, faculty members, and trustees need to recognize the risks involved in pursuing more and more commercial ventures and begin to build sturdier safeguards. To be sure, setting proper limits and providing supportive structures will take a lot of work. Entrepreneurial professors may resist new rules. Boosters may protest athletics reforms. Corporations may balk at strict secrecy limits and refuse to enter into lucrative research contracts.

M EANWHILE, the temptation to push ahead will frequently be great. Most profit-seeking ventures start not with obvious violations of principle but with modest compromises that carry few immediate costs. The problems tend to appear so gradually that their link to commercialization may not even be perceived. Like adolescents experimenting with drugs, campus officials may believe that they can proceed without serious risk.

Before succumbing to such temptations, university leaders should recall the history of intercollegiate athletics and ponder the sobering lessons that it teaches. Once the critical compromises have been made and tolerated long enough, universities will find it hard to rebuild the public's trust, regain the faculty's respect, and return to the happier conditions of earlier times. In exchange for ephemeral gains in the constant struggle for prestige, universities will have sacrificed essential values that are very difficult to restore.

Derek Bok is a university professor and president emeritus of Harvard University. His latest book, Universities in the Marketplace: The Commercialization of Higher Education, *was published April 2003 by Princeton University Press.*

Between Right and Right

GEOFFREY COLVIN

DOES EBITDA NOW STAND FOR "EARNINGS BEFORE I TRICKED THE Dumb Auditors?" As that current Wall Street joke suggests, the scope of corporate ethics has grown a bit wider in the past 12 months. The atmosphere business people breathe has changed so much since the first Enron shocks that a formerly obscure earnings measure is now used to set up a punch line about executive crime. It's time to face the music and realize that a lot of business behavior no one used to think twice about may now be judged on stricter ethical criteria than ever before.

Business behavior no one used to think twice about may now be judged on strict ethical criteria.

Spectacular managerial malfeasance is what has created the new atmosphere, but that's not what I'm talking about. The actions for which CEOs and CFOs are getting indicted and sued are the result of situations where someone faces a choice between right and wrong and chooses to do wrong. When Scott Sullivan at WorldCom capitalized over $3 billion of expenditures of a type that had previously been expensed, I think he knew it was wrong. If Dennis Kozlowski, as alleged in a lawsuit, secretly gave Tyco's lead director $10 million of corporate cash and said, "Let's not tell anyone else about this, shall we?" I think he knew it was wrong.

But most people won't choose to do wrong in situations like those; that's one reason such cases are so newsworthy. As professor Joseph Badaracco of Harvard Business School has

pointed out, the real ethical dilemmas are not choices between right and wrong, but choices between right and right—cases in which both options seem correct for different reasons, yet one must be chosen and one rejected.

These are the ethical dilemmas business people face most often, the kind I think the media, lawmakers, regulators, shareholders, and managers will be looking at in a new light. Here are three specific dilemmas, provoked by recent events, that I believe we'll see being rethought in coming months:

Who suffers? You're newly in charge of a department, a division, or a company; it hasn't been performing, and your mandate is to deliver results. The pressure has never been heavier: Shareholders are angry after 31 months of a bear market, and a new survey shows that 50% of U.S. households own stocks— that's millions of ordinary Americans who won't get much from Social Security, many of whom don't have defined-benefit pension plans. These people desperately need stock performance to pay for retirement. Working for you is a 52-year-old manager with two kids in college. In evaluations, gutless previous executives told him he was doing fine—but he wasn't, and he isn't. To do your job, you've got to fire him. So who's going to suffer: shareholders whose retirement is in jeopardy or a nice guy who's been lied to for 20 years? Your choice.

How far should the CEO go to protect shareholders? As FORTUNE detailed in its Sept. 2 cover story, "You Bought. They Sold" (see fortune.com), CEOs of many of the bull market's highest fliers were furiously selling shares in their own companies back when prices were at or near their apex. In most cases these executives apparently acted within the rules. But their actions confirm that they knew what has since become apparent:

Their companies' shares were in many cases insanely over-priced—not overpriced by 20% or 50%, but overpriced by 20 or 50 times. Question: Isn't the CEO obligated to tell the world that the share price is nuts? Not legally obligated, but ethically obligated? Or would such a statement, which would probably tank the stock, be unfair to the poor dope who bought shares this morning at the egregiously inflated price? CEO statements of this kind aren't unheard of. Warren Buffett has on occasion said Berkshire Hathaway is overpriced, and he wouldn't recommend buying it. But no one else has done it, as far as I know. Why not?

Should you reprice options? You know the story. Your company gave everybody options two or three years ago. Now they're deeper underwater than the *Titanic*. Good employees are leaving for companies where they can get new options at today's low price. You could stop them by repricing your options, but that sends a message that when times turn tough, you lower the bar. Institutional investors, who own at least half your shares, hate it. And governance activists argue that it's just plain wrong to change the rules. But it isn't your employees' fault that we're in a historic bear market. So who takes the hit?

Scandals always put ethics on the front burner, and that's never a bad thing. Let's just not waste too much time cogitating on the ethical dimensions of Raptor limited partnerships or throwing company-financed birthday parties for your wife on Sardinia. We've got far harder problems to deal with than that.

***

GEOFFREY COLVIN, *the editorial director of* FORTUNE, *can be reached at gcolvin@fortunemail.com. Watch him on* Wall $treet Week With Fortune, *Friday evenings on PBS.*

The Padding That Hurts

Auditors cannot ignore expense account cheating by management.

By Joseph T. Wells

Davenport, an independent auditor, had a hot potato on his hands. He had just learned from Robert, his client's internal auditor, that an employee had reported to him possible expense account abuses by one of the company's managers. Robert said that this employee accompanied Murphy, a senior vice-president, on many business trips. The employee said Murphy had some curious habits: When getting out of a taxi, he would ask for extra blank receipts, and in restaurants, he would often do the same.

Robert had followed up this tip. He pulled Murphy's travel file and found numerous irregularities: multiple receipts from the same taxi companies for the same days, extremely expensive meals, duplicate meal receipts for the same days and other suspicious charges for several hundred dollars each billed to an innocuous-appearing, but unknown source. Robert estimated he could safely document a minimum of $30,000 worth of phony charges over the last three years.

When Robert told Davenport what he had found, he said: "The guy makes over half a million a year, and yet he evidently is hitting us for at least $10,000 a year in completely fake expenses." Davenport added, "And if we know he is defrauding the company for $10,000 a year, then

what is he up to that we don't know about?"

The two men decided they would completely document Murphy's abuses and notify the CEO. However, as internal auditor, Robert was concerned—and not without reason. "Look," he said to Davenport, "Murphy outranks me. He and the CEO are very tight. This will look like I am ratting out a valuable company executive, and the CEO won't be happy with me." But Davenport explained to Robert that when it came to high-ranking executives, there was no such thing as an "immaterial" fraud. Davenport knew his duty: He had to report Murphy's conduct to the next highest level in the organization—in this case, the president and CEO and then disclose it to the audit committee.

THE BAD NEWS BEARS

The two auditors met with the CEO, and Robert's intuition about his reaction was correct. After hearing the presentation, the CEO erupted: "Murphy makes millions for this company, and you people are in here claiming he is hitting us for pocket change. Don't you have anything better to do?" But, Davenport stuck to his guns. "I really hate that this has happened," he said, "but my duty as independent auditor is very

clear. Murphy is an executive in this organization, and management fraud can have very serious consequences. Managers must set a proper example. If Murphy can cheat on his expenses and get away with it, then other people will try it, too. And if you discipline one employee and not another, the company opens itself to legal liability. Furthermore, a person in Murphy's position controls millions of dollars in company assets. If he is dishonest about his expenses, what else is he dishonest about?"

But the CEO wouldn't listen. "I'm telling you," he said, shaking his finger in the air, "drop this now and leave him alone. I've known Murphy for over 10 years. I recommended hiring you as the company's auditor. I can just as easily recommend that you should be replaced." It was clear to Davenport the CEO was furious, so he felt it best to end the discussion for the time being.

By the next day, the CEO had relented. He called Davenport and said: "I have thought this over. I even talked to my wife about it last night. Of course you are doing the right thing. I'm sorry I acted the way I did; it's just that Murphy is such a valuable team member, and this thing is embarrassing for the company and me. I'll go ahead and talk to the chairman of the audit committee. You can come with me."

The two men informed the audit committee and the board of directors of Murphy's "petty" thefts. Most members were chagrined that they had to involve themselves in what they saw as such an insignificant matter. It finally was decided that three audit committee members would speak directly to Murphy.

Murphy's attitude was cavalier toward the audit committee. He pointed out the many hundreds of nights he had logged away from home on the company's behalf. He readily admitted submitting inflated and duplicate expense reports, but he said the reason was that he didn't keep track of all of the cash he spent on behalf of the company, and this was just a way of reimbursing himself. The audit committee backed down from any further confrontation with him.

A WAY OUT

To settle the matter, the audit committee chairman offered to strike a compromise with Davenport. Davenport's firm would be authorized to conduct enough additional audit work to satisfy itself that Murphy's sins were confined only to the expense account, new internal controls would be implemented over executive travel and the company would send out a memo to all employees informing them of the company's ethics policies and reminding them of expense account policies.

But then came the tough part of the compromise: The audit committee chairman told Davenport that it was in the company's best interests to keep Murphy and that—notwithstanding Murphy's indiscretions—he was a valuable company asset. Furthermore, the board decided against punishing Murphy to make an example out of him.

Davenport argued that not disciplining Murphy would send the wrong message. The chairman countered that Murphy's actions were not widely known and that morale would suffer more if he was disciplined than if the incident was glossed over. And Murphy agreed to go forth and sin no more. In the end, Davenport gave in; after all, his duties were to ensure the accuracy of the financial statements, not to dictate policy to management.

CAUGHT IN A DILEMMA

There are valuable lessons in this case. First, sometimes it is easy to know but hard to do the "right thing." Decisions in the business world are not always black and white. As a CPA, Davenport knew what ethical course to take and took it. The audit committee chairman and the CEO considered what was in the best interests of the company and made their choice, opting to let Murphy off the hook. Only time will tell whether they made the right decision: Will Murphy mend his ways? Will other employees find out he got away with theft and try it themselves?

Second, there is a double standard in most organizations for employees and for executives. Dismissing a clerical employee for expense account abuse might be done with little thought, but companies naturally are reluctant to get rid of a big revenue-producing executive like Murphy. The result, of course, is that it may send the worst kind of anti-fraud message: "In this company, crime pays."

WHAT COMPANIES SHOULD KNOW ABOUT

Expense account schemes. Employees who cheat on their expense accounts usually do so by one of four methods:

- *Mischaracterized expenses.* Employees produce legitimate documentation for nonbusiness-related transactions. Example: taking a friend to dinner and charging it to the company as "business development."
- *Overstated expense reports.* Employees inflate the amount of actual expenses and keep the difference. Example: altering a taxicab receipt from $10 to $40.

- *Fictitious expenses.* Employees submit phony documentation for reimbursement. Example: producing a fake hotel bill on a home computer.
- *Multiple reimbursements.* Employees copy invoices and resubmit them for payment more than once. Example: copying an airline ticket and claiming the cost again on next month's expense reimbursement.

Preventing expense account abuse. Beyond using tighter internal controls, auditors can put in place some commonsense controls and policy measures at their own and their clients' companies to deter expense account abuse. But it should be a reasonable expense reimbursement policy. If your company's expense account reimbursement policy is too restrictive, employees are more likely to cheat to make up for unreimbursed out-of-pocket costs. A reasonable expense account policy usually gives the benefit of the doubt to the employee. Some companies find it useful to set a fairly liberal per diem rate for employee travel, which should cover all expenses.

Accepting photocopies. There sometimes are legitimate reasons to accept photocopies for small expense items. However, making a copy of an altered document is a common expense account ploy. Pay close attention to the documentation evidence provided in support of the expense claim to see if it appears to contain alterations, particularly if this is the habit of a single employee, as repeat offenders are the rule, not the exception.

Spotting trends. Expense reimbursements, because they are subject to abuse, should be monitored periodically by supervisory personnel or auditors. Look for red flags such as increasing expense reimbursements by employee, variations from budgeted expenses and unreasonable charges.

EXECUTIVES AND FRAUD

When it comes to upper management, there is no such thing as an immaterial fraud; an executive who cheats on his or her expense account may also cheat—big-time—on the company's financial statements.

According to the new fraud standard, Statement on Auditing Standards no. 99, *Consideration of Fraud in a Financial Statement*, whenever the auditor determines there is evidence of fraud, he or she should bring the matter to the attention of the proper level of management. This is appropriate even if the amount might be considered inconsequential, such as a minor defalcation by an employee at a low level in the entity's organization. Fraud involving senior management and fraud (whether caused by senior management or other employees) that causes a material misstatement of the financial statements should be reported directly to the audit committee.

The message to the independent auditor is clear: If the integrity of executives is so low that they would engage in "immaterial" fraud, it is only logical that they would also engage in fraud when something material is at stake. In short, when leaders abuse their organizations for small amounts, we may be seeing only the tip of the iceberg. CPAs should therefore be vigilant in these dangerous waters.

JOSEPH T. WELLS, CPA, CFE, is founder and chairman of the Association of Certified Fraud Examiners in Austin, Texas, and professor of fraud examination at the University of Texas. Mr. Wells' article "So That's Why It's Called a Pyramid Scheme" (JofA, Oct.00, page 91), won the Lawler Award for the best JofA article in 2000. His e-mail address is joe@cfenet.com.

Costco's Dilemma:
Be Kind to Its Workers, or Wall Street?

By Ann Zimmerman

When it comes to workers, companies can be accused of not paying enough — or paying too much.

Wal-Mart Stores Inc.'s parsimonious approach to employee compensation has made the world's largest retailer a frequent target of labor unions and even Democratic presidential candidate John Kerry, who has accused the Bentonville, Ark., chain of failing to offer its employees affordable health-care coverage.

In contrast, rival Costco Wholesale Corp. often is held up as a retailer that does it right, paying well and offering generous benefits.

But Costco's kind-hearted philosophy toward its 100,000 cashiers, shelf-stockers and other workers is drawing criticism from Wall Street. Some analysts and investors contend that the Issaquah, Wash., warehouse-club operator actually is too good to employees, with Costco shareholders suffering as a result.

"From the perspective of investors, Costco's benefits are overly generous," says Bill Dreher, retailing analyst with Deutsche Bank Securities Inc. "Public companies need to care for shareholders first. Costco runs its business like it is a private company."

Costco appears to pay a penalty for its largesse to workers. The company's shares trade at about 20 times projected per-share earnings for 2004, compared with about 24 for Wal-Mart. Mr. Dreher says the unusually high wages and benefits contribute to investor concerns that profit margins at Costco aren't as high as they should be.

Costco, which opened its first store in 1983 and now has 432 locations, disputes the contention that it takes care of workers at the expense of investors. "The last thing I want people to believe is that I don't care about the shareholder," says Jim Sinegal, Costco's president and chief executive since 1993, who owns about 3.2 million Costco shares valued at $118 million. "But I happen to believe that in order to reward the shareholder in the long term, you have to please your customers and workers."

Worker pay, benefits and job quality have been hot topics in the retail industry. While employees in many fields are worried about generally stagnant job growth and spiraling health-care costs, already-meager retail wages also are threatened by retail-pricing pressure, partly fueled by Wal-Mart's growing dominance in toys, electronics, groceries and other categories. Grocery workers in California recently waged a brutal four-month strike to protest health-care cuts that large supermarket chains were imposing to stay competitive with Wal-Mart.

Hourly retail pay grew only 1% in the 12 months ended last month, according to the Bureau of Labor Statistics, compared with a 1.7% gain for private-sector jobs overall.

Wal-Mart last year added 99,000 jobs in the U.S., making it the country's biggest job creator, and nearly all those positions pay by the hour. And since Costco and Wal-Mart's larger Sam's Club warehouse chain increasingly are competing head-to-head on everything from turkeys to tires, the companies have to pay close attention to each other.

Wal-Mart spokeswoman Mona Williams says the company's "entire package of wages, benefits and career opportunities is at least as good as that offered by Costco," including bonuses, company-paid life insurance and a discounted Wal-Mart stock-purchase program. Sam's Club has a "cost advantage" over Costco, she adds, because it can "leverage efficiencies" from Wal-Mart in areas such as merchandise sourcing and logistics, keeping basic membership fees a third cheaper than Costco's.

Costco has won a reputation for having the best benefits in retail, a sector where labor costs account for about 80% of a typical company's total expenses. Costco pays starting employees at least $10 an hour, and with regular raises a full-time hourly worker can make $40,000 annually within 3½ years. Cashiers are paid $10.50 to $17.50 an hour.

Wal-Mart doesn't disclose its wage rates, since they vary by location. According to a recent study funded by Wal-Mart, cashiers at its Supercenters in Las Vegas were paid $7.65 to $11.45 an hour. Supercenters are Wal-Mart's discount grocery and general-merchandise stores.

Costco also pays 92% of its employees' health-insurance premiums, much higher than the 80% average at large U.S.

Clocking In

Comparing some workplace statistics from Costco and Wal-Mart

	COSTCO	WAL-MART
Employees covered by company health insurance	82%	48%
Insurance-enrollment waiting periods		
Full-time	3months	6 months
Part-time	6 months	2 years
Portion of health-care premium paid by	92%	66%
Annual worker turnover rate	24%	50%

Source: the companies

companies. Wal-Mart pays two-thirds of health-benefit costs for its workers. Costco's health plan offers a broader range of care than Wal-Mart's does, and part-time Costco workers qualify for coverage in six months, compared with two years for Wal-Mart part-timers.

"From day one, we've run the company with the philosophy that if we pay better than average, provide a salary people can live on, have a positive environment and good benefits, we'll be able to hire better people, they'll stay longer and be more efficient," says Richard Galanti, Costco's chief financial officer.

Costco has several advantages over Wal-Mart that help it extend such unusually generous pay and benefits. Costco has a more-upscale reputation than Sam's Club, helping it attract shoppers with higher incomes. The average Costco store rings up $115 million in annual sales, almost double the Sam's Club

average. And Costco, which charges $45 to $100 for yearly memberships, doesn't spend any money on advertising.

Costco says its higher pay boosts loyalty: Its employee turnover rate is 24% a year. Wal-Mart's overall employee turnover rate is 50%, about in line with the retail-industry average. Wal-Mart doesn't break out turnover rates at Sam's Club. High turnover creates added expense for retailers because new workers have to be trained and are not as efficient.

Some critics still aren't convinced that lower turnover is worth what it costs Costco in higher wages and benefits. "Their benefits are amazing, but shareholders get frustrated from a stock perspective," says Emme Kozloff, a retail analyst at Sanford C. Bernstein LLC.

Surging health-care costs have forced Costco to make more aggressive moves to control expenses. Moreover, Costco last year raised employees' contribution to about 8% of their health-care costs, up from 4.5%. It was the company's first rise in employee health premiums in eight years. Mr. Sinegal, the Costco CEO, said the company held off from boosting premiums for as long it could, and didn't give in until after it had lowered its earnings forecast twice last year.

Costco also is looking to employees for ideas that could improve efficiency. One suggestion that Costco implemented at stores was to install pneumatic tubes at check-out areas to speed the movement of cash to a store's back office.

Mr. Galanti says company officials want to boost Costco's pretax income closer to 4% of sales, compared with 3% now and 5% at Wal-Mart, without cutting pay. In its fiscal second quarter ended Feb. 15, Costco's net income rose 25% to $226.8 million, or 48 cents a share. Revenue rose 14% to $11.55 billion.

Some longtime Costco fans say the company should stick to its generous wages and benefits. "Happy employees make for happy customers, which in the long run is ultimately reflected in the share price," says John Bowen, an investment manager in Coronado, Calif., who has held Costco shares for eight years.

The Parable of the Sadhu

After encountering a dying pilgrim on a climbing trip in the Himalayas, a businessman ponders the differences between individual and corporate ethics.

by Bowen H. McCoy

This article was originally published in the September–October 1983 issue of HBR. For its republication as an HBR Classic, Bowen H. McCoy has written the commentary "When Do We Take a Stand?" to update his observations.

Last year, as the first participant in the new six-month sabbatical program that Morgan Stanley has adopted, I enjoyed a rare opportunity to collect my thoughts as well as do some traveling. I spent the first three months in Nepal, walking 600 miles through 200 villages in the Himalayas and climbing some 120,000 vertical feet. My sole Western companion on the trip was an anthropologist who shed light on the cultural patterns of the villages that we passed through.

During the Nepal hike, something occurred that has had a powerful impact on my thinking about corporate ethics. Although some might argue that the experience has no relevance to business, it was a situation in which a basic ethical dilemma suddenly intruded into the lives of a group of individuals. How the group responded holds a lesson for all organizations, no matter how defined.

The Sadhu

The Nepal experience was more rugged than I had anticipated. Most commercial treks last two or three weeks and cover a quarter of the distance we traveled.

My friend Stephen, the anthropologist, and I were halfway through the 60-day Himalayan part of the trip when we reached the high point, an 18,000-foot pass over a crest that we'd have to traverse to reach the village of Muklinath, an ancient holy place for pilgrims.

Six years earlier, I had suffered pulmonary edema, an acute form of altitude sickness, at 16,500 feet in the vicinity of Everest base camp—so we were understandably concerned about what would happen at 18,000 feet. Moreover, the Himalayas were having their wettest spring in 20 years; hip-deep powder and ice had already driven us off one ridge. If we failed to cross the pass, I feared that the last half of our once-in-a-lifetime trip would be ruined.

The night before we would try the pass, we camped in a hut at 14,500 feet. In the photos taken at that camp, my face appears wan. The last village we'd passed through was a sturdy two-day walk below us, and I was tired.

During the late afternoon, four backpackers from New Zealand joined us, and we spent most of the night awake, anticipating the climb. Below, we could see the fires of two other parties, which turned out to be two Swiss couples and a Japanese hiking club.

To get over the steep part of the climb before the sun melted the steps cut in the ice, we departed at 3:30 A.M. The New Zealanders left first, followed by Stephen and myself, our porters and Sherpas, and then the Swiss. The Japanese lingered in their camp. The sky was clear, and we were confident that no spring storm would erupt that day to close the pass.

At 15,500 feet, it looked to me as if Stephen were shuffling and staggering a bit, which are symptoms of altitude sickness. (The initial stage of altitude sickness brings a headache and nausea. As the condition worsens, a climber may encounter difficult breathing, disorientation, aphasia, and paralysis.) I felt strong—my adrenaline was flowing—but I was very concerned about my ultimate ability to get across. A couple of our porters were also suffering from the height, and Pasang, our Sherpa sirdar (leader), was worried.

Just after daybreak, while we rested at 15,500 feet, one of the New Zealanders, who had gone ahead, came staggering down toward us with a body slung across his shoulders. He dumped the almost naked, barefoot body of an Indian holy man—a sadhu—at my feet. He had found the pilgrim lying on the ice, shivering and suffering from hypothermia. I cradled the sadhu's head and laid him out on the rocks. The New Zealander was angry. He wanted to get across the pass before the bright sun melted the snow. He said, "Look, I've done what I can. You have porters and Sherpa guides. You care for him. We're going on!" He turned and went back up the mountain to join his friends.

I took a carotid pulse and found that the sadhu was still alive. We figured he had probably visited the holy shrines at Muklinath and was on his way home. It was fruitless to question why he had chosen this desperately high route instead of the safe, heavily traveled caravan route through the Kali Gandaki gorge. Or why he was shoeless and almost naked, or how long he had been lying in the pass. The answers weren't going to solve our problem.

Stephen and the four Swiss began stripping off their outer clothing and opening their packs. The sadhu was soon clothed from head to foot. He was not able to walk, but he was very much alive. I looked down the mountain and spotted the Japanese climbers, marching up with a horse.

When I reached them, Stephen glared at me and said, "How do you feel about contributing to the death of a fellow man?"

Without a great deal of thought, I told Stephen and Pasang that I was concerned about withstanding the heights to come and wanted to get over the pass. I took off after several of our porters who had gone ahead.

On the steep part of the ascent where, if the ice steps had given way, I would have slid down about 3,000 feet, I felt vertigo. I stopped for a breather, allowing the Swiss to catch up with me. I inquired about the sadhu and Stephen. They said that the sadhu was fine and that Stephen was just behind them. I set off again for the summit.

Stephen arrived at the summit an hour after I did. Still exhilarated by victory, I ran down the slope to congratulate him. He was suffering from altitude sickness—walking 15 steps, then stopping, walking 15 steps, then stopping. Pasang accompanied him all the way up. When I reached them, Stephen glared at me and said: "How do you feel about contributing to the death of a fellow man?"

I did not completely comprehend what he meant. "Is the sadhu dead?" I inquired.

"No," replied Stephen, "but he surely will be!"

After I had gone, followed not long after by the Swiss, Stephen had remained with the sadhu. When the Japanese had arrived, Stephen had asked to use their horse to transport the sadhu down to the hut. They had refused. He had then asked Pasang to have a group of our porters carry the sadhu. Pasang had resisted the idea, saying that the porters would have to exert all their energy to get themselves over the pass. He believed they could not carry a man down 1,000 feet to the hut, reclimb the slope, and get across safely before the snow melted. Pasang had pressed Stephen not to delay any longer.

The Sherpas had carried the sadhu down to a rock in the sun at about 15,000 feet and pointed out the hut another 500 feet below. The Japanese had given him food and drink. When they had last seen him, he was listlessly throwing rocks at the Japanese party's dog, which had frightened him.

We do not know if the sadhu lived or died.

For many of the following days and evenings, Stephen and I discussed and debated our behavior toward the sadhu. Stephen is a committed Quaker with deep moral vision. He said, "I feel that what happened with the sadhu is a good example of the breakdown between the individual ethic and the corporate ethic. No one person was willing to assume ultimate responsibility for the sadhu. Each was willing to do his bit just so long as it was not too inconvenient. When it got to be a bother, everyone just passed the buck to someone else and took off. Jesus was relevant to a more individualistic stage of society, but how do we interpret his teaching today in a world filled with large, impersonal organizations and groups?"

I defended the larger group, saying, "Look, we all cared. We all gave aid and comfort. Everyone did his bit. The New Zealander carried him down below the snow line. I took his pulse and suggested we treat him for hypothermia. You and the Swiss gave him clothing and got him warmed up. The Japanese gave him food

and water. The Sherpas carried him down to the sun and pointed out the easy trail toward the hut. He was well enough to throw rocks at a dog. What more could we do?"

"You have just described the typical affluent Westerner's response to a problem. Throwing money—in this case, food and sweaters—at it, but not solving the fundamentals!" Stephen retorted.

I asked, "Where is the limit of our responsibility in a situation like this?"

"What would satisfy you?" I said. "Here we are, a group of New Zealanders, Swiss, Americans, and Japanese who have never met before and who are at the apex of one of the most powerful experiences of our lives. Some years the pass is so bad no one gets over it. What right does an almost naked pilgrim who chooses the wrong trail have to disrupt our lives? Even the Sherpas had no interest in risking the trip to help him beyond a certain point."

Stephen calmly rebutted, "I wonder what the Sherpas would have done if the sadhu had been a well-dressed Nepali, or what the Japanese would have done if the sadhu had been a well-dressed Asian, or what you would have done, Buzz, if the sadhu had been a well-dressed Western woman?"

"Where, in your opinion," I asked, "is the limit of our responsibility in a situation like this? We had our own well-being to worry about. Our Sherpa guides were unwilling to jeopardize us or the porters for the sadhu. No one else on the mountain was willing to commit himself beyond certain self-imposed limits."

Stephen said, "As individual Christians or people with a Western ethical tradition, we can fulfill our obligations in such a situation only if one, the sadhu dies in our care; two, the sadhu demonstrates to us that he can undertake the two-day walk down to the village; or three, we carry the sadhu for two days down to the village and persuade someone there to care for him."

"Leaving the sadhu in the sun with food and clothing—where he demonstrated hand-eye coordination by throwing a rock at a dog—comes close to fulfilling items one and two," I answered. "And it wouldn't have made sense to take him to the village where the people appeared to be far less caring than the Sherpas, so the third condition is impractical. Are you really saying that, no matter what the implications, we should, at the drop of a hat, have changed our entire plan?"

The Individual Versus the Group Ethic

Despite my arguments, I felt and continue to feel guilt about the sadhu. I had literally walked through a classic moral dilemma without fully thinking through the consequences. My excuses for my actions include a high adrenaline flow, a superordinate goal, and a once-in-a-lifetime opportunity—common factors in corporate situations, especially stressful ones.

Real moral dilemmas are ambiguous, and many of us hike right through them, unaware that they exist. When, usually after the fact, someone makes an issue of one, we tend to resent his or her bringing it up. Often, when the full import of what we have done (or not done) hits us, we dig into a defensive position from which it is very difficult to emerge. In rare circumstances, we may contemplate what we have done from inside a prison.

Had we mountaineers been free of stress caused by the effort and the high altitude, we might have treated the sadhu differently. Yet isn't stress the real test of personal and corporate values? The instant decisions that executives make under pressure reveal the most about personal and corporate character.

As a group, we had no process for developing a consensus. We had no sense of purpose or plan.

Among the many questions that occur to me when I ponder my experience with the sadhu are: What are the practical limits of moral imagination and vision? Is there a collective or institutional ethic that differs from the ethics of the individual? At what level of effort or commitment can one discharge one's ethical responsibilities?

Not every ethical dilemma has a right solution. Reasonable people often disagree; otherwise there would be no dilemma. In a business context, however, it is essential that managers agree on a process for dealing with dilemmas.

Our experience with the sadhu offers an interesting parallel to business situations. An immediate response was mandatory. Failure to act was a decision in itself. Up on the mountain we could not resign and submit our résumés to a headhunter. In contrast to philosophy, business involves action and implementation—getting things done. Managers must come up with answers based on what they see and what they allow to influence their decision-making processes. On the mountain, none of us but Stephen realized the true dimensions of the situation we were facing.

One of our problems was that as a group we had no process for developing a consensus. We had no sense of purpose or plan. The difficulties of dealing with the sadhu were so complex that no one person could handle them. Because the group did not have a set of preconditions that could guide its action to an acceptable resolution, we reacted instinctively as individuals. The cross-cultural nature of the group added a further layer of complexity. We had no leader with whom we could all identify and in whose purpose we believed. Only Stephen was willing to take charge, but he could not gain adequate support from the group to care for the sadhu.

Some organizations do have values that transcend the personal values of their managers. Such values, which go beyond profitability, are usually revealed when the organization is under stress. People throughout the organization generally accept its values, which, because they are not presented as a rigid list of commandments, may be somewhat ambiguous. The stories people tell, rather than printed materials, transmit the organization's conceptions of what is proper behavior.

For 20 years, I have been exposed at senior levels to a variety of corporations and organizations. It is amazing how quickly an outsider can sense the tone and style of an organization and, with that, the degree of tolerated openness and freedom to challenge management.

Organizations that do not have a heritage of mutually accepted, shared values tend to become unhinged during stress, with each individual bailing out for himself or herself. In the great takeover battles we have witnessed during past years, companies that had strong cultures drew the wagons around them and fought it out, while other companies saw executives—supported by golden parachutes—bail out of the struggles.

Because corporations and their members are interdependent, for the corporation to be strong the members need to share a preconceived notion of correct behavior, a "business ethic," and think of it as a positive force, not a constraint.

As an investment banker, I am continually warned by well-meaning lawyers, clients, and associates to be wary of conflicts of interest. Yet if I were to run away from every difficult situation, I wouldn't be an effective investment banker. I have to feel my way through conflicts. An effective manager can't run from risk either; he or she has to confront risk. To feel "safe" in doing that, managers need the guidelines of an agreed-upon process and set of values within the organization.

After my three months in Nepal, I spent three months as an executive-in-residence at both the Stanford Business School and the University of California at Berkeley's Center for Ethics and Social Policy of the Graduate Theological Union. Those six months away from my job gave me time to assimilate 20 years of business experience. My thoughts turned often to the meaning of the leadership role in any large organization. Students at the seminary thought of themselves as antibusiness. But when I questioned them, they agreed that they distrusted all large organizations, including the church. They perceived all large organizations as impersonal and opposed to individual values and needs. Yet we all know of organizations in which people's values and beliefs are respected and their expressions encouraged. What makes the difference? Can we identify the difference and, as a result, manage more effectively?

WHEN DO WE TAKE A STAND?

by Bowen H. McCoy

I wrote about my experiences purposely to present an ambiguous situation. I never found out if the sadhu lived or died. I can attest, though, that the sadhu lives on in his story. He lives in the ethics classes I teach each year at business schools and churches. He lives in the classrooms of numerous business schools, where professors have taught the case to tens of thousands of students. He lives in several case-books on ethics and on an educational video. And he lives in organizations such as the American Red Cross and AT&T, which use his story in their ethics training.

As I reflect on the sadhu now, 15 years after the fact, I first have to wonder, What actually happened on that Himalayan slope? When I first wrote about the event, I reported the experience in as much detail as I could remember, but I shaped it to the needs of a good classroom discussion. After years of reading my story, viewing it on video, and hearing others discuss it, I'm not sure I myself know what actually occurred on the mountainside that day!

I've also heard a wide variety of responses to the story. The sadhu, for example, may not have wanted our help at all—he may have been intentionally bringing on his own death as a way to holiness. Why had he taken the dangerous way over the pass instead of the caravan route through the gorge? Hindu businesspeople have told me that in trying to assist the sadhu, we were being typically arrogant Westerners imposing our cultural values on the world.

I've learned that each year along the pass, a few Nepali porters are left to freeze to death outside the tents of the unthinking tourists who hired them. A few years ago, a French group even left one of their own, a young French woman, to die there. The difficult pass seems to demonstrate a perverse version of Gresham's law of currency: The bad practices of previous travelers have driven out the values that new travelers might have followed if they were at home. Perhaps that helps to explain why our porters behaved as they did and why it was so difficult for Stephen or anyone else to establish a different approach on the spot.

Our Sherpa sirdar, Pasang, was focused on his responsibility for bringing us up the mountain safe and sound. (His livelihood and status in the Sherpa ethnic group depended on our safe return.) We were weak, our party was split, the porters were well on their way to the top with all our gear and food, and a storm would have separated us irrevocably from our logistical base.

The fact was, we had no plan for dealing with the contingency of the sadhu. There was nothing we could do to unite our multicultural group in the little time we had. An ethical dilemma had come upon us unexpectedly, an element of drama that may explain why the sadhu's story has continued to attract students.

I am often asked for help in teaching the story. I usually advise keeping the details as ambiguous as possible. A true ethical dilemma requires a decision between two hard choices. In the case of the sadhu, we had to decide how much to sacrifice ourselves to take care of a stranger. And given the constraints of our trek, we had to make a group decision, not an individual one. If a large majority of students in a class ends up thinking I'm a bad person because of my decision on the mountain, the instructor may not have given the case its due. The same is true if the majority sees no problem with the choices we made.

Any class's response depends on its setting, whether it's a business school, a church, or a corporation. I've found that younger students are more likely to see the issue as black-and-white, whereas older ones tend to see shades of gray. Some have seen a conflict between the different ethical approaches that we followed at the time. Stephen felt he had to do everything he could to save the sadhu's life, in accordance with his Christian ethic of compassion. I had a utilitarian response: do the greatest good for the greatest number. Give a burst of aid to minimize the sadhu's exposure, then continue on our way.

The basic question of the case remains, When do we take a stand? When do we allow a "sadhu" to intrude into our daily lives? Few of us can afford the time or effort to take care of every needy person we encounter. How much must we give of ourselves? And how do we prepare our organizations and institutions so they will respond appropriately in a crisis? How do we influence them if we do not agree with their points of view?

We cannot quit our jobs over every ethical dilemma, but if we continually ignore our sense of values, who do we become? As a journalist asked at a recent conference on ethics, "Which ditch are we willing to die in?" For each of us, the answer is a bit different. How we act in response to that question defines better than anything else who we are, just as, in a collective sense, our acts define our institutions. In effect, the sadhu is always there, ready to remind us of the tensions between our own goals and the claims of strangers.

The word *ethics* turns off many and confuses more. Yet the notions of shared values and an agreed-upon process for dealing with adversity and change—what many people mean when they talk about corporate culture—seem to be at the heart of the ethical issue. People who are in touch with their own core beliefs and the beliefs of others and who are sustained by them can be more comfortable living on the cutting edge. At times, taking a tough line or a decisive stand in a muddle of ambiguity is the only ethical thing to do. If a manager is indecisive about a problem and spends time trying to figure out the "good" thing to do, the enterprise may be lost.

Business ethics, then, has to do with the authenticity and integrity of the enterprise. To be ethical is to follow the business as well as the cultural goals of the corporation, its owners, its employees, and its customers. Those who cannot serve the corporate vision are not authentic businesspeople and, therefore, are not ethical in the business sense.

At this stage of my own business experience, I have a strong interest in organizational behavior. Sociologists are keenly studying what they call corporate stories, legends, and heroes as a way organizations have of transmitting value systems. Corporations such as Arco have even hired consultants to perform an audit of their corporate culture. In a company, a leader is a person who understands, interprets, and manages the corporate value system. Effective managers, therefore, are action-oriented people who resolve conflict, are tolerant of ambiguity, stress, and change, and have a strong sense of purpose for themselves and their organizations.

If all this is true, I wonder about the role of the professional manager who moves from company to company. How can he or she quickly absorb the values and culture of different organizations? Or is there, indeed, an art of management that is totally transportable? Assuming that such fungible managers do exist, is it proper for them to manipulate the values of others?

What would have happened had Stephen and I carried the sadhu for two days back to the village and become involved with the villagers in his care? In four trips to Nepal, my most interesting experience occurred in 1975 when I lived in a Sherpa home in the Khumbu for five days while recovering from altitude sickness. The high point of Stephen's trip was an invitation to participate in a family funeral ceremony in Manang. Neither experience had to do with climbing the high passes of the Himalayas. Why were we so reluctant to try the lower path, the ambiguous trail? Perhaps because we did not have a leader who could reveal the greater purpose of the trip to us.

Why didn't Stephen, with his moral vision, opt to take the sadhu under his personal care? The answer is partly because Stephen was hard-stressed physically himself and partly because, without some support system that encompassed our involuntary and episodic community on the mountain, it was beyond his individual capacity to do so.

I see the current interest in corporate culture and corporate value systems as a positive response to pessimism such as Stephen's about the decline of the role of the individual in large organizations. Individuals who operate from a thoughtful set of personal values provide the foundation for a corporate culture. A corporate tradition that encourages freedom of inquiry, supports personal values, and reinforces a focused sense of direction can fulfill the need to combine individuality with the prosperity and success of the group. Without such corporate support, the individual is lost.

That is the lesson of the sadhu. In a complex corporate situation, the individual requires and deserves the support of the group. When people cannot find such support in their organizations, they don't know how to act. If such support is forthcoming, a person has a stake in the success of the group and can add much to the process of establishing and maintaining a corporate culture. Management's challenge is to be sensitive to individual needs, to shape them, and to direct and focus them for the benefit of the group as a whole.

For each of us the sadhu lives. Should we stop what we are doing and comfort him; or should we keep trudging up toward the high pass? Should I pause to help the derelict I pass on the street each night as I walk by the Yale Club en route to Grand Central Station? Am I his brother? What is the nature of our responsibility if we consider ourselves to be ethical persons? Perhaps it is to change the values of the group so that it can, with all its resources, take the other road.

Bowen H. McCoy retired from Morgan Stanley in 1990 after 28 years of service. He is now a real estate and business counselor, a teacher and a philanthropist.

UNIT 3

Business and Society: Contemporary Ethical, Social, and Environmental Issues

Unit Selections

Key Points to Consider

- How well are organizations responding to issues of work and family schedules, day care, and telecommuting?

- Should corporations and executives face criminal charges for unsafe products, dangerous working conditions, or industrial pollution? Why or why not?

- What ethical dilemmas is management likely to face when conducting business in foreign environments?

 **Links: www.dushkin.com/online/**
These sites are annotated in the World Wide Web pages.

CIBERWeb
   http://ciber.centers.purdue.edu
National Immigrant Forum
   http://www.immigrationforum.org
Sympatico: Workplace
   http://sympatico.workopolis.com
United Nations Environment Programme (UNEP)
   http://www.unep.ch
United States Trade Representative (USTR)
   http://www.ustr.gov

Both at home and abroad, there are social and environmental issues that have potential ethical consequences for management. Incidents of insider trading, deaths resulting from unsafe products or work environments, AIDS in the workplace, and the adoption of policies for involvement in the global market are a few of the issues that need to be seriously addressed by management.

This unit investigates the nature and ramifications of prominent ethical, social, and environmental issues facing management today. The unit articles are grouped into three sections. The first article, "Ethical Compass" reveals that companies without a moral compass are cast adrift, or broken on the rocks. "Does it Pay To Be Good?" covers why corporate citizenship is a diffuse concept for many. The next article scrutinizes the importance of companies gaining and maintaining trust in the marketplace. The last two articles in this subsection provide some thoughtful insight on male bastions, glass ceilings, what women want at work, and explores the lingering problem of prejudice and discrimination for minorities in America.

The first article in the second subsection addresses how a tough consumer ethic demands openness and integrity. "A Dose of Denial" reveals how drug makers sought to keep some dangerous drugs on store shelves.

The subsection *Global Ethics* concludes this unit with readings that provide helpful insight on ethical issues and dilemmas inherent in multinational operations. They describe adapting ethical decisions to a global marketplace and offer guidelines for helping management deal with ethical issues in international markets as well as revealing how female entrepreneurs in some Mideastern countries are making some gains—despite scorn and unequal treatment.

Ethical Compass

People want more from work than a paycheck.

By Tim Hatcher

COMPANIES WITHOUT a moral compass are cast adrift, or broken apart on the rocks. Although companies with formal ethical standards perform better, standards is not an ethics "silver bullet." Enron had a well-developed code of ethics. Beyond a fancy proclamation of ethical do's and don'ts a company's moral compass can be firmly set by executives who know the ethical traction that learning, training, and education provide.

Training strategies can do more than supply skills and knowledge—they can change or reinforce attitudes and values. Savvy executives use training to set their moral compass and help people stay an ethical course.

A climate of integrity requires leaders to build an ethical infrastructure that includes seven strategies:

1. View strategic learning initiatives through ethnically and socially responsive lenses. Create and implement learning strategies and objectives to achieve ethically and socially responsive outcomes. As leaders develop and carry out learning initiatives, they meet knowledge, performance and operational goals, and set the moral compass for the future. Companies with good reputations have better financial performance. Strategic learning goals should be weighed against codes of ethics before being implemented.

2. Consider ethical issues and social performance in needs assessments. Assess how the organization is doing ethically and socially. Needs assessments typically pinpoint needs for skills and knowledge, but they can also help to find ethical disconnects and spot learning activities that encourage ethical and socially responsive actions.

3. Use core process analyses to spot ethical bottlenecks and leverage points. Process analyses can identify potential ethical obstacles and times when people are in highly stressful or compromising situations. As processes are probed, look for potentially stressful and compromising conditions. A simple disconnect in a core process like accounting can lead to miscommunication and mistakes, causing stress and conflict that could jeopardize ethical decision-making.

4. Emphasize ethical behavior and social responsibility in training and management development. Orientation training can enhance ethical behaviors. New employees not only learn about policy and benefits, they also learn how serious the company is about ethical behavior and social responsiveness. Tell stories about how people are rewarded for ethical behaviors.

Ethical leaders are not necessarily born; they can be developed. Being ethical is based on a combination of personal, religious, and family-based values, skills, knowledge, and attitudes that can be developed through training and education.

5. Evaluate the effects of technology on ethical issues. More technology is being used to enhance and transform the skills, knowledge, and behaviors of people on the job. Internet and e-mail monitors and surveillance cameras are valuable tools in reducing theft, security breaches, and illegal activities, yet people are more productive in an environment of trust, respect, and dignity. A solution is to use an as-needed policy on employee monitoring. Make it clear that monitoring can happen at any time and will happen if standards are violated.

6. Develop globally conscious people through training. A depth of knowledge and keen abilities to quickly adapt to new situations and diverse worldviews are necessary for employees to handle culturally specific conflicts and master cross-cultural adaptation. This is possible through focused training and educational experiences such as mentoring with host-country professionals, experiential learning activities such as role-playing, and monitored cultural immersion. To support transference of such training, leaders should visibly sustain, rather than override, the ethical mores and ethnic values of a host culture.

7. Consider the importance of work-life issues. Most people are looking for more in their work than a paycheck. Benefits that address employee work-life needs include continuing education and training, opportunities for personal and professional growth, educational reimbursement, career counseling, flexible work schedules, part-time employment (downshifting), and job sharing; dependent-care spending accounts, child-care benefits, and on-site or near-site child care centers; elder-care programs, adoption services, and financial security assistance including financial planning and scholarships. Work-life benefits are related to turnover, absenteeism, employee morale, recruitment, commitment and job satisfaction, and loss of productivity and downtime due to stress and personal business.

Learning-oriented, creative, fast-moving companies with a quality of human spirit have purpose, intention, vision, and common values that create meaning for people. These companies address the needs of people to find meaning in their work. They tend to keep good people and get more from people because they get more from the company.

Unethical and irresponsible leaders and their companies suffer not only from the inevitable nosedive in market value but also from the inability to attract top talent. Leaders need to set a moral compass by developing and maintaining ethical behaviors and building corporate citizens with both financial and moral staying power.

ACTION: Set your ethical compass

Tim Hatcher is a professor, consultant, speaker and author of Ethics and HRD *(Perseus), hatcher@louisville.edu, 502-231-7787.*

From *Executive Excellence*, July 2003 p. 19. Copyright © 2003 by Executive Excellence. Reprinted by permission.

Does It **PAY** To Be **GOOD?**

Yes, say advocates of corporate citizenship, who believes their time has come—finally.

By A.J. Vogl

Corporate citizenship: For believers, the words speak of the dawning of a new era of capitalism, when business, government, and citizen groups join forces for the greater good, to jointly tackle such problems as water shortages and air pollution, to do something about the 1.2 billion people who live on less than a dollar a day.

Corporate citizenship: For critics of today's capitalism, the words smack of hypocrisy, big business' cynical response to charges of greed and corruption in high places, intended to mollify those who say corporations have too much power and that they wield it shamelessly. Critics charge that corporate citizenship is a placebo to the enemies of globalization, a public-relations smoke screen, capitalism's last-ditch attempt to preserve itself by co-opting its opposition.

Corporate citizenship: For many, it remains a diffuse concept, but generally it speaks to companies voluntarily adopting a triple bottom line, one that takes into account social, economic, and environmental considerations as well as financial results. Though some associate corporate citizenship with charity and philanthropy, the concept goes further—it embraces a corporate *conscience* above and beyond profits and markets. David Vidal, who directs research in global corporate citizenship at The Conference Board, comments, "Citizenship is not, as some critics charge, window dressing for the corporation. It deals with primary business relationships that are part of a company's strategic vision, and a good business case can be made for corporate citizenship."

Whether you are a critic or believer, however, there is no question that corporate citizenship—a term that embraces corporate social responsibility (CSR) and sustainability—is no longer a concept fostered by idealists on the fringe. It has entered the mainstream.

But why *now*? Though the era of corporate citizenship was ushered in with the fall of the Berlin Wall and the rise of market capitalism worldwide, current sentiment against big business has given new weight to the cause. Virtually every opinion survey shows that people think corporations have too much power, and that they will do anything in the pursuit of profits. And now, to add to public distrust, we have a flagging economy, a shambolic stock market, and what have been called "pornographic" CEO salaries. These circumstances have given citizenship's champions new planks for their platform, such as accounting and compensation practices. At the same time, attacks on the very nature of business have sent corporate leaders searching for a bright spot, and that spot may very well be the concept of corporate citizenship.

But that makes corporate enthusiasm for citizenship sound like a calculated, even cynical stance that is likely to last only as long as the environment remains hostile. There are grounds for believing that it is more than that, that it speaks to deeper changes in the greater world that make it *necessary* for large corporations to do good. Some of these changes include:

Tightening regulatory pressures. France, for instance, requires all companies listed on the Paris Stock Exchange to include information about their social and environmental performance within their financial statements; the Johannesburg Stock Exchange requires compliance with a CSR-based code of conduct; and the United Kingdom (the first nation with a minister for corporate social responsibility) requires pension-fund managers to disclose the degree to which social and environmental criteria are part of their investment decisions.

Will there be more national legislation? "If you had asked me that three or four years ago, I would have answered, 'Unclear, or probably not,'" says Allen White. White is acting chief executive of Global Reporting Initiative, an Amsterdam-based organization that has developed uniform guidelines for CSR reporting. "But in 2002 we've seen developments that could not have been anticipated several years ago, developments that have challenged companies to reconstruct or restore credibility, challenges to markets to demonstrate to investors that available information is accurate. Governments have taken note and are considering legislative and regulatory action."

Changing demographics. A socially engaged and better-educated population demands that the companies with which they do business—as consumers, employees, or investors—conform to higher standards. Both consumers and employees tell researchers that they prefer to purchase from and work for a company that is a good corporate citizen. On the investor front, activists—including individuals, socially responsible mutual funds, public pension funds, and religious groups—submitted 800 resolutions in 2002, according to Meg Voorhes, director of the social-is-

Investors Are Listening

For companies in sectors not considered exemplars of corporate citizenship—munitions, pornography, gambling, and tobacco (yes); liquor (probably); and oil (maybe)—there's good news: The market hasn't penalized them for their supposed lack of citizenship. For companies at the opposite end of the spectrum, there's also good news: Investors haven't penalized them for their expenditures on social causes.

On balance, the better news is for the socially responsible companies, who have long labored under the assumption that the investor automatically pays a price for investing in a socially responsible company or mutual fund—the price, of course, being a company or fund that doesn't perform as well as its peers that don't fly the socially-responsible banner.

Investors appear to be listening. According to Financial Research Corp., investors added $1.29 billion of new money into socially responsible funds during the first half of 2002, compared to $847.1 million added during all of 2001. Over the year ending July 31, the average mutual fund—including stock, bond, and balanced funds—was down 13 percent, while comparable socially responsible funds were down 19 percent. But advocates point out that different indices—particularly the Domini Social Index, a capitalization-weighted market index of 400 common stocks screened according to social and environmental criteria, and the Citizen's Index, a market-weighted portfolio of common stocks representing ownership in 300 of the most socially responsible U.S. companies, have outperformed the S&P 500 over the last one, three, and five years.

While the $13 billion invested in socially responsible funds (according to Morningstar) comprises only about 2 percent of total fund assets, advocates expect this percentage to climb to 10 percent by 2012, says Barbara Krumsiek, chief executive of the Bethesda, Md.-based Calvert Group, a mutual-fund complex specializing in socially responsible investing. And others' tallies are far higher: The nonprofit Social Investment Forum counts more than $2 trillion in total assets under management in portfolios screened for socially concerned investors, including socially screened mutual funds and separate accounts managed for socially conscious institutions and individual investors.

Plus, recent corporate scandals may have raised many investors' consciousness: In the first half of 2002, socially responsible mutual funds saw their assets increase by 3 percent, while conventional diversified funds lost 9.5 percent in total assets. People may have decided that if their mutual-fund investments were going to lose money, it might as well be for a good cause.

—A.J.V.

---

sues department at Investor Responsibility Research Center, a Washington, D.C.-based organization that tracks proxies.

More opportunity for investors to back their convictions with money. Socially aware investors can choose among some 230 mutual funds, and, according to Steven J. Schueth of the nonprofit Social Investment Forum, more than 800 independent asset managers identify themselves as managers of socially responsible portfolios for institutional investors and high-net-worth individuals. (See "Investors Are Listening,") Indexes of social and environmental performance—like the Dow Jones Sustainability World Indexes and FTSE4Good—are becoming significant market factors in screening for good citizenship. These indexes have teeth in them: They will and do drop companies that fail to meet social-responsibility standards.

Pressure from nongovernmental organizations. Not only are international NGOs growing in number—at last count, there were 28,000 worldwide—their visibility and credibility are on the rise. Last year, PR executive Richard Edelman told the World Economic Forum, "NGOs are now the Fifth Estate in global governance—the true credible source on issues related to the environment and social justice." While Americans generally trust corporations more than NGO "brands," the

opposite is true in Europe. A study conducted by Edelman's firm found that Amnesty International, the World Wildlife Fund, and Greenpeace outstripped by a margin of nearly two to one the four highest-rated corporations in Europe: Microsoft, Bayer, Shell, and Ford. As in other areas, it appears, European public opinion affirming social responsibility is ahead of that of the United States.

The most prominent corporate citizens rarely receive commensurate rewards.

Greater transparency. If good news travels fast, bad news moves faster. The Internet has given a platform to critics who, if they existed before, could be ignored; now they will be heard. There is the by-now-classic story of MIT graduate student Jonah Peretti, who submitted the word *sweatshop* to Nike's personalize-your-shoes iD program. Nike refused the order, terming the word "inappropriate slang."

Peretti replied, "I have decided to order the shoes with a different iD, but I would like to make one small request. Could you please send me a color snapshot of the ten-year-old Vietnamese girl who makes my shoes?" His e-mail correspondence was forwarded around the world and picked up by the mass media. Nike, in its first annual "corporate responsibility report," responded convincingly to charges that it exploited workers—indeed, the company is generally known as a CSR innovator—but inevitably sounded defensive.

All of these factors have led to increasing corporate acceptance of the importance of citizenship. Every three years, BearingPoint, the consultancy formerly known as KPMG Consulting, surveys global *Fortune* 250 companies on corporate-responsibility issues. The latest survey found that 45 percent of the 250 companies surveyed issued environmental, social, and/or sustainability reports in 2001, up from 35 percent in 1998, and the number of U.S. companies that issued such reports increased 14 percent over the same period. Today, too, two-thirds of the world's largest companies use their Websites to trumpet their social and environmental activities.

Which is not to say that all these corporations have become true believers. "[W]e have to acknowledge," writes Steve Hilton, a British CSR consultant, "that fear of

Bringing Standards Up to Code

In May 2000, the International Chamber of Commerce counted more than 40 codes, existing or in preparation, intended to govern the activities of global corporations; among the most prominent are those of the OECD, the U.N. Global Compact, and the International Labor Organization. Companies may be forgiven for having been confused over which set of guidelines to follow.

That confusion appears to be on the way to being lifted through the "2002 Sustainability Reporting Guidelines," introduced at the World Summit in Johannesburg by the Global Reporting Initiative. The guidelines are not another code. Rather, they are an attempt to create a generally accepted reporting framework for social responsibility. The outcome of two years of work by GRI, the guidelines are a rejoinder to the "deep scepticism" that "the creation of new wealth ... will do anything to decrease social inequities," as the document's introduction states. In nearly 100 pages, the guidelines cover such issues as transparency, sustainability, auditability, and comparability.

The last of these issues is critical, argues Eric Israel, a partner at BearingPoint, the consultancy formerly known as KPMG Consulting. "The meaning of citizenship for one particular company can be completely different than for another," he says. "So how do you benchmark an organization and compare it to others in the same industry? Up to now, there's been no equivalent of GAAP for social responsibility. That's where GRI comes in with its guidelines."

How does one verify that GRI guidelines have been met? Since the advent of CSR codes, companies have hired organizations, ranging from consultancies like BearingPoint to single-issue nonprofits, to verify their compliance for onlookers' eyes. Some monitor the companies themselves and attest that standards are being met—for instance, Chiquita Brands International has partnered with the Rainforest Alliance, which sends inspectors to each farm and offers its Better Bananas seal of approval to products from those farms that pass muster.

Other firms simply verify companies' CSR reports, the public face of compliance with codes. Considering the many codes in circulation and the range of organizations hired to verify compliance, it's not easy to put any particular report in broader context. That's where another organization, London-based AccountAbility, enters the picture.

Last June, AccountAbility issued something called the AA1000S Assurance Standard, which outlines principles around verification and CSR auditing—and which the firm hopes will become the gold standard of CSR verification standards. AccountAbility has credibility because of its governing constituencies—businesses, nonprofits, accountancies, researchers and academics, and consultancies—and its endorsement of GRI's reporting guidelines will likely give a boost to acceptance of both. "What we do is entirely complementary to what GRI does," says AccountAbility COO Mike Peirce. "It's a marriage made in heaven." In future, then, expect to see more annual reports that cite GRI guidelines verified by accountants using AccountAbility standards.

But the existence of these codes and organizations is only a first step; there's still a long way to go. According to a recent OECD survey, only one in five companies with codes of conduct share compliance information with the public, and third-party auditing remains the exception rather than the rule.

—A.J.V.

exposure and the need for compliance are the most powerful forces galvanizing the majority of active corporate citizens."

No Good Deed Goes Unpunished

As necessary as corporate citizenship may be, it still faces challenges from both inside and outside the corner office. Perhaps the most disheartening of these hurdles is that the most prominent corporate citizens rarely receive rewards commensurate with their prominence. As Hilton and Giles Gibbons, co-authors of the pro-CSR *Good Business: Your World Needs You*, point out, "Curiously, the companies whose hearts are most visibly fixed to their pinstriped sleeves tend to be the ones that attract the most frequent and venomous attacks from anti-business critics." Is this because critics feel that devious agendas lie behind the enlightened policies? Noreena Hertz, a British critic of corporate citizenship, wonders whether Microsoft, by

putting computers in schools today, will determine how children learn tomorrow.

Is it that corporations haven't gotten their stories across properly, or that they *have*—and are still being vilified? The experience of McDonald's in this arena is revealing. Last April, the fast-food chain published its first social-responsibility report, composed of 46 pages summarizing its efforts in four categories: community, environment, people, and marketplace. Those efforts have been rewarded in some courts of public opinion: In 2000 and 2001 *Financial Times*/PricewaterhouseCoopers surveys of media and NGOs, McDonald's placed 14th among the world's most respected companies for environmental performance.

At the same time, few corporations have been attacked as savagely as McDonald's for its "citizenship." It has been portrayed as an omnivorous monster that destroys local businesses and culture, promotes obesity, treats its employees badly, and despoils the environment. McDonald's goes to great lengths to answer

these charges in its social-responsibility report—which was itself widely criticized—but, like Nike, it can't help looking defensive. It will take a great deal more than a report of its good works to diminish the Golden Arches as a symbol of "capitalist imperialism" in the eyes of antiglobalists or to stanch the vitriol on such Websites as Mcspotlight.

There's no question that the bar is set exceedingly high in the arena of corporate social involvement. Philip Morris Cos. spends more than $100 million a year, most conspicuously in a series of TV commercials, on measures to discourage underage smoking—and still critics charge that the Philip Morris campaign is a cynical PR stunt that actually *encourages* kids to smoke. The company has been accused of having "a profound conflict of interest that cannot be overcome."

Another tobacco company, BAT, the world's second-largest, put some members of the social-responsibility establishment in an uncomfortable position when, last July, it became the industry's first company to publish a social-responsibility report. Few knew what to think upon reading the tobacco company's blunt rhetoric—"[T]here is no such thing as a 'safe' cigarette.... We openly state that, put simply, smoking is a cause of certain serious diseases"—and the 18 pages devoted to the risks of smoking. BAT even had its report audited by an independent verifier. All this wasn't nearly enough to satisfy antismoking groups, of course—they continue to view the company with deep suspicion. Would anyone have predicted otherwise?

When accused of being overly suspicious, critics point to one company that, over the last six years, won numerous awards for its environmental, human rights, anti-corruption, anti-bribery, and climate-change policies; a company prominent on "most admired" and "best companies to work for" lists; a company that issued a report on the good deeds that supported its claim to be a top corporate citizen. That company was Enron.

No one would argue that Enron is typical, yet its debacle has tainted other companies. It also raises a difficult question about CSR: What is the link between how a company is managed—corporate governance—and corporate citizenship? Steve Hilton, speaking from London, says that the link is not really understood in the United Kingdom: "People here have not made the connection between the corporate-governance, executive-compensation, and accounting-fraud issues in the United States and operational issues that come under the heading of corporate citizenship. I would argue they're all part of the same thing."

So would Transparency International's Frank Vogl, co-founder of the anti-corruption NGO. He believes that CSR has been undermined because it has been disconnected from corporate-conduct issues. "Foreign public trust in Corporate America has been diminished," he said, "and there is scant evidence that U.S. business leaders recognize the global impact of the U.S. scandals."

Vogl says that, for most countries in the world, corruption is much more of a social-responsibility issue than either the environment or labor rights. "What U.S. businesspeople see as a facilitating payment may be seen in developing countries as a bribe," he comments, "and I think that provides some insight into why the United States ranks behind 12 other countries on the Transparency International Bribe Payers Index. To me, corporate citizenship means you don't bribe foreign officials. That's the worst kind of hypocrisy."

Will They Be Good in Bad Times?

The specter of hypocrisy raises its head in another quarter as well: Do employees of companies claiming to be good corporate citizens see their employer's citizenship activities as a diversion or cover-up to charges of bad leadership and poor management practices? Certainly, if recent surveys are a guide, top management needs to restore its credibility with employees. In a recent Mercer Human Resource Consulting study, only a third of the 2,600 workers surveyed agreed with the statement, "I can trust management in my organization to always communicate honestly." And a Walker Information survey of employees found that only 49 percent believe their senior leaders to be "people of high personal integrity." If CSR is perceived by employees merely as puffery to make top management look good, it will not get under an organization's cultural skin.

"Businesses needn't apologize for making products that other Americans want to buy."

Even if there is a genuine management commitment, corporations have other obligations that may take precedence, begging the question: Will corporations be good citizens in bad times as well as good? The experience of Ford Motor Co. brings the question to earth. In August, Ford issued its third annual corporate-citizenship report. Previous reports had drawn plaudits from environmentalists, but this one, coming at a time when the automaker faced financial difficulties, was attacked by the same environmentalists for failing to set aggressive goals for reducing greenhouse-gas emissions or improving gas mileage. Sierra Club's executive director called it "a giant step in the wrong direction for Ford Motor Co., for American consumers, and for the environment."

Lingering tough economic conditions may impel other companies to take their own "giant steps" backward. An old business saw has it that when times get tough and cuts have to be made, certain budgets are at the top of the list for cutbacks—advertising for one, public relations for another. For companies in which corporate

citizenship is seen as an extension of public relations, of "image building" or "reputation management," it may suffer this fate.

Which is as it should be, say some critics. As *The Wall Street Journal* lectured CEO William Ford on its editorial page: "We also hope Mr. Ford has learned from his mistake of ceding the moral and political high ground to environmentalists.... Businesses needn't apologize for making products that other Americans want to buy. Their first obligation is to their shareholders and employees and that means above all making an honest profit."

Does the "Business Case" Really Have a Case?

But hold on: What about the so-called business case for corporate citizenship—that it contributes to making "an honest profit"? Unfortunately, it's difficult to quantify in cost-benefit terms what that contribution is. Not something to be concerned about, says Simon Zadek, CEO of AccountAbility, a London-based institute that has established CSR verification standards. (See "Bringing Standards Up to Code.") "It is a fact that the vast majority of day-to-day business decisions are taken without any explicit cost-benefit analysis," he says, pointing to employee training as an example of a corporate expenditure that is difficult to quantify in cost-benefit terms. What he doesn't mention is that, when business is suffering, training is usually among the expenditures to be cut back or eliminated.

Ultimately, Zadek concedes that, in strictly quantifiable terms, one cannot make a cost-benefit case for corporate citizenship. "Although the question 'Does corporate citizenship pay?' is technically right, it is misleading in practice," he says. "Rephrasing the core question as 'In what ways does corporate citizenship contribute to achieving the core business strategy?' is far preferable."

To some hardheaded corporate types, Zadek's reasoning may seem disingenuous, but even the hardheads can't be dismissive—at least publicly. Moreover, they would probably acknowledge that corporate citizenship, in concept and practice, has come too far to be ignored. In the future, it may well become what Steve Hilton calls a "hygiene factor," a condition of doing business. Hilton's firm, Good Business, consults with firms on citizenship issues. "I think business leaders are coming to realize CSR's potential to go beyond

Attacked From All Sides

While many skeptics criticize the ways in which corporate social responsibility is enacted, some take matters a step further by asking if the concept should exist at all. Who would object to the idea of a company doing good, of moving beyond the traditional and literal bottom line, to take a larger view of the reason for its existence? You may be surprised: There are many critics, and they come from various and sometimes unpredictable directions.

First is a group that says corporate social responsibility is flawed at its heart because it's doing the right thing for the wrong reason. The right thing, they believe, is doing the right thing because it is right, as a matter of principle—not because it advances the firm's business interests. The rejoinder, of course, is that if a larger social or environmental good is met, we should not quibble about motivation. As corporate-governance activist Robert A.G. Monks points out: "You can get backing from institutional investors only if you talk a commercial idiom."

Next is a group of dissimilar critics who believe that, in attempting to pursue goals of corporate citizenship, companies are doing things that are none of their business. Paradoxically, these critics come from both the right and the left.

The right feels that the business of business should be business: As Michael Prowse argues in the *Financial Times*, the role of the corporation "is to provide individuals with the means to be socially responsible. Rather than trying to play the role of social worker, senior executives should concentrate on their statutory obligations. We should not expect benevolence of them, but we should demand probity: the socially responsible chief executive is the one who turns a profit without lying, cheating, robbing or defrauding anyone."

The left, on the other hand, feels that corporations are usurping the powers of government, to the detriment of the citizenry and democracy itself. Noreena Hertz, the British academic and broadcaster who wrote of *The Silent Takeover: Global Capitalism and the Death of Democracy*, is not only dubious about business taking over responsibilities that she feels properly belong to government—she is skeptical about business' ability to handle them: "[M]anagers of multinationals operating in the third world are often overwhelmed by the social problems they encounter, and understandably find it difficult to know which causes to prioritize…. Their contributions can be squandered, or diverted through corruption."

And what happens, she asks, when a corporation decides to pull out, if government has allowed private industry to take over its role? Worse still, she worries about situations in which a socially responsible corporation could use its position "to exact a stream of IOUs and quid pro quos, to demand ever more favorable terms and concessions from host governments."

Then there is a group of critics who see corporate citizenship as a diversionary ploy to placate a public outraged at dubious corporate practices. They will concede that Enron, WorldCom, and Tyco are egregious exceptions, but are other companies exemplars of probity? Hardly. Can companies be considered good corporate citizens when they move their headquarters to Bermuda to avoid taxes (and enrich their CEOs in the process)? Can companies like General Electric, Monsanto, Merck, SmithKline Beecham, and Chiquita Brands International claim the moral high ground when they have cut employee benefits in connection with mergers and spinoffs? And what of such companies as Wyeth, Wal-Mart, McKesson, and Merrill Lynch? Can they, ask the critics, be considered high-minded citizens when the top executives accumulate pots of money in their deferred-compensation accounts? This may be why PR *eminence grise* John Budd says, "For at least the next 18 post-Enron months, I certainly would not counsel any CEO to magically appear publicly as an enlightened champion of social responsibility. The circumstances make it automatic that it would be perceived as spinning."

Last, there is a group of critics that says that simply doing more good than we're doing now is not enough, that we have to rethink the nature of the beast—capitalism itself. Steven Piersanti, president of Berrett-Koehler Publishers, is in the thick of this intellectual contretemps. Last fall, his firm published two books that took divergent views on the issue. The first, *Walking the Talk*, was written by Swiss industrialist Stephan Schmidheiny, along with two colleagues at the World Business Council for Sustainable Development, Chad Holliday of DuPont and Philip Watts of Royal Dutch/Shell. "It advances a reformist view that major changes are needed in our business world," says Piersanti, "but that these changes can best be achieved by reforms within our existing economic structures, institutions, and systems." The second book, *Alternatives to Economic Globalization: A Better World Is Possible*, presents "an activist view that existing economic structures are insufficient and that new structures, institutions, and systems are needed in the world."

It's likely that doubts about the nature and purpose of corporate citizenship will continue to be raised from all quarters. But with social-responsibility reporting and verification initiatives in place and likely government regulation down the road, there's reason to think that their voices will become more isolated.

—A.J.V.

a compliance/risk-management issue into a genuine business tool," he says. "That's been the rhetoric all along, but the reality has been that it's been a slightly marginal issue. With few exceptions, it's been seen as an add-on, without being incorporated into core business decision-making."

This is Zadek's point when he argues the case for what he calls "third-generation corporate citizenship." The first generation is defined by cause-related marketing and short-term reputation management. The second occurs when social and environmental objectives become a core part of long-term business strategy; as an example, he points to automakers competing in the arena of emission controls. The third generation is based on collective action, where corporations join with competitors, NGOs, and government "to change the underlying rules of the game to ensure that business delivers adequate social and environmental results."

Changing the rules means, for one thing, a more level playing field. "In CSR," says AccountAbility COO Mike Peirce, "companies that are leaders might suffer a penalty if there's a big gap between themselves and laggards in the field, so they'd like everybody ticking along at at least a basic level." In other words, a socially responsible company does not want to be penalized financially for being socially responsible. Of course, a cynic might reply that if CSR indeed provides the competitive advantage that its proponents insist it does, then it is the laggards that should suffer the severest financial penalty.

Expect citizenship proponents to make corporate governance itself the issue.

To convince doubters, efforts are being made to schematically quantify corporate social responsibility. In a recent *Harvard Business Review* article titled "The Virtue Matrix: Calculating the Return on Corporate Responsibility," Roger L. Martin makes a point of treating corporate responsibility as a product or service like any

other. According to Martin, who is dean of the University of Toronto's Rotman School of Management, his matrix can help companies sort out such questions as whether a citizenship initiative will erode a company's competitive position.

Even if Martin's formula seems overly clinical, it supports the trend toward closer analysis of what social responsibility means and what it brings to corporations practicing it. But analysis will take you only so far. "[I]t is impossible to prove the direction of the flow of causality," writes Chad Holliday, chairman and CEO of Du-Pont and co-author of *Walking the Talk: The Business Case for Sustainable Development.* "Does a company become profitable and thus enjoy the luxury of being able to worry about environmental and social issues or does the pursuit of sustainability make a company more profitable?"

But for large public companies, the question of whether it truly pays to be good will be asked less and less; for them, it will be *necessary* to be good, if only to

avoid appearing Neanderthal. That means that corporate social responsibility, itself nothing less than a growth industry today, will become "normalized" into corporate cultures.

Yes, there will be an effort to level the playing field in CSR, but, further, expect citizenship proponents to attempt to raise the field to a higher level by making corporate governance itself the issue. "Unless we make basic structural changes," says Marjorie Kelly, the editor of *Business Ethics* magazine and a frequent critic of CSR, "it'll be nothing but window dressing. The corporate scandals have given a real-world demonstration that business without ethics collapses, and that has given us an extraordinary opportunity to change the way we do business."

A.J. VOGL is editor of *Across the Board.* He wrote "Worry About the Details" in the Sept/Oct issue.

TRUST
IN THE
MARKETPLACE

**John E. Richardson and
Linnea Bernard McCord**

Traditionally, ethics is defined as a set of moral values or principles or a code of conduct.

> ... Ethics, as an expression of reality, is predicated upon the assumption that there are right and wrong motives, attitudes, traits of character, and actions that are exhibited in interpersonal relationships. Respectful social interaction is considered a norm by almost everyone.
>
> ... the overwhelming majority of people perceive others to be ethical when they observe what is considered to be their genuine kindness, consideration, politeness, empathy, and fairness in their interpersonal relationships. When these are absent, and unkindness, inconsideration, rudeness, hardness, and injustice are present, the people exhibiting such conduct are considered unethical. A genuine consideration of others is essential to an ethical life. (Chewning, pp. 175–176).

An essential concomitant of ethics is of trust. Webster's Dictionary defines trust as "assured reliance on the character, ability, strength or truth of someone or something." Businesses are built on a foundation of trust in our free-enterprise system. When there are violations of this trust between competitors, between employer and employees, or between businesses and consumers, our economic system ceases to run smoothly. From a moral viewpoint, ethical behavior should not exist because of economic pragmatism, governmental edict, or contemporary fashionability—it should exist because it is morally appropriate and right. From an economic point of view, ethical behavior should exist because it just makes good business sense to be ethical and operate in a manner that demonstrates trustworthiness.

Robert Bruce Shaw, in *Trust in the Balance*, makes some thoughtful observations about trust within an organization. Paraphrasing his observations and applying his ideas to the marketplace as a whole:

> 1. Trust requires consumers have confidence in organizational promises or claims made to them. This means that a consumer should be able to believe that a commitment made will be met.
>
> 2. Trust requires integrity and consistency in following a known set of values, beliefs, and practices.
>
> 3. Trust requires concern for the well-being of others. This does not mean that organizational needs are not given appropriate emphasis—but it suggests the importance of understanding the impact of decisions and actions on others—i.e. consumers. (Shaw, pp. 39–40)

Companies can lose the trust of their customers by portraying their products in a deceptive or inaccurate manner. In one recent example, a Nike advertisement exhorted golfers to buy the same golf balls used by Tiger Woods. However, since Tiger Woods was using custom-made Nike golf balls not yet available to the general golfing public, the ad was, in fact, deceptive. In one of its ads, Volvo represented that Volvo cars could withstand a physical impact that, in fact, was not possible. Once a company is "caught" giving inaccurate information, even if done innocently, trust in that company is eroded.

Companies can also lose the trust of their customers when they fail to act promptly and notify their customers of problems that the company has discovered, especially where deaths may be involved. This occurred when Chrysler dragged its feet in replacing a safety latch on its Minivan (Geyelin, pp. A1, A10). More recently, Firestone and Ford had been publicly brought to task for failing to expeditiously notify American consumers of tire defects in SUVs even though the problem had occurred years earlier in other countries. In cases like these, trust might not just be eroded, it might be destroyed. It could take years of painstaking effort to rebuild trust under these circumstances, and some companies might not have the economic ability to withstand such a rebuilding process with their consumers.

A *20/20* and *New York Times* investigation on a recent *ABC 20/20* program, entitled "The Car Dealer's Secret" revealed a sad example of the violation of trust in the marketplace. The investigation divulged that many unsuspecting consumers have had hidden charges tacked on by some car dealers when purchasing a new car. According to consumer attorney Gary Klein, "It's a dirty little secret that the auto lending industry has not owned up to." (*ABC News 20/20*)

The scheme worked in the following manner. Car dealers would send a prospective buyer's application to a number of lenders, who would report to the car dealer what interest rate the lender would give to the buyer for his or her car loan. This interest rate is referred to as the "buy rate." Legally a car dealer is not required to tell the buyer what the "buy rate" is or how much the dealer is marking up the loan. If dealers did most of the loans at the buy rate, they only get a small fee. However, if they were able to convince the buyer to pay a higher rate, they made considerably more money. Lenders encouraged car dealers to charge the buyer a higher rate than the "buy rate" by agreeing to split the extra income with the dealer.

David Robertson, head of the Association of Finance and Insurance Professionals—a trade group representing finance managers—defended the practice, reflecting that it was akin to a retail markup on loans. "The dealership provides a valuable service on behalf of the customer in negotiating these loans," he said. "Because of that, the dealership should be compensated for that work." (*ABC News 20/20*)

Careful examination of the entire report, however, makes one seriously question this apologetic. Even if this practice is deemed to be legal, the critical issue is what happens to trust when the buyers discover that they have been charged an additional 1–3% of the loan without their knowledge? In some cases, consumers were led to believe that they were getting the dealer's bank rate, and in other cases, they were told that the dealer had shopped around at several banks to secure the best loan rate they could get for the buyer. While this practice may be questionable from a legal standpoint, it is clearly in ethical breach of trust with the consumer. Once discovered, the companies doing this will have the same credibility and trustworthiness problems as the other examples mentioned above.

The untrustworthiness problems of the car companies was compounded by the fact that the investigation appeared to reveal statistics showing that black customers were twice as likely as whites to have their rate marked up—and at a higher level. That evidence—included in thousands of pages of confidential documents which *20/20* and *The New York Times* obtained from a Tennessee court—revealed that some Nissan and GM dealers in Tennessee routinely marked up rates for blacks, forcing them to pay between $300 and $400 more than whites. (*ABC News 20/20*)

This is a tragic example for everyone who was affected by this markup and was the victim of this secret policy. Not only is trust destroyed, there is a huge economic cost to the general public. It is estimated that in the last four years or so, Texas car dealers have received approximately $9 billion of kickbacks from lenders, affecting 5.2 million consumers. (*ABC News 20/20*)

Let's compare these unfortunate examples of untrustworthy corporate behavior with the landmark example of Johnson & Johnson which ultimately increased its trustworthiness with consumers by the way it handled the Tylenol incident. After seven individuals, who had consumed Tylenol capsules contaminated by a third party died, Johnson & Johnson instituted a total product recall within a week costing an estimated $50 million after taxes. The company did this, not because it was responsible for causing the problem, but because it was the right thing to do. In addition, Johnson & Johnson spearheaded the development of more effective tamper-proof containers for their industry. Because of the company's swift response, consumers once again were able to trust in the Johnson & Johnson name. Although Johnson & Johnson suffered a decrease in market share at the time because of the scare, over the long term it has maintained its profitability in a highly competitive market. Certainly part of this profit success is attributable to consumers believing that Johnson & Johnson is a trustworthy company. (Robin and Reidenbach)

The e-commerce arena presents another example of the importance of marketers building a mutually valuable relationship with customers through a trust-based collaboration process. Recent research with 50 e-businesses reflects that companies which create and nurture trust find customers return to their sites repeatedly. (Dayal.... p. 64)

In the e-commerce world, six components of trust were found to be critical in developing trusting, satisfied customers:

- State-of-art reliable security measures on one's site
- Merchant legitimacy (e.g., ally one's product or service with an established brand)
- Order fulfillment (i.e. placing orders and getting merchandise efficiently and with minimal hassles)
- Tone and ambiance—handling consumers' personal information with sensitivity and iron-clad confidentiality
- Customers feeling that they are in control of the buying process
- Consumer collaboration—e.g., having chat groups to let consumers query each other about their purchases and experiences (Dayal..., pp. 64–67)

Additionally, one author noted recently that in the e-commerce world we've moved beyond brands and trademarks to "trustmarks." This author defined a trustmark as a

> ... (D)istinctive name or symbol that emotionally binds a company with the desires and aspirations of its customers. It's an emotional connection—and it's much bigger and more powerful than the uses that we traditionally associate with a trademark.... (Webber, p. 214)

Certainly if this is the case, trust—being an emotional link—is of supreme importance for a company that wants to succeed in doing business on the Internet.

It's unfortunate that while a plethora of examples of violation of trust easily come to mind, a paucity of examples "pop up" as noteworthy paradigms of organizational courage and trust in their relationship with consumers.

In conclusion, some key areas for companies to scrutinize and practice with regard to decisions that may affect trustworthiness in the marketplace might include:

- Does a company practice the Golden Rule with its customers? As a company insider, knowing what you know about the product, how willing would you be to purchase it for yourself or for a family member?
- How proud would you be if your marketing practices were made public.... shared with your friends....

or family? (Blanchard and Peale, p. 27)

- Are bottom-line concerns the sole component of your organizational decision-making process? What about human rights, the ecological/environmental impact, and other areas of social responsibility?
- Can a firm which engages in unethical business practices with customers be trusted to deal with its employees any differently? Unfortunately, frequently a willingness to violate standards of ethics is not an isolated phenomenon but permeates the culture. The result is erosion of integrity throughout a company. In such cases, trust is elusive at best. (Shaw, p. 75)
- Is your organization not only market driven, but also value-oriented? (Peters and Levering, Moskowitz, and Katz)
- Is there a strong commitment to a positive corporate culture and a clearly defined mission which is frequently and unambiguously voiced by upper-management?
- Does your organization exemplify trust by practicing a genuine relationship partnership with your customers—*before, during, and after* the initial purchase? (Strout, p. 69)

Companies which exemplify treating customers ethically are founded on a covenant of trust. There is a shared belief, confidence, and faith that the company and its people will be fair, reliable, and ethical in all its dealings. *Total trust is the belief that a company and its people will never take opportunistic advantage of customer vulnerabilities*. (Hart and Johnson, pp. 11–13)

References

ABC News 20/20, "The Car Dealer's Secret," October 27, 2000.

Blanchard, Kenneth, and Norman Vincent Peale, *The Power of Ethical Management*, New York: William Morrow and Company, Inc., 1988.

Chewning, Richard C., *Business Ethics in a Changing Culture* (Reston, Virginia: Reston Publishing, 1984).

Dayal, Sandeep, Landesberg, Helen, and Michael Zeissner, "How to Build Trust Online," *Marketing Management*, Fall 1999, pp. 64–69.

Geyelin, Milo, "Why One Jury Dealt a Big Blow to Chrysler in Minivan-Latch Case," *Wall Street Journal*, November 19, 1997, pp. A1, A10.

Hart, Christopher W. and Michael D. Johnson, "Growing the Trust Relationship," *Marketing Management*, Spring 1999, pp. 9–19.

Hosmer, La Rue Tone, *The Ethics of Management*, second edition (Homewood, Illinois: Irwin, 1991).

Kaydo, Chad, "A Position of Power," *Sales & Marketing Management*, June 2000, pp. 104–106, 108ff.

Levering, Robert; Moskowitz, Milton; and Michael Katz, *The 100 Best Companies to Work for in America* (Reading, Mass.: Addison-Wesley, 1984).

Magnet, Myron, "Meet the New Revolutionaries," *Fortune*, February 24, 1992, pp. 94–101.

Muoio, Anna, "The Experienced Customer," *Net Company*, Fall 1999, pp. 025–027.

Peters, Thomas J. and Robert H. Waterman Jr., *In Search of Excellence* (New York: Harper & Row, 1982).

Richardson, John (ed.), *Annual Editions: Business Ethics 00/01* (Guilford, CT: McGraw-Hill/Dushkin, 2000).

_____, *Annual Editions: Marketing 00/01* (Guilford, CT: McGraw-Hill/Dushkin, 2000).

Robin, Donald P., and Erich Reidenbach, "Social Responsibility, Ethics, and Marketing Strategy: Closing the Gap Between Concept and Application," *Journal of Marketing*, Vol. 51 (January 1987), pp. 44–58.

Shaw, Robert Bruce, *Trust in the Balance*, (San Francisco: Jossey-Bass Publishers, 1997).

Strout, Erin, "Tough Customers," *Sales Marketing Management*, January 2000, pp. 63–69.

Webber, Alan M., "Trust in the Future," *Fast Company*, September 2000, pp. 209–212ff.

Dr. John E. Richardson *is Professor of Marketing in the Graziadio School of Business and Management at Pepperdine University, Malibu, California*

Dr. Linnea Bernard McCord *is Associate Professor of Business Law in the Graziadio School of Business and Management at Pepperdine University, Malibu, California*

GLASS BREAKERS

Are women in business still expected to exceed expectations? What should women ask before accepting a job offer? What does Tupperware have to do with women's lib? Can the number of women on corporate boards really quadruple in the next decade? What does it take to smash through a real, honest-to-god glass ceiling? And what does a businesswoman resemble more: a windmill or a fax machine [and why would we even ask such a question]? All is revealed in our special report.

John Gray

WHAT'S AT THE ROOT OF COMMUNICATION CHALLENGES BETWEEN MEN AND WOMEN AT WORK?

First of all, let's be clear that everything I say is a generalization. I'm not claiming all women or men feel or act any particular way, but these are patterns I see quite commonly.

One way to characterize the way the sexes do business differently is that on Mars there are rules, while on Venus there are manners. Fundamentally, it's the way they approach solutions, starting with the listening process. Men need to win the trust of women by learning how to listen—women claim men never listen, and I've heard 17 reasons why they believe this. One of them is that a woman will start to talk, the man thinks he sees where she is going and gets antsy, so he interrupts and gives her a "solution." She thinks, "He didn't hear me out, he doesn't value what I say." Women want to spend more time sharing thoughts about a problem before looking at a solution. He thinks she's indecisive because she didn't get to the solution right away. He thinks she didn't have a solution, but he didn't actually ask for one, just offered his own. My advice to male managers is that if you don't want to have the whole conversation, interrupt with a question, not a solution.

"Most women are not obsessed with getting to the top, but with being rewarded equally."

THE DIFFERENT APPROACHES TO PROBLEM SOLVING ARE PROBLEMS IN AND OF THEMSELVES.

Right. Let me give another example. Two women are standing by a copy machine talking about how it doesn't work right. A guy comes by, and they ask him why it hasn't been fixed. The women are bonding, building the team, and coming to the best solution through sharing ideas. But the way the man sees it, they're wasting time complaining, so he points out that there's a copier down the hall. That alienates them. If he had had Mars-Venus coaching, he'd have known to say something empathetic before offering a solution. Acknowledge the hassle of getting the copier fixed.

On the other hand, if a female manager had come by, she'd probably have found the guy trying to find out what was wrong with the copier without asking for help. She'd think he was wasting time by letting his macho ego get in the way. Both ways of dealing with the problem are actually due to how the male and female handle stress differently.

IN WHAT WAY?

Women have three basic things that help them cope with stress. First is collaboration—working as a team. Second, harmony—working together in cooperation. Third, communication—sharing so that everyone knows what's going on inside everyone else. These processes actually cause women's bodies to produce a hormone, which is their best way to deal with stress. The best stress-protection mechanism for men is testosterone. It makes them feel they can accomplish things. When men are confident they can solve a problem, their stress levels go down. We're firemen who want to put out the fire as fast as we can. We go immediately to a solution.

HOW DO MEN AND WOMEN DIFFER WHEN IT COMES TO GIVING AND RECEIVING CRITICISM, OR SHOWING APPRECIATION?

Men think that if they don't complain, that shows appreciation. Women say that on Venus, appreciation has to be overtly expressed, and good managers show interest by being involved.

Generally, men handle criticism in a hierarchical fashion. The boss doesn't have to convince a male employee, just tell him what he wants him to do: "Don't call Bill, call Phil." Women prefer to get feedback—"Don't you think you might get a better answer from Phil than Bill?" Men may react, "Why do you ask me what I think when you're the boss?" They feel there is some manipulative agenda, while the female boss is expressing Venusian manners by not being confrontational, asking if together they can't come up with a better solution.

I advise women managers to be more direct. Women managers or even co-workers will also ask questions to gather information because they want to improve things. Men are likely to feel that if it ain't broke, don't fix it, and that the women are wasting time talking about fires that don't exist. Female employees want to discuss the options with their managers. They feel the typical male manager is too authoritarian and makes them feel incompetent. When it comes to criticism, women tend to take it personally; men experience it with more distance. Women feel men should

be asking for help to understand why women do things a certain way.

HOW SOLID IS THE GLASS CEILING?

A survey of the top money-making women in the U.S. asked what was responsible for their success. The answer they most consistently gave was "exceeding expectations." In other words, they have to perform better than a man might in a similar position to be recognized. However, most women are not obsessed with getting to the top, but with being rewarded equally.

> "Women and minorities make the majority of all consumer decisions, and yet, they're not represented at the apex of where policy is made."

What we're really talking about with regard to reaching the very upper levels of management is usually the need for an extreme Type A personality. Many women are not willing to make the sacrifices involved because they value the quality of their personal lives and relationships more than that. They're not as insane as men. —SCOTT SMITH

JOHN GRAY specializes in the communication (or lack thereof) between the sexes. A family therapist, and author of the 1992 bestseller *Men Are from Mars, Women Are from Venus,* he has most recently turned his attention to how gender differences play out at work.

Change of Heart

A landmark survey reveals that most Americans are open to sharing their life, work, and even love with people of a different color. So why do tensions remain?

By Adam Goodheart

The rural Maryland county where I live, barely an hour from the Washington, D.C., Beltway, is a place whose soul is not just divided but fractured. There are still small towns here that feel like the Old South, where whites talk about "colored people" and blacks in their late 40s remember such things as farming with mules and horses and attending segregated schools. But there are newer communities, too: sprawling tracts of identical suburban houses whose middle-class residents—black as well as white—think little about the past and care even less. In their midst, a small but growing Hispanic population has started to thrive, drawn by the economic opportunities that change has brought.

Many parts of our country today look something like this. When President Lyndon Johnson's Kerner Commission famously prophesied in 1968 a future of "two societies, one black, one white," it was wrong. What we have now is a multiplicity of Americas, often sharing the same neighborhood, but rarely the same mindset.

The good news is that in the 50 years since the Supreme Court ruled in favor of school desegregation in the case of *Brown* v. *Board of Education,* there have been some dramatic changes in Americans' attitudes toward race and equality. Today, most Americans—55 percent—think that the state of race relations is either very or somewhat good, according to a landmark telephone survey of 2,002 people conducted last November and December by the Gallup Organization for AARP and the Leadership Conference on Civil Rights (LCCR). Yet disheartening divisions between the races persist. Such is the complicated picture painted by "Civil Rights and Race Relations," the largest and most comprehensive race-relations survey of blacks, Hispanics, and whites that Gallup has ever undertaken.

The most astonishing progress has been made in two areas that hit closest to home for most Americans: interracial relationships and the neighborhoods we live in. Consider that 70 percent of whites now say they approve of marriage between whites and blacks, up from just 4 percent in a 1958 Gallup poll. Such open-mindedness extends across racial lines: 80 percent of blacks and 77 percent of Hispanics also said they generally approve of interracial marriage. Perhaps even more remarkable, a large majority of white respondents—66 percent—say they would not object if their own child or grandchild chose a black spouse. Blacks (86 percent) and Hispanics (79 percent) were equally accepting about a child or grandchild's marrying someone of another race.

When it comes to choosing neighbors, an inclusive spirit again prevails: majorities of blacks, whites, and Hispanics all say they would rather live in racially mixed neighborhoods than surround themselves with only members of their own group. "It's hard now to imagine the level of fear and anxiety that Americans felt about these issues just a few decades ago," says Taylor Branch, who won a Pulitzer Prize in 1989 for his history of the Civil Rights Movement, *Parting the Waters: America in the King Years, 1954-1963.* "The idea [among whites] that you might have a black colleague or customer or neighbor has now become relatively commonplace except in a few scattered pockets." Similarly, slight majorities of whites and Hispanics and a little less than half of blacks think that minorities should try to blend in with the rest of American culture rather than maintain their own separate identities.

The data did show a significant generation gap: young Americans (ages 18-29) of all races were more likely than older respondents (65-plus) to favor the retention of distinctive cultures. But this is not necessarily a step backward. "Younger people are more likely to have been exposed in school to the idea that multiculturalism is a positive thing, that it's not necessarily bad when certain groups desire to be among their own kind," suggests the eminent Harvard sociologist William Julius Wilson. "This is a phenomenon of just the last couple of decades."

When it comes to future expectations, however, in certain respects the picture is as bleak as ever. Sixty-three percent of Americans think that race relations will always be a problem for our country—a view that varies little whether the respondents are white, black, or Hispanic.

Survey Insights

Our respondents told us that they...

1. Would not object to a child or grandchild's marrying someone of another race.

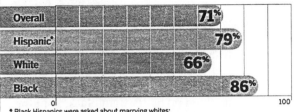

Overall	71%
Hispanic*	79%
White	66%
Black	86%

* Black Hispanics were asked about marrying whites; white Hispanics were asked about marrying blacks.

2. Prefer to live in a neighborhood that is mostly mixed.

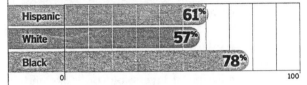

Hispanic	61%
White	57%
Black	78%

3. Believe race relations will always be a problem in the U.S.

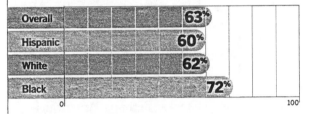

Overall	63%
Hispanic	60%
White	62%
Black	72%

4. Think all or most of the goals of Dr. Martin Luther King Jr. and the Civil Rights Movement have been achieved.

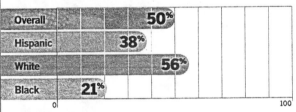

Overall	50%
Hispanic	38%
White	56%
Black	21%

5. Have been denied a rental or an opportunity to buy a home.

Hispanic	19%
White	2%
Black	24%

*Civil Rights and Race Relations," a study commissioned by AARP and the LCCR and conducted by the Gallup Oranization, is based on telephone interviews with 2,002 people 18 years of age or older from households in the continental United States. All polling was conducted between November 11 and December 14, 2003. The respondents included 915 whites and oversamples of 446 blacks and 551 Hispanics. In addition, 90 who belonged to other groups or gave no racial or ethnic affiliation were interviewed. The results were weighted to reflect the actual representation of each group in the U.S. population. ("Whites" refers to non-Hispanic whites; "black" refers to non-Hispanic blacks; and the "Hispanic" category includes all Hispanics, whether they identified as black or as white or did not specify a racial category.) The margin of error at the 95 percent confidence level for that total national sample is +/-5.1 percentage points. +/-6.7 percentage points for whites, +/-8.5 percentage points for blacks, and +/-6.2 percentage points for Hispanics.

That's up sharply from the 42 percent who felt similarly in a study done in 1963, when most Americans were seeing television images of African Americans withstanding police dogs and fire hoses but believed the Civil Rights Movement would eventually prevail. (Indeed, respondents over 65, who remember the 1960s well, were the ones most likely to remain optimistic, while those under 30—of all races—were the least hopeful.)

"There was a sense then that eventually truth and justice would win out," recalls Julian Bond, who as a founder of the Student Nonviolent Coordinating Committee (SNCC) led some of the earliest sit-ins and is now chairman of the National Association for the Advancement of Colored People (NAACP). "Maybe people are looking back and realizing we haven't come as far as we'd hoped."

A large majority of Americans of all ages and races does agree that the 20th-century crusade for civil rights was a watershed in our nation's history. In addition, most people of all backgrounds also believe that the movement has benefited not just blacks and other minorities but all Americans. This is a remarkable degree of unanimity for an issue that violently divided so many families and communities just a generation or two ago.

"The Civil Rights Movement has had enormous collateral effects for everyone from gays to members of religious minorities, and especially for women," Branch says. "These effects have been felt in every university, every corporation, and even, I'd venture to say, almost every American household, down to the level of who does the dishes and changes the diapers."

But when it comes to gauging the ultimate success or failure of the struggle, members of different races diverge sharply. While 56 percent of whites say they believe that "all or most" of the goals of Dr. Martin Luther King Jr. and the 1960s Civil Rights Movement have been achieved, only 21 percent of blacks agree with them. A similar margin divides whites' and blacks' opinions on how much of a role the movement will continue to have: 66 percent of blacks think it will be "extremely important" to the United States in the future, compared with only 23 percent of whites. "Many whites have a misconception of the Civil Rights Movement as something with a few limited goals that have already been achieved," Branch suggests.

Similarly, the AARP-LCCR survey found vast gulfs between different groups' perceptions of how minorities are treated today. Seventy-six percent of white respondents think that blacks are treated "very fairly" or "somewhat fairly," but only 38 percent of blacks agree with them; nearly one-third, in fact, say that members of their race are treated "very unfairly." (Hispanics fall in the middle: they are more or less evenly divided about the treatment of their own group as well as that of blacks.) And while 61 percent of whites believe that blacks have achieved equality in the realm of job opportunities, just 12 percent of African Americans concur.

How is it that we can all share the same land, the same history, and yet reach such different conclusions? The disparities start to make sense when you look at the most fundamental measure of each group's current happiness: economic prosperity.

Blacks are more than twice as likely as whites to say that their personal finances are in "poor shape"; they are also more than twice as likely to say they worry constantly about whether their family's income will be enough to pay the bills. Hispanics appear to be feeling similar or even greater degrees of financial stress. And indeed, their concerns are legitimate: nationally, the median household income is $35,500 among blacks, $40,000 among Hispanics, and $55,318 among whites, according to the most recent figures available from the U.S. Census Bureau.

"Were we to have solved all the problems that we tried to take on, there would be relative parity today," Bond says. "The fact that there is still an enormous wealth gap between blacks and whites is evidence of the continuing legacy of segregation and even of slavery."

What explains these persistent economic disparities? Continued prejudice, plain and simple. Half a century after *Brown*, a minuscule 8 percent of African Americans could claim that they had ever in their lives been denied admittance to a school on account of race. Yet other forms of discrimination persist. A third reported that they had been passed over for a job because they are black, a third said they had been blocked from promotion, and a quarter said they had been denied an opportunity to rent or buy housing. Only slightly fewer Hispanics said they had experienced similar forms of prejudice.

Even more than such dramatic instances of racism, it is the less obvious, day-to-day examples of prejudice that are a continuing, grinding burden on minorities in America. Nearly half of all blacks reported having experienced at least one form of discrimination in the last 30 days, in settings ranging from stores (26 percent) to restaurants and theaters (18 percent) to public transportation (10 per-

cent). The figures for Hispanics were at nearly the same level. Perhaps most troubling of all, a surprising 22 percent of blacks and 24 percent of Hispanics said they had, in the past month, been the victims of prejudice in an interaction with the police.

For the record, a significant number of white Americans maintain that they, too, are sometimes penalized on the basis of race: 21 percent report that they have been the victims of reverse discrimination, especially in the workplace. And many seem unaware or even dismissive of continuing prejudice against other groups: nearly half insist that society treats them no better than blacks. But the majority of whites—52 percent—say they support affirmative action for blacks, as do 81 percent of blacks and 66 percent of Hispanics. So while an uncomfortably large number of Americans remain in denial about persistent discrimination against minorities, an even larger percentage, it seems, want to do the right thing.

Like the American countryside, the AARP-LCCR survey results are a landscape of layers: old outlooks and new perceptions, 20th-century memories and 21st-century expectations. One of the most unexpected results came when the polltakers asked participants to consider the prediction that by 2050 the majority of Americans will be nonwhite. Only about 13 percent of each group said this would be a bad thing; most Americans said it simply won't matter.

So, as their country changes, perhaps Americans—more than they are often given credit for—are ready to change along with it. Indeed, the revolution that *Brown* started will likely continue through the next 50 years and beyond. "We did much," Bond says, "but there's much left to do."

Adam Goodheart is a fellow of the C. V. Starr Center for the Study of the American Experience at Washington College in Chestertown, Maryland.

Privacy in the Age of Transparency

A tough customer ethic demands corporate openness and integrity.

by Jeffrey Rothfeder

It's not often that a blue-chip CEO publicly lectures another CEO from a brand-name company about how he should manage his organization. Then again, it's not often that the practices of one company upset employees of another one so strongly.

The incident occurred in 1999 when Amazon.com introduced *purchase circles*, an online marketing tool that, supposedly for the customer's benefit, revealed what books Amazon's customers from some well-known corporations were buying. For example, customers from Microsoft, it appeared, liked to read *The Microsoft File: The Secret Case Against Bill Gates,* by Wendy Goldman Rohm, a book that was critical of top management at the software giant. A book about operating system upstart Linux was a hit at Intel.

IBM favorites were also exposed on the Amazon site. As a group, IBM employees weren't reading anything particularly heretical, but Big Blue's then–chief executive Louis V. Gerstner Jr. didn't like the voyeuristic aspects of the purchase circles, and polled IBM's workers for their reactions to Amazon's new program. Gerstner was inundated with 5,000 e-mails within hours; more than 90

percent expressed displeasure about having their corporate book-buying behavior displayed online. Gerstner passed this finding along to Amazon, and IBM was removed from the purchase circles.

As an embarrassing coda, an excerpt from a letter Gerstner sent to Amazon CEO Jeff Bezos was leaked to *The New York Times*. In it, Gerstner cautioned: "I'm certainly not going to tell you how to run your business, but I do urge you to view this as an enormously important issue."

That anecdote, related by Don Tapscott and David Ticoll in their new book, *The Naked Corporation: How the Age of Transparency Will Revolutionize Business,* illustrates well the delicate balancing act companies face in satisfying the imperative to provide an increasingly personalized and streamlined relationship with customers, suppliers and other business partners, and simultaneously keeping the data they've collected about them confidential.

Companies are entering an era of information transparency—a result, Tapscott and Ticoll say, of increasingly activist stakeholders, the growing influence of global markets, the spread of communications technology, and a

new customer ethic demanding openness, honesty and integrity from companies. Consequently, risks to privacy are greater, and safeguarding sensitive information has become more significant, and more difficult to do. Among the companies given high marks by privacy advocates for making data protection a priority are Dell, IBM, Intel, Microsoft, Procter & Gamble, Time Warner and Verizon. Some of these companies—such as Microsoft, which has in the past been plagued by security leaks in its operating system and e-commerce programs—have embraced hard-line privacy stances only after experiencing first-hand the potential damage to their businesses that privacy breaches can inflict.

Business-to-consumer companies that fail to protect customer data can lose the trust and loyalty of customers, and drive them to other companies with which they feel more comfortable sharing personal information. That, in turn, has the somewhat ironic effect of providing privacy-friendly companies with the greatest aggregate database of valuable demographic, purchasing, and financial information about customers. This sensitive data can be a goldmine for cross-selling additional products and targeting direct mailings on the basis of customer preferences—as long as these sales campaigns are handled gingerly so that consumers feel that their privacy is respected.

There's persuasive evidence that consumers are becoming even more protective of their personal information with the increased prevalence of Internet shopping and the aggressive data collection about shoppers by consumer product companies. The most thought-provoking statistics have been published by *Privacy and American Business (P&AB)*, a monthly newsletter co-founded by Alan F. Westin, a well-known information privacy expert and professor emeritus of public law and government at Columbia University. *P&AB* is published by the Center for Social & Legal Research, a data-protection think tank. According to the research in *P&AB*'s September 2003 issue, 36 percent of the American public, some 75 million adults, call themselves "Privacy Fundamentalists." These are people who are passionate about threats to their privacy by businesses and favor government regulation of corporate information practices. That's a huge leap from 2000, when only 25 percent of respondents to a similar survey fit this category. Moreover, in 2003, *P&AB* found that 53 percent of Americans (10 percent fewer than in 2000) could currently be categorized as "Privacy Pragmatists," that is, people who will freely exchange personal information if the benefits they receive are perceived as greater than the privacy risks they're taking.

Professor Westin used other survey data to explain the increase in Fundamentalists and decrease in Pragmatists and to draw the following conclusions: Fifty-six percent of Americans don't believe most businesses handle consumers' personal information in a manner they consider to be proper; 59 percent do not think the existing mixed public-private system of protecting consumer privacy is providing a "reasonable" level of assurance.

Consumers have adopted these beliefs after being exposed to a growing array of privacy intrusions. Since 1990, 33.4 million Americans have been victims of identity theft—in this case, defined as the theft of personal information with the intent to use it for fraudulent purposes. Half of these crimes occurred in the last two years, according to *P&AB*. There are also many disconcerting ways individual privacy is invaded. It's impossible for individuals to use the Internet without being interrupted by cookies-based marketing piggybacking on Web surfing and purchasing habits; video and biometric surveillance is unavoidable in public places and at work; and in numerous instances, medical and financial databanks have leaked personal information and cost people their jobs, reputations or both.

The scale and impact of these unwelcome trends is chronicled extensively in *Database Nation: The Death of Privacy in the 21st Century*, by long-time privacy activist Simson Garfinkel. In this book, Garfinkel is implacable about the importance of privacy to individuals and why people are so protective of it: "Privacy is about self-possession, autonomy, and integrity.... Over the next fifty years we will see new kinds of threats to privacy that don't find their roots in totalitarianism, but in capitalism, the free market, advanced technology, and the unbridled exchange of electronic information."

That statement may be a bit harsh, but the *P&AB* surveys, as well as other recent polls, indicate that consumers share many of Garfinkel's concerns. Somewhat surprisingly, considering the depth of consumer wariness, this attitude represents an opportunity for companies, if they're willing to develop robust privacy programs. This is a central theme of *The Naked Corporation* and an earlier book, *The Privacy Payoff: How Suc-*

cessful Businesses Build Consumer Trust, by the privacy commissioner of Ontario, Canada, Ann Cavoukian, and journalist Tyler J. Hamilton. Both books argue that the companies that are open and honest in their communications, adopt privacy policies and are very clear about how they use collected data discreetly to further corporate growth, efficiency and performance will benefit from wider consumer acceptance in international markets. This, they further argue, is what leads to increased revenue, less litigation from the aggrieved, enhanced reputations for their brands and more prospective partners willing to enter into lucrative cooperative ventures that require a deep well of trust.

Privacy Payoff points readers to a very powerful instrument for determining how well their companies are complying with fair information practices and to what extent these businesses promote the protection of customer privacy. It's called the Privacy Diagnostic Tool Workbook (www.ipc.on.ca/english/resources/resources.htm), and it assesses such essential privacy principles as limiting the collection, disclosure and retention of records; instituting customer consent procedures to opt in or opt out of data-sharing programs; verifying accuracy of records; and protecting data from hackers. In addition, *Privacy Payoff*'s authors provide a Privacy Impact Assessment questionnaire in the book that companies can use to ensure that new technology—whether databank, biometric security system, video camera, ERP system or others—complies with privacy requirements.

Importantly, the authors of *Privacy Payoff* note, privacy policies and systems are just as pivotal to the success of business-to-business relationships as they are to business-to-consumer interactions. More and more companies are entering into joint ventures, either Internet- or extranet-based, to increase efficiency and innovation in supply chains, inventory management, customer relations and other business

PRIVACY RESOURCES

Works mentioned in this review.

Ann Cavoukian and Tyler J. Hamilton, *The Privacy Payoff: How Successful Businesses Build Consumer Trust* (McGraw-Hill, 2002), 288 pages, $24.95.

Michael Erbschloe and John Vacca, *Net Privacy: A Guide to Developing and Implementing an Ironclad E-Business Privacy Plan* (McGraw-Hill, 2001), 318 pages, $24.95.

Simson Garfinkel, *Database Nation: The Death of Privacy in the 21st Century* (O'Reilley & Associates, 2001), 336 pages, $16.95.

Albert J. Marcella Jr. and Carol Stucki, *Privacy Handbook: Guidelines, Exposures, Policy Implementation, and International Issues* (John Wiley & Sons, 2003), 384 pages, $80.

Don Tapscott and David Ticoll, *The Naked Corporation: How the Age of Transparency Will Revolutionize Business* (Free Press, 2003), 368 pages, $28.

Guide to Consumer Privacy in Japan and the New Japanese Personal Information Protection Law, by Alan F. Westin and Vivian van Gelder (Privacy & American Business, 2003). For a free copy, e-mail Irene Oujo at ioujo@pandab.org

Privacy & American Business newsletter: www.pandab.org

Privacy Diagnostic Tool Workbook: www.ipc.on.ca/english/resources/resources.htm

U.S. Department of Commerce Safe Harbor site: www.export.gov/safeharbor

business around the world, companies have had to adapt to local cultures and regulations. Privacy rules vary wildly throughout the globe, and navigating this thicket of laws is critical to international commerce. This is particularly important for American companies, because the U.S. has weak data-protection rules. As a result, a U.S. firm with toothless, but legal, privacy policies could be forbidden from, for instance, sending payroll files or customer purchasing records to an affiliate in a country where shipping data from one place to another is strictly regulated.

Privacy Handbook: Guidelines, Exposures, Policy Implementation, and International Issues, by IT experts Albert J. Marcella Jr. and Carol Stucki, provides an overview of global data protection regulations and laws, and a large number of resources for staying on the right side of them. The book's country-by-country breakdown of privacy regulations is particularly well researched, covering small nations as well as large ones. Bulgaria's constitution explicitly states that "the privacy of citizens shall be inviolable," and in 1997 Bulgaria enacted a tough Personal Data Protection Act. This law requires that organizations collecting personal information must inform people why their data is being gathered and what it will be used for; allow people access to information about themselves and give them the right to correct it; ensure that the information is securely held and cannot be improperly used; and limit the use of personal information for purposes other than the original reason unless they have the consent of the person affected.

The effort that Bulgaria and other nations with similarly tough policies have put into enacting strong privacy policies places in stark relief how little the U.S. has done: The term *privacy* doesn't appear in the Constitution, and no specific set of laws in the U.S. governs the level of data protection companies must provide. In fact, the lack of mandated privacy safeguards has gotten U.S.

companies into hot water with the European Union.

In 2000, after months of negotiation with U.S. Department of Commerce officials, the United States devised a series of privacy policies that reward American companies that voluntarily agree to adhere to them. In exchange for following these rules, U.S. companies have the right to collect data from E.U. citizens, which can include anything from consumer credit information to personnel records of employees at subsidiary operations.

Fifty-six percent of Americans believe most businesses don't handle consumers' personal information properly.

These so-called safe harbor rules, which are essentially a slightly watered-down version of the E.U.'s landmark 1995 Directive on Data Protection and are similar to the four principles in the Bulgaria example, are detailed in *Privacy Handbook, Privacy Payoff,* and at www.export.gov/safeharbor, a Department of Commerce site. Safe harbor companies are automatically granted permission to transfer data anywhere in Europe, streamlining communications between their U.S. headquarters and overseas affiliates and avoiding the cumbersome process of having to negotiate a potentially stricter privacy contract with each E.U. firm to which they want to send data. To date, nearly 500 U.S. companies have been certified by the Commerce Department as having adopted privacy policies consistent with E.U. requirements.

Few U.S. companies will be able to avoid Europe's strict view of how data must be protected, say information strategy consultants Michael Erbschloe and John Vacca in *Net Privacy: A Guide to Developing and Implementing an Ironclad E-Business Privacy Plan.* Japan also recently passed its

operations. As part of these cooperative undertakings, sensitive and proprietary corporate data is shared among all partners. If strict measures and rules are not in place to safeguard private information—such as customer, manufacturing, design and marketing files—companies can end up unwittingly broadcasting some of their most valuable intellectual assets.

Globalization is another noteworthy factor behind the increased attention being paid to privacy. To do first omnibus privacy law, which Professor Westin at P&AB accurately describes as "a 'middle way' between the industry-sector-based privacy laws of the U.S. and the comprehensive data protection laws of the European Union." *P&AB* offers the *Guide to Consumer Privacy in Japan and the New Japanese Personal Information Protection Law* to explain the data-protection climate in Japan and help companies navigate the legislation.

Although many U.S. companies initially fought consumers' efforts to make companies pay attention to privacy, almost no major businesses today feel they can completely neglect data protection rules. That doesn't always mean that leading companies make the right privacy choices. (Recall the JetBlue episode in 2003, in which the airline ran afoul of customers when it shared flight records with a Pentagon contractor that was building a travel security database.) It is also interesting to see how some companies are using privacy to enhance their brand images. The Internet service provider (ISP) EarthLink has run a humorous ad campaign accusing other unnamed ISPs of sharing personal information and promising to be much more discreet. Microsoft has launched a project called Trustworthy Computing, under which Chairman Bill Gates has challenged the company to be certain that availability, security, privacy and trustworthiness are key components of every software and service product the company develops.

These are just a few examples of how seriously companies today look upon privacy. There's a strong indication that, because of scrupulous motives, strategic imperatives or the cynical notion that privacy sells, in the future there aren't likely to be any more embarrassing CEO-to-CEO rebukes like the one Jeff Bezos received.

Jeffrey Rothfeder [jrothfeder@comcast.net] writes frequently for *Strategy + Business* and other leading business publications. He is the author of *Privacy for Sale: How Computerization Has Made Everyone's Private Life an Open Secret* [Simon & Schuster, 1992]. His most recent book is *Every Drop for Sale: Our Desperate Battle Over Water in a World About to Run Out* [Penguin Putnam, Jeremy P. Tarcher, 2001].

A Dose of Denial

How drug makers sought to keep popular cold and diet remedies on store shelves after their own study linked them to strokes.

By Kevin Sack and Alicia Mundy

Tracy Patton had just arrived at a community theater rehearsal in August 2000 when she felt such a searing explosion in the back of her head that it knocked her to her knees.

At the hospital in Louisville, Ky., doctors said Patton, then 37, had suffered a catastrophic stroke, and they predicted she wouldn't survive the night.

Patton defied the odds. But nearly four years later, she is so overwhelmed by simple tasks that she must post a "personal hygiene checklist" in her bathroom to remind herself to brush her teeth and flush the toilet.

At 15, Tricia Newenham was full of promise when she suffered her stroke in October 2000 while hanging out in her bedroom with a cousin. A Down East Mainer from a family of woodsmen and lobstermen, she had been named her middle school's student of the year and was on track to become the first Newenham to attend college.

She spent a month in a coma, and emerged totally blind and profoundly mentally impaired. When reminiscing about her former self, about her prom dates and nights at the movies, she dissolves into inconsolable sobbing, condemned to remember just enough of what her life was like then to understand how much less it is now.

Only hours before these devastating strokes, each victim had washed down a seemingly innocuous over-the-counter cold medicine, one of billions of doses consumed annually nationwide. The medicines contained phenylpropanolamine, or PPA, the active ingredient in scores of popular nonprescription decongestants and diet aids until November 2000, when the Food and Drug Administration declared PPA unsafe and asked drug companies to stop selling it.

By then, the drug industry had spent more than two decades fending off growing evidence of a possible link between PPA and hemorrhagic stroke. But Patton and Newenham were among hundreds of PPA consumers who suffered attacks after a landmark study—sponsored by the drug industry itself—concluded in October 1999 that the use of PPA was associated with an increased risk of that deadliest form of stroke.

Recently obtained internal company documents show that rather than alerting the public during cold season, drug makers launched a yearlong campaign to keep the results quiet and stall government regulation. By the time the FDA acted, 13 months and hundreds of strokes later, the companies had reformulated their brand names with little interruption in sales. The market for PPA has been estimated at $500 million to $1 billion annually.

In the interim, Americans continued to purchase PPA products right off the shelf and assume they were safe.

"It never even dawned on us," said Tim A. Bybee, Newenham's stepfather, speaking of the Triaminic cold syrup Tricia took shortly before her stroke. "It was in the store. Everyone uses it. It must be all right."

The Times reviewed thousands of pages of documents produced through discovery in PPA lawsuits and obtained from the FDA through a Freedom of Information Act request. The documents demonstrate that the pharmaceutical industry consistently challenged any notion that PPA could be dangerous and dismissed evidence to the contrary. They also show that the manufacturers assured the public that PPA was safe even as some FDA scientists and industry officials were raising concerns.

As early as 1982, an FDA report warned that PPA had "the ability to cause cardiovascular effects, cerebral hemorrhage and cardiac arrhythmias." Two years later, a memo from the medical services department at Sandoz Pharmaceuticals, which made the PPA products Triaminic and Tavist-D, referred to PPA as "an agent known to cause hypertension and stroke."

Yet the drug companies accelerated their marketing of PPA, winning FDA approval to sell prescription PPA products on an over-the-counter basis and introducing flavorful new formulas for children.

Upon learning that the 1999 study had found a stroke link, the drug makers opened a relentless assault on its methodology and on the integrity of the Yale University researchers who conducted it. They did so despite having paid for the five-year, $5-million study themselves, approving its protocol and handpicking investigators who had previously expressed skepticism about a link between PPA and stroke.

Some documents show that the companies hoped to survive the 2000 cold season without pulling PPA products. Rarely do the internal memos indicate concern by corporate officials that PPA might pose a threat to the public.

Early in November 2000, for instance, two weeks after an FDA advisory panel concluded that PPA could be hazardous, an official with Bayer, which made Alka-Seltzer Plus with PPA, drafted a proposed "PPA Crisis Action Plan." Its stated objectives: "Delay mandatory implementation of FDA recommendation. Blunt PR impact by highlighting questionable study conclusions as they pertain to cough/cold products. Begin shipping PPA-free product as soon as possible."

Terry O. Tottenham, a lawyer for Bayer, said the plan was not implemented. But records and interviews show the industry largely followed that course.

The FDA eventually recommended the withdrawal of more than 100 PPA products, including popular cough and cold brands such as Robitussin CF and Dimetapp, and appetite suppressants such as Dexatrim and Acutrim. FDA officials said they did not move faster because the industry's efforts to discredit the Yale results effectively delayed the delivery of a final report.

"There were obvious concerns that we weren't getting the data because it was being held up by the people who sponsored the study," said Dr. Charles J. Ganley, director of the FDA's Division of Over-the-Counter Drug Products.

Left in the Dark

Once the FDA stepped in, the manufacturers issued press releases, posted notices on websites and wrote letters to doctors, pharmacists and retailers advising them of the agency's action. But after the products were withdrawn, neither the companies nor the FDA mounted major advertising or direct-mail campaigns to warn Americans they might have dangerous products in their handbags and homes.

A survey commissioned by plaintiffs in lawsuits over PPA estimated that 3.5 million U.S. households still possessed PPA formulations a full 15 months after the withdrawals were requested in November 2000.

The wife of a Mississippi stroke victim says she purchased Alka-Seltzer Plus with PPA from a convenience store in April 2001, six months after it was supposed to have been removed. Her 45-year-old husband took two packets over two days, began convulsing, and now is confined to a wheelchair, according to his lawyer. Both the retailer and the wholesaler have testified in depositions that they were never alerted by Bayer or the FDA. The couple

are suing Bayer and Double Quick Inc., the retailer.

Even now, the industry's attacks on the study it commissioned are its primary defense against more than 2,500 lawsuits filed by plaintiffs who say they suffered strokes shortly after taking products with PPA.

Spokespersons for each of the major manufacturers of PPA products said in interviews or written responses that they continued to believe PPA was safe, despite the study's findings.

"We did not believe then, nor do we believe now, that PPA was dangerous," wrote Tottenham, the Bayer lawyer. "In fact, we believe the PPA in those medications was safe and effective and did not, in any way, cause or contribute to hemorrhagic stroke or any other circulatory disease, when used as directed." Tottenham said that there was "no valid scientific evidence" of an association and that the Yale study, when "properly analyzed, does nothing to change this conclusion."

The Consumer Healthcare Products Assn. (CHPA), the leading nonprescription drug trade group, declined to comment for this article.

But its former longtime president, James D. Cope, who took a previously scheduled retirement shortly after the study's completion, said the drug companies would have been well-advised to accept the findings. "Industry was convinced that if a proper study would be done, the results would come out where they wanted them: safe and effective," he said. "It didn't. And since it didn't, and they designed the best study they could, I think they have to live with it."

The manufacturers include some of the largest drug companies in the world— Bayer; Novartis, which absorbed Sandoz in a merger; Wyeth, which makes Dimetapp and Robitussin CF; Glaxo-SmithKline, which makes Contac; and the former Thompson Medical Co., which made Dexatrim until Chattem Inc. bought the line late in 1998.

Doctors and scientists cannot say for sure that PPA caused Patton, Newenham or any other victim to have a stroke. Many of those who suffered strokes after taking PPA were particularly susceptible to blood pressure spikes because they suffered from one of several conditions affecting tens of millions of Americans.

Some had hypertension, which afflicts one in five Americans. Patton was among the estimated 3% of Americans with cerebral aneurysms, which can pop if blood pressure rises suddenly. Newenham had an

arteriovenous malformation, a circulatory defect that can make vessels prone to rupture. Neither Patton nor Newenham knew about their conditions before their strokes.

If PPA had been a lifesaving drug, the benefits might have more clearly outweighed the risks to such a large segment of the population. But though it unclogged countless stuffy noses and helped millions of dieters shed a few pounds, PPA was neither essential nor irreplaceable.

What made it worth fighting for were its sales, estimated at several billion doses a year. In a deposition, Robert G. Donovan, the former head of Sandoz Consumer Health Care, said the profitability of the company's two PPA products was about 75% to 80% of revenue.

Years before the Yale Hemorrhagic Stroke Project, clinical studies and individual cases published in medical journals began to raise concerns about PPA.

Sandoz was among several companies that considered reformulating their cold products with comparably effective ingredients, primarily pseudoephedrine, which had been used safely for years and gained final FDA approval in 1994. But pseudoephedrine cost more than PPA. And it had a bitter taste that was more difficult to mask, an important consideration for the pediatric market. The manufacturers concluded there was no reason to switch.

"There appears to be little, if any, upside business potential in reformulating from both a consumer and professional standpoint," wrote the marketing director of pediatric cough and cold products for Sandoz in a 1988 memo included in litigation records.

"Few consumers are aware of [over-the-counter] cough/cold products' active ingredients," he wrote. "Fewer still would be aware of any safety issues with PPA."

In depositions, many industry officials have tried to shift responsibility to the FDA.

"My assumption was that if there was an issue of safety, supported by sound evidence, that the Food and Drug Administration would exercise their responsibility and take the product off the market," Donovan testified. But FDA officials said that until they received the final results of the industry study, there was not sufficient evidence of PPA's dangers to take it off the market or demand prominent stroke warnings on labels.

The agency does not require manufacturers to report cases of adverse reactions to certain drugs, like PPA, that have long been available over the counter. That makes it virtually impossible to track potentially dangerous trends as they develop.

Example of drug makers' strategy

On Oct. 6, 1999, with the Yale study of PPA and hemorrhagic stroke nearing completion, a Wyeth executive e-mailed a colleague about the need to prepare for the worst. John Incledon was vice president of the respiratory business unit of Wyeth's Whitehall-Robins division.

Per the discussion at the team meeting on 9/28, what is going to be our counter strategy if this data proves to be negative? In other words do we have anyone lined up to review these studies and temper them? I know CHPA is "working" on this but a quick check of the PDR for OTC's shows WHR, Bayer (Alka-Selzer Plus), and Novartis (Triaminic) have the most to lose, especially the Dimetapp brand. We need to be thinking Offense here not just defense. While not a scientist myself, I can certainly formulate a series of questions regarding their findings in cough cold given the change from studying diet supplements initially. I don't think we should be passive on this and allow CHPA to exclusively manage this. We need an adjunct/complimentary approach to CHPA in case they fall short. Do you think Carol is adequately prepared if this thing breaks quick? The timing of this is ideal for news stations to pick up on it in droves. It's Yale, it's cold season, and it's in children's products we are likely to get some q's if the research is negative.

What are your thoughts?

John

Sources: Times research

Some companies provide such data voluntarily, but research has shown that underreporting is widespread.

As a result, there are no reliable figures for how many strokes may have been associated with PPA use. But in 2000, FDA epidemiologists estimated that between 200 and 500 hemorrhagic strokes a year could be attributed to PPA in people 18 to 49.

Although products with PPA are no longer for sale, Sen. Ron Wyden, an Oregon Democrat who held hearings on PPA safety as a congressman in 1990, said in an interview that he hoped FDA officials would learn from the PPA experience.

"In 1990, there was already essentially a decade of evidence that PPA could be causing health problems, and it was 10 years after I opened up these hearings that PPA came off the shelf," he said. "There are real human consequences of slow, stalling tactics. Loved ones don't come back, disabilities don't disappear, just because PPA is off the shelf after years of foot-dragging."

The 'Big Soldier'

Tracy Patton could never have imagined such a tentative life.

Though only 5 feet 2, she was the first player off the bench for her Scottsburg, Ind., high school basketball team when it went to the state semifinals. She held the town's high school long jump record—16 feet, 8 inches—and won a track and field scholarship to college. Before her stroke, she mowed the yards at seven of her father's rental properties every week.

Whenever Patton faced adversity as a child, when she skinned a knee or was dragged to the dentist, her father would tell her to "be a big soldier," and she took his instruction to heart. Within her family and in her job as the director of a foster care agency, she had a reputation for determination and grit.

Patton says that on the drive to nearby Louisville for her play rehearsal that night, she took a single tablet of Tavist-D to unclog her sinuses. She hemorrhaged an hour later.

At the hospital, Patton's doctor told family members to expect the worst, and advised them to say their goodbyes. "She'll probably bleed out," he said. "We'll try to make her as comfortable as we can." To their astonishment, just before sunrise, she began to wake from her coma.

The surgeons cut a scythe-shaped incision in her head, repaired her aneurysm with two metal clips and inserted three metal plates in her skull. She lost 85% of the vision in her left eye, leaving her to view the world as if through Vaseline-smeared glasses.

These days, Patton struggles with simple math and the concept of time. She keeps a printed inventory of her own odd behaviors: "I have been found talking to pictures on the wall. I have 'thanked' myself after I have poured myself a drink." One day, she thought she saw a reindeer driving a car.

Patton, who is single, tries to present a patina of normalcy, but her daily routine taxes her strength. She has recurring nightmares, often about brains. "Shopping for brains, brains of all shapes and colors and

sizes, brains in jars," she said. "And then there's brain surgery. They want me to go in and look at other people having brain surgery. I wake up in a panic."

Patton still holds down her job, where her office computer has been programmed with large-print type. But she acknowledges she is able to work only because a colleague has assumed many of her responsibilities. "She does it all and acts like I did it," Patton said. "We hide it really well."

On the day she came home from the hospital, a month after her stroke, Patton celebrated her 38th birthday with family and friends. She held an ice pack to her head as her sister, Kim, read her cards aloud and handed her gifts—a scented candle, a collectible race car, and, most utilitarian, a collection of hats. Then Kim presented the cake she had baked in the shape of a brain. "Can you imagine how many times it took me to make gray icing?" she asked with a laugh.

But the day's most meaningful gift came from her father. It was a simple sliver of silver, and he had had it engraved: "#1 Big Soldier."

Hidden Dangers

Researchers estimate that hemorrhagic strokes, which occur when blood vessels rupture and bleed into the brain, kill more than a third of all victims within a month and leave more than a third of survivors severely disabled. They account for only 12% to 17% of the 700,000 strokes in the U.S. each year, according to the American

Stroke Assn., but play a disproportionate role in making stroke America's third leading killer.

Phenylpropanolamine, which was first synthesized around 1910, is one of a class of drugs that stimulate the sympathetic nervous system, not unlike amphetamine and cocaine. It also can constrict blood vessels and increase the force of heart contractions. By narrowing blood vessels in nasal mucous membranes, PPA allows air passages to open up. The very same mechanism can, according to the FDA, produce transient spikes in blood pressure.

Whether PPA can raise blood pressure to dangerous levels has been the subject of extensive debate. After dozens of studies and case reports, the cumulative weight of scientific evidence suggests that PPA is not necessarily dangerous to everybody, but that it can trigger lethal reactions in some.

Studies found that the degree of blood pressure elevation attributable to PPA depended on the type and quantity of product taken, whether it was taken in combination with stimulants like caffeine, whether the patient was otherwise susceptible to high blood pressure, and whether it was consumed while upright or lying down, when the impact apparently is greatest.

Of particular concern was that PPA could produce adverse effects in quantities that were only two or three times the FDA's recommended dosing limits—150 milligrams per day for decongestants and 75 milligrams per day for diet drugs.

The FDA takes the position that over-the-counter drugs, while not risk-free, should be "relatively hard to get in trouble with," said Dr. Robert J. Temple, the agency's associate director for medical policy.

Some researchers, many of them bankrolled by drug manufacturers, have held that PPA has minimal effects on blood pressure. Most prominent is Dr. George L. Blackburn, whose chair in nutrition medicine at Harvard was endowed by the founder of Thompson Medical Co., which created Dexatrim. Another is Dr. John P. Morgan, who was Thompson Medical's part-time medical director and who defended PPA in a 1985 text that was heavily underwritten by the company.

Morgan acknowledged in an interview that he was paid "an enormous amount of money" over the years by Thompson. "I know some people thought that influenced the research, but that was not the case," he said. He added that he still did not believe PPA caused strokes. "But I've always been afraid I'd be proved wrong," he said. "Maybe it does."

When the FDA began evaluating PPA in the 1970s, the agency's expert panels recommended it be categorized as safe and effective, while also noting reports of "idiosyncratic reactions of central nervous system stimulation and/or blood pressure rise." There was enough uncertainty about safety to keep the agency from issuing a final ruling, placing PPA in a regulatory limbo that allowed its continued marketing.

As the body of research about PPA's potential hazards expanded, the industry maintained there was no health risk. In 1989, the Proprietary Assn.—a forerunner of the CHPA—declared in a statement that PPA was safe, and asserted that "clinically recommended doses of PPA produce no clinically significant changes in blood pressure, heart rate or EKG."

But even as the companies were publicly defending PPA, one internal report after the next referred to its potential dangers.

In 1989, for instance, a manager in the Sandoz medical services department wrote that both PPA and pseudoephedrine were "viable for use" in over-the-counter products but that "each have had dire outcomes in small doses." The manager then added: "It isn't only abuse or overdoses which cause problems. Adverse effects are rare but can be serious."

By 1996, a confidential Sandoz "safety update" warned: "It is conceivable that the intake of drugs containing this active ingredient predisposes to or even causes cerebrovascular accidents."

Some manufacturers had begun exploring the possibility of reformulating their brands with other ingredients in the early 1980s. But at Dorsey Laboratories, a division of Sandoz, officials calculated in 1983 that a switch to pseudoephedrine, which was more than twice as expensive as PPA, would cost $1.4 million. Furthermore, a company marketing survey concluded that awareness of PPA's possible side effects was not yet widespread among physicians and pharmacists.

"Based on the reaction of these professionals, reformulation to pseudoephedrine is not an urgent matter," wrote a staffer in Dorsey's marketing research division.

Birth of a Study

In 1990, prompted by reports of PPA's dangers and its growing use in diet drugs,

then-Rep. Wyden held his hearings. Some of the testimony was devastating.

After enumerating a laundry list of ailments, including cerebral hemorrhage, that had been associated with PPA in medical literature, Dr. Thaddeus E. Prout, then the chairman of medicine at Greater Baltimore Medical Center, issued a challenge: "I defy anyone to find another unregulated drug that has such a record of disaster." Prout, an authority on drugs, blamed the FDA for not moving against PPA. "Thousands of people will suffer as a result of our negligence," he predicted.

From the FDA's vantage point, the only way to truly determine whether PPA users were at disproportionate risk of stroke was to conduct an extensive epidemiologic study. But since the agency does not itself sponsor research for drug reviews, it had to rely on PPA manufacturers to investigate the safety of their own products.

There was incentive for the companies as well. A long-term study would keep PPA on the market, at least temporarily.

The industry sponsors—Thompson Medical and Ciba Consumer Pharmaceuticals (then the maker of the diet drug Acutrim)—were involved in all major methodological decisions, as was the CHPA. They chose investigators who were highly credible with the FDA, but who also were known to be skeptical of any connection between PPA and stroke.

Lawrence M. Brass, the Yale neurologist initially enlisted for the study, said in an interview that he told the industry sponsors in an early meeting that he "really didn't see a lot of evidence for an association."

Similarly, the sponsors approved Dr. Louis C. Lasagna, who had endorsed PPA's safety in a 1988 textbook, as chairman of the study's three-member oversight committee.

In April 1994, as the investigators and the companies applied the finishing touches to the study's design, Timothy R. Dring, Ciba's assistant director of regulatory affairs, wrote to one of the Yale researchers that the protocol "will serve our research purposes quite admirably."

At the same time, Dexatrim's maker, Thompson Medical, broke with the rest of the industry by disclosing on labels that there had been reports that stroke and other conditions "might be associated" with PPA.

It seemed a purely defensive move. Thompson's president, Daniel N. Horwitz, stressed in a letter to the FDA that the company "in no way believes that these reports are correct." And CHPA officials made it clear that they disagreed with the decision.

The companies not only continued to sell their products, but also introduced new PPA brands, like Bayer's Alka-Seltzer Plus children's cold medicine with "fizzy fresh cherry taste."

Unexpected Findings

To the astonishment of the drug companies, the study conducted by its hand-picked researchers using their industry-approved protocol produced bombshell results.

An examination of 702 stroke cases in people 18 to 49 years old identified 27 victims, mostly women, who had taken PPA shortly before their attacks. Their experience was compared to a control group of 1,376 people.

The most significant finding was that women who had taken an appetite suppressant with PPA were 16 times more likely to have a stroke within three days than those in a control group who had not taken any.

The study also found that the risk of stroke was three times greater for women who had used PPA products for the first time in the last 24 hours. "First use" meant that the subject had not taken a PPA product in the previous two weeks. All the first-users in the study had taken PPA cough and cold remedies.

In their final report to the FDA, the investigators concluded that "the association of PPA with risk for hemorrhagic stroke is present for both customary indications for PPA (as a cough-cold remedy and an appetite suppressant)."

For all subjects—regardless of gender, the type of product taken or the timing of ingestion—the risk of stroke increased by 50%. But that finding, like some others, fell short of statistical significance.

Upon learning the results on Oct. 17, 1999, the members of the study's oversight committee—including Lasagna, who had previously written so confidently about PPA's safety—unanimously approved the findings and instructed the researchers to notify the FDA immediately.

The next day they did, placing telephone calls to officials at the agency and to the leaders of the trade association. Industry officials feared that the study would prompt FDA action against all forms of PPA, and began mounting a counteroffensive.

Even before the Yale results were disclosed, the industry had started considering worst-case scenarios. "We need to be thinking offense here not just defense," wrote John Incledon, vice president of the respiratory business unit of Wyeth's Whitehall-Robins Healthcare division, in an e-mail to a colleague on Oct. 6, 1999. "The timing of this is ideal for news stations to pick up on it in droves. It's Yale, it's cold season and it's in children's products."

Once the study was finished, the FDA asked the doctors to summarize their findings in a letter. Dr. R. William Soller, then the senior vice president of the CHPA, wrote to one of the researchers to insist that any report to the FDA stress PPA's overall safety record. The next day, he wrote again, this time warning that the Yale investigators may have violated their contract by communicating results to the FDA before fully vetting them with the industry sponsors. Two days later, a lawyer for Novartis accused the Yale doctors in a letter of committing "a serious breach" by prematurely disclosing the results.

The doctors were taken aback. "We contend that we were in full compliance with the contract," Dr. Walter N. Kernan, one of the Yale researchers, said in an interview. "Neither the university nor the investigators were going to allow anything to get between us and what we perceived as the best interest of the public."

The FDA, meanwhile, told the researchers that any communication with the agency would have to be public. It quickly scheduled an open meeting of its Nonprescription Drugs Advisory Committee, a panel of experts whose recommendations were almost always endorsed by the FDA commissioner.

But the doctors said their data needed further refining and analysis before public release. And the industry told the FDA it could not prepare a public defense so quickly.

In the end, the panel's meeting was pushed off by more than 10 months, with much of that time marked by parrying between the Yale doctors and the industry over the research methods they had agreed to five years earlier. In the meantime, the public remained unaware of the study's findings, and products with PPA stayed on the market.

"I think the companies wished that we'd never reach the final stage," said Dr. Ralph I. Horwitz, a clinical epidemiologist who helped lead the Yale team, "because the longer the process was underway, they were able to avoid finally dealing with the consequences of the research."

Horwitz, who is now dean of the Medical School at Case Western Reserve University, said the delay left issues of consumer safety in suspension. "I do think that had they been able to see the study findings as soon as the data were available, that the FDA would have felt obliged to issue a warning in the interest of public health and safety," he said.

The FDA's Ganley said the agency could not act without a final report. "Why would we put out something like that when we didn't really have the data in hand?" he asked. "We would be criticized, and justifiably so."

Circling the Wagons

As the clock ticked toward some form of FDA regulation, the companies enlisted a battalion of consultants to analyze the study. They hired a public relations firm, Ruder Finn, which suggested in a draft memo that the industry argue that PPA-related jumps in blood pressure were "within the range of increases associated with routine daily activities, such as climbing stairs or mowing the lawn," according to correspondence from CHPA's Totman.

One Bayer memo about a meeting of an industrywide PPA task force said it had been noted that the FDA's Temple had an unfavorable position on PPA and that "efforts should be made to steer the media away from him."

At Chattanooga, Tenn.-based Chattem, which had just bought Dexatrim, President A. Alexander Taylor II wrote to Soller that he feared "an avalanche of negative publicity" if the study were to become public before it could be reviewed by the industry sponsors.

Taylor appealed to his home-state senator, Tennessee Republican Bill Frist, a physician, to intervene with the FDA. Taylor began a Feb. 4, 2000, letter by mentioning that a prominent Frist donor served on the Chattem board of directors and that the company's chief executive officer was the brother of a Frist county reelection chairman. "I am a very proud contributor to your current campaign," Taylor continued.

"A few more months of study before any public release of this data will not harm the public health, and may benefit it," he wrote.

Frist never responded. "It fell on deaf ears," Taylor said in a deposition.

As the months passed, the companies saw that it was time to reformulate.

In December 1999, Novartis had kick-started its efforts to remake Triaminic with pseudoephedrine. Wyeth also set a quick timetable for reconstituting Dimetapp, then slowed down as the FDA postponed its advisory committee meeting.

"It appears that we have a bit more time than we originally expected on a decision from the FDA on PPA," wrote Wyeth's senior product manager for Dimetapp in an April 2000 memo. "By launching in January 2001 instead of September 2000 (the peak of the cough/cold season), we will be able to better manage open stock and display inventories."

In May, a draft memo from Wyeth's Whitehall-Robins division addressed whether retailers should return stocks of Robitussin CF when they began receiving shipments of PPA-free replacements. The answer: "NO. Again, the decision to reformulate was voluntary. Therefore, current stock is perfectly safe and effective for use. We will not be accepting returned product for the new formula."

David E. Dukes, a lawyer for Wyeth, stressed in an interview that the companies and the FDA were still evaluating the Yale study at that point. "At the senior levels, where decisions were being made about Dimetapp and Robitussin CF, safety was the primary concern," he said.

Meanwhile, even the consultants brought in by industry found it difficult to dismiss the study's conclusions.

Dr. James Lewis, a University of Pennsylvania epidemiologist who had been commissioned by Bayer, wrote that the Yale researchers showed "fairly convincing evidence of an association between PPA use and the risk of hemorrhagic stroke."

Like other consultants hired to critique the study, however, he also guided his client toward a strategy for attacking the fragility of the findings. With such a small number of PPA-related stroke cases, he wrote, any methodological bias could affect the statistical significance of a result.

The industry seized on that approach. "We came out and said we don't like our own study," said Cope, the former CHPA president. "It's predictable: If the results don't come out the way you like, since there's no such thing as a bulletproof study, you point out the weaknesses in it."

Under increasing pressure from the FDA, the Yale doctors submitted their final report on May 10, 2000. Though they stopped short of saying PPA could cause hemorrhagic stroke, they later emphasized

that "causation is one explanation for that association."

The FDA staff quickly sided with the researchers. An FDA statistician praised the study as one of the best he had reviewed in the last decade. A pair of FDA epidemiologists were so persuaded that they took the unusual step of recommending that PPA-containing appetite suppressants be banned as over-the-counter products.

"The study demonstrated a statistically significant increased risk of hemorrhagic stroke among both appetite suppressant users and first time users of PPA as a cough/cold remedy," their report concluded. The recommendation for a ban infuriated industry officials, who complained it would unfairly sway the advisory panel, now scheduled to meet on Oct. 19.

At the advisory committee meeting, Dr. Noel S. Weiss, a University of Washington epidemiologist who had been hired by the CHPA, honed in on the disparity in the study's findings for different types of products. "Why an association with appetite suppressant drugs and not for colds and such when the typical doses given for colds are higher than for appetite suppressants?" he asked.

But the attack on the study was so broad that it ultimately undercut the industry's cause, FDA officials said. "They essentially trashed the study, even though they are the ones who designed it and financed it," Ganley said.

The advisory panel voted unanimously, with a few abstentions, that PPA could not be considered safe. A few weeks later, the agency told manufacturers it expected to classify PPA as not safe for over-the-counter use and asked that they voluntarily discontinue marketing the products. The evidence of an association, while not conclusive, had been persuasive.

"If someone wanted you to swear it must be true, I wouldn't do that," said the FDA's Temple. "But we thought it was enough. Look, if the drug were lifesaving, if it was something of immense value and had no replacements, you'd have to think about it. But it wasn't."

Stolen Youth

Tricia Newenham suffered her stroke the week before the advisory committee met. As her neurosurgeon prepared to remove the damaged tissue from her brain, he warned her parents she might not survive her eight hours on the table. Three

days later, before a second operation to remove a blood clot, her mother had her baptized, just in case.

Tricia made it through, but she would never be the same.

Before her stroke, she stood a gangly 5 feet 6 and weighed 106 pounds. She was becoming a woman, and had developed a serious case of the boycrazies (login: kissable98; password: puckerup). She never left her house in Steuben, Maine, without her hair and makeup just right. She had given up basketball and softball and swimming in vanity over her skinny legs.

Now 18, Newenham weighs 196 pounds, the consequence of medication and a captive life in which junk food provides a rare escape. Once a promising artist who had imagined a career in design, she passes the time rocking gently in a blue recliner, listening to the drone of soap operas.

Newenham can brush her teeth and wash her hands, but she does not always know when to stop. Clinging fast to her femininity, she insists on shaving her own legs, but leaves them scabby with cuts.

She hears a lot and comprehends much, but she has difficulty processing thought and even more in communicating it. When asked a question, she struggles to find the most economical answer, usually a word or two, often a guttural "I don't know," with little intonation.

Is she in physical pain? "No." Is she angry? "No." Is she sad? "No." Is she frustrated? "Yeah."

What are her favorite things to do? "Sleep and eat." What does she like to eat? "Chop suey." What else? "I don't know."

What does she remember about her old life? "Boys."

Is she content or bored with her life? "I get bored." What does she wish she were doing? "I don't know. Going out with friends."

And then she begins to cry. And cry and cry.

While Newenham lingered in a coma after her stroke, the doctors advised her parents to consider a nursing home. Even if Tricia came to, she would not be the daughter they had known.

But ever so slowly, Tricia started waking up. First, a tear would form in the crease of her eye. Sometimes, when her mother talked to her, Tricia would reward her with a muffled, choking cry.

Patricia Bybee told the doctors she was taking her daughter home. "I just sensed that she was in there," she said. Two months later, Tricia had spoken her first word: "M-m-m-om." Three months after that, she could walk.

When the paramedics came to the house on the day of the stroke, they asked Bybee what medications Tricia had taken. "Only Triaminic," she said. It was months later, after the FDA had asked drug companies to withdraw their PPA products, that she learned of the possible connection between cold medicines and stroke.

Bybee, a nurse's assistant, and her husband, Tim, a plumber, went deep into debt to pay off medical bills. They say a settlement reached last year with Novartis will relieve their debts and cover the cost of Tricia's attendance at a school for the blind near Boston.

After three years, they have slowly adapted to their new reality, and lowered their expectations.

"We would give anything to have her back the way she was," said Tim Bybee. "But we have grown to love her and accept her the way she is."

Softening the Blow

The withdrawal of PPA was a tough loss for the companies, but they had succeeded brilliantly in minimizing the impact. The study's long duration bought five years to market PPA products without restriction. And the post-study delay provided time to formulate products without PPA, which began shipping within days of the withdrawal.

Throughout, the manufacturers remained defiant.

As late as Oct. 25, 2000, six days after the FDA advisory committee voted that PPA was unsafe, Novartis' director of medical affairs sought to reassure doctors about the safety of PPA, particularly for children, who he pointed out were not included in the Yale study.

"As you know, hemorrhagic stroke is exceedingly rare in the pediatric population," Dr. Geoffrey Ross wrote.

"Particular to the pediatric population, PPA plays a significant role in reducing missed school days and in promoting effective symptom relief."

The researchers submitted a scientific article on their PPA study to the *New England Journal of Medicine,* reporting a statistically significant risk of stroke for women taking PPA diet drugs and a possible association between decongestant use and stroke in women. The Journal considered the findings important enough to post the article on its website Nov. 6, six weeks before it came out in print.

The same day, the FDA issued a public health advisory that consumers should not use PPA products. Health officials in a number of countries, from Canada to Malaysia, quickly followed suit.

Finding herself stuck with millions of dollars' worth of useless pills Chattem's Dexatrim brand manager suggested to a colleague in an e-mail—produced by the company for litigation—that they sell the inventory to a sampling and promotion company known as Box of Brands.

Andrea M. Crouch, the vice president of toiletries marketing, responded enthusiastically. "I think using Box of Brands is an excellent idea!" she wrote. "I see no downside—so what if they divert! I will be surprised if they don't have a problem with PPA but let's go for it!"

Crews Townsend, a lawyer for Chattem, called the proposal "part of the brainstorming process" and said the company never sold its Dexatrim inventory to Box of Brands. Instead, he said, it was destroyed.

At Wyeth, gallows humor set in. When a speech was drafted for an executive to deliver at an awards banquet several weeks before Christmas 2000, it included a line about the need to dispose of large quantities of Dimetapp and Robitussin CF: "When you're sorting this year's holiday gift list by 'naughty and nice,' don't think 'lump of coal,' think 'product with PPA.' " By the time a final draft had been prepared, that opening had been replaced by an off-color joke about the 2000 presidential campaign, according to a copy provided by lawyers for Wyeth.

Virtually all of the firms took one-time accounting losses because of the withdrawals—$80 million for Wyeth, $54 million for Bayer, $50 million for Novartis and $8 million for Chattem, according to corporate filings and statements.

But for the most part, the losses were short-lived. Thanks to the quick reformulation and shipment of PPA-free Dimetapp, domestic sales of the product rose 50% in the first quarter of 2001. Meanwhile, 2001 sales of Dexatrim Natural, the non-PPA version of Chattem's diet aid, "more than made up for lost sales" due to the discontinuation of Dexatrim with PPA, according to an annual report.

The Battle Continues

Chattem announced in December that it would seek to settle most of its 332 PPA lawsuits. It had already agreed last year to

pay $3.5 million to Jennifer Villarreal, a Texas hairstylist who collapsed at a gym on March 6, 2000, allegedly after taking a Dexatrim pill.

The company also said it had reached settlements with insurers who alleged in lawsuits that Chattem had applied for liability policies without disclosing the Yale results. Townsend, the Chattem lawyer, said the settlements did not indicate that the company had changed its belief that Dexatrim with PPA was a safe and effective product.

Novartis agreed to make payments to Tricia Newenham and her family last year on the condition that the terms remained confidential, according to her mother. Novartis would not answer questions about Newenham, and neither Novartis nor the other companies would disclose details about other settlements.

Thousands of plaintiffs, including Tracy Patton, have lawsuits pending against PPA drug makers, but only a few of those cases have made it to trial. This year, juries in New Jersey and California rejected claims by plaintiffs that Novartis products had caused their strokes. In both trials, the victims had had a variety of risk factors for stroke, and their strokes occurred before the Yale study was completed.

"Our company is extremely gratified that two diverse juries, from opposite ends of the country, reached the same conclusions after an exhaustive airing of all the evidence," said Nancy Fitzsimmons, vice president for global communications of Novartis Consumer Health.

The industry's efforts to discredit the Yale study have continued in court, with defense lawyers trying to poke holes in enough of the study's PPA-related stroke cases to negate its findings.

The dispute has become increasingly personal. Drug company lawyers have hypothesized a conspiracy that has the Yale doctors manipulating data to strengthen their chances of finding an association. Such a finding, the industry lawyers suggest, would help the researchers win promotions and publication in a top journal.

"Those investigators were very vulnerable to human frailty, to human desires and human error; driven by a desire to succeed, to obtain recognition," said Jan E. Dodd, a lawyer for Novartis, in her closing argument in the California trial.

In constructing their theory, defense lawyers have focused on a midcourse shift by the researchers in defining when a stroke begins.

In one case, the investigators set the onset of a stroke one hour after the patient had taken PPA, even though the patient had begun suffering a headache—potentially an early sign of stroke—six days earlier. The companies have made much of a 1998 e-mail sent by Yale researcher Kernan to his colleagues saying the strategy of shifting the time of onset "effectively increases our likelihood of finding an association" between PPA and hemorrhagic stroke.

Kernan said in an interview that he was just stating the obvious, and not suggesting that data could be tweaked to produce a desired result.

"Sloppy research does not get you promoted at Yale," he said. "Lack of integrity gets you fired. The investigators had no stake in the outcome of the research."

Brass, the Yale neurologist, joked that given the drug industry's financial support for friendly scientists, the researchers would have had more incentive to skew the study in PPA's favor. "If we were thinking payoff, we should have shown PPA as safe," he said. "I would have had a chair. Yale would have a whole division dedicated to the study of obesity. But we don't fix studies. We just do them."

Some in academic medicine worry that the industry's attacks on the Yale doctors might discourage researchers from pursuing similar studies. "With the amount of hassle and harassment that they had to endure, I'm sure the next time they're asked to undertake something like this, they'll wonder if it's worth the cost," said former FDA Commissioner David A. Kessler, now the dean of medicine at UC San Francisco.

The Yale doctors, said Horwitz, clearly were naive about the industry's willingness to assail their integrity. "I love arguing about the science," he said, "but this is outrageous, especially considering who was making the accusations. It was their study."

Kevin Sack is a Times staff writer based in Atlanta; Alicia Mundy is a special correspondent based in Virginia. Researcher Janet Lundblad in Los Angeles contributed to this report.

Values in Tension: Ethics Away from Home

When is different just different, and when is different wrong?

by Thomas Donaldson

When we leave home and cross our nation's boundaries, moral clarity often blurs. Without a backdrop of shared attitudes, and without familiar laws and judicial procedures that define standards of ethical conduct, certainty is elusive. Should a company invest in a foreign country where civil and political rights are violated? Should a company go along with a host country's discriminatory employment practices? If companies in developed countries shift facilities to developing nations that lack strict environmental and health regulations, or if those companies choose to fill management and other top-level positions in a host nation with people from the home country, whose standards should prevail?

Even the best-informed, best-intentioned executives must rethink their assumptions about business practice in foreign settings. What works in a company's home country can fail in a country with different standards of ethical conduct. Such difficulties are unavoidable for businesspeople who live and work abroad.

But how can managers resolve the problems? What are the principles that can help them work through the maze of cultural differences and establish codes of conduct for globally ethical business practice? How can companies answer the toughest question in global business ethics: What happens when a host country's ethical standards seem lower than the home country's?

Competing Answers

One answer is as old as philosophical discourse. According to cultural relativism, no culture's ethics are better than any other's; therefore there are no international rights and wrongs. If the people of Indonesia tolerate the bribery of their public officials, so what? Their attitude is no better

or worse than that of people in Denmark or Singapore who refuse to offer or accept bribes. Likewise, if Belgians fail to find insider trading morally repugnant, who cares? Not enforcing insider-trading laws is no more or less ethical than enforcing such laws.

The cultural relativist's creed—When in Rome, do as the Romans do—is tempting, especially when failing to do as the locals do means forfeiting business opportunities. The inadequacy of cultural relativism, however, becomes apparent when the practices in question are more damaging than petty bribery or insider trading.

In the late 1980s, some European tanneries and pharmaceutical companies were looking for cheap waste-dumping sites. They approached virtually every country on Africa's west coast from Morocco to the Congo. Nigeria agreed to take highly toxic polychlorinated biphenyls. Unprotected local workers, wearing thongs and shorts, unloaded barrels of PCBs and placed them near a residential area. Neither the residents nor the workers knew that the barrels contained toxic waste.

We may denounce governments that permit such abuses, but many countries are unable to police transnational corporations adequately even if they want to. And in many countries, the combination of ineffective enforcement and inadequate regulations leads to behavior by unscrupulous companies that is clearly wrong. A few years ago, for example, a group of investors became interested in restoring the SS *United States*, once a luxurious ocean liner. Before the actual restoration could begin, the ship had to be stripped of its asbestos lining. A bid from a U.S. company, based on U.S. standards for asbestos removal, priced the job at more than $100 million. A company in the Ukranian city of Sevastopol offered to do the work for less than $2 million. In October 1993, the ship was towed to Sevastopol.

The Culture and Ethics of Software Piracy

Before jumping on the cultural relativism bandwagon, stop and consider the potential economic consequences of a when-in-Rome attitude toward business ethics. Take a look at the current statistics on software piracy: In the United States, pirated software is estimated to be 35% of the total software market, and industry losses are estimated at $2.3 billion per year. The piracy rate is 57% in Germany and 80% in Italy and Japan; the rates in most Asian countries are estimated to be nearly 100%.

There are similar laws against software piracy in those countries. What, then, accounts for the differences? Although a country's level of economic development plays a large part, culture, including ethical attitudes, may be a more crucial factor. The 1995 annual report of the Software Publishers Association connects software piracy directly to culture and attitude. It describes Italy and Hong Kong as having "'first world' per capita incomes, along with 'third world' rates of piracy." When asked whether one should use software without paying for it, most people, including people in Italy and Hong Kong, say no. But people in some countries regard the practice as *less* unethical than people in other countries do. Confucian culture, for example, stresses that individuals should share what they create with society. That may be, in part, what prompts the Chinese and other Asians to view the concept of intellectual property as a means for the West to monopolize its technological superiority.

What happens if ethical attitudes around the world permit large-scale software piracy? Software companies won't want to invest as much in developing new products, because they cannot expect any return on their investment in certain parts of the world. When ethics fail to support technological creativity, there are consequences that go beyond statistics—jobs are lost and livelihoods jeopardized.

Companies must do more than lobby foreign governments for tougher enforcement of piracy laws. They must cooperate with other companies and with local organizations to help citizens understand the consequences of piracy and to encourage the evolution of a different ethic toward the practice.

A cultural relativist would have no problem with that outcome, but I do. A country has the right to establish its own health and safety regulations, but in the case described above, the standards and the terms of the contract could not possibly have protected workers in Sevastopol from known health risks. Even if the contract met Ukranian standards, ethical businesspeople must object. Cultural relativism is morally blind. There are fundamental values that cross cultures, and companies must uphold them. (For an economic argument against cultural relativism, see the insert "The Culture and Ethics of Software Piracy.")

At the other end of the spectrum from cultural relativism is ethical imperialism, which directs people to do everywhere exactly as they do at home. Again, an understandably appealing approach but one that is clearly inadequate. Consider the large U.S. computer-products company that in 1993 introduced a course on sexual harassment in its Saudi Arabian facility. Under the banner of global consistency, instructors used the same approach to train Saudi Arabian managers that they had used with U.S. managers: the participants were asked to discuss a case in which a manager makes sexually explicit remarks to a new female employee over drinks in a bar. The instructors failed to consider how the exercise would work in a culture with strict conventions governing relationships between men and women. As a result, the training sessions were ludicrous. They baffled and offended the Saudi participants, and the message to avoid coercion and sexual discrimination was lost.

The theory behind ethical imperialism is absolutism, which is based on three problematic principles. Absolutists believe that there is a single list of truths, that they can be expressed only with one set of concepts, and that they call for exactly the same behavior around the world.

The first claim clashes with many people's belief that different cultural traditions must be respected. In some cultures, loyalty to a community—family, organization, or society—is the foundation of all ethical behavior. The Japanese, for example, define business ethics in terms of loyalty to their companies, their business networks, and their nation. Americans place a higher value on liberty than on loyalty; the U.S. tradition of rights emphasizes equality, fairness, and individual freedom. It is hard to conclude that truth lies on one side or the other, but an absolutist would have us select just one.

The second problem with absolutism is the presumption that people must express moral truth using only one set of concepts. For instance, some absolutists insist that the language of basic rights provide the framework for any discussion of ethics. That means, though, that entire cultural traditions must be ignored. The notion of a right evolved with the rise of democracy in post-Renaissance Europe and the United States, but the term is not found in either Confucian or Buddhist traditions. We all learn ethics in the context of our particular cultures, and the power in the principles is deeply tied to the way in which they are expressed. Internationally accepted lists of moral principles, such as the United Nations' Universal Declaration of Human Rights, draw on many cultural and religious traditions. As philosopher Michael Walzer has noted, "There is no Esperanto of global ethics."

The third problem with absolutism is the belief in a global standard of ethical behavior. Context must shape ethical practice. Very low wages, for example, may be considered unethical in rich, advanced countries, but developing nations may be acting ethically if they encourage investment and improve living standards by accepting low wages. Likewise, when people are malnourished or starving, a government may be wise to use more fertilizer in order to improve crop yields, even though that means settling for relatively high levels of thermal water pollution.

When cultures have different standards of ethical behavior—and different ways of handling unethical behavior—a company that takes an absolutist approach may find itself making a disastrous mistake. When a manager at a large U.S. specialty-products company in China caught an employee stealing, she followed the company's practice and turned the employee over to the provincial authorities, who executed him. Managers cannot operate in another culture without being aware of that culture's attitudes toward ethics.

If companies can neither adopt a host country's ethics nor extend the home country's standards, what is the answer? Even the traditional litmus test—What would people think of your actions if they were written up on the front page of the newspaper?—is an unreliable guide, for there is no international consensus on standards of business conduct.

What Do These Values Have in Common?

Non-Western	Western

Kyosei (Japanese):
    Living and working
    together for the
    common good.
	Individual liberty

Dharma (Hindu):
    The fulfillment of
    inherited duty.
	Egalitarianism

Santutthi (Buddhist):
    The importance of
    limited desires.
	Political participation

Zakat (Muslim):
    The duty to give
    alms to the Muslim poor.
	Human rights

Balancing the Extremes: Three Guiding Principles

Companies must help managers distinguish between practices that are merely different and those that are wrong. For relativists, nothing is sacred and nothing is wrong. For absolutists, many things that are different are wrong. Neither extreme illuminates the real world of business decision making. The answer lies somewhere in between.

When it comes to shaping ethical behavior, companies must be guided by three principles.

- Respect for core human values, which determine the absolute moral threshold for all business activities.
- Respect for local traditions.
- The belief that context matters when deciding what is right and what is wrong.

Consider those principles in action. In Japan, people doing business together often exchange gifts—sometimes expensive ones—in keeping with long-standing Japanese tradition. When U.S. and European companies started doing a lot of business in Japan, many Western businesspeo-

ple thought that the practice of gift giving might be wrong rather than simply different. To them, accepting a gift felt like accepting a bribe. As Western companies have become more familiar with Japanese traditions, however, most have come to tolerate the practice and to set different limits on gift giving in Japan than they do elsewhere.

Respecting differences is a crucial ethical practice. Research shows that management ethics differ among cultures; respecting those differences means recognizing that some cultures have obvious weaknesses—as well as hidden strengths. Managers in Hong Kong, for example, have a higher tolerance for some forms of bribery than their Western counterparts, but they have a much lower tolerance for the failure to acknowledge a subordinate's work. In some parts of the Far East, stealing credit from a subordinate is nearly an unpardonable sin.

People often equate respect for local traditions with cultural relativism. That is incorrect. Some practices are clearly wrong. Union Carbide's tragic experience in Bhopal, India, provides one example. The company's executives seriously underestimated how much on-site management involvement was needed at the Bhopal plant to compensate for the country's poor infrastructure and regulatory capabilities. In the aftermath of the disastrous gas leak, the lesson is clear: companies using sophisticated technology in a developing country must evaluate that country's ability to oversee its safe use. Since the incident at Bhopal, Union Carbide has become a leader in advising companies on using hazardous technologies safely in developing countries.

Some activities are wrong no matter where they take place. But some practices that are unethical in one setting may be acceptable in another. For instance, the chemical EDB, a soil fungicide, is banned for use in the United States. In hot climates, however, it quickly becomes harmless through exposure to intense solar radiation and high soil temperatures. As long as the chemical is monitored, companies may be able to use EDB ethically in certain parts of the world.

Defining the Ethical Threshold: Core Values

Few ethical questions are easy for managers to answer. But there are some hard truths that must guide managers' actions, a set of what I call *core human values*, which define minimum ethical standards for all companies.[1] The right to good health and the right to economic advancement and an improved standard of living are two core human values. Another is what Westerners call the Golden Rule, which is recognizable in every major religious and ethical tradition around the world. In Book 15 of his *Analects*, for instance, Confucius counsels people to maintain reciprocity, or not to do to others what they do not want done to themselves.

Although no single list would satisfy every scholar, I believe it is possible to articulate three core values that incorporate the work of scores of theologians and philosophers around the world. To be broadly relevant, these values must include elements found in both Western and non-Western cultural and religious traditions. Consider the examples of values in the insert "What Do These Values Have in Common?"

At first glance, the values expressed in the two lists seem quite different. Nonetheless, in the spirit of what philosopher John Rawls calls *overlapping consensus*, one can see that the seemingly divergent values converge at key points. Despite important differences between Western and non-Western cultural and religious traditions, both express shared attitudes about what it means to be human. First, individuals must not treat others simply as tools; in other words, they must recognize a person's value as a human being. Next, individuals and communities must treat people in ways that respect people's basic rights. Finally, members of a community must work together to support and improve the institutions on which the community depends. I call those three values *respect for human dignity, respect for basic rights*, and *good citizenship*.

Those values must be the starting point for all companies as they formulate and evaluate standards of ethical conduct at home and abroad. But they are only a starting point. Companies need much more specific guidelines, and the first step to developing those is to translate the core human values into core values for business. What does it mean, for example, for a company to respect human dignity? How can a company be a good citizen?

I believe that companies can respect human dignity by creating and sustaining a corporate culture in which employees, customers, and suppliers are treated not as means to an end but as people whose intrinsic value must be acknowledged, and by producing safe products and services in a safe workplace. Companies can respect basic rights by acting in ways that support and protect the individual rights of employees, customers, and surrounding communities, and by avoiding relationships that violate human beings' rights to health, education, safety, and an adequate standard of living. And companies can be good citizens by supporting essential social institutions, such as the economic system and the education system, and by working with host governments and other organizations to protect the environment.

The core values establish a moral compass for business practice. They can help companies identify practices that are acceptable and those that are intolerable—even if the practices are compatible with a host country's norms and laws. Dumping pollutants near people's homes and accepting inadequate standards for handling hazardous materials are two examples of actions that violate core values.

Similarly, if employing children prevents them from receiving a basic education, the practice is intolerable. Lying about product specifications in the act of selling may not affect human lives directly, but it too is intolerable because it violates the trust that is needed to sustain a corporate culture in which customers are respected.

Sometimes it is not a company's actions but those of a supplier or customer that pose problems. Take the case of the Tan family, a large supplier for Levi Strauss. The Tans were allegedly forcing 1,200 Chinese and Filipino women to work 74 hours per week in guarded compounds on the Mariana Islands. In 1992, after repeated warnings to the Tans, Levi Strauss broke off business relations with them.

Creating an Ethical Corporate Culture

The core values for business that I have enumerated can help companies begin to exercise ethical judgment and think about how to operate ethically in foreign cultures, but they are not specific enough to guide managers through actual ethical dilemmas. Levi Strauss relied on a written code of conduct when figuring out how to deal with the Tan family. The company's Global Sourcing and Operating Guidelines, formerly called the Business Partner Terms of Engagement, state that Levi Strauss will "seek to identify and utilize business partners who aspire as individuals and in the conduct of all their businesses to a set of ethical standards not incompatible with our own." Whenever intolerable business situations arise, managers should be guided by precise statements that spell out the behavior and operating practices that the company demands.

Many companies don't do anything with their codes of conduct; they simply paste them on the wall.

Ninety percent of all *Fortune* 500 companies have codes of conduct, and 70% have statements of vision and values. In Europe and the Far East, the percentages are lower but are increasing rapidly. Does that mean that most companies have what they need? Hardly. Even though most large U.S. companies have both statements of values and codes of conduct, many might be better off if they didn't. Too many companies don't do anything with the documents; they simply paste them on the wall to impress employees, customers, suppliers, and the public. As a result, the senior managers who drafted the statements lose credibility by proclaiming values and not living up to them. Companies such as Johnson & Johnson, Levi Strauss, Motorola, Texas Instruments, and Lockheed Martin, however, do a great deal to make the words meaningful. Johnson & Johnson, for example, has become well known for its Credo Challenge sessions, in which managers discuss ethics in the context of their current business problems and are invited to criticize the company's credo and make suggestions for changes. The participants' ideas are passed on to the company's senior managers. Lockheed Martin has created an innovative site on the World Wide Web and on its local network that gives employees, customers, and suppliers access to the company's ethical code and the chance to voice complaints.

If a company declared all gift giving unethical, it wouldn't be able to do business in Japan.

Codes of conduct must provide clear direction about ethical behavior when the temptation to behave unethically is strongest. The pronouncement in a code of conduct that bribery is unacceptable is useless unless accompanied by guidelines for gift giving, payments to get goods through customs, and "requests" from intermediaries who are hired to ask for bribes.

Motorola's values are stated very simply as "How we will always act: [with] constant respect for people [and] uncompromising integrity." The company's code of conduct, however, is explicit about actual business practice. With respect to bribery, for example, the code states that the "funds and assets of Motorola shall not be used, directly or indirectly, for illegal payments of any kind." It is unambiguous about what sort of payment is illegal: "the payment of a bribe to a public official or the kickback of funds to an employee of a customer...." The code goes on to prescribe specific procedures for handling commissions to intermediaries, issuing sales invoices, and disclosing confidential information in a sales transaction—all situations in which employees might have an opportunity to accept or offer bribes.

Codes of conduct must be explicit to be useful, but they must also leave room for a manager to use his or her judgment in situations requiring cultural sensitivity. Host-country employees shouldn't be forced to adopt all home-country values and renounce their own. Again, Motorola's code is exemplary. First, it gives clear direction: "Employees of Motorola will respect the laws, customs, and traditions of each country in which they operate, but will, at the same time, engage in no course of conduct which, even if legal, customary, and accepted in any such country, could be deemed to be in violation of the accepted business ethics of Motorola or the laws of the United States relating to business ethics." After laying down such absolutes, Motorola's code then makes clear when individual judgment will be necessary. For example, employees may sometimes accept certain kinds of small gifts "in rare circumstances, where the refusal to accept a gift" would injure Motorola's "legitimate business interests." Under certain circumstances, such gifts "may be accepted so long as the gift inures to the benefit of Motorola" and not "to the benefit of the Motorola employee."

Striking the appropriate balance between providing clear direction and leaving room for individual judgment

makes crafting corporate values statements and ethics codes one of the hardest tasks that executives confront. The words are only a start. A company's leaders need to refer often to their organization's credo and code and must themselves be credible, committed, and consistent. If senior managers act as though ethics don't matter, the rest of the company's employees won't think they do, either.

Conflicts of Development and Conflicts of Tradition

Managers living and working abroad who are not prepared to grapple with moral ambiguity and tension should pack their bags and come home. The view that all business practices can be categorized as either ethical or unethical is too simple. As Einstein is reported to have said, "Things should be as simple as possible—but no simpler." Many business practices that are considered unethical in one setting may be ethical in another. Such activities are neither black nor white but exist in what Thomas Dunfee and I have called *moral free space*.[2] In this gray zone, there are no tight prescriptions for a company's behavior. Managers must chart their own courses—as long as they do not violate core human values.

Many activities are neither good nor bad but exist in *moral free space*.

Consider the following example. Some successful Indian companies offer employees the opportunity for one of their children to gain a job with the company once the child has completed a certain level in school. The companies honor this commitment even when other applicants are more qualified than an employee's child. The perk is extremely valuable in a country where jobs are hard to find, and it reflects the Indian culture's belief that the West has gone too far in allowing economic opportunities to break up families. Not surprisingly, the perk is among the most cherished by employees, but in most Western countries, it would be branded unacceptable nepotism. In the United States, for example, the ethical principle of equal opportunity holds that jobs should go to the applicants with the best qualifications. If a U.S. company made such promises to its employees, it would violate regulations established by the Equal Employment Opportunity Commission. Given this difference in ethical attitudes, how should U.S. managers react to Indian nepotism? Should they condemn the Indian companies, refusing to accept them as partners or suppliers until they agree to clean up their act?

Despite the obvious tension between nepotism and principles of equal opportunity, I cannot condemn the practice for Indians. In a country, such as India, that emphasizes clan and family relationships and has catastrophic levels of

The Problem with Bribery

Bribery is widespread and insidious. Managers in transnational companies routinely confront bribery even though most countries have laws against it. The fact is that officials in many developing countries wink at the practice, and the salaries of local bureaucrats are so low that many consider bribes a form of remuneration. The U.S. Foreign Corrupt Practices Act defines allowable limits on petty bribery in the form of routine payments required to move goods through customs. But demands for bribes often exceed those limits, and there is seldom a good solution.

Bribery disrupts distribution channels when goods languish on docks until local handlers are paid off, and it destroys incentives to compete on quality and cost when purchasing decisions are based on who pays what under the table. Refusing to acquiesce is often tantamount to giving business to unscrupulous companies.

I believe that even routine bribery is intolerable. Bribery undermines market efficiency and predictability, thus ultimately denying people their right to a minimal standard of living. Some degree of ethical commitment—some sense that everyone will play by the rules—is necessary for a sound economy. Without an ability to predict outcomes, who would be willing to invest?

There was a U.S. company whose shipping crates were regularly pilfered by handlers on the docks of Rio de Janeiro. The handlers would take about 10% of the contents of the crates, but the company was never sure which 10% it would be. In a partial solution, the company began sending two crates—the first with 90% of the merchandise, the second with 10%. The handlers learned to take the second crate and leave the first untouched. From the company's perspective, at least knowing which goods it would lose was an improvement.

Bribery does more than destroy predictability; it undermines essential social and economic systems. That truth is not lost on businesspeople in countries where the practice is woven into the social fabric. CEOs in India admit that their companies engage constantly in bribery, and they say that they have considerable disgust for the practice. They blame government policies in part, but Indian executives also know that their country's business practices perpetuate corrupt behavior. Anyone walking the streets of Calcutta, where it is clear that even a dramatic redistribution of wealth would still leave most of India's inhabitants in dire poverty, comes face-to-face with the devastating effects of corruption.

unemployment, the practice must be viewed in moral free space. The decision to allow a special perk for employees and their children is not necessarily wrong—at least for members of that country.

How can managers discover the limits of moral free space? That is, how can they learn to distinguish a value in tension with their own from one that is intolerable? Helping managers develop good ethical judgment requires companies to be clear about their core values and codes of conduct. But even the most explicit set of guidelines cannot always provide answers. That is especially true in the thorniest ethical dilemmas, in which the host country's ethical

standards not only are different but also seem lower than the home country's. Managers must recognize that when countries have different ethical standards, there are two types of conflict that commonly arise. Each type requires its own line of reasoning.

In the first type of conflict, which I call a *conflict of relative development*, ethical standards conflict because of the countries' different levels of economic development. As mentioned before, developing countries may accept wage rates that seem inhumane to more advanced countries in order to attract investment. As economic conditions in a developing country improve, the incidence of that sort of conflict usually decreases. The second type of conflict is a *conflict of cultural tradition*. For example, Saudi Arabia, unlike most other countries, does not allow women to serve as corporate managers. Instead, women may work in only a few professions, such as education and health care. The prohibition stems from strongly held religious and cultural beliefs; any increase in the country's level of economic development, which is already quite high, is not likely to change the rules.

To resolve a conflict of relative development, a manager must ask the following question: Would the practice be acceptable at home if my country were in a similar stage of economic development? Consider the difference between wage and safety standards in the United States and in Angola, where citizens accept lower standards on both counts. If a U.S. oil company is hiring Angolans to work on an offshore Angolan oil rig, can the company pay them lower wages than it pays U.S. workers in the Gulf of Mexico? Reasonable people have to answer yes if the alternative for Angola is the loss of both the foreign investment and the jobs.

Consider, too, differences in regulatory environments. In the 1980s, the government of India fought hard to be able to import Ciba-Geigy's Entero Vioform, a drug known to be enormously effective in fighting dysentery but one that had been banned in the United States because some users experienced side effects. Although dysentery was not a big problem in the United States, in India, poor public sanitation was contributing to epidemic levels of the disease. Was it unethical to make the drug available in India after it had been banned in the United States? On the contrary, rational people should consider it unethical not to do so. Apply our test: Would the United States, at an earlier stage of development, have used this drug despite its side effects? The answer is clearly yes.

But there are many instances when the answer to similar questions is no. Sometimes a host country's standards are inadequate at any level of economic development. If a country's pollution standards are so low that working on an oil rig would considerably increase a person's risk of developing cancer, foreign oil companies must refuse to do business there. Likewise, if the dangerous side effects of a drug treatment outweigh its benefits, managers should not accept health standards that ignore the risks.

When relative economic conditions do not drive tensions, there is a more objective test for resolving ethical problems. Managers should deem a practice permissible only if they can answer no to both of the following questions: Is it possible to conduct business successfully in the host country without undertaking the practice? And Is the practice a violation of a core human value? Japanese gift giving is a perfect example of a conflict of cultural tradition. Most experienced businesspeople, Japanese and non-Japanese alike, would agree that doing business in Japan would be virtually impossible without adopting the practice. Does gift giving violate a core human value? I cannot identify one that it violates. As a result, gift giving may be permissible for foreign companies in Japan even if it conflicts with ethical attitudes at home. In fact, that conclusion is widely accepted, even by companies such as Texas Instruments and IBM, which are outspoken against bribery.

Does it follow that all nonmonetary gifts are acceptable or that bribes are generally acceptable in countries where they are common? Not at all. (See the insert "The Problem with Bribery.") What makes the routine practice of gift giving acceptable in Japan are the limits in its scope and intention. When gift giving moves outside those limits, it soon collides with core human values. For example, when Carl Kotchian, president of Lockheed in the 1970s, carried suitcases full of cash to Japanese politicians, he went beyond the norms established by Japanese tradition. That incident galvanized opinion in the United States Congress and helped lead to passage of the Foreign Corrupt Practices Act. Likewise, Roh Tae Woo went beyond the norms established by Korean cultural tradition when he accepted $635.4 million in bribes as president of the Republic of Korea between 1988 and 1993.

Guidelines for Ethical Leadership

Learning to spot intolerable practices and to exercise good judgment when ethical conflicts arise requires practice. Creating a company culture that rewards ethical behavior is essential. The following guidelines for developing a global ethical perspective among managers can help.

Treat corporate values and formal standards of conduct as absolutes. Whatever ethical standards a company chooses, it cannot waver on its principles either at home or abroad. Consider what has become part of company lore at Motorola. Around 1950, a senior executive was negotiating with officials of a South American government on a $10 million sale that would have increased the company's annual net profits by nearly 25%. As the negotiations neared completion, however, the executive walked away from the deal because the officials were asking for $1 million for "fees." CEO Robert Galvin not only supported the executive's decision but also made it clear that Motorola would neither accept the sale on any terms nor do business with those government officials again. Retold over the decades, this story demonstrating Galvin's resolve has

helped cement a culture of ethics for thousands of employees at Motorola.

Design and implement conditions of engagement for suppliers and customers. Will your company do business with any customer or supplier? What if a customer or supplier uses child labor? What if it has strong links with organized crime? What if it pressures your company to break a host country's laws? Such issues are best not left for spur-of-the-moment decisions. Some companies have realized that. Sears, for instance, has developed a policy of not contracting production to companies that use prison labor or infringe on workers' rights to health and safety. And BankAmerica has specified as a condition for many of its loans to developing countries that environmental standards and human rights must be observed.

Allow foreign business units to help formulate ethical standards and interpret ethical issues. The French pharmaceutical company Rhône-Poulenc Rorer has allowed foreign subsidiaries to augment lists of corporate ethical principles with their own suggestions. Texas Instruments has paid special attention to issues of international business ethics by creating the Global Business Practices Council, which is made up of managers from countries in which the company operates. With the overarching intent to create a "global ethics strategy, locally deployed," the council's mandate is to provide ethics education and create local processes that will help managers in the company's foreign business units resolve ethical conflicts.

In host countries, support efforts to decrease institutional corruption. Individual managers will not be able to wipe out corruption in a host country, no matter how many bribes they turn down. When a host country's tax system, import and export procedures, and procurement practices favor unethical players, companies must take action.

Many companies have begun to participate in reforming host-country institutions. General Electric, for example, has taken a strong stand in India, using the media to make repeated condemnations of bribery in business and government. General Electric and others have found, however, that a single company usually cannot drive out entrenched corruption. Transparency International, an organization based in Germany, has been effective in helping coalitions of companies, government officials, and others work to reform bribery-ridden bureaucracies in Russia, Bangladesh, and elsewhere.

Exercise moral imagination. Using moral imagination means resolving tensions responsibly and creatively. Coca-Cola, for instance, has consistently turned down requests for bribes from Egyptian officials but has managed to gain political support and public trust by sponsoring a project to plant fruit trees. And take the example of Levi Strauss, which discovered in the early 1990s that two of its suppliers in Bangladesh were employing children under the age of 14—a practice that violated the company's principles but was tolerated in Bangladesh. Forcing the suppliers to fire the children would not have ensured that the children received an education, and it would have caused serious hardship for the families depending on the children's wages. In a creative arrangement, the suppliers agreed to pay the children's regular wages while they attended school and to offer each child a job at age 14. Levi Strauss, in turn, agreed to pay the children's tuition and provide books and uniforms. That arrangement allowed Levi Strauss to uphold its principles and provide long-term benefits to its host country.

Many people think of values as soft; to some they are usually unspoken. A South Seas island society uses the word *mokita*, which means, "the truth that everybody knows but nobody speaks." However difficult they are to articulate, values affect how we all behave. In a global business environment, values in tension are the rule rather than the exception. Without a company's commitment, statements of values and codes of ethics end up as empty plati-tudes that provide managers with no foundation for behaving ethically. Employees need and deserve more, and responsible members of the global business community can set examples for others to follow. The dark consequences of incidents such as Union Carbide's disaster in Bhopal remind us how high the stakes can be.

Notes

1. In other writings, Thomas W. Dunfee and I have used the term *hypernorm* instead of *core human value*.

2. Thomas Donaldson and Thomas W. Dunfee, "Toward a Unified Conception of Business Ethics: Integrative Social Contracts Theory," *Academy of Management Review*, April 1994; and "Integrative Social Contracts Theory: A Communitarian Conception of Economic Ethics," *Economics and Philosophy*, spring 1995.

Mideast Businesswomen Fight for Respect

Female Entrepreneurs in Region, Despite Scorn and Unequal Treatment, Make Some Gains

By Amy Teibel

SOUTHERN SHUNEH, JORDAN—Loula Zaklama was 20 years old in 1962, married with two children, when Gamel Abdel Nasser's regime abruptly detained her husband. Finding herself without support, she opened what now is one of Egypt's leading public-relations firms.

"It was damn tough," Ms. Zaklama said. "There was no such thing as women in the workplace."

Things have changed enormously, said Ms. Zaklama, president of Rada Research & Public Relations Co. If a woman is professional and conducts her business professionally, the men respect her, she said, adding, "But in whatever she is doing, she has to excel. She cannot be average."

Almost 40 years later, Yasmine Shihata, 29, is a measure of change since Ms. Zaklama launched her business. Ms. Shihata launched Egypt's first glossy lifestyle magazine, Cleo, six years ago, and in January 2000, started her second, Enigma. Things have changed for Middle Eastern women since Ms. Zaklama opened her business, but not nearly enough, she says.

"Once you get into the business world in the Middle East, it's a real fight," she said. "A woman as an entrepreneur is just not encouraged. . . . Any encouragement I got was from my years abroad," said Ms. Shihata, who was born in Kuwait to Egyptian parents and grew up in Vienna and Washington.

Ms. Zaklama's and Ms. Shihata's experiences—similarities as well as differences—illustrate tangible but tenuous advances of women in the Middle East, where many remain politically disenfranchised and without an economic voice.

Both attended a World Economic Forum conference in Jordan recently.

Big strides in health and education between 1970 and 2000 haven't brought commensurate employment gains, the World Bank said in a September 2003 report. If women's participation in the labor force were in keeping with education and age structure, household earnings could rise as much as 25%, the bank said.

"For many families, this is a ticket to the middle class," said Nadereh Chamlou, a senior adviser at the bank.

If female participation rates had been at levels their education and age structure would suggest, then annual growth of gross domestic product, or the total value of all goods and services produced in a nation, per capita might have been

0.7% higher than the 1.9% posted in the 1990s, says the World Bank, citing calculations for a subset of the region's countries.

In many countries in the Middle East, there are signs of change that could remove some of the economic and political obstacles.

In Morocco, a new family code has stripped men of their sweeping authority over women. In Kuwait, the cabinet again is considering whether to give women the right to vote, after rejecting the notion in 1999. Jordan recently guaranteed that six women would get seats in the 110-member lower chamber of Parliament. In Lebanon, Nayla Moawad is campaigning to become the country's first female president.

Such efforts are coming up against the pressure of tradition and Islamic fundamentalists, who resist notions such as Western-style equality for women.

Nabeela al-Mulla can cast a vote at the United Nations, where she is Kuwait's ambassador, but she can't vote in her own country. Prince Turki al-Faisal, the Saudi Arabian ambassador to the United Kingdom, is fond of saying nothing is more desirable in his country than a woman with a job. But that woman can't go to work without a male escort, never mind drive herself in a country that won't allow her a license.

Without her husband's consent to work, a woman can risk a great deal more than a man's wrath: In many Middle East countries, a husband has a unilateral right of divorce and often is granted custody of children.

Women across the Middle East now serve as ministers, ambassadors and university deans. Still, a duty barrier keeps many women from achieving as much in the workplace as their abilities would suggest.

In Egypt, women such as Ms. Zaklama and Ms. Shihata demonstrate, over two generations, how pervasive such influences are. "A woman's first duty in our culture is towards her family," Ms. Zaklama said. "She cannot be there if she has to run a business."

"Entrepreneurial spirit is not an asset of Egyptian women," she said. "If you work for yourself, there's no such thing as 9-to-5. And it's at the cost of children, husband, family life."

The sheer number of women in the workplace has helped change things in Egypt, she said, adding that some are working because they want to take advantage of the education they have received, and others need the money in increasingly expensive times.

The World Bank estimates women constituted about 30% of the Egyptian work force in 2000, the latest year for which figures were available.

Across the region, women's participation has risen to 28% in 2000 from 24% in 1980, the World Bank says. That still leaves the region with the lowest participation rates in the world. The regional average encompasses figures as low as 16% in Saudi Arabia and as high as 35% in Morocco.

Many women who work before they marry drop out of the work force once they start raising children, the World Bank said.

Ms. Zaklama broke the mold in more ways than that when she opened her business in the 1960s. "I came from a very conservative upper Egyptian family. Women in my background never worked, no matter what," she said. "There was no such thing as women in business. So the family did not like this at all."

Her husband, released from detention after a few months, was an exception, she said. "When he came out, he said, 'If you did this well, carry on.'"

Today, Ms. Zaklama's business, which started as an advertising agency, employs 45 people, including two daughters, and has revenue of about $2 million a year, she said.

Even today, however, such entrepreneurial energy in a traditional Egyptian family is rare. The women who are breaking out of this box and starting businesses for the most part are those who have been raised abroad, "or have amazing parents," Ms. Shihata said.

For Ms. Shihata, the big problem at Cleo, her first magazine, was getting the businessman who helped finance the venture to treat her like a partner. Men bristle at taking orders from women, especially younger ones, she said.

"It was a power struggle the whole time," she said. "I had zero leeway. I was being treated like an employee. I didn't have any access to the money, even though I had invested in it."

Ms. Shihata said she sold her shares in that first magazine at a loss because of clashes with her partner over authority.

With her second magazine, Enigma, she rejected the idea of a single business partner and works with four investors. All are Egyptian businessmen, but the company structure prevents any one partner from dominating the others, or her. "I think the biggest problem is being underestimated," she said. "People don't expect a woman to be really determined. And it's not their own fault, because there aren't that many women doing their own thing."

Ms. Shihata makes a point of profiling a businesswoman or celebrity in her magazine every other month to increase the visibility of role models.

Although families can be an obstacle, they can—when they are supportive—be essential to success. Ms. Zaklama said banks are apprehensive about lending to women, and Ms. Shihata said many women with small businesses, typically enterprises such as flower shops and boutiques, are funded by their parents.

"For a woman to actively go out and seek investors and all that is very rare," Ms. Shihata said, adding that it also is a matter of who you know.

Navigating such terrain is difficult in countries where there is little legal or institutional infrastructure to pave the way. Women are careful about their approach, relying on their wits to find their way through obstacles.

Even Ms. Zaklama isn't interested in overthrowing tradition, but rather, co-opting it.

"Even I, as a successful [business]woman, advocate that a woman's role first and foremost is to be a mother to her children," she says.

UNIT 4

Ethics and Social Responsibility in the Marketplace

Unit Selections

Key Points to Consider

- What responsibility does an organization have to reveal product defects to consumers?

- Given the competitiveness of the business arena, is it possible for marketing personnel to behave ethically and both survive and prosper? Explain. Give suggestions that could be incorporated into the marketing strategy for firms that want to be both ethical and successful.

- Name some organizations that make you feel genuinely valued as a customer. What are the characteristics of these organizations which distinguish them from their competitors? Explain.

- Which area of marketing strategy is most subject to public scrutiny in regard to ethics—product, pricing, place, or promotion? Why? Give some examples of unethical techniques or strategies involving each of these four areas.

 **Links: www.dushkin.com/online/**
These sites are annotated in the World Wide Web pages.

Business for Social Responsibility (BSR)
http://www.bsr.org/
Total Quality Management Sites
http://www.nku.edu/~lindsay/qualhttp.html
U.S. Navy
http://www.navy.mil

From a consumer viewpoint, the marketplace is the "proof of the pudding" or the place where the "rubber meets the road" for business ethics. In other words, what the company has promulgated about the virtues of its product or service has little meaning if the company's actual marketing practices and its treatment of the consumer contradict its claims.

At its core, marketing has a very noble and moral purpose: to satisfy human needs and wants and to help people through the exchange process. Marketing involves the coordination of the variables of product, price, place, and promotion to effectively and efficiently address the needs of consumers. Unfortunately, at times the unethical marketing practices of some firms have cast a shadow of suspicion over marketing in general. Since marketing is the aspect of business that is most visible to the public, it has perhaps taken a disproportionate share of the criticism directed toward the free-enterprise system.

This unit takes a careful look at the strategic process and practice of incorporating ethics into the marketplace. The first subsection, *Marketing Strategy and Ethics*, contains articles describing how marketing strategy and ethics can be integrated in the marketplace. The article, "A Matter of Trust," describes how some companies are leveraging their salespeople as positive examples of their ethical stance. The next article reveals how Saks' diversity training has had positive organization results. The last article in this subsection reflects why learning to manage angry customers is a crucial part of today's service landscape.

In the next subsection, *Ethical Practices in the Marketplace*, the first article delineates the importance of having an organizational culture which encourages and supports sound ethical behavior and socially responsible business practices. The next selection wrestles with the assumption that compliance with generally accepted principles (GAAP) is the equivalent of transparent reporting. The last article elucidates how Fetzer Vineyard places an emphasis on having a good product, providing a good work environment, and having a good partnership with its distributors.

The Perils of Doing the Right Thing

By Andrew W. Singer

At a May 11 press conference, Ford Motor Co. released its first-ever "corporate citizenship" report. In the 98-page document, titled "Connecting With Society," the company acknowledged serious concerns about its highly profitable sport utility vehicles. Not only do SUVs pollute the air and guzzle gas at rates far higher than conventional automobiles, the report conceded, they may be hazardous to other drivers.

Ford's was an unusual announcement. SUVs, after all, contribute about half of the company's earnings. The public's taste for these vehicles has shown no sign of waning. And even though they're three times as likely as cars to kill the other driver in a crash, the government has yet to declare these vehicles inherently unsafe.

What, then, was the company doing announcing that it had problems with these immensely popular, high-margin vehicles?

The front page of the next day's *New York Times* noted that Ford scion and chairman William Clay Ford Jr., whose family controls 40 percent of the company's voting shares, "has been active in environmental causes since his days at prep school and at Princeton" and was now worried "that car makers could get reputations like those of tobacco companies" if they ignored these problems. (The company did *not* pledge to stop producing SUVs, however.)

The company has been lauded for its candor. Veteran automobile-industry analyst Mary Ann Keller, now an executive with Priceline.com Inc., calls the announcement a "welcome instance of leadership." Norman Bowie, Dixons Professor of Business Ethics and Social Responsibility at London Business School, describes Ford's decision as "significant and courageous."

What makes the company's action noteworthy is that it carries real risks. According to Bowie, the biggest danger is a "backlash" among current and prospective SUV owners, who could begin to think the cars dangerous.

"Public tastes are fickle," says Brock Yates, editor-at-large of *Car and Driver*. "No one anticipated the surge in interest in SUVs, and like all fads it could disappear." And credit agency Standard & Poor's has warned that "[t]he automaker's stability could be affected if the sport-utility market slumped."

Before one proclaims a new era of social responsibility, then—as some did in the wake of the Ford press conference—one would do well to pause. Good corporate citizenship is praiseworthy, of course. But it isn't always easy. Indeed, if one looks at the experiences of other companies once acclaimed as "leaders," it is a decidedly mixed history. For all their high promise and initial acclaim, many firms later emerged scarred and chastened, victims of public derision, consumer boycotts, shareholder rebellion, and even bankruptcy.

If Ford does follow through on its exemplary course, it might do well to consider some of the lessons learned by other companies—often the hard way:

Lesson No. 1: Make sure what you are doing is really leadership— and not just self-adulation.

When asked about Ford's quandary—financial dependence on a product that carries potential environmental and safety problems—Bentley College business ethicist W. Michael Hoffman responds, "You can be ethical, and smart too."

Hoffman recalls a story recounted at a 1977 Bentley ethics conference, about a small paper company located on a polluted

New England stream. At a celebration of the first Earth Day, the mill's owner "got religion." He spent $2.5 million in an effort to clean up the company's effluent and, several months later, went broke, since he couldn't compete with other paper companies that didn't follow his example. He was unrepentant, though, "encased in a kind of angelic halo as he spoke of the necessity of clean water and sacrificing material things for spiritual ends." When it was pointed out that the water was no cleaner overall, he said, "Well, that's those other 17 fellows upstream."

"He went out of business, and he put 500 people out of work," Hoffman says. "But he felt ethically pure. That's just crazy." He describes the mill owner's attempt to "do it on his own" as a typically individualistic, American response.

Ford Motor could behave like the mill owner—act alone—and simply stop making SUVs. But that could be financially disastrous. "Ford's executives can do other things," Hoffman continues. "If they are truly concerned about a product but know they can't disarm unilaterally, then they have to work diligently within their industry and with government."

Cornell University economist Robert H. Frank says that the fact that Ford is concerned "is a positive thing." But this is "a collective-action problem," he says. "It's not a matter of Ford breaking any law." The solution Frank suggests: William Clay Ford should sit down with the U.S. secretary of transportation and work something out; a possible solution might involve instituting new passenger-vehicle taxes based on weight, emission levels, and fuel economy.

In late July, Ford took another step, announcing that it had decided to increase the fuel economy of its SUVs by 25 percent over the next five years. Its main competitor, General Motors, bristled: Vice chairman Harry Pearce expressed annoyance at Ford's claim of being "somehow the environmental leader." GM, he insisted, is and will be far superior to Ford in the area of fuel economy. On the other hand, the company is proceeding with full production of the 7,000-plus-pound Hummer, a version of the Humvee, a military transport made famous in the Gulf War.

Lesson No. 2: Be prepared to be attacked by virtue of your virtue.

H.B. Fuller Co., a Minneapolis-based adhesives manufacturer, enjoyed a reputation as one of America's most socially responsible companies. It endowed a chair in the study of business ethics at the University of Minnesota and established a charitable foundation dedicated to the environment, the arts, and social programs. Minnesotans regarded longtime president Elmer L. Andersen so highly that they elected him governor in 1960.

But beginning in the late 1980s, the company was dogged by reports that one of its adhesives, Resistol, had become the drug of choice for glue-sniffing street kids in Central America.

H.B. Fuller seemed unprepared for the furor that arose over the abuse of one of its products. "It's a social problem. It's not a product problem," the company argued. Still, it pulled the product off retail shelves in Guatemala and Honduras.

That didn't stop activists from protesting Fuller's continued marketing of Resistol to industrial customers, and to retailers in neighboring countries. Activists picketed annual shareholder meetings and brought wrongful-death suits against the company. "At risk are millions of dollars and the reputations of the company's top leaders," noted the Minneapolis *Star Tribune*.

How could such a well-regarded company become ensnared in such a circumstance? After all, Fuller's competitors were manufacturing and marketing glue in Latin America at the time, and impoverished street kids were abusing their products too. "But no one expected much of those companies," says Bowie. Social critics mostly gave them a free pass.

Unfortunately, "If you do something ethical, and then market it, and there's a little failure, you get hammered," says Bowie, who adds that company leaders were perhaps not as "proactive as they should have been."

Michael G. Daigneault, president of the nonprofit Ethics Resource Center in Washington, D.C., observes, "There are risks inherent in being perceived as, or fostering the perception of being, an exceptionally ethical or socially responsible organization. People will hold you to that standard."

This isn't to say that such a reputation is not positive. But it can backfire, particularly if a company is "overzealous" in promoting itself in this area. Daigneault says that companies that have made absolute statements—like Wal-Mart Stores Inc. claiming that all of its products are made in the United States, or Tom's of Maine Inc. insisting that all of its products are "natural"—have sometimes invited criticism. "The irony," he says, "is that a lot of these organizations have the best intentions, and many actually walk the talk—99 percent of the time." But the 1 percent of the time that they slip up, someone will be waiting for them.

Lesson No. 3: Expect to have your motives questioned and your leadership credentials challenged.

"The only thing good without qualification is a good will," wrote Immanuel Kant. In business, however, it's often difficult to distinguish goodwill from economic self-interest.

Consider the case of Smith & Wesson, the nation's largest handgun manufacturer. In March, the company entered into an agreement with federal, state, and local governments to restrict the sale of handguns. The company agreed to sell only to "authorized dealers and distributors" that would conform to a code of conduct. Among other things, this required dealers to conduct background checks on buyers at gun shows, and it put some restrictions on multiple gun sales. No other gun manufacturer signed the agreement.

On some fronts, Smith & Wesson was celebrated for its commitment. President Clinton observed that "it took a lot of courage" for the company to sign the agreement in the face of industry resistance. Housing and Urban Development secretary Andrew Cuomo described the settlement as "the most important announcement" during his tenure at HUD, and added, "The principles of the agreement will provide a framework for a new, enlightened gun policy for this nation."

Target of Criticism

"No loaded firearms or live ammunition beyond this point," reads the sign on the front door of Smith & Wesson's headquarters in Springfield, Mass.—a reminder that this is not your average business. Nor was there anything quite ordinary about the industry reaction to the firearms manufacturer's decision to accept some restrictions on its handgun sales.

Smith & Wesson CEO Edward Shultz says he wasn't surprised by the response to the firm's March 17 settlement announcement. "When you take this sort of step, you don't do it without a lot of thought. Certainly, it would have been easier to go with the crowd."

The National Rifle Association denounced Smith & Wesson, the nation's largest gun maker, for surrendering to the Clinton administration. NRA president Charlton Heston asserted that Smith & Wesson's British owner, Tomkins PLC, places less value on the Second Amendment right to bear arms than Americans do. The attorney general of Connecticut warned of "extreme elements that want to punish [Smith & Wesson] or retaliate against it for doing the right thing."

Why such a strong reaction? "We're dealing with the most anti-gun administration in recent history," says Shultz. The fact that S&W is even talking to the Clinton administration "irritates folks."

Still, Shultz says, he hadn't counted on the breadth of the detractors. The majority of S&W customers agree with the company's actions, he asserts. But its move seems to have "had an impact on anyone who owns a firearm." It's as if an automaker had installed safety air bags before any of its competitors and "it angered not just its customers but anyone who owned a car."

Shultz says he understands the emotions of the critics. As a boy in eastern Iowa, he "grew up with guns as a part of [his] daily life. But my head says that the world is changing and we will have to get in harmony with it."

Lawsuits against gun makers—who are being held partly responsible for bloodshed like that which rocked Columbine High School last year—will continue for the next five to 10 years, he predicts. "When you have the federal government after you, and the states, and lots of the cities, it's hard to say that all these people are wrong and you're right."

Will the company be stronger in the long run for signing the agreement? "Our belief was that if we didn't make this decision, we would go out of business," due to ceaseless, costly litigation. "This way, we can still prosper."

Significantly, perhaps, when New York became the first state to take the firearms-manufacturing industry to court in late June, Smith & Wesson was not named in the lawsuit. Local governments have since dropped S&W from lawsuits, too. Meanwhile, though, "The rest of the industry has held fast," noted *The New York Times*. No other gun maker signed the agreement, which requires manufacturers to take steps such as installing safety locks on guns.

Shultz has been working in the consumer-goods sector for 37 years, the last nine of which he has spent in the firearms industry. "I came from the outside to make a change here" because the company was in some financial trouble in 1992. At that time, "I never dreamed of the things that we face today in the legal and political arena."

He says that what S&W is doing is viewed as a huge compromise because it's voluntary, rather than mandated by laws and regulations. Inevitably, though, the firearms industry has to go through change. "Change is expensive, it's painful, and it involves some risk," he says.

"I've spent most of my career dealing with conflicts relating to change," Shultz says. "If I retire, it will probably be from one change too many."

—A.W.S.

Reaction was somewhat less approving in other quarters, however. The National Rifle Association and the National Shooting Sports Foundation (NSSF) denounced Smith & Wesson for "selling out" the industry and called for an immediate boycott of the company's products. (See "Target of Criticism.")

Still, Smith & Wesson CEO Edward Shultz says he's comfortable with his decision. Standards of social responsibility change, he says: "We can't operate as we did in 1935 or 1955 or 1975 and still be described as responsible." In 1955, a customer could order a gun out of a catalog, and the weapon would be delivered to that person's house. "Today, that would be viewed as totally irresponsible," he says.

"From a pure business standpoint, it makes sense to find a solution," Shultz continues. "To understand what's going on, you have to get in a conversation with the people trying to put you out of business," like anti-handgun groups. It also made sense to "settle," given the numbers of lawsuits being brought against the firearms industry in the wake of the Columbine shooting and other acts of carnage. "Rather than go out of business paying for lawsuits, if we go out of business, it will be because customers refuse to buy our products," he says.

Opposition to the company's position proved more lasting and damaging than anticipated. Some dealers refused to sell S&W products, incensed by the code of conduct that the manufacturer imposed on them. In June, Smith & Wesson announced that it was suspending firearms manufacturing at two New England factories for three weeks. It acknowledged that a contributing factor was "the reaction of some consumers to the agreement Smith & Wesson signed with federal, state and local government entities."

"I don't think they anticipated the severity of the response," says Robert Delfay, president and CEO of the NSSF, the largest firearms-industry trade group. Many members saw it as an infringement of their Second Amendment right to bear arms.

Also, inevitably, some critics saw the firm's actions as a matter of sheer expediency. "I don't view what Smith & Wesson did as leadership," Delfay says. "We think it was capitulation to strong-arm tactics by government officials." As he sees it, the gun makers showing real leadership are those that haven't "capitulated to government blackmail."

"Was that a decision of conscience?" asks ethicist Mark Pastin, president of the Council of Ethics Organizations in Alexandria, Va., of the S&W action. "Or a response to what the market demands of the company?"

Consultant Eileen Shapiro, author of *The Seven Deadly Sins of Business*, insists that Smith & Wesson's decision *did* represent a leadership position, because it involved real action: "They did something that matched their rhetoric."

It's not exceptional that some ambiguity attends the gun maker's action. Few business actions, after all, are ethically "pure." Most are a kind of double helix: one strand virtue, the other economic self-interest. It is almost impossible to disentangle the two.

Shapiro, for one, disputes that Ford Motor took any leadership position with its May announcement. Ford isn't redeploying any of its assets. It will still build SUVs. Moreover, she says, "This guy [William Ford] actually drives an SUV!"

A week after the Ford press conference, automobile-industry watcher Brock Yates said, "Internally, we're hearing a lot of concern and confusion. It's seen as a hollow gesture. The grandest gesture would have been to cancel the Excursion, which has become a paradigm for SUV evil."

In sum, even when a company takes a socially responsible stance, it should still expect to have its moral bona fides questioned. Ed Shultz speaks from experience: "Leadership is never very popular, particularly if decisions are made to change and to move forward."

Lesson No. 4: Circumstances beyond your control—including public hysteria—can undermine your position.

In the early 1990s, chemicals manufacturer Monsanto Co. placed a big bet on an exciting new business: sustainable agriculture. It committed its resources to developing seemingly miraculous genetically altered crops—cotton that could be grown without pesticides, tomatoes altered to ripen slowly, potatoes that were insect-resistant.

"Monsanto is in a unique position to contribute to the global future," gushed prominent biodiversity advocate Peter Raven at

a "global forum" in 1995. "Because of your skills, your dedication, and your understanding, you are equal to the challenge."

The first breakthrough had come two years earlier, in November 1993. After nine years of investigation, the FDA approved the use of Monsanto's bovine growth hormone (marketed under the name of Posilac), which when injected into a cow's pituitary gland increased milk output by 25 percent.

Monsanto spent $1 billion to develop Posilac, with Wall Street's approval. Posilac, after all, was the first of perhaps dozens of genetically altered agricultural products to be introduced in years ahead. The profits anticipated would fill company coffers.

The company's CEO, Robert B. Shapiro, was acclaimed as a visionary. "Bob Shapiro displayed enormous vision in committing the company to sustainable business practices" that neither deplete the world of resources nor damage the environment, noted Robert H. Dunn, president of Business for Social Responsibility, a San Francisco-based membership organization.

Only a few years later, however, things had gone terribly wrong with Monsanto's new direction. A wave of protesters had arisen to campaign against Posilac, and foreign governments were beginning to pay attention. In 1998, a British researcher declared on television that eating genetically modified (GM) potatoes could stunt rats' growth. A Cornell University study contended that pollen from GM corn harmed butterflies.

Europe resisted the U.S.-dominated GM crop business; supermarket chains rejected foods containing GM ingredients. France, citing the precautionary principle, ordered the destruction of hundreds of hectares of rapeseed that had been accidentally planted with seeds containing GM material. Brazil sent out police to burn GM crops. U.S. food processors, such as Archer Daniels Midland Co., advised suppliers to segregate GM from non-GM crops.

Environmentalists turned on Monsanto. Greenpeace told the European Union that it "cannot continue to let GMOs [genetically modified organisms] contaminate our food and environment."

All of this battered the company's share price. Early this year, one analyst noted that "investors have valued Monsanto's $5 billion-a-year agricultural-business unit at less than zero dollars during the past week."

What happened? "In ethics, some stands look appropriate at the time," Bowie observes. But then circumstances change, or science changes, "or people get hysterical—so what looked like a good decision at one time no longer looks like a good decision."

When Bowie asked his London students this past summer why the reaction against GM foods was so severe—why the "hysteria"—they answered: "We don't trust the government." In part, this was because of the British government's belated response to the dangers of "mad cow" disease, which it long downplayed. Asks Bowie: "How could Monsanto anticipate that students wouldn't trust their government because of mad cow disease?"—and by extension, that they wouldn't believe the government when it insisted that GM foods were safe?

"You can't rationalize emotions," says one analyst who follows the company but asked not to be identified in this article.

"[Robert] Shapiro felt that the Green Movement didn't have a rational case," and so the company was reluctant to modify its position. "They should have been more sensitive to the perception of these bold moves. They didn't lay the groundwork."

Ironically, in June, the Paris-based Organization for Economic Cooperation and Development—once at the heart of the GM opposition—announced that genetically modified crops approved for human consumption are as safe as other foods. The announcement may have come a bit late, however, for Robert Shapiro and Monsanto. The company was acquired by Pharmacia & Upjohn Inc. last December—for a price considerably lower than what it could have fetched a few years earlier. Robert Shapiro was slated to be "non-executive" chairman of the merged company for 18 months, and then give way to a successor.

"In the end, Shapiro was a trailblazer," concludes the analyst. One day, the world may view positively the company's technological achievement, the medical applications, the improved yields from these crops. "There is a future, but perhaps the market wasn't ready for them."

Given the costs that some of the companies mentioned here—H.B. Fuller, Monsanto, Smith & Wesson, the New England mill owner—have paid, one might well ask: Does social responsibility pay? Does it make economic sense to take a leadership position where the environment or corporate citizenship is involved?

For years, many have asserted that good ethics is good business, Pastin observes. "But there were no examples. Now there are examples, but they are hard to interpret." There has never been systemic, credible evidence that good ethics indeed leads to good financial results, he notes.

That said, some view Ford Motor's May announcement as evidence of a new era of social responsibility. "Ford has definitely demonstrated leadership as one of the first large, global companies to file a social report as a companion to its financial report," says Dunn of Business for Social Responsibility. The company "instilled in the report a spirit of candor, acknowledging the issues it must address."

Ford has "obviously learned the lesson" of the last 20 years regarding such matters—namely, "that companies that are honest and forthright are forgiven by the public, but those that stonewall earn the public's enmity," says Booz-Allen & Hamilton leadership consultant James O'Toole, whose guess is that Ford has enough data to conclude that the safety and environmental problems regarding SUVs are real. Moreover, the automaker might have a similar problem to that of the tobacco industry: By sitting on the data, it risks lawsuits later.

By acting in an honest, straightforward manner, the companies expect to be treated accordingly by the public. "Ford is trying to establish its credentials, give itself credibility," O'Toole says. "Young William Ford is laying the foundation of trust."

"I think we're entering a new age of corporate citizenship in which candor will be rewarded," says veteran PR executive Robert Dilenschneider. "Younger people—young CEOs—are willing to stick their necks out farther than the older generation. Bill Ford is a perfect example."

Others note a certain irony here. "It's interesting that it's the Ford Motor Co. that has seen fit to come forward to talk about some safety and environmental problems with SUVs," says Bentley College's Hoffman. "Maybe it has something to do with the lessons learned from the business-ethics movement."

One of the landmark cases in that movement, after all, was the 1979 Ford Pinto case, in which the state of Indiana indicted Ford on charges of criminal homicide after a rear-ended Pinto burst into flames, killing a passenger. "It made world headlines and sent reverberations through Corporate America," Hoffman says.

Even though Ford was eventually acquitted, it "was found guilty in the court of public opinion, as well as in civil cases," particularly when it was disclosed that the company had conducted a cost-benefit analysis to determine whether it should improve safety by adding a $5.08 bladder to fuel tanks—and opted not to do so. The negative public reaction "sent a message to Corporate America," Hoffman says, "that the American public would be watching corporations more carefully in terms of their social responsibility and ethical commitment."

Given the history of other companies that took a lead in "doing the right thing," though, Ford shouldn't expect an unhindered path toward an enlightened future. There are real risks with tampering with the SUV business model: risks to the company's profits, its share price, and its reputation.

ANDREW W. SINGER is publisher and co-editor of Ethikos, *a Mamaroneck, N.Y.-based publication that examines ethical and compliance issues in business. He is writing a book on the perils of corporate leadership. His last article was a review of* When Pride Still Mattered *in the February issue.*

A MATTER OF TRUST

In the aftermath of highly publicized corporate scandals, all eyes are on company executives and the way they do business. Here's how some are leveraging their salespeople as the first line of defense against skeptics

BY JENNIFER GILBERT

Gary Welch was hoping his early December meeting with a prospective business partner, a local builder, would go well. What he didn't expect was that he'd all but closed the deal in that one meeting on the strength of his company's ethical reputation.

"We were just wanting to build a relationship with him where we would act as his exclusive lender," says Welch, vice president of HomeBanc Mortgage Corporation, an Atlanta-based retail mortgage lender. For HomeBanc, prospective business partners are essentially prospective customers. When a deal is signed, HomeBanc becomes a builder's preferred lender—allowed to put marketing materials in the builder's homes and offices, and recommended to the builder's home buyers.

What sealed the deal in the meeting wasn't some knock 'em dead presentation—it was an article the builder had read in *The Atlanta Journal-Constitution* the previous day about Home-Banc's new chief people officer; Dwight "Ike" Reighard, an ordained minister. HomeBanc hired Reighard in December to maintain the quality of its workforce as the company expands.

"The builder said that if HomeBanc was willing to invest its money and its human capital in keeping employees happy, he had no questions as to how we would treat his customers," Welch says.

Such an example supports Welch's belief that customers do care about companies' ethical standards—and that it's in a company's best interest to have salespeople make such standards known. "That value has been heightened by all the negative things that have happened; it's a growing appreciation," Welch says. "If you can provide people with service and trust, they are willing to pay for that."

It's an issue that's coming up more and more during sales calls: An increasing number of sales managers are telling their reps to address the issues of ethics, corporate responsibility, and even financial viability in interactions with clients. In this business climate, some experts say, touting ethics during sales meetings is a golden opportunity to bolster a company's image.

While most companies have ethics codes already in place, some are taking a second look at them, says John Boatright, professor of business ethics at Loyola University Chicago and executive director of the Society for Business Ethics, in Chicago.

"But they're also looking at the need to increasingly focus on the code and use that code in decision making."

One potential use of the code, Boatright says, is "to make customers aware of it and to transmit this through the sales force. If companies are failing to do this, they are missing a good opportunity, because it increases the credibility of the company."

According to a recent *SMM*/Equation Research survey, 83 percent of 220 respondents said they train their reps to sell their companies' ethics and integrity along with their products and services. Nearly 70 percent said they believe their clients consider a company's ethical reputation when deciding whether to make a purchase. And while 48 percent said their companies haven't changed their emphasis on ethics and values in this economic climate, another 48 percent said they are placing somewhat more or much more emphasis on ethics.

"If corporations are not trying to promote, advertise, and sell their integrity through customers, employees, investors, and potential investors, then they are really missing a tremendous opportunity," says W. Michael Hoffman, executive director of the Center for Business Ethics at Bentley College, in Waltham, Massachusetts. Companies that develop strategies to convince those stakeholders to trust them will have a major competitive advantage over those that cannot, he says. "We are in an economic environment in which trust is at a premium. It's like air: When it's present, you don't think about it. When it's not present, you think about it all the time," Hoffman says. "We're in a financial market where there isn't a lot of air."

Speaking Up

Salespeople today are being told by their managers that a company's integrity can be as much of a selling point as low prices. So they talk about it.

HomeBanc's salespeople, for example, like to speak at length with customers about the company's commitment to keeping its employees happy. They hope that in every interaction, clients ask, "Why should we do business with you?" Welch says. HomeBanc's mission statement is: "To enrich and

DENS OF INIQUITY

What aspects of corporate culture foster unethical behavior among employees, particularly salespeople?

An environment in which employees don't have a clear understanding of what is expected of them "The ideal approach is for an organization to have a written code of conduct that everyone receives and reads," says Jim Eskin, a public affairs consultant in San Antonio, Texas. It doesn't have to be formal; expectations regarding ethical conduct can be effectively communicated in meetings, orientation, bulletins, and e-mail. "The employer is asking for trouble when there is no communication at all," he says.

A communication breakdown Employees need to feel comfortable talking to supervisors. Otherwise, they will be less inclined to report ethics violations.

Rules dictated from the top down Smart employers bring their people together to talk about common issues such as gifts and entertainment, and the use of e-mail and other company resources. "The most effective rules result from employee input and feedback," Eskin says.

A win-at-any-price attitude from management Management leads by example, and if executives send signals that grabbing short-term profits is desirable regardless of the consequences, workers throughout the organization will reflect that attitude in their behavior.

A commission-centric environment Commissions can be tricky and run the risk of distorting judgment, especially when they put salespeople's personal interests at odds with those of the customer or client.

The cog-in-the-wheel trap If employees are proud of their organization and feel a sense of loyalty, their conduct is far more likely to be ethical. "But if they feel management is making profits at their expense, there could be a mindset of getting even," Eskin says.

—J.G.

fulfill lives by serving each other, our customers and communities… as we support the dream of homeownership." The company's list of values includes, "We have integrity—do the right thing, always!" and "We deliver world-class service—serve all customers as they wish to be served." The company's mission and values are printed on cards that marketing materials sales associates carry with them to pass out to potential customers, and HomeBanc's marketing packages include reprints of newspaper articles high-lighting the company's ethical initiatives.

Welch, who manages 10 salespeople and also engages in direct selling, says he has experienced a customer's appreciation for a company's integrity and ethical reputation and how that affects his or her buying decision. "There's been a real awakening to the question of, 'Who can we trust?'" in the wake of recent corporate scandals, he says. "What we're finding is that as people learn and see us live by our mission statement, they are attracted to doing business with us, because we fall in line with what their mission statement is."

Nancy Sparks, vice president of sales and marketing for Marietta, Georgia–based builder Homes by Williamscraft Inc., says her company chose HomeBanc as its exclusive lender for

that reason. "We wanted to be associated with just them," she says. "They deliver as promised."

Sparks says HomeBanc also promotes itself positively in the community through its advertising and salespeople and clearly sends the message that it is a well-established, reputable company. "In the corporate climate that we're in right now, any kind of business is suspect," she says. "Companies have to get out there every day and prove themselves. You don't want to be associated with any company that might not be doing that."

A big part of HomeBanc's ethical agenda is keeping employees honest and satisfied. It's on the right track, at least according to one expert: "The best indicator of how sales organizations are going to treat their clients is how they treat their employees," says Brian Clapp, managing principal of the mid-Atlantic region for Right Management Consultants, based in Philadelphia.

HomeBanc stages day-long orientation programs for new salespeople, during which reps learn about how to best treat customers—by providing service guarantees and full refunds for unsatisfactory services, for example. Training is a seven-week process that teaches salespeople how to identify the best loans for customers. And to make sure all reps are behaving ethically, HomeBanc set up a hotline eight years ago that salespeople can use to report behavior that would reflect negatively on the company.

"We've been Atlanta's number-one mortgage lender for eleven straight years and if we weren't ethically responsible, I don't think we'd be here," HomeBanc's Chief People Officer Reighard says.

Another company, Memphis, Tennessee–based Inventory Locator Service (ILS), also tries to promote its ethical standards—inside and out. "When I saw some of our new dot-com competitors come out in 1999, one of the things I developed for our sales team was a white paper that focused on integrity, because at the time, the competitors were using less-than-ethical business practices," says James Sdoia, vice president of sales and service at the company, which runs an electronic marketplace for the aviation, marine, and industrial gas turbine industries and the U.S. Department of Defense.

Salespeople give the two-page sheet to customers. It addresses ILS's fiscal integrity, data integrity, and client integrity, Sdoia says, and has been "quite effective in several cases—even more so when the competitors started using high-pressure tactics such as those you'd get from a door-to-door salesman."

Recently revised, the two-pager details the company's new products and services and has been reformatted into a question-and-answer structure. The handout answers questions such as, "What makes up your financial strength and stability?" And while his company's business-to-business customer base hasn't been rocked by corporate scandals reported in the news to the extent that he believes consumers have, Sdoia insists that his salespeople address the issue of ethics.

"Certainly, the corporate integrity of any company should be reflected by the salespeople when they talk about the company," he says. "You don't have to come out and say 'Our company's trustworthy'; you show how long you've been in business, that you are financially stable, and that you have long-term relationships with clients. Salespeople should say those things in pitches."

Bill Morales, president of Tracer Corporation, a Milwaukee-based aircraft parts company, says he's proud to be a 10-year ILS customer because of its ethical and professional reputation. "They back up what they say they can do," he says. "From an ethics standpoint, they are extremely open and forward-thinking. They are willing to stand behind their product."

Uphill Battle

WorldCom is one company working overtime to show its customers that it has a soul. The bankrupt Clinton, Mississippi-based telecommunications company has been rebuilding itself following the admission of multibillion-dollar accounting fraud in summer 2002 and the investigation into its accounting and management practices.

Despite WorldCom's initiative to put new people in place, including a new CEO, and a renewed commitment to integrity, Chris Atkins, director of global corporate practice at New York-based public relations firm Ketchum, thinks the telecom giant has a steep climb ahead. "It's going to take years before people stop thinking of WorldCom as an unethical institution," he says. "On the other hand, I'm often surprised by how short America's memory really is."

WorldCom is banking on that short-term memory—and an overhaul of internal practices. In its quest to reinvent its image, the sales organization has become a critical vehicle for relaying the company's new commitment to customers and financial integrity in both words and action, says Jonathan Crane, president of U.S. sales, marketing, and services.

"We are probably the safest company in the U.S. right now because of what we've done internally and what's been done to us externally" by the courts, Crane says. He has led the charge to address ethics and corporate responsibility within the sales ranks via such programs as town-hall meetings. He also enforces the company's zero-tolerance ethics policy.

As part of sales training, all employees are asked to read, sign, and abide by the ethics policy or risk termination, Crane says. And WorldCom's commitment to integrity "is something salespeople want to make sure they get out on the table," he says.

Salespeople tell customers about new ethics programs, the independent ethics office, the new board structure and corporate governance, the hiring of a new corporate controller, and the expansion of its internal department audit staff.

"We tell people exactly what we're doing," Crane says. Salespeople also provide customers with written materials, and WorldCom posts detailed information regarding its efforts on its Web site. "We have to convince our client base that there will not be a reoccurrence of this behavior," Crane says. That

has to be a priority, he says, because customers care about WorldCom's integrity more than that of other companies.

"Because we are the company accused of perpetrating the largest fraud in the history of American business, customers are asking, 'Well, what are you doing to make sure it doesn't happen again in the future?'" Crane says. "As we enter this new year, we get a sense from our client base that our approach to this has helped us. We're starting to see an opening up of buying decisions."

Loose Lips Sink Ships?

Some experts, of course, caution managers against having their salespeople talk too much about their company's integrity and ethical responsibility in pitches, advocating a show-don't-tell approach. Broaching the subject, they argue, can actually backfire and raise suspicion.

"The least effective way to be seen as trustworthy is to say, 'I'm trustworthy.' You have to behave in a way that inspires confidence," Atkins says, rather than say, "'We're really honest.' It sounds a little disingenuous."

Like Atkins, Bill Cook, vice president of sales at Santa Clara, California-based Sun Microsystems, is an advocate of the actions-speak-louder-than-words philosophy. A 17-year alumnus of Sun's sales team, Cook says his company's ethical reputation has been built over time through its employees' actions.

Indeed, it's the small stuff that often means more to customers than words, Right's Clapp says. These include following up on commitments, not being cavalier, honoring noncompetes, and not selling empty promises.

Still, Cook acknowledges that the latest corporate scandals have shed new light on the issues of corporate and financial responsibility. Last October, Sun rolled out the Fiduciary Boot Camp, a special training program for all senior-level managers worldwide. The boot camp is designed to educate executives on the new rules and regulations included in the Sarbanes-Oxley Act of 2002, which holds companies to higher corporate governance standards, and informs them of Sun's view of ethical leadership. Executives who attend share the lessons with salespeople.

Sun's boot camp has boosted reps' recognition of the issues. But salespeople still interact with customers as they always have, Cook says. Customers do perceive Sun to be an ethical company with which to do business, Cook says, but that's because of the way its salespeople conduct themselves. "You just show it, day in and day out," he says. "We tell our customers about our products and offerings, and then we make sure we deliver against those. It's part of Sun's culture."

Senior Editor Jennifer Gilbert can be reached at jgilbert@salesandmarketing.com

Diversity Training Ups Saks' Sales

By JOANNE CLEAVER

When people think of Saks Fifth Avenue, a number of adjectives pop into their heads: exclusive, expensive, designer.

What they don't think of is just as telling: welcoming, warm, approachable.

Jay Redman, Saks' vice president for service, selling and training, is changing that.

While Saks relies on 200,000 heavy-spending, loyal core customers, there just aren't enough of them to fuel sales growth at the 62-store chain. That must come from the other 1.8 million occasional customers.

Unfortunately, those customers weren't spending enough time or money at Saks even when they did stop by. While researching that problem, Saks executives found that the company needed a heart transplant. Many occasional shoppers were essentially being ignored by Saks sales associates who made sweeping, erroneous judgments about who was a likely customer, and why.

The solution: Customer service training that focused not just on diversity, but effectively replaced a poorly performing service culture with one that is inclusive and friendly.

The effort is paying off, says Myrna Marofsky, president of diversity training firm ProGroup Inc., which created the training program for Saks, the New York-based unit of Saks Inc. retail holding company, based in Birmingham, Ala. Last year—the first full year in which the training has been in effect— Saks' sales increased at least $1 million due directly to better customer service, Marofsky says. (Saks officials

won't release financial results linked to the program but also don't argue with Marofsky's assessment.)

Back in the late 1990s, Saks concentrated on deepening the loyalty of its core customers. Its 12,000 associates caught on quickly to the notion that cultivating relationships with regular, heavy spenders was a sure way to increase sales and commissions.

An unintended consequence of that training, though, was that some associates figured it wasn't in their job descriptions to greet customers who weren't spending thousands every time they came by.

Ongoing research conducted by an external firm in 2001 revealed the scope of the problem. "We found that our brand, by its nature being exclusive, was also keeping customers from coming in the store," Redman reports. "The brand is so strong as a high-end luxury retailer that a lot of people didn't see it as the store for them. They wanted a store where they would not be intimidated. Everyone should have the chance to splurge and indulge regardless of their income, lifestyle or background."

Advertising reinforced Saks as a good prospect for finding a classy suit for a job interview or a beautifully detailed evening dress for an anniversary celebration. Shoppers would come in hoping that their experience in the store would be as tailor-made as the clothes they wanted to buy, but the reality was often the opposite.

"Customers felt that their service level was based on their appearances, including their race," says Marofsky, whose firm is based in Minneapolis. "All of us have had experiences of dressing up and going

into a store and being treated differently than if you popped in dressed down, but when you combine that with race and ethnicity, (the difference is) magnified."

Essentially, associates were assessing potential customers' spending capacity based on their first impressions. Though company research shows that even occasional shoppers have average incomes of $200,000, the associates' images of the preferred customer didn't translate to the occasional customers. Not only did Saks associates lose immediate sales when customers left right away, but they also lost the chance to convert occasional shoppers to core customers.

It wasn't hard to build a business case for a change of heart. Redman shrewdly drew a short, straight line from a culture of inclusiveness to increased sales commissions.

That was the hook that got associates' attention, but the look-in-the-mirror training strategy won their hearts. Marofsky and Redman collaborated on the presentation, which showcased numerous "customers" (portrayed by actors) who might have easily been dismissed—such as a portly man in traditional Middle Eastern dress—replicating scenarios that researchers had observed in actual situations on the floor. The customers were videotaped in a real store, browsing and being ignored, then told viewers how they felt.

Their comments pulled at associates' heartstrings, but the kicker that grabbed their purse strings at the end of the video was the dollar figure shown with each videotaped customer, representing the lost sales she represented.

For instance, one vignette showed a sales associate working with a young woman while a middle-aged woman wearing denim gets the cold shoulder. The middle-aged woman walks out of the store and tells the camera, "It was like I was invisible." Then a "lost opportunity" figure flashes on the screen: several hundreds of dollars in cosmetic sales that the woman represents.

Redman believes that the program is successful because it helps associates relate to that universal feeling of being unsure whether or not you belong in what looks like an exclusive club. "The psychology of the exclusive brand and the anxiety it creates—that you have to be a member to be accepted—that's not true, but it's the impression that people have" of Saks, he says. "The associates need to understand what people are thinking when they come here."

The occasional customer, he says, doesn't just want a suit or dress, but also craves a bit of validation. They want to know that they are shopping at a place where they'll get the right look for an important life event, and that the sales staff will enjoy helping them.

As the training program rolled out in 2001 and 2002, Redman followed up immediately by surveying customers at stores where associates had just participated in the sessions. Benchmarked against the earlier survey results, he saw an immediate lift in customer satisfaction scores. Employee service has shown improvement for the last four consecutive measurement periods, he adds.

That's not to say that there aren't some snobby holdouts. "Certain stores are a problem. And some customer bases still don't feel welcome," he says.

Ultimately, the diversity training doesn't have to carry the entire load for transforming the Saks culture. It is one of more than 60 initiatives that Redman is putting into place, including the new concierge desks prominently placed by the main entrance at each store, specifically to greet shoppers and help them find what they need.

"The core customers won't use it because they have associates (dedicated to them)," Redman says. "But for everyone else, this is a friendly associate just for you."

Joanne Cleaver is a Chicago-based freelance writer.

SURVIVING IN THE AGE OF RAGE

Learning to manage angry customers is a crucial part of today's service landscape.

By Stephen J. Grove, Raymond P. Fisk, and Joby John

We seem to live in an age of rage. What once were isolated incidents of volatile customer behavior have become commonplace. News reports from around the world chronicle a growing number of customer rage incidents. These incidents create serious problems for managers of service organizations. Consider the following episodes:

Checkout counter rage: A woman had half her nose bitten off by a fellow shopper when she insisted on remaining in an express lane with more than the 12 permitted items.

Parking rage: Youths screamed, swore at, and verbally abused a man in a dispute over a parking space in front of a Costco store and later severely scratched his automobile.

Air rage: A disruptive passenger who attempted to break into the cockpit on a Southwest Airlines flight to Salt Lake City was beaten, choked, and eventually killed by other passengers. (This happened before Sept. 11, 2001.)

Snowplow rage: Frustrated by the never-ending snowfall and the snowplow generated mountain of white blocking his driveway, a Framingham, Mass., man beat the town's plow driver with his snow shovel.

Pub rage: Incensed for being refused service at a pub at closing time, a man with a tractor repeatedly smashed into the establishment, causing the pub's walls to crumble.

ATM rage: When a bank machine at a convenience store swallowed his card, an enraged patron stuck the ATM machine with a utility knife, cursed a nearby clerk, hurled the knife at a cashier, and smashed an adjacent fax machine to the ground.

These incidents only hint at the breadth and severity of customer rage. Damage caused by rage episodes varies from verbal indignation, to vandalism, to physical injury, and even death. Fellow patrons and workers alike have been unsuspecting targets of rage. Clearly, disruptive customer behaviors pose severe problems for businesses afflicted by rage episodes. These problems might include negative publicity, costs of legal actions, and the untold ramifications of traumatized customers and employees. Service organizations should have policies and procedures to prevent or reduce the occurrence of customer rage.

Many customer rage incidents go unreported, so the precise number of rage episodes is difficult to determine. Indications are, however, that customer rage is on the upswing. Consider the airline industry prior to Sept. 11. A *New York Times* article reported that Swissair witnessed nearly a 100% increase over a three-year period in the occurrence of passenger interference with crew members' in-flight duties. CNN reported that an estimated 4,000 air rage episodes occurred in the United States (where airlines are not required to register such instances) in the year 2000 alone. While the number of air rage incidents has declined since 2001 according to the Federal Aviation Administration, a new phenomenon called "ground rage" is growing. Aggressive behavior toward airline personnel on the ground is now so prevalent that British Airways issues soccer-style yellow cards as a final warning to disruptive travelers that any further disturbance will result in refusal of service.

On another front, a recent survey of call center personnel found that nearly 60% of the respondents reported an increased incidence of phone rage over the past five years. Regardless of the range or severity of customer rage, it's the service sector that is most frequently afflicted with rage incidents. Service organizations, such as hotels, banks, restaurants, airlines, and theme parks, require interaction between customers and employees, often in the presence of multiple consumers sharing a common service setting. In addition, service

EXECUTIVE briefing	With civility on a seemingly downward path, customer rage has become a common problem for many service organizations. This article discusses "the four Ts of customer rage," which include the targets of customer rage behavior, the influence of temperament on customers expressing rage, the triggers that spark customers' rage, and the treatments for preventing or managing customer rage. In this environment, smart service managers are doing all they can to improve the service environment for their customers.

quality provided by such organizations is notoriously variable due to the "real time" character of service delivery and the many uncontrollable elements that combine to create customers' service experience. Further, service organizations are often capacity constrained. It's not surprising then that service encounters are a veritable petri dish for customer rage. According to a 2002 study by the Public Agenda research group, shopping malls, airports, airplanes, and government offices are particularly vulnerable to rude or disrespectful behavior.

Customer behaviors in service settings can range from those that are too friendly to those that constitute rage. Obviously, pleasant interactions between customers and employees are desirable. However, if customers are excessively friendly, they can be a major distraction to employees and may delay service to subsequent customers. Under such circumstances, the service process bogs down and workers search for ways to chill customers' friendly advances. Hence, we label the boundary line between too friendly and the range of acceptable behaviors as the freezing point. Toward the other extreme of acceptable behaviors, unfriendly situations occur when customers are irritating or rude to employees. Unfriendly interactions can escalate to rage if the customer or the employee hits the other's hot button with an inappropriate comment, misguided gesture, or other affront. We label the boundary line between rage and the range of acceptable behaviors as the boiling point.

The Four Ts of Customer Rage

Targets. Since customer rage is a common service phenomenon, it's not surprising that the targets of customer rage are other customers, employees, or elements of the service environment. In reality, no aspect of a service organization is immune from rage. In most cases, the rage exhibited far exceeds the transgression that triggered the anger. An unsolicited comment or an accidental bump by a fellow patron may unleash astonishing fury. Harried employees who snub or overlook demanding customers may experience their uncontrolled wrath. Not even innocent bystanders are sheltered from customer rage. Bottled up angst may find an outlet in the nearest unsuspecting soul. Sometimes it's the adjacent passenger, fellow shopper, or exuberant fan that draws the rage of nearby customers. Sharing the service setting with one who is predisposed to rage is not unfathomable.

When fellow customers or employees are not targets of rage, fury may be directed at inanimate objects or others' possessions. Angry ATM users relentlessly pound the machine that swallowed their debit card. Frustrated golfers hurl the clubs that humiliate them into the nearest water hazard. Enraged diners slam tables and toss food on the floor when offended by a waiter. Clearly, when anger boils over, neither people nor property is safe.

Temperament. Service organizations that cater to large numbers of customers simultaneously must be aware that some people are prone to customer rage. Most people know somebody who can "go off" at the slightest provocation. Perhaps it can be traced to personality or maybe other personal factors are at play. Regardless, not all service customers are equally likely to exhibit rage.

Unfriendly interactions can escalate to rage if the customer or the employee hits the other's hot button with an inappropriate comment, misguided gesture, or other affront.

Modern technology has created a world where the boundaries between work and leisure are blurred. Where can one escape the responsibilities of the workplace? Cell phones, pagers, laptop computers, and Internet access keep us tethered to obligations that follow us everywhere. We seem to live in a world where we're on stage 24 hours a day, seven days a week, and 365 days a year. These stressful circumstances provide ample kindling to ignite rage in some customers.

Is it possible that some people fly into rage more quickly? Perhaps. There is some evidence that anger is inherited, yet it seems more likely that rage behaviors are learned via socialization as appropriate responses to certain situations. Some people may have internalized rage as a typical response for some occasions, possibly through a previous experience or by observing others. Further contributing to the likelihood of rage may be the absence of one's spouse or close friends, whose presence might normally keep one's aggressive behavior in check. At the very least, the enraged customer may lack strong social or personal norms that prevent them from boiling over when faced with challenging circumstances.

Many other temperament factors can make some people susceptible to rage. Aggressive personality types are prone to heated verbal exchanges and attempt retribution for even the smallest perceived transgressions. Customers who exhibit type A behavior patterns (i.e., intense achievement strivings, strong sense of competition) often find themselves in situations where their impatience or obsessive nature sparks confrontation. Those who feel controlled by circumstances may be prone to display aggression as well. Even physiological conditions, such as reduced amounts of serotonin and low levels of cholesterol in one's blood system, have been linked with aggressive tendencies. These are just a handful of individual characteristics associated with rage. In short, some customers enter a service encounter with their rage sensors loaded and ready.

The task of identifying likely candidates for rage is fraught with issues. There is an important but subtle difference between engaging in customer segmentation and discrimination. Customer segmentation involves offering different customers different service based on their distinctive characteristics. (Service businesses that provide a more protective environment for parents with small children engage in customer segmentation.) Discrimination occurs when customers are given poor service because of their race, age, sex, religion, or other distinctive characteristic. Discrimination can take the form of "profiling." For instance, a business may decide that males with beards are prone to rage and subject such customers to obtrusive scrutiny. Since Sept. 11, profiling has become a controversial issue. The U.S. Transportation Security Administration's computer-assisted passenger profiling system (or CAPPS II) classifies prospective passengers with a three-level rating—green, yellow, or red. A green rating yields minimal security screening, a yellow rating leads to extensive searches and interrogation, and a red rating prevents boarding the plane.

Triggers. The interactive nature of services offers many potential triggers for customer rage. Some of the strongest triggers occur when customers believe they have been treated unfairly, neglected, or negated in a service encounter. Perceived unjust treatment, such as a later-arriving patron being seated first at a restaurant, may fuel rage. Customers sometimes become angry when their needs are neglected. One who endures a long wait at an unattended customer service counter may commence yelling when the service representative finally arrives. If customers believe they are being treated with disrespect, hostility may ensue. A patronizing attitude from an employee tells customers that they are unimportant and can send the customer into a fury. Ironically, it seems that some organizations knowingly trigger "righteous indignation" from customers and may deserve the rage responses they prompt.

Situational influences on customer behavior, such as those described by Russell Belk, may play a role in triggering rage in any service encounter. Consider the rage-generating effect of these in the following:

- *Physical surrounding:* Aspects of the service environment may rub customers the wrong way. Room temperatures can be oppressively warm or chillingly cold, noise levels can be

painfully loud, filthy service settings can anger customers, and/or cramped facilities can make the service setting seem too crowded.
- *Social surroundings:* Other customers often negatively affect each other by violating normative expectations (e.g., standing too close in line or smoking in nonsmoking areas). Crowded service settings can push customers to their limits and may initiate jostling among customers.
- *Temporal perspective:* Long delays or being rushed for time can ignite rage. Time is one of the most sensitive of situational triggers. For example, most customers detest waiting in line, and time delays can cause tempers to rushed often become aggravated and lash out.

We seem to live in a world where we're on stage 24 hours a day, seven days a week, and 365 days a year. These stressful circumstances provide ample kindling to ignite rage in some customers.

- *Task definition:* Extraordinary obligations Heightened expectations and desires can increase customer sensitivity. For example, a married couple celebrating a special occasion may become quite agitated when things don't go as planned at a fancy restaurant.
- *Antecedent states:* Temporary conditions that customers experience, such as hunger or thirst, may cause people to become easily enraged. But the most troubling of such antecedent states is drunkenness, a circumstance that escalates when businesses such as bars, nightclubs, or sporting events serve large numbers of drinking customers.

Treatment. People's emotions can soar during a rage-precipitating incident to the point where management must get involved during or after the episode. Less astute organizations occasionally find themselves tackling uncomfortable negative publicity and possibly liability issues. Clearly, it's in any organization's best interest to have a well-designed set of procedures and policies to manage customer rage.

The first management step is to prevent customer rage by preempting such situations. To do this, firms should focus on the triggers that activate rage. Organizations that understand the triggers that prompt rage can institute procedures to manage outbursts. For example, an unfulfilled promise of a "freebie" supplemental service, an unbearably long wait for service due to unforeseen circumstances, an aggressive customer in a bad mood, or a poorly trained employee serving an "important customer" may each require different treatment. Consider how Disney Corp. successfully manages waiting time for rides at its theme parks. For years, Disney has communicated average waiting times, kept lines moving, and made the wait entertaining. But the most significant improvement is Disney's Fastpass virtual queue system that allows guests to reserve a place in line without having to queue up.

When rage incidents occur, frontline service staff must scramble to defuse the situation and protect the personal safety of those present. At the very least, customer rage may have harmful effects on frontline employees, on customers who share the service setting, and on the perception of service quality. If an employee is the target of rage, this can affect subsequent encounters with future customers. If other patrons are present, they may witness the rage incident and their own experience may be affected negatively. The 2002 Public Agenda study found that nearly three of every four customers report seeing fellow customers behaving badly toward service personnel, and more than 60% said such incidents bothered them a lot. All in all, the costs of mishandling customer rage are too great to be ignored.

Once a rage episode has occurred, organizations are faced with the difficult task of determining the appropriate remedial action for that specific incident and learning from the event to prevent future occurrences. Service organizations should be attuned to how the nature of services can affect customer rage. Since services occur in real time, the risk of failure is always high. Therefore, it is imperative that organizations take a systematic approach to managing rage incidents. For example, the C.H.A.R.M. School provides lessons in Customer Hostility and Rage Management. Employees learn various identification techniques to spot potential incidents before they happen and plausible tactics to defuse potentially dangerous customers. Forward thinking organizations that prepare employees for rage through such programs are making a commitment to a better service experience.

In Exhibit 1, we suggest how firms might establish customer rage management protocols.

There are several managerial actions that organizations can take before, during, or after a customer rage incident occurs.

Exhibit 1
Living with customer rage

BEFORE

Ensure that people and processes are in place to recognize customers who are prone to rage and potential customer rage situations

DURING

Empower employees with the skills and reward mechanisms to manage customer rage as it occurs

AFTER

Investigate, analyze, and learn from customer rage incidents

"Before" Actions

Before customer rage occurs, managers can take preemptive actions to lock the trigger. First, organizations should identify and institute early warning mechanisms and procedures for handling rage episodes. The specific devices involved may vary across service types. Nevertheless, frontline employees need to be trained, motivated, and rewarded for handling difficult customer rage incidents. These actions demonstrate to employees and customers that management takes rage situations seriously. It also facilitates any legal defense if an unfortunate event should occur. As a manager, you might do the following:

- Train employees to anticipate and manage service failures and customer rage.
- Empower employees to act on the incidents without waiting for supervisory assistance.
- Establish reward systems that motivate all employees to attend to customer rage incidents.
- Design early warning mechanisms to anticipate circumstances and situations leading to customer rage.

As an example, Caterpillar Inc. depends a great deal on service enhancements to its products. The company monitors customer equipment remotely, sending electronic warning signals to its service technicians when necessary. These employees are given information indicating the parts and tools needed to make the repair.

"During" Actions

During a rage incident, other procedures may be engaged. Such procedures might include employee actions that seek to respond to the situation. The status of the customer could dictate the type of procedure to invoke. For example, an important client might be handled by senior management with a just amount of apologies and offers for redemption. During a rage incident, you should do the following:

- Take immediate action
- Maintain decorum and remain calm
- Listen to the customer, show empathy, assume responsibility, apologize, and make amends
- Separate or isolate the enraged customer, especially in a shared customer experience
- Document everything about the incident including witness reports
- Involve superiors, if necessary

Marriott, for example, specifies the situations that call for empowered actions based on the nature of the customer problem and the value of the customer to the company. Employees are given "safe zones" for spending up to $2,500 to compensate a customer grievance or inconvenience.

Exhibit 2
Phases in the treatment of customer rage

1
Analysis of rage incidents
Understand customer rage triggers

2
Process Design
Design and install prevention methods to preempt customer rage

3
Action during rage incident
Employ prevention methods to manage raging customers

4
Action after rage incident
Follow-up at the individual level after customer rage incidents

5
Process improvement
Follow-up at the organization level after customer rage

"After" Actions

After a rage incident, management must analyze each episode and follow up with the individuals involved. For long-term actions, incidents must be recorded, categorized by level of severity and frequency of occurrence, stored as information, and then analyzed so that systemic improvements might be designed into the service delivery processes. Managers should take the following steps after an episode of customer rage:

- Investigate causes of the incident
- Follow-up with customers by apologizing, explaining, and reinstating the organization's commitment to preventing similar occurrences in the future
- Depending on the severity and pervasiveness of an incident, involve upper management If service failure was the reason, determine what can be done to prevent it in the future
- If a customer is at fault, determine if an individual or a customer segment should be avoided
- If a service employee is at fault, determine if screening, hiring, training, or supervision is to be changed or improved

Westpac Bank of Melbourne, Australia, has adopted an innovative way to respond to customer rage. It recruits "middle-aged mums" to cool customer rage since mothers tend to have the proper skills from managing their families. They have a general willingness to listen, an increased level of patience, and are naturally empathetic.

Exhibit 2 outlines the series of steps that firms might formally establish to manage customer rage. Step 1 is to rage. Process design is Step 2, which requires designing and implementing methods for preempting customer rage. Step 3 stresses action during rage incidents by employing prevention methods to manage raging customers. Taking action after a rage incident is Step 4, following up with individuals who became enraged. This is essentially a damage control step. If the customer was enraged about legitimate complaints, then corrective actions must be taken. If, however, the customer was primarily to blame for the rage incident, then it might be necessary to ask the customer to take their patronage elsewhere. Step 5 is process improvement. The organization should follow up on any lessons learned regarding managing customer rage.

The Prognosis

In some ways, it's surprising that the customer rage problem isn't worse. Civility seems to be scarce in modern times. The 2002 Public Agenda study documented a perception of growing rudeness in America with 80% of Americans surveyed viewing rudeness as a very serious problem. Among the reasons that customers become rude or even enraged is that their public and private lives leave them pressed for time. In addition, rising education levels have led to rising customer expectations. Information age technology will continue to present opportunities for customer rage as it provides new methods for interaction between firm and customer, and for interaction among customers. Against this backdrop, it's clear that more needs to be done to manage and prevent customer rage.

Will service encounters in the future contain even more hostility than today? We believe that customer rage is more likely unless service managers reduce common targets of customer rage, manage customer temperaments, prevent triggers, and pursue treatments for customer rage. Smart services managers will do everything possible to make sure that their customer interactions are characterized by civility rather than marred by rage. They know that customers prefer businesses that provide predictably pleasant service environments.

About the Authors

Stephen J. Grove is professor, department of marketing, college of business, Clemson University, Clemson, S.C. He may be reached at groves@clemson.edu. **Raymond P. Fisk** is professor and chair of marketing, department of marketing, college of business administration, University of New Orleans. He may be reached at rfisk@uno.edu. **Joby John** is professor and chair, marketing department, Bentley College, Waltham, Mass. He may be reached at jjohn@bentley.edu.

From *Marketing Management*, March/April 2004, pp. 41–46. Copyright © 2004 by American Marketing Association. Reprinted by permission.

Managing for Organizational Integrity

By supporting ethically sound behavior, managers can strengthen the relationships and reputations their companies depend on.

Lynn Sharp Paine

Many managers think of ethics as a question of personal scruples, a confidential matter between individuals and their consciences. These executives are quick to describe any wrongdoing as an isolated incident, the work of a rogue employee. The thought that the company could bear any responsibility for an individual's misdeeds never enters their minds. Ethics, after all, has nothing to do with management.

In fact, ethics has *everything* to do with management. Rarely do the character flaws of a lone actor fully explain corporate misconduct. More typically, unethical business practice involves the tacit, if not explicit, cooperation of others and reflects the values, attitudes, beliefs, language, and behavioral patterns that define an organization's operating culture. Ethics, then, is as much an organizational as a personal issue. Managers who fail to provide proper leadership and to institute systems that facilitate ethical conduct share responsibility with those who conceive, execute, and knowingly benefit from corporate misdeeds.

Managers must acknowledge their role in shaping organizational ethics and seize this opportunity to create a climate that can strengthen the relationships and reputations on which their companies' success depends. Executives who ignore ethics run the risk of personal and corporate liability in today's increasingly tough legal environment. In addition, they deprive their organizations of the benefits available under new federal guidelines for sentencing organizations convicted of wrongdoing. These sentencing guidelines recognize for the first time the organizational and managerial roots of unlawful conduct and base fines partly on the extent to which companies have taken steps to prevent that misconduct.

Prompted by the prospect of leniency, many companies are rushing to implement compliance-based ethics programs. Designed by corporate counsel, the goal of these programs is to prevent, detect, and punish legal violations. But organizational ethics means more than avoiding illegal practice; and providing employees with a rule book will do little to address the problems underlying unlawful conduct. To foster a climate that encourages exemplary behavior, corporations need a comprehensive approach that goes beyond the often punitive legal compliance stance.

An integrity-based approach to ethics management combines a concern for the law with an emphasis on managerial responsibility for ethical behavior. Though integrity strategies may vary in design and scope, all strive to define companies' guiding values, aspirations, and patterns of thought and conduct. When integrated into the day-to-day operations of an organization, such strategies can help prevent damaging ethical lapses while tapping into powerful human impulses for moral thought and action. Then an ethical framework becomes no longer a burdensome constraint within which companies must operate, but the governing ethos of an organization.

How Organizations Shape Individuals' Behavior

The once familiar picture of ethics as individualistic, unchanging, and impervious to organizational influences has not stood up to scrutiny in recent years. Sears Auto Centers' and Beech-Nut Nutrition Corporation's experiences illustrate the role organizations play in shaping individuals' behavior—and how even sound moral fiber can fray when stretched too thin.

In 1992, Sears, Roebuck & Company was inundated with complaints about its automotive service business. Consumers and attorneys general in more than 40 states had accused the company of misleading customers and selling them unnecessary parts and services, from brake jobs to front-end alignments. It would be a mistake, however, to see this situation exclusively in terms of any one individual's moral failings. Nor did management set out to defraud Sears customers. Instead, a number of organizational factors contributed to the problematic sales practices.

In the face of declining revenues, shrinking market share, and an increasingly competitive market for undercar services, Sears management attempted to spur the performance of its auto centers by introducing new goals and incentives for employees. The company increased minimum work quotas and introduced productivity incentives for mechanics. The automotive service advisers were given product-specific sales quotas—sell so many springs, shock absorbers, alignments, or brake jobs per shift—and paid a commission based on sales. According to advisers, failure to meet quotas could lead to a transfer or a reduction in work hours. Some employees spoke of the "pressure, pressure, pressure" to bring in sales.

Under this new set of organizational pressures and incentives, with few options for meeting their sales goals legitimately, some employees' judgment understandably suffered. Management's failure to clarify the line between unnecessary service and legitimate preventive maintenance, coupled with consumer ignorance, left employees to chart their own courses through a vast gray area, subject to a wide range of interpretations. Without active management support for ethical practice and mechanisms to detect and check questionable sales methods and poor work, it is not surprising that some employees may have reacted to contextual forces by resorting to exaggeration, carelessness, or even misrepresentation.

Shortly after the allegations against Sears became public, CEO Edward Brennan acknowledged management's responsibility for putting in place compensation and goal-setting systems that "created an environment in which mistakes did occur." Although the company denied any intent to deceive consumers, senior executives eliminated commissions for service advisers and discontinued sales quotas for specific parts. They also instituted a system of unannounced shopping audits and made plans to expand the internal monitoring of service. In settling the pending lawsuits, Sears offered coupons to customers who had bought certain auto services between 1990 and 1992. The total cost of the settlement, including potential customer refunds, was an estimated $60 million.

Contextual forces can also influence the behavior of top management, as a former CEO of Beech-Nut Nutrition Corporation discovered. In the early 1980s, only two years after joining the company, the CEO found evidence suggesting that the apple juice concentrate, supplied by the company's vendors for use in Beech-Nut's "100% pure" apple juice, contained nothing more than sugar water and chemicals. The CEO could have destroyed the bogus inventory and withdrawn the juice from grocers' shelves, but he was under extraordinary pressure to turn the ailing company around. Eliminating the inventory would have killed any hope of turning even the meager $700,000 profit promised to Beech-Nut's then parent, Nestlé.

A number of people in the corporation, it turned out, had doubted the purity of the juice for several years before the CEO arrived. But the 25% price advantage offered by the supplier of the bogus concentrate allowed the operations head to meet cost-control goals. Furthermore, the company lacked an effective quality control system, and a conclusive lab test for juice purity did not yet exist. When a member of the research department voiced concerns about the juice to operating management, he was accused of not being a team player and of acting like "Chicken Little." His judgment, his supervisor wrote in an annual performance review, was "colored by naïveté and impractical ideals." No one else seemed to have considered the company's obligations to its customers or to have thought about the potential harm of disclosure. No one considered the fact that the sale of adulterated or misbranded juice is a legal offense, putting the company and its top management at risk of criminal liability.

An FDA investigation taught Beech-Nut the hard way. In 1987, the company pleaded guilty to selling adulterated and misbranded juice. Two years and two criminal trials later, the CEO pleaded guilty to ten counts of mislabeling. The total cost to the company—including fines, legal expenses, and lost sales—was an estimated $25 million.

Acknowledging the importance of organizational context in ethics does not imply forgiving individual wrongdoers.

Such errors of judgment rarely reflect an organizational culture and management philosophy that sets out to harm or deceive. More often, they reveal a culture that is insensitive or indifferent to ethical considerations or one that lacks effective organizational systems. By the same token, exemplary conduct usually reflects an organizational culture and philosophy that is infused with a sense of responsibility.

For example, Johnson & Johnson's handling of the Tylenol crisis is sometimes attributed to the singular personality of then-CEO James Burke. However the decision to do a nationwide recall of Tylenol capsules in order to avoid further loss of life from product tampering was in reality not one decision but thousands of decisions made by individuals at all levels of the organization. The "Tylenol decision," then, is best understood not as an isolated incident, the achievement of a lone individual, but as the reflection of an organization's culture. Without a shared set of values and guiding principles deeply ingrained throughout the organi-

Corporate Fines Under the Federal Sentencing Guidelines

What size fine is a corporation likely to pay if convicted of a crime? It depends on a number of factors, some of which are beyond a CEO's control, such as the existence of a prior record of similar misconduct. But it also depends on more controllable factors. The most important of these are reporting and accepting responsibility for the crime, cooperating with authorities, and having an effective program in place to prevent and detect unlawful behavior.

The following example, based on a case studied by the United States Sentencing Commission, shows how the 1991 Federal Sentencing Guidelines have affected overall fine levels and how managers' actions influence organizational fines.

Acme Corporation was charged and convicted of mail fraud. The company systematically charged customers who damaged rented automobiles more than the actual cost of repairs. Acme also billed some customers for the cost of repairs to vehicles for which they were not responsible. Prior to the criminal adjudication, Acme paid $13.7 million in restitution to the customers who had been overcharged.

Deciding before the enactment of the sentencing guidelines, the judge in the criminal case imposed a fine of $6.85 million, roughly half the pecuniary loss suffered by Acme's customers. Under the sentencing guidelines, however, the results could have been dramatically different. Acme could have been fined anywhere from 5% to 200% the loss suffered by customers, depending on whether or not it had an effective program to prevent and detect violations of law and on whether or not it reported the crime, cooperated with authorities, and accepted responsibility for the unlawful conduct. If a high ranking official at Acme were found to have been involved, the maximum fine could have been as large as $54,800,000 or four times the loss to Acme customers. The following chart shows a possible range of fines for each situation:

What Fine Can Acme Expect?

	Maximum	Minimum
Program, reporting, cooperation, responsibility	$2,740,000	$685,000
Program only	10,960,000	5,480,000
No program, no reporting, no cooperation, no responsibility	27,400,000	13,700,000
No program, no reporting, no cooperation, no responsibility, involvement of high-level personnel	54,800,000	27,400,000

Based on Case No.: 88-266, United States Sentencing Commission, *Supplementary Report on Sentencing Guidelines for Organizations.*

zation, it is doubtful that Johnson & Johnson's response would have been as rapid, cohesive and ethically sound.

Many people resist acknowledging the influence of organizational factors on individual behavior—especially on misconduct—for fear of diluting people's sense of personal moral responsibility. But this fear is based on a false dichotomy between holding individual transgressors accountable and holding "the system" accountable. Acknowledging the importance of organizational context need not imply exculpating individual wrongdoers. To understand all is not to forgive all.

The Limits of a Legal Compliance Program

The consequences of an ethical lapse can be serious and far-reaching. Organizations can quickly become entangled in an all-consuming web of legal proceedings. The risk of litigation and liability has increased in the past decade as lawmakers have legislated new civil and criminal offenses, stepped up penalties, and improved support for law enforcement. Equally—if not more—important is the damage an ethical lapse can do to an organization's reputation and relationships. Both Sears and Beech-Nut, for instance, struggled to regain consumer trust and market share long after legal proceedings had ended.

As more managers have become alerted to the importance of organizational ethics, many have asked their lawyers to develop corporate ethics programs to detect and prevent violations of the law. The 1991 Federal Sentencing Guidelines offer a compelling rationale. Sanctions such as fines and probation for organizations convicted of wrongdoing can vary dramatically depending both on the degree of management cooperation in reporting and investigating corporate misdeeds and on whether or not the company has implemented a legal compliance program. (See the insert "Corporate Fines Under the Federal Sentencing Guidelines.")

Such programs tend to emphasize the prevention of unlawful conduct, primarily by increasing surveillance and control and by imposing penalties for wrongdoers. While plans vary, the basic framework is outlined in the sentencing guidelines. Managers must establish compliance standards and procedures; designate high-level personnel to oversee compliance; avoid delegating discretionary authority to those likely to act unlawfully; effectively communicate the company's standards and procedures through training or publications; take reasonable steps to achieve compliance through audits, monitoring processes, and a system for employees to report criminal misconduct without fear of retribution; consistently enforce standards through appropriate disciplinary measures; respond appropriately when offenses are detected; and, finally, take reasonable steps to prevent the occurrence of similar offenses in the future.

There is no question of the necessity of a sound, well-articulated strategy for legal compliance in an organization. After all, employees can be frustrated and frightened by the complexity of today's legal environment. And even managers who claim to use the law as a guide to ethical behavior often lack more than a rudimentary understanding of complex legal issues.

Managers would be mistaken, however, to regard legal compliance as an adequate means for addressing the full range of ethical issues that arise every day. "If it's legal, it's ethical," is a frequently heard slogan. But conduct that is lawful may be highly problematic from an ethical point of view. Consider the sale in some countries of hazardous products without appropriate warnings or the purchase of goods from suppliers who operate inhumane sweatshops in developing countries. Companies engaged in international business often discover that conduct that infringes on recognized standards of human rights and decency is legally permissible in some jurisdictions.

Legal clearance does not certify the absence of ethical problems in the United States either, as a 1991 case at Salomon Brothers illustrates. Four top-level executives failed to take appropriate action when learning of unlawful activities on the government trading desk. Company lawyers found no law obligating the executives to disclose the improprieties. Nevertheless, the executives' delay in disclosing and failure to reveal their prior knowledge prompted a serious crisis of confidence among employees, creditors, shareholders, and customers. The executives were forced to resign, having lost the moral authority to lead. Their ethical lapse compounded the trading desk's legal offenses, and the company ended up suffering losses—including legal costs, increased funding costs, and lost business—estimated at nearly $1 billion.

A compliance approach to ethics also overemphasizes the threat of detection and punishment in order to channel behavior in lawful directions. The underlying model for this approach is deterrence theory, which envisions people as rational maximizers of self-interest, responsive to the personal costs and benefits of their choices, yet indifferent to the moral legitimacy of those choices. But a recent study reported in *Why People Obey the Law* by Tom R. Tyler shows that obedience to the law is strongly influenced by a belief in its legitimacy and its moral correctness. People generally feel that they have a strong obligation to obey the law. Education about the legal standards and a supportive environment may be all that's required to insure compliance.

Discipline is, of course, a necessary part of any ethical system. Justified penalties for the infringement of legitimate norms are fair and appropriate. Some people do need the threat of sanctions. However, an overemphasis on potential sanctions can be superfluous and even counterproductive. Employees may rebel against programs that stress penalties, particularly if they are designed and imposed without employee involvement or if the standards are vague or unrealistic. Management may talk of mutual trust when unveiling a compliance plan, but employees often receive the message as a warning from on high. Indeed, the more skeptical among them may view compliance programs as nothing more than liability insurance for senior management. This is not an unreasonable conclusion, considering that compliance programs rarely address the root causes of misconduct.

Even in the best cases, legal compliance is unlikely to unleash much moral imagination or commitment. The law does not generally seek to inspire human excellence or dis-tinction. It is no guide for exemplary behavior—or even good practice. Those managers who define ethics as legal compliance are implicitly endorsing a code of moral mediocrity for their organizations. As Richard Breeden, former chairman of the Securities and Exchange Commission, noted, "It is not an adequate ethical standard to aspire to get through the day without being indicted."

Integrity as a Governing Ethic

A strategy based on integrity holds organizations to a more robust standard. While compliance is rooted in avoiding legal sanctions, organizational integrity is based on the concept of self-governance in accordance with a set of guiding principles. From the perspective of integrity, the task of ethics management is to define and give life to an organization's guiding values, to create an environment that supports ethically sound behavior, and to instill a sense of shared accountability among employees. The need to obey the law is viewed as a positive aspect of organizational life, rather than an unwelcome constraint imposed by external authorities.

Management may talk of mutual trust when unveiling a compliance plan, but employees often see a warning from on high.

An integrity strategy is characterized by a conception of ethics as a driving force of an enterprise. Ethical values shape the search for opportunities, the design of organizational systems, and the decision-making process used by individuals and groups. They provide a common frame of reference and serve as a unifying force across different functions, lines of business, and employee groups. Organizational ethics helps define what a company is and what it stands for.

Many integrity initiatives have structural features common to compliance-based initiatives: a code of conduct, training in relevant areas of law, mechanisms for reporting and investigating potential misconduct, and audits and controls to insure that laws and company standards are being met. In addition, if suitably designed, an integrity-based initiative can establish a foundation for seeking the legal benefits that are available under the sentencing guidelines should criminal wrongdoing occur. (See the insert "The Hallmarks of an Effective Integrity Strategy.")

But an integrity strategy is broader, deeper, and more demanding than a legal compliance initiative. Broader in that it seeks to enable responsible conduct. Deeper in that it cuts to the ethos and operating systems of the organization and its members, their guiding values and patterns of thought and action. And more demanding in that it requires

The Hallmarks of an Effective Integrity Strategy

There is no one right integrity strategy. Factors such as management personality, company history, culture, lines of business, and industry regulations must be taken into account when shaping an appropriate set of values and designing an implementation program. Still, several features are common to efforts that have achieved some success:

• *The guiding values and commitments make sense and are clearly communicated.* They reflect important organizational obligations and widely shared aspirations that appeal to the organization's members. Employees at all levels take them seriously, feel comfortable discussing them, and have a concrete understanding of their practical importance. This does not signal the absence of ambiguity and conflict but a willingness to seek solutions compatible with the framework of values.

• *Company leaders are personally committed, credible, and willing to take action on the values they espouse.* They are not mere mouthpieces. They are willing to scrutinize their own decisions. Consistency on the part of leadership is key. Waffling on values will lead to employee cynicism and a rejection of the program. At the same time, managers must assume responsibility for making tough calls when ethical obligations conflict.

• *The espoused values are integrated into the normal channels of management decision making and are reflected in the organization's critical activities*: the development of plans, the setting of goals, the search for opportunities, the allocation of resources, the gathering and communication of information, the measurement of performance, and the promotion and advancement of personnel.

• *The company's systems and structures support and reinforce its values.* Information systems, for example, are designed to provide timely and accurate information. Reporting relationships are structured to build in checks and balances to promote objective judgment. Performance appraisal is sensitive to means as well as ends.

• *Managers throughout the company have the decision-making skills, knowledge, and competencies needed to make ethically sound decisions on a day-to-day basis.* Ethical thinking and awareness must be part of every managers' mental equipment. Ethics education is usually part of the process.

Success in creating a climate for responsible and ethically sound behavior requires continuing effort and a considerable investment of time and resources. A glossy code of conduct, a high-ranking ethics officer, a training program, an annual ethics audit—these trappings of an ethics program do not necessarily add up to a responsible, law-abiding organization whose espoused values match its actions. A formal ethics program can serve as a catalyst and a support system, but organizational integrity depends on the integration of the company's values into its driving systems.

---

an active effort to define the responsibilities and aspirations that constitute an organization's ethical compass. Above all, organizational ethics is seen as the work of management. Corporate counsel may play a role in the design and implementation of integrity strategies, but managers at all levels and across all functions are involved in the process. (See the chart, "Strategies for Ethics Management.")

During the past decade, a number of companies have undertaken integrity initiatives. They vary according to the ethical values focused on and the implementation approaches used. Some companies focus on the core values of integrity that reflect basic social obligations, such as respect for the rights of others, honesty, fair dealing, and obedience to the law. Other companies emphasize aspirations—values that are ethically desirable but not necessarily morally obligatory—such as good service to customers, a commitment to diversity, and involvement in the community.

When it comes to implementation, some companies begin with behavior. Following Aristotle's view that one becomes courageous by acting as a courageous person, such companies develop codes of conduct specifying appropriate behavior, along with a system of incentives, audits, and controls. Other companies focus less on specific actions and more on developing attitudes, decision-making processes, and ways of thinking that reflect their values. The assumption is that personal commitment and appropriate decision processes will lead to right action.

Martin Marietta, NovaCare, and Wetherill Associates have implemented and lived with quite different integrity strategies. In each case, management has found that the initiative has made important and often unexpected contributions to competitiveness, work environment, and key relationships on which the company depends.

Martin Marietta: Emphasizing Core Values

Martin Marietta Corporation, the U.S. aerospace and defense contractor, opted for an integrity-based ethics program in 1985. At the time, the defense industry was under attack for fraud and mismanagement, and Martin Marietta was under investigation for improper travel billings. Managers knew they needed a better form of self-governance but were skeptical that an ethics program could influence behavior. "Back then people asked, 'Do you really need an ethics program to be ethical?'" recalls current President Thomas Young. "Ethics was something personal. Either you had it, or you didn't."

The corporate general counsel played a pivotal role in promoting the program, and legal compliance was a critical objective. But it was conceived of and implemented from the start as a companywide management initiative aimed at creating and maintaining a "do-it-right" climate. In its original conception, the program emphasized core values, such as honesty and fair play. Over time, it expanded to encompass quality and environmental responsibility as well.

Today the initiative consists of a code of conduct, an ethics training program, and procedures for reporting and investigating ethical concerns within the company. It also includes a system for disclosing violations of federal pro-

Strategies for Ethics Management

Characteristics of Compliance Strategy

Ethos	conformity with externally imposed standards
Objective	prevent criminal misconduct
Leadership	lawyer driven
Methods	education, reduced discretion, auditing and controls, penalties
Behavioral Assumptions	autonomous beings guided by material self-interest

Characteristics of Integrity Strategy

Ethos	self-governance according to chosen standards
Objective	enable responsible conduct
Leadership	management driven with aid of lawyers, HR, others
Methods	education, leadership, accountability, organizational systems and decision processes, auditing and controls, penalties
Behavioral Assumptions	social beings guided by material self-interest, values, ideals, peers

Implementation of Compliance Strategy

Standards	criminal and regulatory law
Staffing	lawyers
Activities	develop compliance standards train and communicate handle reports of misconduct conduct investigations oversee compliance audits enforce standards
Education	compliance standards and system

Implementation of Integrity Strategy

Standards	company values and aspirations social obligations, including law
Staffing	executives and managers with lawyers, others
Activities	lead development of company values and standards train and communicate integrate into company systems provide guidance and consultation assess values performance identify and resolve problems oversee compliance activities
Education	decision making and values compliance standards and system

curement law to the government. A corporate ethics office manages the program, and ethics representatives are stationed at major facilities. An ethics steering committee, made up of Martin Marietta's president, senior executives, and two rotating members selected from field operations, oversees the ethics office. The audit and ethics committee of the board of directors oversees the steering committee.

The ethics office is responsible for responding to questions and concerns from the company's employees. Its network of representatives serves as a sounding board, a source of guidance, and a channel for raising a range of issues, from allegations of wrongdoing to complaints about poor management, unfair supervision, and company poli-

cies and practices. Martin Marietta's ethics network, which accepts anonymous complaints, logged over 9,000 calls in 1991, when the company had about 60,000 employees. In 1992, it investigated 684 cases. The ethics office also works closely with the human resources, legal, audit, communications, and security functions to respond to employee concerns.

Shortly after establishing the program, the company began its first round of ethics training for the entire workforce, starting with the CEO and senior executives. Now in its third round, training for senior executives focuses on decision making, the challenges of balancing multiple responsibilities, and compliance with laws and regulations critical to the company. The incentive compensation plan for executives makes responsibility for promoting ethical conduct an explicit requirement for reward eligibility and requires that business and personal goals be achieved in accordance with the company's policy on ethics. Ethical conduct and support for the ethics program are also criteria in regular performance reviews.

Today top-level managers say the ethics program has helped the company avoid serious problems and become more responsive to its more than 90,000 employees. The ethics network, which tracks the number and types of cases and complaints, has served as an early warning system for poor management, quality and safety defects, racial and gender discrimination, environmental concerns, inaccurate and false records, and personnel grievances regarding salaries, promotions, and layoffs. By providing an alternative channel for raising such concerns, Martin Marietta is able to take corrective action more quickly and with a lot less pain. In many cases, potentially embarrassing problems have been identified and dealt with before becoming a management crisis, a lawsuit, or a criminal investigation. Among employees who brought complaints in 1993, 75% were satisfied with the results.

Company executives are also convinced that the program has helped reduce the incidence of misconduct. When allegations of misconduct do surface, the company says it deals with them more openly. On several occasions, for instance, Martin Marietta has voluntarily disclosed and made restitution to the government for misconduct involving potential violations of federal procurement laws. In addition, when an employee alleged that the company had retaliated against him for voicing safety concerns about his plant on CBS news, top management commissioned an investigation by an outside law firm. Although failing to support the allegations, the investigation found that employees at the plant feared retaliation when raising health, safety, or environmental complaints. The company redoubled its efforts to identify and discipline those employees taking retaliatory action and stressed the desirability of an open work environment in its ethics training and company communications.

Although the ethics program helps Martin Marietta avoid certain types of litigation, it has occasionally led to other kinds of legal action. In a few cases, employees dismissed for violating the code of ethics sued Martin Marietta, arguing that the company had violated its own code by imposing unfair and excessive discipline.

Still, the company believes that its attention to ethics has been worth it. The ethics program has led to better relationships with the government, as well as to new business opportunities. Along with prices and technology, Martin Marietta's record of integrity, quality, and reliability of estimates plays a role in the awarding of defense contracts, which account for some 75% of the company's revenues. Executives believe that the reputation they've earned through their ethics program has helped them build trust with government auditors, as well. By opening up communications, the company has reduced the time spent on redundant audits.

The program has also helped change employees' perceptions and priorities. Some managers compare their new ways of thinking about ethics to the way they understand quality. They consider more carefully how situations will be perceived by others, the possible long-term consequences of short-term thinking, and the need for continuous improvement. CEO Norman Augustine notes, "Ten years ago, people would have said that there were no ethical issues in business. Today employees think their number-one objective is to be thought of as decent people doing quality work."

NovaCare: Building Shared Aspirations

NovaCare Inc., one of the largest providers of rehabilitation services to nursing homes and hospitals in the United States, has oriented its ethics effort toward building a common core of shared aspirations. But in 1988, when the company was called InSpeech, the only sentiment shared was mutual mistrust.

Senior executives built the company from a series of aggressive acquisitions over a brief period of time to take advantage of the expanding market for therapeutic services. However, in 1988, the viability of the company was in question. Turnover among its frontline employees—the clinicians and therapists who care for patients in nursing homes and hospitals—escalated to 57% per year. The company's inability to retain therapists caused customers to defect and the stock price to languish in an extended slump.

At NovaCare, executives defined organizational values and introduced structural changes to support those values.

After months of soul-searching, InSpeech executives realized that the turnover rate was a symptom of a more basic problem: the lack of a common set of values and aspirations. There was, as one executive put it, a "huge disconnect" between the values of the therapists and clinicians and those of the managers who ran the company. The therapists and clinicians evaluated the company's success in terms of its delivery of high-quality health care. InSpeech management, led by executives with financial services and venture capital backgrounds, measured the company's worth exclusively in terms of financial success. Management's single-minded emphasis on increasing hours of reimbursable care turned clinicians off. They took management's performance orientation for indifference to patient care and left the company in droves.

CEO John Foster recognized the need for a common frame of reference and a common language to unify the diverse groups. So he brought in consultants to conduct interviews and focus groups with the company's health care professionals, managers, and customers. Based on the results, an employee task force drafted a proposed vision statement for the company, and another 250 employees suggested revisions. Then Foster and several senior managers developed a succinct statement of the company's guiding purpose and fundamental beliefs that could be used as a framework for making decisions and setting goals, policies, and practices.

Unlike a code of conduct, which articulates specific behavioral standards, the statement of vision, purposes, and beliefs lays out in very simple terms the company's central purpose and core values. The purpose—meeting the rehabilitation needs of patients through clinical leadership—is supported by four key beliefs: respect for the individual, service to the customer, pursuit of excellence, and commitment to personal integrity. Each value is discussed with examples of how it is manifested in the day-to-day activities and policies of the company, such as how to measure the quality of care.

To support the newly defined values, the company changed its name to NovaCare and introduced a number of structural and operational changes. Field managers and clinicians were given greater decision-making authority; clinicians were provided with additional resources to assist in the delivery of effective therapy; and a new management structure integrated the various therapies offered by the company. The hiring of new corporate personnel with health care backgrounds reinforced the company's new clinical focus.

The introduction of the vision, purpose, and beliefs met with varied reactions from employees, ranging from cool skepticism to open enthusiasm. One employee remembered thinking the talk about values "much ado about nothing." Another recalled, "It was really wonderful. It gave us a goal that everyone aspired to, no matter what their place in the company." At first, some were baffled about how the vision, purpose, and beliefs were to be used. But, over time, managers became more adept at explaining and using them as a guide. When a customer tried to hire away a valued employee, for example, managers considered raiding the customer's company for employees. After reviewing the beliefs, the managers abandoned the idea.

NovaCare managers acknowledge and company surveys indicate that there is plenty of room for improvement. While the values are used as a firm reference point for decision making and evaluation in some areas of the company, they are still viewed with reservation in others. Some managers do not "walk the talk," employees complain. And recently acquired companies have yet to be fully integrated into the program. Nevertheless, many NovaCare employees say the values initiative played a critical role in the company's 1990 turnaround.

The values reorientation also helped the company deal with its most serious problem: turnover among health care providers. In 1990, the turnover rate stood at 32%, still above target but a significant improvement over the 1988 rate of 57%. By 1993, turnover had dropped to 27%. Moreover, recruiting new clinicians became easier. Barely able to hire 25 new clinicians each month in 1988, the company added 776 in 1990 and 2,546 in 1993. Indeed, one employee who left during the 1988 turmoil said that her decision to return in 1990 hinged on the company's adoption of the vision, purpose, and beliefs.

Wetherill Associates: Defining Right Action

Wetherill Associates, Inc.—a small, privately held supplier of electrical parts to the automotive market—has neither a conventional code of conduct nor a statement of values. Instead, WAI has a *Quality Assurance Manual*—a combination of philosophy text, conduct guide, technical manual, and company profile—that describes the company's commitment to honesty and its guiding principle of right action.

Creating an organization that encourages exemplary conduct may be the best way to prevent damaging misconduct.

WAI doesn't have a corporate ethics officer who reports to top management, because at WAI, the company's corporate ethics officer *is* top management. Marie Bothe, WAI's chief executive officer, sees her main function as keeping the 350-employee company on the path of right action and looking for opportunities to help the community. She delegates the "technical" aspects of the business—marketing, finance, personnel, operations—to other members of the organization.

Right action, the basis for all of WAI's decisions, is a well-developed approach that challenges most conventional management thinking. The company explicitly rejects the usual conceptual boundaries that separate morality and self-interest. Instead, they define right behavior as logically, expediently, and morally right. Managers teach employees to look at the needs of the customers, suppliers, and the community—in addition to those of the company and its employees—when making decisions.

WAI also has a unique approach to competition. One employee explains, "We are not 'in competition' with anybody. We just do what we have to do to serve the customer." Indeed, when occasionally unable to fill orders, WAI salespeople refer customers to competitors. Artificial incentives, such as sales contests, are never used to spur individual performance. Nor are sales results used in determining compensation. Instead, the focus is on teamwork and customer service. Managers tell all new recruits that absolute honesty, mutual courtesy, and respect are standard operating procedure.

Newcomers generally react positively to company philosophy, but not all are prepared for such a radical departure from the practices they have known elsewhere. Recalling her initial interview, one recruit described her response to being told that lying was not allowed, "What do you mean? No lying? I'm a buyer. I lie for a living!" Today she is persuaded that the policy makes sound business sense. WAI is known for informing suppliers of overshipments as well as undershipments and for scrupulous honesty in the sale of parts, even when deception cannot be readily detected.

Since its entry into the distribution business 13 years ago, WAI has seen its revenues climb steadily from just under $1 million to nearly $98 million in 1993, and this is an industry with little growth. Once seen as an upstart beset by naysayers and industry skeptics, WAI is now credited with entering and professionalizing an industry in which kickbacks, bribes, and "gratuities" were commonplace. Employees—equal numbers of men and women ranging in age from 17 to 92—praise the work environment as both productive and supportive.

WAI's approach could be difficult to introduce in a larger, more traditional organization. WAI is a small company founded by 34 people who shared a belief in right action; its ethical values were naturally built into the organization from the start. Those values are so deeply ingrained in the company's culture and operating systems that they have been largely self-sustaining. Still, the company has developed its own training program and takes special care to hire people willing to support right action. Ethics and job skills are considered equally important in determining an individual's competence and suitability for employment. For WAI, the challenge will be to sustain its vision as the company grows and taps into markets overseas.

At WAI, as at Martin Marietta and NovaCare, a management-led commitment to ethical values has contributed to competitiveness, positive workforce morale, as well as solid sustainable relationships with the company's key constituencies. In the end, creating a climate that encourages exemplary conduct may be the best way to discourage damaging misconduct. Only in such an environment do rogues really act alone.

Lynn Sharp Paine is associate professor at the Harvard Business School, specializing in management ethics. Her current research focuses on leadership and organizational integrity in a global environment.

Transparent Reporting?

It doesn't equal GAAP compliance.

By John P. McAllister, CPA

IF A TITLE (like a picture) is worth a thousand words, then IMA President Margaret Butler's "Can Financial Professionals Be Trusted?" (Perspectives, August 2002, p. 5) must be a perfect example. Who would have thought that such a question would ever be raised—even for the express purpose of responding affirmatively?

The financial reporting scandals dominating the news seem to have at least two things in common: greed and dishonesty. Beyond those very disturbing and embarrassing traits, I believe we should consider the possibility of the presence of a pervasive weakness in U.S. accounting and financial reporting, specifically the assumption that compliance with generally accepted accounting principles (GAAP) is the equivalent of transparent reporting.

To facilitate this discussion, I propose several assumptions:

1. Readers of financial statements are reasonably sophisticated investors and creditors.
2. Readers of financial statements expect to receive high-quality information about a company's operating, investing, and financing activities.
3. Information about those activities is reported in the income statement, balance sheet, statement of cash flows, and notes to the financial statements.
4. Preparers and auditors of financial statements have a shared obligation to the readers of financial statements.
5. That obligation is to assure that financial statements are transparent.

While reasonable people might argue for or against one or more of these assumptions, let's save those arguments for another day. This will allow us to focus our attention on transparent financial reporting.

Consistent with the fourth assumption, my use of "we" will refer jointly to preparers and auditors of financial statements. I'll come back to the notion of a shared obligation later.

TRANSPARENCY IN FINANCIAL REPORTING

The term transparent is used in many countries to describe high-quality financial statements. In the wake of the scandals, the term is fast becoming a regular part of our U.S. business vocabulary. My very old college dictionary offers several meanings for this word. Most directly relevant to financial reporting are "... easily understood... very clear... frank... candid." Transparent is further described as being the opposite of opaque, one meaning of which is "... hard to understand, obscure."

When asked by my Kennesaw State University students to relate the "idea" of transparency to the realm of financial reporting, I suggest they consider two extremes:

- Transparency is present when the readers can "see" a company through the financial statements.
- Transparency is absent when readers either can't "see" a company at all through the financial statements or get a distorted view of the company.

Transparency may be a relatively new word in U.S. financial reporting circles, but it certainly isn't a new idea:

- As financial professionals, we have always been expected to choose substance over form.
- The Financial Accounting Standards Board's (FASB) Conceptual Framework includes "representational faithfulness" as one of the essential qualitative characteristics of accounting information.
- The second paragraph of a standard audit report informs readers that "an audit also includes assessing... the overall financial statement presentation."
- The third paragraph of the audit report includes the assertion that "... the financial statements... present fairly... the financial position... results of operations and cash flows."

So, yes, we have always been challenged to communicate in a transparent manner with readers of financial statements.

In my opinion, the likelihood of transparency has been inhibited by our supposition that GAAP compliance is its equivalent. Accounting standards address individual measurement and reporting issues (business combinations, leases, income taxes, and the like) and tend to be quite detailed. From an historical perspective, our seemingly insatiable thirst for detail is understandable in light of two related pressures:

- Criticism that alternative treatments permitted under GAAP facilitated manipulation of results, and
- Our vulnerability to legal liability.

Unfortunately, highly detailed standards and transparency may not be very good bedfellows. The former often results in a checklist/minimalism mentality as in: "Compliance with the details is all we need." The latter calls for a high-quality/best-possible mentality as in: "Let's find the best way to communicate this economic reality." I suggest that our concentration on GAAP compliance has overwhelmed much (if not all) of the concern that we may have with respect to transparency.

Both groups must accept the fact that GAAP compliance is not equivalent to transparency. Financial statements must allow readers to "see" the company.

Enron's accounting and reporting treatment of special-purpose entities (SPEs) offers an appropriate example. This may be difficult, but, just for a moment, let's presume integrity on the part of Enron's preparers and auditors. Enron's accounting for its SPEs may have complied with the detailed requirements of existing GAAP. But could readers "see" Enron through its financial statements? Of course not. High-quality information about the company's operating, investing, and financing activities wasn't made available to readers. The financial statements were opaque, not transparent. (Note: In January, the FASB issued Interpretation No. 46, "Consolidation of Variable Interest Entities," regarding SPEs, off-balance-sheet structures, and similar entities to offer new guidance on these issues.)

The domination of GAAP compliance over transparency also is evident in a not so obvious context: our general condemnation of the reporting of pro-forma operating results. Criticism is certainly appropriate in those cases where companies sought to use other-than-GAAP presentations to mislead readers. Yet one of the most common pro-forma reporting adjustments (and, in many cases, the largest in sheer dollar size) has been the exclusion of goodwill amortization from the calculation of profit. And now, after careful study, the FASB has concluded that goodwill should *not* be amortized. Hence, is

it possible that, at least with respect to this issue, pro-forma reporting might have been more transparent than GAAP reporting?

THE CHALLENGE FOR THE FUTURE

Our challenge for the future emanates clearly from IMA President Butler's question: "Can Financial Professionals Be Trusted?" Yes, I agree with her conclusion that we can be trusted. But—and I'm returning to my idea of shared obligations—I suggest that the following steps are needed to reestablish trust in the financial reporting process:

- CFOs will have to explain to their CEOs and boards of directors that the days of "gaming accounting standards" are over.
- Audit partners will have to explain to their executive offices that audits dominated by accounting standard checklists are over.
- Both groups must publicly acknowledge that they have a shared purpose with respect to financial reporting: *transparency*. A shared purpose should be relatively easy to deal with since we come from common educational, experience, and, perhaps most important, ethical roots.
- Both groups must accept the fact that GAAP compliance is not equivalent to transparency. Financial statements must allow readers to "see" the company. Hence, GAAP compliance is a necessary but not a sufficient condition for high-quality financial reporting.
- The FASB must begin a 100% reconsideration of its standards with the purpose of establishing a "transparency theme" throughout. Furthermore, to assure its continuing consideration, transparency should be defined within the Conceptual Framework's sections on objectives and qualitative characteristics.

Is all of this simply a question of words and theories? I think not. Shareholder litigations are real. Improved transparency should lower their occurrence. Market value penalties for opaque reporting are real. Improved transparency should permit the markets to assess company value more fairly. And last, but certainly not least, our reputations as finance professionals are real. It is up to us to assure that those who rely on us are not disappointed.

John P. McAllister, Ph.D., CPA, is chair and professor of accounting at Kennesaw State University in metro-Atlanta. You can reach him at (770) 423-6317 or john_mcallister@coles2.kennesaw.edu.

From *Strategic Finance*, March 2003 pp. 47-48. Copyright © 2003 by PARS International Corp. Reprinted by permission.

Using Conversation to Change the World

How Paul Dolan of Fetzer Vineyards is using conversation to create sustainability inside a major corporation and across his industry.

BY MARJORIE KELLY

It was a dark and stormy night, as a dozen business people huddled by the light of the kerosene lamp. The year was 1992 and the place was a remote homestead—sans electricity—20 miles off the main road, deep in the forest of northern California. In the group were seven newly minted managers from Fetzer Vineyards in Hopland, plus three corporate folks from the Louisville, KY. headquarters of Brown-Forman, the public corporation that had acquired Fetzer just two months earlier. Leading the group was the audacious Paul Dolan, who after 15 years at Fetzer had just been appointed president. He was out to change the world. Fetzer was his vehicle.

"Why are we in business?" he asked the gathering. The obvious answers came quickly—to produce quality wine, to make money—but he urged them to go deeper. Tired of the question, some tried to change the subject. But they were stuck in the woods with nowhere to go, and Dolan kept asking the same question. Eventually they found agreement. They wanted to produce great quality wine at a good price, and they wanted a good work environment, as well as good partnerships

with distributors, and they wanted to farm responsibly. Ultimately, they crystalized their core purpose: *Fetzer people, enhancing the quality of life.*

It's one of the stories Dolan tells in his book, *True to Our Roots,* which chronicles how he and his staff transformed Fetzer into a genuinely sustainable company—and made plenty of money along the way. Through the 1990s, Fetzer earnings grew an average of 15 percent a year as sales doubled. Fetzer is now the largest selling brand in the U.S. for premium wines in the $7 to $10 range, and it makes nearly 4 million cases a year. In Fetzer's price and volume category, *Wine & Spirits* magazine name Fetzer the "Winery of the Year" seven times in the 1990s for its category.

While sales were doubling, Fetzer reduced the amount of waste hauled to the landfill by 97 percent. In 2002 production facilities sent less than 40 cubic yards to the landfill—compared to the starting volume of 1700 cubic yards. Fetzer now farms its grapes entirely organically, and is helping dozens of other independent growers convert to organic farming. Fetzer's commitment is to use only organic grapes by 2010.

The company has a Sustainability Team, called E3, which manages for the triple bottom line. E3 has helped find more efficient motors, insulate better, switch from petroleum to biodiesel fuel and start an employee commuter van program. Fetzer also sponsors English-as-a-Second-Language programs for its Spanish-speaking workers and has opened its organic garden to local educators.

> "I used to try to guilt growers into organic farming. But now I see it improves quality, and is more cost-effective. We're farming organic at the same cost as conventional, with better yields."

In 1994, Dolan challenged his team to build a new administration building that didn't deplete natural resources in its construction or operation. They did it—with a building that's won architectural awards, and which cost the same as a conventional building. The main construction material is rammed earth, which needs no further insulation. It has solar panels on the roof for energy, and ceilings finished with staves from an old beer tank. Much of the wood was reused from existing structures—including oak floors salvaged from a condemned office building.

More broadly, Dolan has led an effort to spread organic farming in the wine industry. As a board member of the Wine Institute, he helped spearhead an effort—in partnership with the California Association of Winegrape Growers—to create a Code of Sustainable Winegrowing Practices for California, announced in November 2002. The idea is to advance organic farming in the wine industry and make it an example for all of agriculture.

The key to it all, Dolan writes in *True to Our Roots,* is conversation. Conversation about sales and profits, he notes, is one of the most well-developed conversations on Earth. We need to insert a conversation about sustainability into the conversation about profits, and keep it there until they become the same conversation. Talking is vital, he believes, because there is no roadmap for what we're trying to do. Conversation is one of the few processes almost guaranteed to produce new insights and ideas.

As leaders, we need to structure conversations about sustainability so they take place without us, he says. We need to schedule regular get-togethers. We need to mention sustainability at every gathering. And we need to remember that a report about a conversation is not a conversation, because it's lifeless.

That first meeting by kerosene lamp, Dolan writes, was really about generating conversation. Similarly, when the company decided to go all-organic, its first move was to gather 25 managers for a conversation.

Today, Dolan is taking the conversation into the larger Brown-Forman family of consumer product companies. With $2.4 billion in 2003 sales, Brown-Forman owns such brands as Hartmann luggage, Lenox china, Jack Daniels Tennessee whis-

key, Southern Comfort, and Finlandia vodka.

Business Ethics editor Marjorie Kelly caught up with Dolan after he returned from a two-day sustainability conference for Brown-Forman managers that he instigated.

Paul Dolan: Yesterday we spent the day having our first Chairman's Conference on Sustainability. In the room were people like farmer-poet Wendell Berry, Bob Scrowcroft, director of the Organic Farming Research Foundation, plus people from Interface, Gap, and Ben & Jerry's. We did small panels with about 100 people from Brown-Forman, which was all their senior management, from the CEO on. They were so engaged. And it was the chairman Owsley Brown who set the context by saying, "This is important to me, and it's important enough that we're having a complete conference on it." When I left they were breaking into small groups and looking at how to go forward and jump into this.

It sounds like you're taking your social mission into the rest of Brown-Forman.

Well, that was always my audacious commitment. I wanted to transform them before they had the chance to change us! And it's happening. Since the Brown family is so involved they have a different culture than many companies. They own over 50 percent and have been with the company many generations. They approach business from a longer term perspective. They are driven very much by the bottom line, but they are also involved with their local community. And they see opportunities on the environmental side.

Marjorie: Does Brown-Forman set your goals for the year? How does it work being part of a larger company?

Dolan: We set our own goals—not only financial, but environmental and social goals. A key goal is being 100 percent organic by 2010, which means educating our growers, because there is still some fear.

With UC Davis we put together a 3-day symposium for our farmers and had 50 attendees with 65 on the waiting list. We'll do another soon with 100 farmers. Growers are no longer asking, "Why do I need to do this?" but, "How do I do this?"

> "When our E3 Team meets, we go around the room and check in on what occurred last week and what we're planning next month. The results just show up. It's not necessary to set individual goals."

We walk them through the code of sustainable business practices. It's a 490-page self-assessment guide that is being taken around to all wine communities in the state. They see this is the future and they better get up to speed.

Marjorie: I know you started on the organic road because you were convinced it made better grapes.

Dolan: Early on, I would try to guilt the growers into organic—saying, you should do this for your kids. It wasn't until we converted our own vineyards that I saw it improved quality. Now we can demonstrate it's also more cost-effective. We farm organic at basically the same cost as conventional. Plus we get better yields. If you get an extra ton per acre, you get a better return.

Marjorie: Is that how you tell the story to Brown-Forman? Do you wrap this in a profit story?

Dolan: We were just recently able to wrap it in a profit story. I was questioned pretty hard recently, having made the statement we would be 100 percent organic by 2010. They questioned what that would mean for the corporation. We had to look at our cost structures and do comparative studies. So we were able to demonstrate cost-effectiveness.

But were also able to demonstrate the shift among consumers, who are interested in health and nutrition. We're putting together plans to position ourselves as "a good choice for you." We can't make health claims, but we can describe the healthy practices we use in the vineyards, and the good stewardship inside the winery.

Marjorie: What do you think will come of the Brown-Forman conference?

Dolan: If you keep sustainability in the everyday conversation, you'll focus on it. If not, you won't do much. That's what we will organize around at Brown-Forman. In the production area, teams will be challenged to organize themselves so they discuss it and set goals for themselves that they can measure.

I'm a pretty unstructured guy, I have to admit, and at Fetzer I don't necessarily look at the metrics. It's important to see change though. What's important is to create an environment in which conversation can occur. When E3 meets, we go around the room and check in on what's going on, and the results show up. We announce what happened last week and what we're planning next month. It's not necessary to set individual goals. We set broad-range goals like zero waste, or recycling 100 percent of the water back into the vineyards.

> ## "We don't have waste baskets anymore. When you finish a meal, you have either a paper basket, a plastic basket, a metal basket, or a scrap food basket—it's gotta fit in one of those."

It's part of our culture. We recycle 97 percent of our waste. We don't even have wastebaskets anymore. When you finish a meal, you either have a paper basket, a plastic basket, a metal basket, or a scrap food basket —it has to fit in one of those, because there's nowhere else for it to go!

Marjorie: In your book, you write about reaching out beyond Brown-Forman, to change business as a whole.

Dolan: I feel strongly that business is where change can be made in the world. It's where the answers will be found, through the resources business has and its leadership potential.

Marjorie: Why do you think business is the place where change will come from?

Dolan: It has to, because business manages and controls all the resources. For us to make this a world that works for everybody, it will come through expanded awareness of business leaders.

And it starts with conversation. Once that kicks in, things will happen. Conversation shifts mindsets. This is, ultimately, how we will change the world.

> ## "I wanted to transform our parent company before they had the chance to change us. And it's happening."

True to Our Roots: Fermenting a Business Revolution, by Paul Dolan, was published in November 2003 by Bloomberg Press.

Learn more about Fetzer: `www.fetzer.com` Marjorie Kelly is editor of Business Ethics. Contact her: marjorie.`kelly@business-ethic.com`

UNIT 5

Developing the Future Ethos and Social Responsibility of Business

Unit Selections

Key Points to Consider

- In what areas should organizations become more ethically sensitive and socially responsible in the next five years? Be specific, and explain your choices.

- Obtain codes of ethics or conduct from several different professional associations (for example, doctors, lawyers, CPAs, etc.). What are the similarities and differences between them?

- How useful do you feel codes of ethics are to organizations? Defend your answer.

 **Links: www.dushkin.com/online/**
These sites are annotated in the World Wide Web pages.

Brazil's Instituto Ethos
http://www.ethos.org.br/docs/ingles/index.shtml
International Business Ethics Institute (IBEI)
http://www.business-ethics.org/index.asp
UNU/IAS Project on Global Ethos
http://www.ias.unu.edu/research/globalethos.cfm

Business ethics should not be viewed as a short-term, "knee-jerk reaction" to recently revealed scandals and corruption. Instead, it should be viewed as a thread woven through the fabric of the entire business culture—one that ought to be integral to its design. Businesses are built on the foundation of trust in our free-enterprise system. When there are violations of this trust between competitors, between employer and employees, or between businesses and consumers, the system ceases to run smoothly.

From a pragmatic viewpoint, the alternative to self-regulated and voluntary ethical behavior and social responsibility on the part of business may be governmental and legislative intervention. From a moral viewpoint, ethical behavior should not exist because of economic pragmatism, governmental edict, or contemporary fashionability—it should exist because it is morally appropriate and right.

This last unit is composed of articles that provide some ideas, guidelines, and principles for developing the future ethos and social responsibility of business. In the first article, Archie Carroll discusses some of the ethical challenges that business will face in the current environment of fraud and corruption. The next article discloses how trust, integrity, and fairness are crucial to the bottom line. "SOX Alone Won't Stop Fraud" relates that while the Sarbanes-Oxley Act (SOX) may deter corporate fraud, corruption is not going to disappear completely. The next three articles reflect why managers and leaders must take a more active role in addressing ethical issues within the organization. The last article, "Ensuring Ethical Effectiveness" discloses that new rules and legislation mean that virtually every company will need a code of ethics.

Business Ethics In The Current Environment Of Fraud And Corruption

WILL OUR MORAL COMPASS FAIL?

by Archie B. Carroll and Robert W. Scherer

The past two years (2002-2003) may be characterized as the most serious period of ethical scandal on the part of business since the 1980s. Then, Michael Milkin and Ivan Boesky were the headliners. Today, a host of companies and CEOs have been at center stage. The current period may be the worst ever for business ethics—certainly in my memory.

In most respects, the current environment of fraud and corruption is far worse than the insider trading scandals and greed we saw manifested in the 1980s because the current situation has caused such significant financial harm for tens-of-thousands of employees and millions of investors. Many of you have seen your lifetime investments drop by 30% or more or you have lost it all. In addition, it all came to light around the time of 9-11 and so our country was hit with a pretty serious one-two punch at about the same time. We were, in fact, hit with terrorism of two kinds.

What has been amazing about the recent rash of scandals during the past two years is how quickly they came to light and how many of them there have been. With each passing day we don't know whether we'll be hit with more or not. We are constantly "waiting for the (next) shoe to drop."

At about the time the Enron scandal came to light in Fall of 2001, my coauthor and I were wrapping up the 5th edition of our business ethics textbook (Business and Society: Ethics and Stakeholder Management, 2003) and had shipped it off to the publisher. Well, guess what? There is no reference in our just published book to Enron, World-Com, Arthur Andersen, Tyco, Quest, Global Crossings, Imclone, and the whole host of scandals that have come to light in the past year or so. I guess this will give the professors using the book something to talk about in bringing their students up to date. In any event, this example shows how quickly this tide of scandal surfaced.

Furthermore, even though we had a chapter in the book on corporate governance, we both had commented about how "quiet" things had been on the corporate gov-

ernance front. In fact, my co-author, Ann Buchholtz, who is a corporate governance specialist, said there wasn't really much we needed to add on that subject because it had almost become a non-issue. How wrong this turned out to be. Now, with the recent revelations, it has become obvious there was an appalling amount going on beneath the surface—we just didn't know about it. Corporate governance has quickly become a number one topic in business ethics.

Two questions come to mind that are worthy of comment: (1) What went wrong and who's to blame and (2) What should be done about it?

First, "What went wrong and who is to blame?"

It is challenging to completely get your arms around an answer to this question. There is a lot of blame and responsibility to spread around to a number of different groups.

First, we need to place the blame on the greed and dishonesty of many senior executives. In the final analysis, these are the people who controlled the decisions and had the knowledge of what was going on. They were the leaders. Leaders bear responsibility. We have heard a lot recently about "infectious greed." There is no question this must have been at work and maybe one reason was the tens and hundreds of millions of dollars that were at stake for them personally. As Ralph Nader recently observed, it's been a period of "greed on steroids." We have been subjected to a "supermarket of white-collar crime" and the senior executives in business must bear primary responsibility. The public seems to agree. A July 2002 poll published by the Barna Research Group found that 39% of those surveyed thought greed was the root of these problems. Other reasons were distant-seconds.

Some of my colleagues in corporate finance and economics have said that "greed is good" (sound familiar?). My response has been that "self interest" is good, but greed is bad. Greed is "excessive self interest" or self interest run amok.

As a result of CEO and CFO behavior, new terms have entered the financial vocabulary. I hear that CEO now refers to "chief embezzlement officer" and CFO now stands for "corporate fraud officer". We are also now learning that EPS no longer just stands for earnings per share, but also "eventual prison sentence," as we have seen former CEOs handcuffed and hauled off to jail where they trade their business attire for orange jump suits.

For decades, business ethics professors have been talking about how the moral tone of the organization is set at the top—and by the same logic—the immoral tone is also set at the top. Interestingly, business ethics training is what top execs want their middle managers to take, but they don't take it themselves!

Second, the greed and dishonesty of many auditors and accountants must be identified as a major contributor to the current environment. I don't need to detail how many companies Arthur Andersen got in trouble with because of its questionable audit work. In many respects, this upsets me more than the executives' fraud and corruption. Why? It is because you and I depend on accountants and auditors to be ethical agents in society. They are one of the few checks and balances we have had in a free market economy, and when they go wrong we are in deep trouble. Who can you trust if you can't trust a major accounting firm? And don't say your lawyer or your banker, because they have been implicated too!

The accounting firms have been rife with conflicts of interest. If you were anArthur Andersen partner and your firm was pulling in $50 million a year from Enron alone for consulting services, wouldn't you be tempted to "go along" with their devious schemes? Any human would be tempted by this blatant conflict of interest when there is so much at stake. Accounting firms, however, should not be tempted to compromise their standards in these situations. They, especially, should develop policies and attitudes that would root out unethical practices.

Third, we need to point out the failure of government regulators and agencies to enforce existing laws and to prosecute those who broke the law. In a capitalistic system such as ours, however, government regulators are not funded sufficiently to have the resources to offset the cleverness and scheming of the executives and the accountants who have colossal sums of money at their disposal to hide their crimes. Regardless, they should have been more aggressive.

Fourth, and I could easily argue that this group is the most accountable of all, are the boards of directors which have failed to do their jobs. For decades we have been concerned about lax corporate governance and oversight—about boards being co-opted and compromised by CEOs, and their not providing compliance and ethical leadership for their companies. Boards also have been responsible for permitting CEOs to become chairmen of the board, a blatant conflict of interest. In addition, excessive and unjustified CEO compensation have set the stage of opportunism for the top execs' greed and accumulation of wealth.

Recent statistics have documented how CEO compensation has grown disproportionately to average worker compensation over the past 30 years. Following are statistics that have been reported. In 1973, the average CEO earned 45 times the average worker. By 1991, this had grown to 145 times the average worker. And, in 2001, the average CEO earned 500 times the average worker. (By contrast, some European countries set a cap at 20x the earnings of the least paid worker). These ratios should have raised some red flags. Boards have allowed this to happen. Who do the boards think they have at the helm? Tiger Woods? Who else makes that kind of money!

Board memberships have become cushy jobs frequently occupied by people serving on more boards than they can handle and simply going along with management as they collect their own perks. This clubbish atmosphere, with few independent outside directors, has created weak boards incapable of governing their corporations.

In this connection, I cannot tell you how disappointed I was to learn that one of Enron's board members, Robert Jaedicke, a former Stanford University business school dean and professor of accounting, was on the board and involved in decision making when all this was going on. Thirty five years ago, I took an accounting course in my MBA program, and we used some of the publications authored by Jaedicke. And, now we learn this. How disappointed I am to learn that a business school professor and former dean was a part of the Enron debacle.

Many of you are aware that my business school colleague, Dennis Beresford, has been named to the board of WorldCom. The newspaper said it was because of his vast experience as a former chair of the Federal Accounting Standards Board, the FASB, and that he was squeaky clean. I think he will make an excellent board member. As he stated, one of his major jobs is to help WorldCom emerge out of bankruptcy.

Not everyone understands his role, however. The UGA campus newspaper, the Red and Black, had a headline implying that Beresford was chosen to "help fix" WorldCom's ethics. I don't think this is what he had in mind and I'm sure the company's ethics can't be fixed by one, new person. If they really wanted to fix their ethics, how about appointing a business ethics professor to the board? Do you think that would ever happen?

Finally, there are other culprits that have been named to the corruption and fraud lineup. Some want to blame President Bush and his administration, former-President Clinton and his administration, the current political campaign finance system, and some want to blame the business schools for not educating moral leaders. However, I think these have been primarily backdrop factors to the scandals that have occurred.

However, let me comment further on the business school's role in all this since I am a business school professor. Some of us who teach business ethics, and there are not many of us, maybe one or two at most business schools, have been teaching these courses for ten to twenty years. Personally, I have been teaching business ethics at UGA for over twenty years.

Those of us who teach these courses have done a decent job. The problems are that one course is just a drop in the bucket when you consider the process of moral maturity. Furthermore, business ethics courses are typically not required. At UGA, for example, I teach business ethics to undergrads but my course is only required for management majors (about 300 of our 7,000 students) and the course serves as an elective for other business majors and very few of them can get into the course because of limited seating capacity. In short, not many business undergraduates get exposure to business ethics education.

At the MBA level, our business ethics course is basically half-a-course, a decision that I have never approved of, but I'm not on the curriculum committee. A major problem is that in academe the faculty control the curriculum and many of the business school faculty don't regard business ethics courses as very important, especially relative to their own courses. We always have to fight for shelf-space in the curriculum and then the course often gets reduced to a mini-course or a micro-course that many students quickly get out of the way, or don't take seriously because of its limited role in the curriculum.

A professor at George Washington University, Amitai Etzioni, wrote a newspaper column in the Washington Post in which he said the nation's business schools get an "F" for their teaching of business ethics. I don't totally disagree with Etzioni. On a good day I might give B-schools a "C" for their efforts, but overall, ethics just doesn't play a big role in B-school education. This is a fact I regret admitting. Even if the course were to play a more important role, there is so much else that must be addressed as well.

I recently read that the University of Maryland is adding an interesting twist to its business ethics courses this fall. The class will visit a federal prison which will give the MBA students a unique opportunity to speak with former executives-turned-inmates about the serious consequences of compromising ethical standards. Maybe this will get the students' attention.

Amazingly, a recent Aspen Institute study of MBA students revealed that most of them are less ethical at the end of their MBA programs than they were before they entered the program. Most MBA students learn quickly that the amoral pursuit of the bottom line is what is rewarded by their employers-to-be.

Let me interject an ironic story at this point. Back in the 1980s, a major accounting firm put significant money into a program designed to integrate business ethics into the B-school curriculum. For several years they held all-expenses paid seminars at their corporate training center outside of Chicago to help B-school professors learn about how to teach business ethics. I attended one of these programs and remember clearly being picked up in Chicago in a big limousine and being driven to nearby St. Charles, Illinois. After 5 years or so, the program was sus-

pended and we never heard of it again. Guess who that accounting firm was? Yes, it was Arthur Andersen, the same company that now is history due to illegal and unethical practices. If you want to read more about the sad collapse of Arthur Andersen, I recommend Final Accounting: Ambition, Greed, and the Fall of Arthur Andersen (2003) by Barbara Ley Toffler.

Second, "What should be done about the current climate of fraud, deception and scandal in business?"

Again, there are no simple answers. I don't like government intervention any more than most business people, but I can certainly understand why Congress felt they had to do something and that the Sarbanes-Oxley Act was quickly passed by Congress in the Summer of 2002. A recent Harris poll (July 2002) found that 82% of Americans thought tough new laws were needed to prevent future corporate fraud. The Sarbanes-Oxley law increased accounting regulation with an oversight board, prohibits auditors from offering consulting services to audit-clients, provides for new criminal penalties for securities fraud, including jail sentences; requires CEOs/CFOs to certify financial reports and to forfeit profits and bonuses when earnings are restated due to securities fraud, and provides for some other key provisions.

This latter point contained in the new law is vital; namely, that once earnings restatements come to light and fraud has been detected, executives who are convicted may be forced to pay restitution. Before, "crime paid," and the execs walked off with the winnings. Corporate criminals that raid their companies are no better than crooks that rob the local minute market for their cash on hand.

In my business ethics classes, I teach something known in the literature as the "iron law of responsibility." It has to do with the abuse of corporate power. Articulated over 30 years ago, the iron law of responsibility states that "in the long run, those who do not use power in a manner which society considers responsible will tend to lose it." Stated another way, "whenever power and responsibility become substantially out of balance, forces will be generated to bring them back into closer balance."

This explains one major reason why government regulation comes into being. Government regulation, along with investor lawsuits and crushing media blows to corporate reputations are "forces" that kick in to bring power and responsibility back into balance.

To wrap up, there are three major ways by which society can get solid corporate citizenship and ethical behavior out of business. First, there is the market. The market works efficiently for many purposes. However, it has not worked in controlling illegal and unethical behavior. Certain firms beat the market (or maybe it's more correct that some of the executives beat the market—many of the firms are in bankruptcy and their owners/employees are paying the price). So, the market is good for some purposes, but not for controlling ethical behavior.

Second, there is government regulation. Few of us want this except government. But when the people think there is nothing else they can do to control illegal and unethical behavior of companies and executives, they turn to government regulation. It is amazing that business has not figured this out and kept its record clean. Ethical practices, not lobbying, is the surest way for business to keep government off its backs.

Third, there is business ethics. Business and executives can monitor themselves. They can do what is right, what is fair, and what is just, all the while earning an excellent profit. There is nothing antithetical about profits and ethics.

But, in the final analysis, business ethics is all about personal ethics. After all is said and done, no amount of laws, regulations, policies, or even corporate ethics codes can surpass in effectiveness one's own personal ethics. If a leader does not possess the character to lead, one cannot be acquired and developed in business school and one assuredly cannot be "caught" in the executive suite, and it certainly won't be won over by a new corporate governance law.

As someone recently said, "a dog is a dog and a greedy coward is a greedy coward, whether in Levi's or a Brooks Brothers suit."

My personal concern is that as religion and faith are being driven out of the public square, the Judeo-Christian ethical foundations that have sustained our country since its beginning, are being lost and are being replaced with a humanistic amorality, a self-centered, pragmatic indifference that will ensure that our moral compasses will fail to point us in the right direction in the future.

In conclusion, we need to get back to our spiritual roots if we want business ethics to get better rather than worse. This is one time when going backwards is moving forward.

Ethics for a Post-Enron America

John R. Boatright

The high-profile scandals at Enron, WorldCom, Global Crossing, and Tyco, among others, combined with the spectacular dissolution of the accounting firm Arthur Andersen, are more than business failures. Numerous and voluminous news reports have revealed egregious failures by top executives and their advisers—including accountants, investment bankers, and lawyers—to fulfill their basic fiduciary duties to serve the interests of shareholders and the public.

A fiduciary duty is a duty of a person in a position of trust to serve the interests of others. Accordingly executives are fiduciaries who are pledged to serve the interests of shareholders. Yet, some have manipulated earnings, hidden debts, and falsified accounting records, all in order to exercise their lavish stock options at their shareholders' expense. Accountants who perform audits for the benefit of the investing public have permitted many instances of so-called "aggressive accounting" and approved financial statements that subsequently proved false. Investment bankers have helped executives to develop complex financial transactions that generated phantom earnings or removed unwanted debts from the balance sheet.

All the while, the banks' analysts, who are supposed to be objective, were giving favorable evaluations of the securities of companies with which the banks were doing deals, and the banks' brokers were filling their customers' portfolios with these same securities, even as they sometimes denigrated them in internal communications. And the lawyers who blessed many of these accounting and financial shenanigans were acting as though their clients were the executives who hired them and not the shareholders, who were ultimately paying for their services.

In each of these cases, the moral wrong is simple: a failure to fulfill a fiduciary duty, generally because of a serious conflict of interest. That this kind of behavior is immoral, and often illegal, is clear, but what challenge does it pose beyond recognizing that it is wrong and attempting to prevent it? Some argue that existing laws and the force of the marketplace are sufficient, so that nothing more needs to be done. Indeed, many of the wrongs in the recent scandals are slowly being rectified. Congress has mandated new rules to ensure that directors and auditors are "independent," which is another way of saying "free of conflicting interests." Among the many provisions of the Sarbanes-Oxley bill, for example, are the requirements that audit committees be composed entirely of independent directors with no ties to man-

agement and that accounting firms doing audits refrain from performing certain nonaudit services that could bias an audit. Similarly, Eliot Spitzer, the New York State attorney general, has forced some major investment banks to increase the independence of analysts to reduce the risk that their ratings of stocks will be influenced by the banks' deal-makers.

Although these efforts to reinforce fiduciary duties by removing conflicts of interest and restoring objectivity may produce some improvements, they do not address the most important challenge posed by the recent scandals. The effectiveness of fiduciary duties as a regulator of business conduct has been seriously undermined in the past two decades by several developments in the American business system. In particular, executive compensation tied to performance, the combining of auditing and consulting by accounting firms, and consolidation in the financial-services industry have produced powerful new incentives that have been major factors in the recent scandals. Restoring the traditional fiduciary duties in the face of these developments will be a difficult, if not impossible, task.

There are alternatives, however. Imposing fiduciary duties is one form of regulation that relies heavily on moral force, but market-based regulation that seeks to alter the incentives is another form. The challenges in this post-Enron era, then, is to determine which form of regulation, or what combination of these forms, can best secure the kind of ethical business environment in which future Enrons will not occur.

WHAT WENT WRONG?

We cannot propose reforms to prevent another Enron, much less understand the post-Enron world, without a firm grasp of why the recent scandals occurred. The stories are complex, and each one is different, but they all share some common features. Each case involves a business strategy gone awry, executives determined to boost short-term stock price by any means, directors who failed to detect warning signs, accountants who acquiesced in aggressive accounting, investment bankers who structured questionable financial deals, and lawyers who showed how to achieve the desired results with a plausible legal veneer.

A major factor in the scandals of 2001 is an increased focus on share price. This greater attention to stock price began in the early 1980s during a period of hostile takeovers, when a high share price was the best defense against a takeover. The impetus for high executive compensation tied to performance came originally from companies taken over that needed to raise share price quickly. Institutional investors encouraged this trend because it seemed to promote good corporate governance by aligning executives' interests more closely with those of shareholders. Finance theorists, most notably Michael Jensen, further supported this idea with arguments drawn from agency theory, which studies the problems of a principal (in this case the shareholders) controlling an agent (the CEO). Reducing the loss from an inadequately controlled CEO would more than offset the high executive compensation—or so the theory goes. Executives also became enamored of rising stock prices, not only because of their option-rich pay packages, but also because a high stock price opened up a growth strategy of making acquisitions.

A second important factor is the deregulation that occurred in the past two decades. Market deregulation, especially in energy and telecommunications, began a scramble to develop business models for a future that no one could accurately predict. It is significant that the biggest bankruptcies occurred at Enron (an energy-trading company) and at WorldCom and Global Crossing (in telecommunications). The novelty of these companies required new accounting methods that tested generally accepted accounting principles (GAAP). How should Enron price long-term contracts for delivery of energy, for example? Or how should WorldCom and Global Crossing classify unused telephone lines and optic-fiber cable? (WorldCom counted lease payments for idle capacity as capital investments, which is garden-variety accounting fraud.) At the same time, investment banks were developing sophisticated financial instruments that permitted, to cite just one example, loans that could be booked as trades. In this deregulated financial environment, Enron became more like a hedge fund than an energy company.

In addition to market deregulation, in the 1990s the legal liability of accounting firms and investment banks was reduced. It is difficult for a company to commit massive fraud without the complicity of its accountants, bankers, and lawyers. However, a 1994 court decision held that accounting firms and investment advisers could not be held liable for "aiding and abetting" fraud in securities transactions, and the 1995 Private Securities Litigation Reform Act protected investment banks from class-action suits for alleged securities fraud. Although this liability deregulation was introduced to make business more efficient, it had the unintended consequence of weakening a powerful constraint on accounting firms and investment banks.

The third factor, and perhaps the most significant, is simultaneous changes in the compensation structures for executives, accountants, and investment bankers. The rapidly escalating pay for CEOs has become heavily weighted with stock options that must be exercised within a narrow period. This time limit, combined with the importance of meeting analysts' expectations, produced great pressure to achieve short-term results. To achieve the needed results, earnings management, which has long been used to iron out small wrinkles in financial statements, was now used to fashion figures out of whole cloth.

Further, accounting firms had discovered that it was far more lucrative to sell consulting services to their audit clients, thus tempting the firms to go easy on audits lest they lose the consulting business. And investment banks found that they could make more money doing deals with large companies than by servicing individual brokerage clients. As a result, analysts touted the stock of companies with which the deal-makers were doing business and encouraged the firm's brokerage customers to stuff their portfolios with these stocks. Individual investors were further shunted aside as investment banks made their most lucrative opportunities, such as shares in hot initial-public offerings (IPOs), available to their CEO-clients. These CEOs received thinly disguised kickbacks for bringing their company's business to the investment bank.

> **The American business system is schizophrenic in that it combines a market system built on the pursuit of self-interest with a system of fiduciary duties, in which one party is pledged to serve the interests of another. This system has worked because of the compartmentalized professional roles of those with fiduciary duties.**

The effect of these changes is that what had previously been a system of healthy checks and balances became a united front, at the expense of investors. Instead of having opposed interests that served to protect investors, these entities now had an unhealthy common interest. The fiduciary duty that executives owed to shareholders took a back seat to the pursuit of a short-term increase in stock price. Accountants, who had formerly policed financial reports to protect the public, now had a strong incentive to help executives to do whatever was necessary to boost share price so as to keep them as consulting clients. And investment bankers no longer served as trusted advisers to their customers, scouting out the best securities. They found it more advantageous to work with executives and accountants to finance deals that raised stock prices, even if this meant selling out their customers.

This broad-brush indictment also overlooks many factors, but it does paint a picture of a systematic failure with multiple causes. It is like a major industrial accident that happens when

177

a number of small mishaps, inconsequential by themselves, occur together with catastrophic results. Although the individual failures are predictable, their occurrence together is highly improbable and hence not easily foreseen. Lacking an understanding of the convergence of factors that led to the Enron collapse and to other bankruptcies, the people involved could not easily appreciate the risks they were taking. For the most part, they were playing the game with which they were familiar, unaware of how treacherous the playing field had become.

WHAT IS TO BE DONE?

The American business system is schizophrenic in that it combines a market system built on the pursuit of self-interest with a system of fiduciary duties, in which one party is pledged to serve the interests of another. This system has worked because of the compartmentalized professional roles of those with fiduciary duties. Public accountants, stock brokers, and lawyers have operated as professionals who serve clients—or, in the case of public accountants, the public. Even CEOs and other top executives have generally viewed themselves as quasi-professionals and have taken their fiduciary duties seriously.

However, the compartmentalization of those with professional roles has been seriously eroded in recent years by several factors. One is the enormous compensation packages that have become common in recent years. These are designed to align executives' interests with those of shareholders so as to solve the agency problem of how to induce executives to serve the shareholders' interests. Whatever the merits of this strategy, one effect is to replace a moral and legal mechanism with a purely market mechanism. Fiduciary duties are now less important as a means for restraining executive behavior because the market is now being employed to achieve the same end.

Another factor is the consolidation of multiple services in accounting firms and investment banks. Accounting firms now provide many internal accounting and financial-information systems, advise on tax strategies, and offer appraisals and fairness opinions. In a similar manner, investment banks that mainly served large corporate clients merged with those that offered brokerage services mostly to small individual clients. As a result, brokers and analysts, who have always operated with both fiduciary duties and market mechanisms, now find themselves with even greater conflicts.

A third factor is the devaluation of some professional services. Auditing is a cost to companies that must be borne because the service is mandated by law. The cost is passed along to the intended beneficiaries, the investing public, but investors have little control over the price or the quality of audits. Similarly, securities analysis is a cost for brokerage firms that is also passed on to investors. Thus, corporations have an incentive to skimp on audit costs, and investment banks on the costs of analysis. In the recent bull market, investors had less interest in both

the quality of audits and the quality of research because they found that everything they bought unfailingly increased in price. As a result, accounting firms and investment banks have tended to treat auditing and analysis, respectively, as loss leaders to attract more lucrative business. These professional services have thus become peripheral to the more basic business services of consulting and investment banking.

> **This erosion of professional roles and decline of fiduciary duties is the reality of the post-Enron era. Although efforts can be made to reverse this development, doing so might require changing executive compensation and breaking up accounting firms and investment banks.**

This erosion of professional roles and decline of fiduciary duties is the reality of the post-Enron era. Although efforts can be made to reverse this development, doing so might require changing executive compensation and breaking up accounting firms and investment banks. Congress has grappled unsuccessfully with the issue of executive compensation, and the proposal by Arthur Levitt, the former chairman of the SEC, to separate auditing and consulting services was soundly rejected. And the consolidation of the banking industry has so collapsed the distinctions between investment banks that serve large clients and those engaged in retail brokerage that any return to the past would be very difficult.

Would we really be better off if we could put on the brakes and return to the pre-Enron period? After all, high executive compensation tied to performance might actually provide greater protection for shareholders than would a sense of fiduciary duty. The problem in the recent scandals is not that the pay packages were too large, but that they did not create the right incentives. Arguably, corporations and shareholders are better served by multipurpose accounting firms that can attract the best people and provide economies of both scale and scope. And financial supermarkets that offer a multitude of services also might serve everyone better. In any event, the market is telling us that these kinds of consolidation are more efficient and that they can be undone only at a price.

What is the alternative? Despite their importance, fiduciary duties are a second-best means of regulation. They are generally employed in relations in which one party agrees to serve the interests of another. If the obligations in question can be fully specified and embodied in contacts, then there is no need for fiduciary duties. Fiduciary duties, which are general, open-ended obligations to act for the benefit of another, are employed, then, when precise rules are not possible. For example, the main reason for imposing a fiduciary duty on executives to serve the shareholders' interests is that shareholders cannot specify in detail what executives should do to serve their interests because the situations that might arise are unpredictable. However, tying executive compensation to performance gets around this problem without the need for fiduciary duties+. A market mechanism that appeals to self-interest, rather than an ethical and legal duty, is used instead.

> **An alternative to more rules is the European approach of employing accounting principles instead of rules. A principle-based accounting system, which prescribes general goals instead of specific means, allows accountants to choose, and auditors to approve, the accounting methods that provide the truest picture of a firm's financial situation. However, the European system requires a greater reliance on the integrity of the persons doing accounting and auditing.**

Although accounting is a highly rule-bound activity, the rules still leave considerable discretion that accountants can use to benefit one party over another. The fiduciary duty of public accountants to serve the public is one way of ensuring that the public is served. However, the new Public Company Accounting Oversight Board, which was created by the Sarbanes-Oxley bill, is charged with creating even more rules and with conducting reviews of audits. The result of such efforts may further constrain the accounting profession and reduce the need for fiduciary duties. In addition, more accounting information is now available from corporations, and it may be possible in the near future for investors to have real-time access to company books. Such a development would reduce the need for audits and provide an external check on their quality.

Some people argue that there are already too many rules in accounting and that their number merely encourages the search for creative ways of getting around them. An alternative to more

rules is the European approach of employing accounting principles instead of rules. A principle-based accounting system, which prescribes general goals instead of specific means, allows accountants to choose, and auditors to approve, the accounting methods that provide the truest picture of a firm's financial situation. However, the European system requires a greater reliance on the integrity of the persons doing accounting and auditing. American accountants already have the authority to depart from GAAP if doing so provides a truer picture, but few take advantage of this opportunity because it imposes a burden of proof that can be avoided by merely following the rules. In addition, the pursuit of principles should lead to the best methods of accounting, which can then be codified in rules. In return, these rules prevent unnecessary disagreements over the best methods. It is probably better to have precise rules wherever they are possible and to leave principles for difficult cases that are less amenable to rules.

The problem of biased analysis by investment banks has a very easy solution. Instead of guarding the independence of analysts or requiring analysts to disclose any conflicts, which are among the current proposals, encourage the development of a larger market for analysis. If analysis has value, then it will be purchased by investors, and analysis from a provider with a reputation for objectivity will bring a higher price. Part of the problem with analysis at investment banks is that top-notch analysts receive more in salary than brokerage customers are willing to pay for, and so the money for their high pay can be generated only by adding value to the bank's deal-makers, which creates a conflict of interest. The best solution, then, may be to invest only as much in analysis as buyers will pay for in the marketplace.

CONCLUSIONS

Both fiduciary duties and market-based regulation aim at a common goal, which is to reduce risk. In particular, investors run the risk that executives will enrich themselves at the shareholders' expense, that a company's financial statements will not be accurate, and that a broker's advice will not be sound. In each case, the solution has been to impose fiduciary duties that reduce the risk with a promise, in effect, not to take advantage of investors. Executives, accountants, and brokers each promise to act in the investors' interests. Rules on conflict of interest further reduce the risk to investors by prohibiting situations in which the parties might be tempted to break this promise.

However, the goal of reducing risk can be achieved in a number of ways. A market-based system of regulation would shift the risk away from investors and back to the parties that now have fiduciary duties. For example, if accounting firms cannot be held liable for "aiding and abetting" clients in fraud, then they bear little risk in facilitating "aggressive accounting." Removing this protection would require accounting firms to engage in more extensive risk management so that they would, in effect, be regulating themselves more closely. In short, if accounting firms and investment banks bore more of the risk of the activities for which they now have a fiduciary duty, then investors would have less need to rely on this kind of obligation to serve their interests.

There are drawbacks to such a regulatory approach. An increased risk burden would lead to less risky behavior, which might not be in investors' interest given that greater risk leads to higher returns. This burden involves a cost that would most likely be passed along to investors because accounting firms, for example, might spend more money on audits or buy more insurance. However, fiduciary duties also have a cost, and so in the end the choice of regulatory approaches may depend on a trade-off between effective protection and the cost of that protection.

However this issue is ultimately decided, it is clear that in this post-Enron era the fiduciary duties of the various players in the American business system have become less-effective protections for investors and the public. This erosion of a traditional means of regulation has resulted from many changes that have taken place in recent years, some of them highly beneficial. The challenge we face, then, is deciding whether to strengthen these fiduciary duties, in part by effectively reducing conflicts of interest, or to find other means of protecting against the kinds of scandal that Enron represents.

John R. Boatright is the Raymond C. Baumhart, S.J., Professor of Business Ethics in the Graduate School of Business at Loyola University Chicago. He currently serves as the executive director of the Society for Business Ethics, and is a past president of the Society. He is the author of the books *Ethics and the Conduct of Business* and *Ethics in Finance*. His current research focuses on ethics in finance and corporate governance. He received his PhD in philosophy from the University of Chicago.

SOX Alone Won't Stop FRAUD

The most recent litany of SEC investigations—from HealthSouth to Ahold's U.S. Foodservice to AOL—are vivid reminders that the Sarbanes-Oxley Act (SOX) and related legislation may deter corporate fraud, but corruption is not going to disappear completely.

BY ARLEN S. LASINSKY

Employee misconduct and fraud are sadly commonplace among members of today's savvy, highly mobile workforce. In nearly every organization, there is at least one person who is willing to step over the line and engage in fraudulent activity. Approximately $600 billion will be lost annually due to corporate fraud, with one in six cases costing the affected organization more than $1 million, according to the Association of Certified Fraud Examiners.

While the stricter penalties proposed by the Sarbanes-Oxley Act may discourage some fraud, the most effective deterrents must be established at the company level through good corporate governance and effective business controls.

CAUSE AND EFFECT

Every fraud scheme has three common components: motivation, opportunity and rationalization. Most perpetrators are motivated to commit fraud because of a "perceived" need, such as medical bills, alcoholism, gambling, drugs, divorce or simply living beyond their means. Work pressures can also elicit fraud—for example, if an executive is having trouble reaching profit goals in order to receive a bonus, that may motivate him to falsify financial statements. As long as executive incentives are linked to financial performance, they will continue to be a strong motivating factor of fraudulent behavior.

With respect to opportunity, if a company allows an employee to be put in a position where he can easily misappropriate assets, that employee is more likely to commit fraud. Opportunity is most often created by a lack of internal controls.

The third component of fraud is rationalization. Fraudsters use rationalization to justify their activities, believing they have a good reason to commit bad behavior. For example, an individual troubled by high medical bills may rationalize fraud by believing that she is only "borrowing" the funds and "deserves" the money because she is sick. Perpetrators rationalize fraud by adapting their personal beliefs or codes of ethics to explain their behavior. Typical rationalizations include insufficient salary increases, lower-than-expected bonuses, unfair treatment, "I deserve it," "no one will get hurt" and "the company owes me."

So how can executives safeguard company assets while preventing financial loss, avoiding fees associated with legal and other professional services and escaping the embarrassment of being a victim?

MINIMIZE THE RISK

There are a number of techniques to employ that significantly reduce the risk of fraud:

Make everyone aware of the threat. The most common method for detecting fraud is a tip; the second most common is by accident. Therefore, it is essential to explain to managers and employees the areas in which your organization is most susceptible. Employees need to understand that when a fraud occurs, it can hurt the entire organization, right down to the individual employees. Enron is a vivid example of how the actions of a just a few executives led to the demise of an entire organization, costing retirement savings and hundreds of employees their jobs.

Become familiar with fraud symptoms. Fraud symptoms may include obvious clues, such as missing documents, poor accounting records and excessive balance sheet adjustments. But there are also subtler hints, such as employees who never take a vacation or who use photocopies instead of original documents. Be on the lookout for employees whose behavior creates a "need" to commit fraud, such as living beyond their means, gambling and drug and alcohol abuse. For example, an employee who earns $35,000 per year but drives a $50,000 automobile and has a home in the most expensive part of town may be funding his extravagant lifestyle by milking corporate funds. Although there may be a plausible explanation for his unusual circumstances, there is a good chance that his employer has been taken for a ride. Clearly, the employee's actions should be reviewed.

Assess risks and test controls. Conducting a thorough risk analysis before establishing internal controls is an essential but commonly overlooked way to reduce fraud. A thorough risk analysis asks, "What's important?" and "How is it controlled?" When assessing risks, executives must carefully scrutinize problem areas, such as accounts payable, payroll, expense reports, consulting fees, reconciliations, end-of-period adjustments and vendor master files.

After risks have been identified, it is equally important to periodically reassess and test internal controls.

> Beyond the risk of fraud, an employee with a history of ethical lapses can significantly compromise a company, its reputation, assets and intellectual property.

Internal audit committees, whose financial reporting responsibilities are outlined in Section 301 of the Sarbanes-Oxley Act, play a critical role in periodically testing controls to ensure that prescribed procedures are being followed. Based on the work of the internal audit committee, procedures can be enhanced to better control the finance and reporting environment.

Develop a fraud policy. A written policy, distributed to all employees and vendors, can be a strong deterrent against fraud. The policy should state zero tolerance for violations. In addition, the establishment of a "fraud hotline" is vital for detecting fraud, since most schemes are discovered through tips.

Fraud hotlines make a lot of sense. According to the Association of Certified Fraud Examiners, organizations with fraud hotlines cut their losses by approximately 50% per scheme.

Regulators have also acknowledged the importance of hotlines: The Sarbanes-Oxley Act proposes audit committees establish procedures for the receipt, retention and treatment of anonymous and confidential complaints about accounting or auditing matters.

Establish "tone at the top." Good corporate governance, the Holy Grail of the Sarbanes-Oxley Act, can only be achieved in an environment where employees follow the example set by senior management. For example, when senior managers file expense reports, they should submit only legitimate, business-related expenses and provide the same proper and original documentation that they expect all employees to submit. If a top manager files a report that includes questionable or exorbitant charges, more junior employees can easily rationalize similar behavior in their own reports.

Segregate duties in critical areas. The segregation of duties is the bedrock of effective internal controls. No one employee should be able to initiate and consummate a transaction and then be in a position to record it without involving someone else.

The vast majority of assets misappropriations involve failures in this area. For example, those employees responsible for creating customer invoices should not also receive customer payments.

Unfortunately, employees who collude can circumvent even the most sound accounting controls. Consequently, other controls should be instituted beyond those.

CONDUCT PRE-EMPLOYMENT SCREENING

Taking time to check out the backgrounds of potential hires is a lot like exercising—you know you are supposed to do it but it is easy to find excuses not to do so. Unfortunately, too many companies conduct only perfunctory investigations or none at all, assuming that background verifications have already been done because candidates previously held positions of responsibility at other companies or because they were already well-known in their fields.

A recent study by ADP Screening and Selection Services revealed an epidemic of resume fraud—an astounding 44% of the resumes submitted to prospective employers contained false or misleading information.

Does it matter if someone stretches the truth on a resume? Absolutely. Lies on a resume are often a harbinger of other forms of deception. Beyond the risk of fraud, an employee with a history of ethical lapses can significantly compromise a company, its reputation, assets and intellectual property.

SCREEN AND MONITOR VENDORS

Many executives are surprised to learn that corporate fraud is frequently initiated by outsiders. When considering new vendors, screenings should be as thorough and exhaustive as employee background checks. Investigate vendors' ownership, clients, references and litigation history.

Reconciliation of vendor invoices against company transactions is essential. One of the most common vendor-initiated schemes uses fake invoices to charge a client for goods or services that were never delivered. The vendor recruits an employee from within the customer's organization and provides that individual with financial kickbacks in exchange for approving the spurious charges.

PASSWORD SECURITY

The open architecture of modern systems makes password security a critical control.

Inappropriate system access makes it possible to steal large amounts of money or other assets quickly and, in many cases, without detection. For example, many passwords are easily guessed (e.g., the user's birthday) or may even be written down and kept near the computer keyboard or monitor. If one of those passwords falls into the hands of a fraudster or, worse, the password belongs to a system administrator, access to critical data is often unlimited—so is the potential damage. Company policy should require passwords to be changed periodically, every two or three months. This provides an essential layer of security in the computer system, where most critical business information is stored today.

Enron, WorldCom and other high-profile business scandals have given executives and investors a crash course in corporate fraud. We've also learned that the best time to assess risk and implement internal controls is before fraud occurs, not after. To protect your organization, adopt active defensive measures and adhere to a system of internal controls that protects hard-earned profits. In today's business climate, you can't afford not to.

Arlen S. Lasinsky is a director in the Chicago office of Citigate Global Intelligence & Security, an international business intelligence, corporate investigations and business controls/security consulting firm.

Are You Serious About Ethics?

For companies that **can't guarantee confidentiality**, the answer is no.

By Patrick J. Gnazzo and George R. Wratney

You did the right thing. You created an ethics program for your organization built around a workable and enforceable code of behavior for employees. You appointed compliance or ethics officers to administer the program, and you built a structure to receive employee allegations and feedback.

Have you done enough? No.

Here's a simple truth: A certain number of your employees will not raise issues to management unless they are promised confidentiality throughout the process, including in any potential litigation. Under current law, your ethics program cannot guarantee that protection. Consequently, you will not hear some things that you should.

Of course, ethics officers (EOs) can, and do, assure employees who raise issues that the EO will do everything possible to keep the employee's identity confidential. Such assurances often are all that's needed inside the organization. But when a subpoena crosses the company threshold (or when a request from a regulator does the same), the assurance of confidentiality is jeopardized. Suddenly, the employee who had earlier contacted the EO and heard, "We will do everything possible to keep your identity confidential" learns that his name may have to surface in court.

Here's how that could happen. An employee (the source) suspects that Ralph is cheating the company on his expense report. The company's code of conduct asks (and some demand) employees to report suspected violations and illegalities. The source works next to Ralph in the office and lives in the same neighborhood. Their children attend school together. Yet the employee wants to do the right thing.

The employee approaches the EO about Ralph and asks for confidentiality. The employee does not want to fracture his relationship with Ralph at work and with Ralph's family on Maple Street. The EO gives the source the usual "we will do our best" assurance.

The EO investigates the allegation, deems that Ralph is guilty and should be fired, and Ralph is dismissed. In turn, Ralph hires an attorney and sues the employer. The compliance officer ends up on the witness stand, and the source's identity is revealed under examination. And then, as they say, "There goes the neighborhood."

We recently received a call at United Technologies from an ethics officer at another well-known U.S. company. The EO knew that we have successfully defended ombudsman privilege (the idea that a neutral, independent organizational ombuds should not be compelled to reveal the identity of a source) and asked whether we knew of such a privilege for EOs. We said, "There is none." At that, the EO replied, "My program and I are in trouble. An employee visited my office to raise an issue. I offered the usual qualified assurance of confidentiality, and now I am being subpoenaed over the issue. I will be compelled to reveal his identity; he will lose all confidence in me, and it will wreck our program."

Kevlar, Not Spandex

Employees who seek to raise issues but are timid or fearful want more than a conditional assurance of confidentiality. They want a guarantee made of Kevlar, not Spandex. How can you make that guarantee? First of all, realize that unlike attorney-client, doctor-patient, priest-penitent, and other limited privileges, no law covers the relationship between ethics or compliance officers and employees. While compliance and ethics officers can suggest they will "keep this confidential," they risk much if they suggest a privilege they cannot defend later. As Supreme Court Justice William Rehnquist wrote in the 1981 decision on *Upjohn Co. v. United States*, "An uncertain privilege, or one which purports to be certain but results

Alternatives to Ombuds

The process works. But what about those organizations that choose not to employ an ombuds? A potential solution would be a national source-protection law that would prevent third-party litigants from forcing any organization to reveal the name(s) of sources who raise allegations of wrongdoing or any other issue in the workplace (with the understanding that company-union contracts and certain other situations might be excluded).

Discussions around this sort of source-protection law within the Fellows Program of the Washington, D.C.-based nonprofit Ethics Resource Center led to the idea that a new organization should be formed to address the public-policy issues surrounding ethics programs, including source protection. Thus, in 2000, the Coalition for Ethics and Compliance Initiatives was born. The coalition's primary focus is "to support changes in government policy and law that will recognize privileges for the good faith use of effective compliance programs to discover and report suspected misconduct and potential illegalities."

A source-protection law would not exempt the source from discipline should he be party to the offense. But neither would he ever be revealed as the source and therefore would not be subject to the threats (and potential realities) of workplace retribution.

Some in the legal profession object to the idea. "We want to interview the source," they might say. The counterargument is that it's better to have the issue surfaced for examination, and not have the source's name, than to have no issue at all.

Suppose five employees dump a barrel full of toxic substances from the plant into the state park rather than cart it to a proper disposal site. They forge the required paperwork so no one will know. Then one of the five gets a guilty conscience and wants to report the wrongdoing but knows his colleagues will hammer him if they find out. What does he do if he has no confidential outlet to report the deed? Is the public better served if he reports or does not report?

—P.J.G. and G.R.W.

in widely varying applications by the courts, is little better than no privilege at all."

Second, realize that if the guarantee does not exist, a certain portion of the workforce will not raise an issue, however troubling, through official channels. They will sit, and perhaps suffer, in silence, that suffering seeming more bearable than retribution. An organization can have a policy that prohibits retribution, but a manager who wants to "get even" with a reporting employee can write performance appraisals that gradually build a case for the

employee's termination for "poor performance." Slow, deliberate retribution is difficult to prove. Their employers will suffer as well—they will not receive knowledge of issues occurring in the workplace.

So how can your company offer a genuine guarantee of confidentiality to employees? One way that has worked is to establish an ombudsman office such as we have had since 1986 at United Technologies, where corporate ombuds are available to hear employees' concerns in confidence.

Organizational ombudsman's offices are structured to protect the identity of the reporting source. Those ombuds receive information from employees, convey that information to management with the employees' permission, and pledge to not reveal the employees' identities. Organizational ombuds are neutrals. They do not investigate, act on behalf of management, make recommendations regarding discipline, or keep official records of the organization. They act as a confidential, neutral conduit for the flow of information and possess no information that is not discoverable elsewhere. The position offers a contrast to that of an ethics officer, who is obligated to take action once the EO has received notice of an issue; unlike an ombudsman, an ethics officer investigates the complaint and can get involved in any disciplinary outcome. Most importantly, ethics officers, like other staff organizations, cannot unequivocally offer confidentiality.

We have used the legal process successfully a half-dozen times in order to defend our ability to protect confidentiality. Here's an example of how it works. A former employee sues the company, alleging unfair dismissal. His attorney asks him, "Who in the company was aware of your issue?" And the employee replies, "Well, there was my boss, and my HR rep. And, oh yes, I did discuss my issue with the ombudsman."

"The ombudsman! Let's subpoena him along with the others."

Our ombuds have successfully resisted having to testify by asserting that we have an implied bilateral contract based on the understanding that communications with the ombuds are confidential. Our position is that the confidentiality contract is held by both the company and the employee who calls the ombuds, that it takes both sides to agree to break the contract, and the company never will. We argue, as stated above, that the ombuds is neutral and therefore is not involved in management actions such as discipline and investigations. The ombudsman's files are not files of official company actions.

Also, we assert ombuds' confidentiality privilege, based on Federal Rule of Evidence 501. This allows U.S. federal courts to recognize privileges as developed on a case-by-case basis under common law. We do this not only to keep our promises to past employees who have contacted us but also to assure those who are thinking of contacting us that we will not reveal their names.

The recent enactment of the Sarbanes-Oxley Act expands corporate whistleblower protections, but the act's coverage of whistleblowers relates basically to those who raise concerns regarding questionable accounting, auditing, or similar internal controls. In addition, the act's requirements for procedures to provide "the confidential, anonymous submissions by employees" ask for something the law does not now provide: a guarantee of confidentiality for the source.

The dilemma is rooted in the fact that responsible organizations create ethics and compliance programs to help guide and limit employee behavior. The organizations provide feedback mechanisms for employees to report suspected wrong-doing. The nature of the workplace, which can include vengeful managers and co-workers, is partially overlooked.

It takes both sides to agree to break the contract, and the company never will.

"It is never easy for subordinates to be honest with their superiors," wrote Warren Bennis in *The New York Times* last year. "After a string of box-office flops, Samuel Goldwyn is said to have told a meeting of his top staff, 'I want you to tell me exactly what's wrong with me and M.G.M.—even if [it] means losing your job.'"

The Guarantee on the Job

Here's an example of the way the process works at United Technologies. One of our administrative staff called the ombudsman's office with terror in her voice. Reluctant to provide her name, she said, "My boss is cheating the company. Only he and I know it. If I report him, as I am supposed to do, he will find out and fire me—or worse." She truly feared for her physical safety as well as continued employment. She hoped the confidential ombudsman office could help but doubted that the company could safely investigate a situation in which only two people knew of the offense—and one was the alleged culprit.

After three weeks of calls to the ombudsman and assurances that the company would do a blanket, "routine" audit, she agreed to reveal what she knew. The information was passed to the ethics officer for investigation, but the source was never revealed to anyone, including the ethics officer. The investigation proved she was correct, the boss was fired, she's still with us, and no one ever knew. Had we not been able to offer a guaranteed, confidential outlet, we think she would never have called in the first place.

Without guaranteed confidentiality, employees can find themselves with nowhere to take their issues. Sometimes, particularly at smaller plants and offices in remote locations, local management controls the flow of information so tightly that employees are left with no recourse unless the ombudsman option exists.

We think our company is no different than most. Every employee of every company has issues that he would like to raise to management's attention. What helps set us apart from most is that our employees have this alternate mechanism through which issues can be raised under a Kevlar umbrella of identity protection. We will not divulge the identity of a source, period.

He told her, "If you are not married by the time your baby is born, we will fire you."

Consider the following situations, all of which were resolved successfully and fairly from both the employees' and management's perspective:

- Our ombuds office received a call from an employee in Asia whose supervisor told her that she was going to be fired because she was seven months pregnant and unmarried. Her condition offended the supervisor's sense of morality, and he said, "If you are not married by the time your baby is born, we will fire you." The inquiry revealed that the supervisor's boss had agreed in advance with the decision to fire her.
- A U.S.-based employee called after first being given a 90-day performance-improvement plan, which was then cut by 30 days, with the threat of discipline "up to and including dismissal" for failure to comply. The performance-improvement plan, concocted by his manager and HR representative, contained no specific goals, measurements, or objectives. He was told to "get better," but no one defined what "getting better" looked like.
- A managing director in Central Europe decided he could save money in his budget by not telling employees about a new tuition-assistance program offered by the company. An employee who learned of the program through the grapevine, and who felt there was no way he could raise the issue within his company, called the ombudsman.

If the individuals referred to above had failed to report, who would have suffered? The answer is simple: everyone associated with that organization—except the perpetrators. The kind of behaviors cited can lead to workplace tensions and anxiety, lower morale, reduced productivity, increased costs, and possibly costly litigation.

Keeping the Peace

Surveys by the Ethics Resource Center and the Society for Human Resources Management are consistent in finding that a third of employees observe misconduct at work—and half of those decide not to report it. Reasons cited for failing to report: fear of retribution or retaliation, lack of trust that the organization will keep their reporting confidential, and concern about being labeled a whistleblower.

Overall, in 2002, we learned of 2,569 issues from United Technologies employees worldwide via our confidential ombudsman program. Five percent involved allegations of waste, fraud, abuse, and other actions that negatively affect company assets. Each issue was turned over to our Business Practices Organization for investigation. The remaining 95 percent involved issues and allegations about management practices, misapplications of company policy, concerns over environmental issues and product quality, and a host of other topics.

We are convinced that organizations and their ethics programs can be strengthened if a defendable promise of confidentiality can be made. If such a promise were available, more employees would feel comfortable coming forward, more allegations would be available for review, more opportunities for corrective action would be created, stronger organizations would result, and customers, shareowners, trustees, and other stakeholders would benefit. The source who reported about Ralph's expense report would not need to fear being labeled a "whistleblower," for no one would know his name. And there would be peace in the neighborhood, back on Maple Street.

PATRICK J. GNAZZO is vice president of business practices at United Technologies Corp. GEORGE R. WRATNEY is corporate ombudsman at United Technologies Corp.

"See No Evil, Hear No Evil, Speak No Evil"—Leaders Must Respond to Employee Concerns About Wrongdoing

BOB GANDOSSY AND ROSABETH MOSS KANTER

It wasn't the first time he discovered fraud committed by his boss—also the owner of the company. A year after he joined the firm, as the head of accounting, he came across several loans that were financed, not once, but two and three times. The owner claimed the loans were obtained "inadvertently" and, further, "it was no big deal and won't happen again." A year later, the accountant discovered it did happen again. This time his boss said, "don't worry" and promised, "I'll take care of it." Over the next few years, more signs of trouble surfaced: serious cash flow difficulties, officers' loan accounts exceeding net worth, doctored financial statements, incomplete documentation on multimillion-dollar transactions, and extravagant spending by the principals. Then, some seven years after he first came to the company, the firm pleaded guilty to check kiting and received the maximum penalty under the law.

Why would the accountant stay under these circumstances? Clearly, the company was in deep financial trouble and a principal had resorted to fraud and other forms of misconduct in the past, and, therefore, was quite capable of doing it again. Why not get out? The accountant eventually did leave, but only after he and other inside accountants had discovered hard evidence of fraud amounting to more than $40 million—and that was for only one year. On leaving, the accountant did not reveal what he knew to the authorities. Nor did the other accountants, who continued to work for the company. A year after he resigned, a massive fraud was uncovered—19 financial institutions had been swindled out of more than $220 million during a ten-year period. Could the fraud have been prevented? Why didn't the accountant and many others, who either knew or strongly suspected the fraud, take action?

Over the past several decades the business press has reported dozens of scandals, often involving leading companies that have been involved in improprieties for years before anyone took steps to bring them to an end. Why weren't illegal activities discovered earlier? And, if they were, why didn't people act to bring the crimes to a halt? How can responsible managers and professionals be so blind to such massive misconduct?

As we've seen, the aftermath of scandals usually involves numerous people sifting through evidence, discovering "retrospective errors" and unheeded warnings on the part of particular players associated with the fraudulent operators. Signs of trouble are typically present, but simply missed by the persons involved. So, the question becomes, why? What factors prevent us from seeing and acting on signs of misconduct? As important, what steps can we take to reduce the likelihood of becoming a victim—or worse, blindly aiding and abetting the perpetrator? And, as leaders, what steps should we take to reassure our employees that we are what we say?

There is no single answer to these questions. Human and organizational behaviors are complex, and explanations for our actions rarely come in tidy packages. Likewise, there is no single step to protect corporations from wrongdoing, but several steps will decrease the probability that managers will become either victimized or otherwise involved in such frauds. Said differently, there are certain things we as leaders do that *can* foster criminal wrongdoing. As well, there are no simple steps to ensure leadership integrity on such matters, but we must take seriously the workforce uneasiness that ripples the corporate landscape in the wake of recent scandals.

Most of the attention in leadership today is primarily focused on the positive side of corporate life—strategies for getting results through people, the organizational value of giving people more responsibility and accountability, and the virtue of trusting in people to do the "right thing." However, alongside this "people-are-trustworthy" theme is yet another emerging set of stories about corporate crime.

In many corporate circles today, managers and leaders are writing off instances of wrongdoing as aberrations without relevance to them. *This is a mistake.* Corporate crime anchors one end of a continuum of performance problems, ranging from outright theft to more subtle instances of ripping off the company for supplies, padding expense accounts, ignoring product defects, or simply failing to perform all duties in a quality manner.

Seen in this way, the ability of leaders to detect and prevent corporate crime is related to their ability to correct ineffective performance more generally. We should look closely at corporate wrongdoing and rip-offs for lessons about how to get the *best* out of people by preventing the *worst*.

COMMON WARNING SIGNS OF FRAUD

How do you know a fraud is being committed by a client, customer, or someone within your own organization?

- Insufficient working capital or credit

- Extremely high debt with rigid restrictions imposed by creditors
- Dependence on few products, services, or customers
- Unfavorable and declining industry or business conditions

Situational

- Profit squeeze (costs rising higher and faster than sales and revenues)
- Difficulty collecting receivables
- Significant inventories
- Long business cycles
- Urgent and intense need to report favorable earnings to support high stock price, lure customers, or obtain credit
- Unrealistic sales projections
- Extremely rapid expansion of business

Opportunity

- Management of the organization or department dominated by one or a few individuals
- Understaffed or inexperienced financial and accounting functions
- Weak internal control system
- Rapid turnover in key financial positions and/or frequent change in auditors
- Numerous unexplained and undocumented transactions
- Apparent tolerance by management of unethical and even illegal conduct

Personal

- Key personnel had rapid rise to top (responsibility and remuneration) and have considerable fear of falling from their perch
- Prior history of unethical or illegal conduct by suspects

NO ONE KNEW

"But I'd shut my eyes in the sentry box so I didn't see nothing wrong." —Rudyard Kipling

In most cases of corporate wrongdoing, we hear that no one "knew" and no one took action. Why? How is it possible for accounting firms, other professional service providers, internal staff, and executives to remain blind to such malfeasance for so long?

In fact, in many of these cases, a number of people either knew about the infractions or strongly suspected them, but they failed to take the necessary steps to bring the crimes to an end. In some situations, individuals saw troubling signs of wrongdoing but considered them less serious than they actually were—the signals were ignored. In other situations, people tried to respond—to further investigate a sign of misconduct—but eventually gave up.

IMPORTANT LESSONS

Stories of corporate scandal make headlines and are interesting studies of wrongdoing, but there are important lessons that extend well beyond the prevention of illegal activity. For instance, is the ineffectiveness of managers and professionals in these cases so different from a production manager closing his eyes to substandard products about to be shipped? Or a design engineer ignoring obvious flaws in a new product design? Or the loan officer who approves credit to a customer with suspect financial records simply to get more loans on the books?

Surely there are differences, make no mistake. But our examination of many cases of corporate wrongdoing, in light of our work with dozens of ethical organizations provides some similarities. The same pressures and opportunities that encourage otherwise responsible managers to become apathetic bystanders to fraud and other forms of misconduct also encourage blindness and paralysis to ineffective performance more generally.

First, senior and middle managers often are rewarded for short-term performance. "What have you done for me lately is a common phrase in corporate corridors for a reason. If salaries, bonuses, and promotions are tied to quarterly profits, it is difficult for managers to call a halt to practices that affect their bottom-line performance. Where reward systems have a performance trigger that provides multiple targets, then pressure is even greater. Corporations that don't permit admitting mistakes (without a penalty) force managers to conceal errors—they simply sweep evidence of poor performance under the rug rather than call attention to themselves.

This overriding concern for financial ends rather than means, coupled with insufficient moral and ethical guidance from senior executives, often leads managers to bend the rules or look the other way if doing otherwise prevents them from achieving their goals.

The second lesson stems from the complexity of business life today. There is virtually no significant transaction or project today that does not involve dozens of specialists, or perhaps even dozens of organizations. Specialists are used to reduce risk. But reducing risk by using multiple actors creates a structure wherein it is easy to conceal poor performance—or fraud.

Organizations that come together for a particular project, joint venture, or series of transactions generally have specific, often very narrow, concerns. And within each organization, the aspects of the deal that occupy an individual's time are further differentiated. Information is diffused and fragmented. No one pays attention to the big picture—each player has a piece of the action, but no one makes sure they are all working together on the same team. The materials managers do not seem to care about complaints from the shop floor. The marketing folks ignore the sales team, and so on.

Because many people are involved, each is quick to assume that others are responsible for certain aspects of the deal or project. When trouble appears—whether poor quality products or services or the slightest sign of misconduct—it is relatively easy to shift responsibility for acting to someone else—and claim later that no one "knew."

INATTENTION TO DETAIL AND LACK OF ACCOUNTABILITY

The third factor is somewhat "softer": inattention to detail and lack of accountability. Sometimes managers at many companies ignore the small things—the "minor" defect in the product, the "insignificant" liabilities of a credit applicant, or the avoidance of a "small" audit step.

These practices set a standard, a pattern others come to follow in a sort of mindless way, making it tolerable—indeed, acceptable—for managers to close their eyes to poor performance. It becomes more important to close the sale than to deliver a quality product or service. Production and service shortcuts are the norm at some companies—hustling new business is more important than delivering on the business they have.

STEPS YOU CAN TAKE TO REDUCE YOUR VULNERABILITY TO FRAUD

- Develop a code of ethics—disseminate widely and hold discussion meetings.
- Conduct unscheduled audits of your business practices to determine where you are vulnerable to foul play.
- Discuss with colleagues ways to shore up weak links thereby obtaining not only better solutions, but also solutions that clearly communicate your concerns.
- Discuss acceptable and unacceptable business practices with colleagues at every opportunity.
- Discuss with employees ways to resolve ethical dilemmas and the alternative courses of action if they discover wrongdoing.
- Discuss ethical issues in performance appraisals.
- Review performance and incentive programs. Minimize the overemphasis on bottom-line performance to the neglect of other factors. Set performance targets that can be met without cheating.
- Establish a reward program for exemplary ethical conduct.
- Discuss fiduciary responsibility with your accountants, lawyers, investment bankers, and other financial advisers. Find out exactly what they do to protect you. Obtain a written understanding of their responsibilities. Monitor carefully for potential conflicts of interest.
- Hold joint meetings with fiduciaries so each clearly understands the roles and responsibilities of each other.

- Ask your lawyer, accountant, and investment bankers to hold question and answer sessions with your managers and supervisors.
- Act swiftly when foul play occurs in your organization. Make the penalty fit the crime, publicize the incident, and hold discussions with employees so there is a clear understanding of what transpired.
- Hire an outsider to periodically raise ethical questions with your staff.

Organizations that live and breathe quality, that set high standards, that pay attention to detail are less vulnerable to misconduct and general ineffectiveness. Senior executives who convey a sense of moral integrity and provide opportunities to openly discuss ethical and operational dilemmas reduce confusion over proper and improper behavior.

Companies that provide multiple, and balance, rewards and forms of recognition, that tolerate reasonable mistakes, are more likely to correct problems when they occur, not after they have been ignored for so long they have become disasters. Where teamwork and shared, overlapping responsibilities are encouraged there is less "passing the buck," and more joint resolution of problems. Individuals are able to discuss and resolve dilemmas common to the group.

To improve performance and reduce costly misbehaviors, leaders can build these factors into the organization: quality, as opposed to inattention to detail; multiple rewards and forms of recognition; rewards for individuals and teams; a tolerance for well-intended mistakes; and integrative cultures rather than segmented units.

Leaders who want to create a great company need to look on the dark side—at the possibility of "evil"—as well as the positive values of faith in people and trust in their integrity. They need to devote personal time and attention to making sure that performance problems do not slip by unnoticed and unpunished. Corporate philosophies saying that achievement is rewarded and good performance is valued mean nothing unless, simultaneously, bad performance is rendered impossible.

Bob Gandossy is a Global Leader for the Hewitt Associates Talent and Organization Consulting Practice, with expertise in improving organizational effectiveness, human resource strategy and increasing growth through innovation. Bob has written a variety of articles and books on related topics, and has been a speaker at Harvard Business School, Human Resources Planning Society and Tom Peters Group, to name a few. Bob holds a B.S. degree from Harpur College and a Ph.D. degree from Yale University where he specialized in the study of organizational behavior.

Rosabeth Moss Kanter is the Ernest L. Arbuckle Professor at Harvard Business School, adviser to businesses and governments worldwide, and the best-selling author of 15 books, including her more recent. *Evolve!: Succeeding in the Digital Culture of Tomorrow.*

From *Business and Society Review*, Vol. 107, No. 4, pp. 415–422. Copyright © by Blackwell Publishers, Ltd. Reprinted by permission.

Why corporations can't control chicanery

Saul W. Gellerman
Management Consultant, Denver, Colorado

> Sadly, as this issue went to press, we learned that Dr. Gellerman had passed away from post-surgical complications. We hope that this article stands in tribute to his wit, insight, and professional dedication. And we extend our condolences to his family.

Business ethics is taught , to one extent or another, one guise or another, in most business schools. But many complain that the schools are not teaching enough of it, or not teaching it well, given the many recent instances of mischief in high places in corporate America. Such a position is naive; personal ethics are "made" well before people reach the point of attending a business school. There are ways, however, to think realistically about the causes of corporate malfeasance and to guard against them.

Recent corporate scandals prove that the lessons of previous scandals have not yet been learned. Management still blames rogue employees, and pundits still blame business schools. Most companies would rather not touch the real cause: pressures that push management to test the boundaries of the permissible. As a result, some executives are inevitably confronted with more temptation to do the wrong thing, and more opportunity to do it, than they can resist. Policies that assume everyone will nobly rise above that combination are unrealistic. The best defense lies in painful structural changes that minimize both the temptation and the opportunity to loot the company and defraud investors.

It happens, on average, about every 12 years: Someone who works for a big company gets caught cooking the books. In a smaller company, the same offense might not be newsworthy. But if the company is well-known, the media—whose job, after all, is to sniff out headlines—react swiftly. Swarms of reporters descend on the company, with prosecutors and politicians not far behind. In a matter of hours, another of corporate America's household names is all over Page One, mired in a messy, potentially damaging scandal.

Management usually defines its predicament as being primarily a problem in public relations, and calls in the damage-control experts. And right there—in diagnosing the problem as a mere crisis in reputation, rather than the inevitable result of the way they do business—the seeds of yet another corporate disaster, due to sprout in about another 12 years, are sown. It will probably strike a different company, but that makes it all the more dangerous, because the next corporate victim will be blind to the lesson not learned by the first one. The next big scandal, in other words, could strike any big company.

Short-term effects

Next, top executives, taking their cue from the wily police chief played by Claude Raines in Casablanca, proclaim themselves to be "shocked, shocked!" at the unauthorized misconduct of a few rogue employees—who promptly become ex-employees. Public relations consultants then prescribe massive doses of good works, such as well-publicized sponsorships of socially beneficial programs (prenatal health care? adult literacy?), to associate the company's name in the public's mind with doing the right thing—conspicuously. Thanks to the public's notoriously short memory, the whole unpleasant episode is soon forgotten. Today's horrendous scandal inevitably becomes tomorrow's stale news—unless, that is, the prosecutors or the regulators strike pay dirt during the discovery phase of their investigation, and if the company's attorneys can't head them off. That could cause the company to implode, which is what happened to financial giants E.F. Hutton and Drexel Burnham about a dozen years ago. Their current counterparts include the once-mighty Arthur Andersen and WorldCom.

He was expressing the essence of the dilemma in which executives find themselves: to go as far as they dare in a lucrative but dangerous direction without ever quite going too far.

Convictions are, of course, the ultimate PR disaster. Firms do not want to do business with a demonstrably crooked company, if only because their own stockholders would surely question their sanity for even thinking of it.

Avoiding corporate destruction is the best reason for companies to rein in the chicanery of their own employees. But as that continuing 12-year cycle indicates, their track record is not very good. There are three reasons for that. First, management is ambivalent about really clamping down on the kinds of mischief that can get a company into serious trouble. Second, when they do try to get a handle on it, they are likely to use ineffective methods. Third, they are likely to shrink from the kinds of drastic structural changes that could halt these abuses altogether.

Managerial ambivalence

A corporation's executives are caught between avoiding the sanctions of the authorities and the displeasure of the stock market. They are forever in the gray zone between maximizing profits and risking the incursions of inquisitive reporters and ambitious prosecutors. (Rudy Giuliani, be it remembered, made his reputation by sending Michael Milken to jail.)

Executives are also in competition with those of other companies, whose profit performance becomes the standard by which their own is judged. They are thus constantly pushed toward the fuzzy, indistinct line that separates barely acceptable practices from those that are intolerable. It should not be surprising, then, that they send mixed messages to the middle managers who make the company's day-to-day, tactical decisions.

I once attended a management meeting of a company that had to walk a fine line between competitiveness and a looming antitrust injunction. A top executive, addressing an audience of middle managers, pounded the lectern for emphasis as he shouted at the top of his lungs, "We want our competitors to survive!" To which he added, in a clearly audible stage whisper, "barely."

He was, I think, expressing the essence of the dilemma in which executives find themselves: to go as far as they dare in a lucrative but dangerous direction without ever quite going too far. You can bet that when the Enron scandal hit the headlines, many a corporation ordered an immediate review of its own accounting practices and put any questionable tactics on hold. How much document-shredding went on in companies that were not (at least not then) the targets of investigation is a fascinating but unanswerable question.

This much is certain: When executives send mixed messages, their subordinates are left to decipher their real meaning. The usual translation is: "If the rewards are not enough to motivate you, we don't need you. Just do whatever you have to do to make your numbers. And remember, anyone stupid enough to get caught will be hung out to dry."

Of course, hardly anyone is foolish enough to say such things for the record. But all that executives really have to do is hint to their subordinates that the race will be won by the most audacious among them, rather than by the most deliberate, and then leave them to draw the necessary inferences. So it should not be surprising when subordinates decide that lifting debts from the balance sheet and stashing them somewhere else, or masking ordinary expenses as long-term investments, is what their bosses really had in mind. Most executives are likely to welcome the results such tactics bring, and do not condemn them until someone outside the company finds out, or until an insider blows the whistle.

For all these reasons, executives tend to approach internal reforms with mixed feelings. For many of them—perhaps most—the bottom line is their highest priority, especially if their own compensation is tied to it. That makes them reluctant to give up a tactic that has already worked to their advantage. But from a longer-range perspective, any given quarter's bottom line is a secondary goal. The primary goal, always, is corporate survival. In the long run, you can make a lot more money from a steadily profitable company that is still in business than from a spectacularly profitable company that lost the confidence of its customers and is now deservedly defunct.

Ineffective methods I: Preaching ethics

When executives undertake to prevent future scandals, they usually seek to prevent "misunderstandings" of their policy guidance. The most common way of doing this is to provide employees with a written "Code of Ethics," most of which states boldly, but imprecisely, that the highest standards of decency, honesty, and fairness are demanded of everyone at all times, and that deviations from those standards will not be tolerated. The main problem with these codes is that they are seldom referred to after the hoopla with which they are introduced has died down. For all practical purposes, they are forgotten after a few months simply for lack of emphasis.

Recognizing the inadequacy of trying to control behavior by merely distributing documents, many companies have gone one step further by bringing in consultants to provide ethics training. Usually these are academics with credentials in philosophy who have "majored," so to speak, in the study of ethics. Their objective is to arm employees with analytical methods that enable them to discern where a line can be drawn between right and wrong.

These consultants illustrate their message with case examples of how easily one can be tempted, or deceived, into taking the wrong turn when making what appears on the surface to be an ordinary business decision. But these courses usually amount to little more than highly sophisticated Sunday School lessons.

There is no question but that an intelligent student will come out of them with an intellectual grasp of ethical principles and how they apply to on-the-job decision making. That such an understanding will beget ethical behavior on the job—especially when the actual challenge occurs long after the course has ended, under heavy pressure for results, in the presence of dangled temptation, and in a culture that stresses winning at all costs—is at best dubious.

Giving the right answer to an ethical problem in a classroom, and applying that same answer in the heat of battle, are two very different things. Unless a way can be found to make what are usually near-instantaneous, gut-level decisions in an atmosphere of classroom-like serenity, under the benign guidance of a professor who has your best interests at heart (as distinct from a demanding boss who will not take "no" for an answer), providing employees with formal training in ethics will be an exercise in futility.

Training does not get at the root of the problem, which is not a lack of ethical intent or ethical wisdom, but rather the circumstances in which most critical managerial decisions are made. Thus, a student may in fact be conversant with such advanced ethical concepts as the Categorical Imperative of Immanuel Kant, or the Utilitarianism of Jeremy Bentham, but will either completely forget them at the moment of decision or discard them as irrelevant when that decision must be made under fire. Knowing full well that what you contemplate doing is wrong is not, alas, an effective deterrent when the rewards of wrongdoing are extravagant, the risks of being found out seem remote, and the consequences of not doing what your superiors seem to want can be devastating to your career.

Ineffective methods II: Excluding unethical employees

Another popular but equally ineffective method used by companies that want to avoid potentially dangerous scandals is to try to prevent unscrupulous people from getting into positions in which they could harm the company. Psychologists are brought in to try to weed out executive candidates who seem overly predisposed to cutting corners or bending rules. The psychologists attempt to peer, as it were, into the innermost psyches of candidates for high-level positions, usually by administering various tests, studying their life histories, and/or interviewing people who have known them well at various stages of their lives.

Giving the right answer to an ethical problem in a classroom, and applying that same answer in the heat of battle, are two very different things.

To authorize such screening requires a great deal more faith in the predictive powers of psychological methods than their record would justify. Many executives are aware of that but reason that in the event of another failure they can always say they did all they could to prevent it.

Psychologists operate on the (correct) assumption that some people are more likely than others to simply brush rules aside and let the consequences be damned. If individuals carrying that trait can be screened out before they acquire the power to make fateful decisions, the company will be spared the disastrous consequences of their rashness. (The flip side of that screening is that you also eliminate people of uncommon initiative.) The psychologists survey candidates for jobs in which critical decisions can be made, hoping to ensure that only men and women of probity, wisdom, and self-restraint get to make the really big ones.

The sad truth seems to be that when it pays to do the wrong thing, someone will. Singling out that "someone" in advance is at best impractical and at worst improbable.

In practice, there are two severe problems with this approach, either of which is enough to invalidate it. The first concerns its feasibility: Can executive crooks actually be weeded out before they do irreparable harm? The second concerns the realism of its underlying premise: Is corporate misconduct actually the work of just a few "bad apples"—that is, a handful of incorrigibly unscrupulous executives? When you dig down into the details, the feasibility question turns out to be tougher than it may appear at first. There are not just one but two types of potential offenders whom the psychologists have to detect.

First, there are those for whom self-serving, irresponsible acts are a way of life. Clinically, these people are usually diagnosed as psychopaths. Fortunately for society, they are relatively rare. Fortunately for employers, most of them quickly acquire the kinds of records that human resource departments routinely screen out. But their very scarcity makes hunting for them among the employees of a big company rather like hunting for a few needles in an enormous haystack. There may not be any of them there in the first place; and if there are, their disdain for rules is likely to be blatantly obvious without tests.

The second target for the psychologists are people whose morals are not especially rigid and who might not be above doing the wrong thing if they encountered sufficiently permissive conditions. This group is likely to be quite large. The practical problem they present is that excluding them from positions of power would probably make a majority of employees, virtually all of whom are innocent, the targets of discrimination. Many a capable, promising, and heretofore honorable employee would be ruled ineligible for higher-level posts if the absence of a stern, steely character were considered a disqualification.

Among the remaining few—those whose characters were deemed "impervious" to temptation (the quotation marks are unavoidable)—it might be difficult to find those who were also sufficiently imaginative and decisive to handle executive responsibilities. The practical result is that management has little choice but to take its chances on executive candidates who might, under the wrong circumstances, present risks of wrongdoing.

Then there is the question of whether psychologists can actually make all those distinctions accurately and reliably. The long answer requires at least a semester in a good psychology program, because of the inherent difficulty in trying to demonstrate such things incontrovertibly. The short answer is: Probably not.

The origins of unethical conduct

The sad truth seems to be that when it pays to do the wrong thing, someone will. Singling out that "someone" in advance is, for the reasons just discussed, at best impractical and at worst improbable. Many employees—possibly even most—will resist the temptation, but in a large enough group, someone will give in. And it only takes one aggressive risk-taker, or a few, to ease a company onto the initially lucrative but inevitably slippery slope that leads, all too readily, to its own destruction.

Why do they do it? What motivates people who usually have a lot to lose (in most cases, a career that was off to an excellent start) to risk everything on a fast buck? Every corporate scoundrel probably had his own set of motives. But the one common denominator that influenced all of them is that they did it because they could. The opportunity was there, and they seized it. Had there been no opportunity, they would still be what they were before the fatal temptation presented itself: highly regarded, promising employees with a great future and perfectly clean records.

In other words, whether one's behavior is going to be ethical or unethical is, to a large extent, situational. It is not the result of an inadequate understanding of ethics, or of fault lines within one's character, but of being in the wrong place at the wrong time.

A wise sociologist once observed, "The main reason there aren't more affairs is that there aren't more opportunities." The same can be said of resorting to creative accounting, of bribing employees to put their own interests above those of clients, even of defrauding widows and orphans. Opportunity, not ignorance or inherent evil, is the culprit. If that thought strikes you as too cynical, answer this question for yourself: Suppose you are out of town, alone, in a city where you know no one and no one knows you. You enter a taxi cab, and as it rushes off toward your destination you notice beside you, on the back seat, the wallet of a previous passenger. It is stuffed with hundred-dollar bills. What will you do?

Obviously, there will be some kind of identification in that wallet, so what you should do is contact its owner and arrange to return the wallet and its contents to him. But the question I am asking is not what you should do, but what you *would* do. If you returned the wallet, many would applaud your honesty. Yet many others would call you a fool. (After all, they might note, those would be tax-free dollars.)

The only way to get a definitive answer to the question would be to put you in a taxi in a strange city, with no one but yourself in a position to see what actually happened. Absent that ultimate test, all of us have a right to be at least somewhat skeptical about what each of the rest of us would do. And if that is the case, it should not be surprising if circumstances that management deliberately creates, or knowingly tolerates, can lead people with previously unblemished records to reach for those fast bucks.

Exalted ideas about human nature have no place in a realistic plan to control employee misconduct. To achieve that goal, you have to start with the following assumptions: that everyone (with no exceptions) is at least potentially dishonest; that temptation and opportunity are the two main contributors to potential dishonesty; and that the best way to keep everyone honest is to eliminate, or at least severely restrict, both of them.

Bad apples or bad barrels?

An old saying has it that a few bad apples, if not removed, can spoil all the other apples in the barrel. That is the principle underlying the attempt to screen out unreliable managers before they rise too high in the hierarchy. But the attempt itself is probably futile. To pursue the analogy, the problem is not with the apples (that is, the individual executives themselves) but rather with the barrel (the system of constraints and licenses in which they operate).

John C. Coffee, Jr., a professor at the Columbia Law School, dealt with exactly that problem in analyzing the reasons why auditors at Enron and elsewhere acquiesced in their clients' attempts at "earnings management." During the 1990s, he noted, the costs to auditors of doing that went down, while the benefits went up:

> The costs declined because in several decisions the Supreme Court made it harder to sue accountants, while Congress passed legislation that, among other things, reduced their maximum liability.… In any profession, but especially for custodians of the public trust, advocacy and objectivity cannot be safely combined. (Coffee 2002)

In other words, the government, not just greedy executives, had a hand in this. Constraints designed to dissuade accountants from colluding with clients to misrepresent their earnings, or at least to present them in an extremely optimistic light, had eroded because of decisions taken by both the judicial and legislative branches. Risks that had been thought foolish under prior rules now seemed worth thinking about. Inevitably, someone experimented with tactics that had previously been discouraged, just to see what would happen. And when nothing happened, others followed suit. Soon, methods that might once have been considered unthinkable became, instead, the norm.

The need for structural change

Bigger fines and stricter enforcement of existing rules are not the answer. That is because so many minds are virtually programmed to seek ways around restrictions on personal freedom—especially when it pays to evade them. Ingenuity always wins out over regulation. Instead, the way to keep all those perfectly clean records as clean as ever lies in structural changes that remove either the incentive to misbehave or the opportunity to do so, or (preferably) both. Of course, such changes come with a price tag attached.

The solutions suggested here are hardly panaceas. They cannot make any of these problems disappear altogether, and they certainly are not painless. But the present sorry situation of American business demands challenges to the kinds of established thinking that got us into this mess. Four areas seem especially ripe for structural change: boards of directors, organization structure, executive pay, and the auditor-client relationship.

Boards of directors

In theory, boards are the shareholder's (and the public's) last line of defense against managerial chicanery. In practice, they have been overly acquiescent and (in too many cases) insufficiently inquisitive about what is really going on in the companies they allegedly govern. For both reasons, boards have come under fire from critics who see them as too chummy with, and therefore too easily conned by, management.

Much has been written about the role of inside directors, whose service on the board of a company they also manage would appear to involve an inherent conflict of interest—not unlike that of a fox guarding a hen house. It is true that inside directors bring with them a detailed, expert knowledge of company operations to which outside directors often need access. On the other hand, there is no good reason why outside directors could not question any manager who had information they needed without having to give him a vote on the board's policy decisions.

Inevitably, someone experimented with tactics that had previously been discouraged, just to see what would happen. And when nothing happened, others followed suit. Soon, methods that might once have been considered unthinkable became, instead, the norm.

But another issue regarding board performance, though at least as important as the "inside vs. outside" question, has received less attention: the board's competence to carry out its duties. Some boards appear to have been asleep at the switch while great harm was being done to their companies. Enron's board, for example, got into an unseemly finger-pointing contest with management once the extent of the firm's accounting shenanigans began to emerge.

Do boards consist chiefly of semi-informed, easily satisfied figureheads capable of presiding over a company but not actively steering it? I doubt that. But to the extent that there may be any truth at all in that stereotype, it is probably because directors are simply playing the role they have been given to play. Keeping their hands off, leaving the heavy lifting to management, and being satisfied with only a general overview of how the company is achieving its reported results is what is commonly expected of them. Nevertheless, we must ask whether it is indeed possible for anyone to bear the ultimate responsibility for a company's fortunes with such a loose grip on its reins.

Another issue that has not received enough attention is the fact that board members (with the frequent exception of the chairman) serve on only a part-time basis. Outside directors, of whom so much more is now expected than before, usually have full-time jobs elsewhere and necessarily treat their directorships as secondary responsibilities.

If boards are to do what they are supposed to do—control their firms, rather than merely preside over them—they will have to become the antithesis of what they have been. And if we are to have active, hands-on, fully informed boards of directors, a majority of them will have to serve full-time. They will also have to be given the authority of a military inspector-general: the right to go anywhere, ask any question of anyone, and apply appropriate sanctions to whoever attempts to conceal information from them.

Will management like this? Of course not. Will relationships between such a board and its management become tense and adversarial? Possibly. But are these prices worth paying to put the representatives of the owners actually in charge of their company? That is a question on which reasonable people may differ. For myself, I suggest that fewer scandals, and fewer bear markets prolonged and worsened by shareholder disgust, would make all that discomfort well worth it in the end.

Organization structure

Organizations with built-in conflicts of interest have tried to enjoy the best of both worlds by erecting so-called "Chinese Walls" (prohibited contacts or discussions) in order to separate employees who could collaborate too easily in ways that could compromise the firm's integrity.

The most striking recent example of an unsuccessful attempt to prevent corruption by merely forbidding it was Merrill Lynch.

Investment bankers realized that having securities analysts under the same roof with them could be a huge competitive advantage when seeking corporate underwriting accounts. So the "wall" was breeched by giving analysts a financial stake in obtaining underwriting business, simply by inducing them to add some undeserved luster to their evaluations of the prospective client's company.

Trying to repair the wall by punishing those who have breeched it or by increasing the penalties for those who try it in the future are probably futile, simply because the incentive is still there. The problem at Merrill Lynch was not the villainy of a few investment bankers, or the willing collaboration of a few financial analysts, but rather the common corporate roof over both of them. Their ready access to each other made the deception of the company's brokerage clients possible, and perhaps even inevitable.

The only way to eliminate both the incentive and the opportunity for this kind of gambit is to spin off one of the two units into a separately owned and managed company. Of course, that would also eliminate opportunities for perfectly legitimate synergy.

Like the executive who wanted his competitors to survive (barely), brokerages that are also investment bankers have to walk a fine line between maximizing their profits and risking the loss of their reputation. It would be a hard choice, because in all probability the sum of the profits generated by two totally separated units would be less than those produced by those same units under a single but perpetually endangered corporate ownership.

Executive pay

Some CEOs and other high-level executives have been grossly overpaid, at the ultimate expense of the companies' shareholders. During the stock market boom of the late 1990s, this attracted little comment because everyone else was prospering too. But when stock prices fell early in the new century, questions arose about whether the earnings of the 1990s that had pumped up those prices were real—and complacency over executive pay quickly changed to outrage.

How much are top executives worth? In the real world, they are worth whatever a board of directors, conscious of its fiduciary responsibility to shareholders, sees fit to pay them. The real issue is not the pay package itself but the basis on which it is calculated, usually a fiscal year. But as we have learned to our sorrow, earnings often have to be recalculated long after they were first officially announced, and fiscal "skeletons" sometimes don't emerge from wherever they were buried until years afterward.

In other words, the problem is not so much in the size of the pay package as in the payment schedule. The only way for the directors of a big company to be reasonably certain that the performance on which an executive's pay is based has been accurately measured is to let enough time pass between its initial calculation and the actual transfer of funds. That means sequestering the incentive component of an executive's pay for several years, and then paying it out gradually over a period of several more years. Boards might even consider attaching strings to those payouts, in the form of mandatory reimbursement, in the event subsequent discoveries make those initial reports questionable. Until those initially reported earnings are no longer uncertain, these executives can live on their salaries (an arrangement that most non-executives would consider neither cruel nor unusual).

Will CEOs and other beneficiaries of lucrative pay packages like this? Of course not. But it will give them an incentive to see to it that there are no hidden accounting tricks, errors, or omissions in the reports they pass on to their boards. And if a board has to stiffen its spine to face down a CEO who finds these restrictions too onerous, that is exactly what their shareholders have a right to expect of them.

Auditors and the audited

The incentive for external auditors to collaborate with a client's attempts to present its financial reports in the most favorable light is to keep the client's auditing business. In the past, there was often an even bigger incentive: to keep the client's consulting business. But even if—as now seems likely—auditing firms have to get out of the consulting business, the temptation for auditors to please the people they are paid to police will still be there. The problem is not that corporate accountants (or their boss, the chief financial officer) are inherently dishonest. Instead, the problem lies in the structure of their relationship with their auditors. The auditors are hirelings whom the company can dispense with as it pleases and simply replace with other auditors. The effect is that the company is expected to police itself, which places both the temptation and the opportunity to coerce the auditors squarely in the hands of the client's financial staff. It should not be surprising that some people on that staff, realizing how much power they have, decide to exercise it.

The solution is term limits for auditors. They should contract with their clients to prowl through their books for a fixed number of years, with no options for renewal. Since there is no point in trying to hold on to a client you are going to lose anyway, auditors would have no incentive to bend over backwards to please the client. They could then return to the at least quasi-adversarial relationship that their respective roles require of them.

All of the changes prescribed here are strong medicine. They won't taste good, and they probably won't go down easily. But boards and management must recognize that the likely alternative is yet another round of scandals, possibly even worse than this one, perhaps a dozen or so years down the road. Sooner or later, the public and its elected representatives will declare that enough is enough and force changes like these (or even tougher ones) down the throats of both guilty and innocent companies. It would be much better for all concerned if companies undertook the necessary reforms by themselves, now, without waiting for that.

References and selected bibliography

Coffee, John C., Jr. 2002. Guarding the gatekeepers. *New York Times* (13 May): A17.

Ensuring Ethical Effectiveness

New rules mean virtually every company will need a code of ethics.

BY RANDY MYERS

Stung by the high-profile accounting scandals that drove some the nation's leading companies into bankruptcy court, Congress and other regulatory authorities have taken up their pens in an attempt to legislate business behavior. The Sarbanes-Oxley Act, which President Bush signed into law in July of 2002, requires publicly traded companies to disclose whether they have adopted a code of ethics for their senior financial officers, and if not, why. They also must report promptly any amendments to or waivers from the code.

The New York Stock Exchange, meanwhile, proposed new corporate governance standards which—if the SEC approves them—would require companies traded on that exchange to adopt corporate governance guidelines and a code of business conduct and ethics for *all* employees. CPAs can help employers or clients navigate these new rules and create a code of ethics that complies with all of the requirements.

NUTS AND BOLTS

For companies that choose to adopt a set of ethics guidelines in response to Sarbanes-Oxley—and few will run the risk of not doing so given the negative message it would send to investors, regulators and potential litigants—section 406 of the act says the code should seek to ensure that senior financial executives

- Conduct themselves honestly and ethically, particularly in handling actual or apparent conflicts of interest.
- Provide full, fair, accurate, timely and understandable disclosure in the periodic reports their employers file with the SEC.
- Comply with all applicable government laws, rules and regulations.

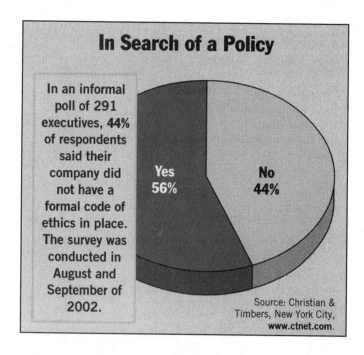

In Search of a Policy

In an informal poll of 291 executives, 44% of respondents said their company did not have a formal code of ethics in place. The survey was conducted in August and September of 2002.

Yes 56%

No 44%

Source: Christian & Timbers, New York City, www.ctnet.com.

Even for CPAs who don't toil as principal financial officers, comptrollers or principal accounting officers—job titles Sarbanes-Oxley specifically targets—the new law introduces a raft of issues. As interpreted by the SEC in the proposed rulemaking notice it issued on October 16, 2002, Sarbanes-Oxley does more than suggest companies have a code of ethics for senior financial executives.

Once SEC rules are finalized, section 404 of the act will require publicly traded companies to file in their annual reports an "internal control report" that outlines what steps management has taken to establish and maintain adequate internal controls and financial reporting procedures, as well as management's conclusions about the effectiveness of those controls and procedures—a report CPAs and corporate finance departments likely will have a hand in drafting. The report must say the company's public accountant has attested to, and reported on, management's evaluation of the company's internal controls and financial reporting procedures. The company must include a copy of the auditor's attestation in its annual report.

> **The Sarbanes-Oxley Act now requires publicly traded companies to disclose whether they have adopted a code of ethics for senior financial officers. The New York Stock Exchange is considering new rules that would require listed companies to have a code of business conduct that applies to all employees.**

What's not clear, says CPA Sherrie McAvoy, national director of corporate compliance and ethics services for Deloitte & Touche in Dallas, is whether an external auditor would be required to formally audit a client's compliance with its own code of ethics. While her initial suspicion is it would not, she says it won't be clear until the SEC issues final regulations. An SEC spokesman notes that Sarbanes-Oxley gave the agency 180 days from the date of the law's enactment, or roughly until the end of January 2003, to issue final rules.

CPA Richard Steinberg, head of the corporate governance practice for PricewaterhouseCoopers in Florham Park, New Jersey, takes a similar view. "As they look at internal controls, the external auditors are going to focus on this (the code of ethics)," he says. "Not that they're going to audit it, but they'll consider it as they assess the company's control environment."

INCREMENTAL CHANGE

Those counting on ethics codes to change corporate behavior may be surprised to learn that most public companies—at least those in the *Fortune* 1000—already have them. When the U.S. Federal Sentencing Guidelines became law in 1991, they listed seven elements of an effective corporate compliance program judges could take into consideration when sentencing corporations for federal offenses. Most large public companies quickly realized the value of incorporating these elements into their operations, if only as risk-management tools. Among them was establishing compliance standards and procedures—otherwise known as a code of conduct or ethics.

Today, says McAvoy, surveys her firm conducted show approximately 95% of *Fortune* 1000 companies have a code of conduct. Stuart C. Gilman, president of the nonprofit Ethics Resource Center in Washington, D.C., says many private companies have such guidelines as well; he estimates that altogether

there are more than 3,000 ethics officers working in the United States.

What's different now that Sarbanes-Oxley is on the books? According to McAvoy, the new law puts more emphasis on financial reporting, particularly its accuracy. This could translate into more responsibility for CPAs. Section 301 also mandates that companies put in place a mechanism for employees to raise concerns about financial reporting matters—confidentially and anonymously. The SEC's proposed rules for implementing section 406 go on to say the code of ethics should identify the person or persons to whom employees should deliver those anonymous reports.

Establishing a process for rank-and-file employees to confidentially report code violations is a critical component of any ethics program, according to McAvoy. Most of the companies that already have established such procedures assign a case number to each complaint or tip an employee makes so he or she can track its progress. In addition, the person to whom employees report alleged violations is generally someone outside the ordinary chain of corporate command—an ethics or compliance officer, for example, or an ombudsman—who nonetheless has access to the company's top executives and its board of directors.

> **CPA Sherrie McAvoy says that while most companies already have ethics codes, Sarbanes-Oxley puts more emphasis on the financial reporting aspects**

The WorldCom case amply illustrated the perils of having employees report complaints to a senior executive with routine corporate responsibilities. Internal auditors who uncovered the company's accounting fraud reported it to the company's then CFO Scott Sullivan. The federal government now alleges Sullivan instigated the fraud and attempted to block the internal investigation. According to an in-depth report *The Wall Street Journal* published in October of 2002, WorldCom didn't finally acknowledge, make public and address the fraud until its vice-president of internal audit, Cynthia Cooper, took damaging evidence to the company's audit committee.

Many CPAs will have a role in helping companies comply with Sarbanes-Oxley. Certainly, those in corporate finance departments can be expected to be involved in drafting or reviewing those portions of their company's code dealing with financial matters, says Nancy Wilgenbusch, president of Marylhurst University in Portland, Oregon, and a member of the AICPA ethics committee. The portions of the code CPAs might handle would range from insider trading to appropriate and accurate expense reporting, acting as good stewards of company assets, avoiding conflicts of interest and assuring accurate corporate communications with the public. To the extent the code of ethics includes quantifiable measures of accountability concerning items such as insider trading or entertainment expense reporting, for example, Wilgenbusch says CPAs are ideally suited, by virtue of their training and professional expertise, to evaluate or test the results.

EXECUTIVE SUMMARY

- **THE SARBANES-OXLEY ACT NOW REQUIRES PUBLICLY** traded companies to disclose whether they have adopted a code of ethics for senior financial officers. In addition, the New York Stock Exchange is considering new rules that would require listed companies to have a code of business conduct that applies to all employees.

- **UNDER THE ACT THE SEC REQUIRES COMPANIES** to file an internal control report with their annual report outlining management's responsibilities for establishing and maintaining adequate internal controls as well as its conclusions about the effectiveness of those controls. The company's auditor must attest to management's evaluation.

- **MANY COMPANIES ALREADY HAVE ETHICS CODES.** With the emphasis in Sarbanes-Oxley on financial reporting, CPAs may want to help employers and clients review these codes to make sure they comply with the new regulations. Companies will need to establish a process for rank-and-file employees to report code violations confidentially to someone outside the ordinary corporate chain of command.

- **THE BEST WAY TO DRAFT A CODE OF ETHICS** all employees will follow is to bring together a multidisciplinary team from all parts of the organization. Employees must then be trained in what the code means using real-life dilemmas they might encounter on the job. Regular refresher courses are important because ethics training is perishable—people forget.

- **COMPANIES WITH AN EXISTING ETHICS CODE UNLIKELY** will need a new one. Still, businesses may want to revisit the code to make sure they have a full-blown compliance program in place. Even though the act focuses on the CFO, the SEC expects the entire organization to comply with the law.

External auditors would also appear to have a role in assessing compliance with codes of ethics, if only in the context of a code's being part of a company's internal control process. Gilman encourages outside auditors to go a step further: For each client, the auditor should sign a statement noting that it understands and accepts the client's code of ethics. "This allows the outside auditing firm to comport with the company's internal environment," Gilman says. "It permits a level of independence and says, 'We're willing to obey and abide by the same set of standards the organization holds itself to.'"

DOING IT RIGHT

A number of companies—including Raytheon and Texas Instruments—have been widely recognized for the scope and quality of their ethics programs. Raytheon makes ethics training a requirement for every employee, all the way up to the CEO. Texas Instruments' employee ethics handbook dates to 1961 and the company has received three ethics awards for its leadership in the field. Texas Instruments also provides employees with a business-card-sized pamphlet that serves as a "quick test" for workers faced with an ethical dilemma.

- Is the action legal?

- Does it comply with our values?
- If you do it, will you feel bad?
- How will it look in the newspaper?
- If you know its wrong, don't do it.
- If you're not sure, ask.
- Keep asking until you get an answer.

Companies should put together a multidisciplinary team from all parts of the organization to draft a code and communicate it to employees.

While it's difficult to calculate a hard return on investment for drafting and implementing a code, Bruce Pfau, national practice leader for organization measurements at Watson Wyatt Worldwide has tried. A survey his consulting company conducted in 2000 found workers who believed their company operated with honesty and integrity showed higher levels of commitment to their employer in terms of job satisfaction and company pride than those who judged their employer to have low ethical values. Pfau also found companies highly rated by their employees for honesty and integrity produced, over the previous three years, a higher return to shareholders (112%) than poorly rated companies (76%).

PUTTING TOGETHER A CODE

With virtually all companies needing a code of ethics so they can avoid having to report they don't have one under Sarbanes-Oxley, the task of developing one from scratch need not be too involved. The Financial Executives Institute has drafted a one-page model code of ethics for senior financial executives it says conforms to the new law; it can be found on the organization's Web site at **www.fei.org**. Another code developed by Parson Consulting, a national consulting company specializing in finance, accounting and business systems is available at **www.parsongroup.com/sarbanes-market_position.asp**.

But most experts say it would be far better to create a code of ethics for the entire company, one that applies to all employees and builds on their input. Under the proposed changes to the NYSE listing requirements, such a policy would be required of all companies trading on the Big Board.

AICPA ethics committee member Nancy Wilgenbusch says CPAs will help draft ethics code provisions dealing with financial matters.

The challenge companies face—whether creating an entirely new code or reassessing and upgrading an existing one to reflect Sarbanes-Oxley—is to draft a document that isn't just decoration on the company bulletin board but instead helps employees live up to the ethical standards investors, legislators and regulators demand. "We're terrified here of what we call the three Ps—the print, post and pray syndrome," says Gilman. "You print a code of conduct, post it on the wall and pray people actually read it."

According to Gilman and other ethics professionals, the correct approach is to bring together a multidisciplinary team from all parts of the organization—finance, sales, human resources, operations, marketing, executive—to draft a code, communicate its importance to employees and then involve them in seminars to help understand how the code applies to them and their colleagues. Finally, says Minneapolis-based ethics trainer Nan DeMars, author of *You Want Me To Do What?* (Fireside, 1998), senior management must follow through and hold people accountable for complying with the code.

One way to make a code of ethics come alive for employees, DeMars says, is for human resources to plan training sessions that engage them in discussions about real-life or theoretical ethical dilemmas they might expect to handle on the job. The more specific the situations are to the particular company, the more valuable they will be. DeMars gives these examples of the types of questions she might pose in a seminar: "You are the assistant to David Duncan, lead auditor for Arthur Andersen. You know the firm is about to be subpoenaed. He asks you to shred documents. What would you do? Or, you are Sharon Watkin's assistant at Enron and you type her memo to Ken Lay warning him of the possibility Enron will implode if its current accounting practices continue. Now that you know the company is in trouble and your boss is aware of this, what do you do?"

"You've got to take the words as well as the legal requirements and translate them into understandable practices," agrees John J. Castellani, president of The Business Roundtable, an association of CEOs of leading corporations. "Ultimately, doing so gives you a very strong tool. When employees violate the policy, they are dismissed."

DeMars and others agree ethics programs don't achieve much when they are handed down by senior management with little input from other employees or when senior managers themselves fail to abide by the code or neglect to stress its importance. Enron had a rigorous code of ethics, for example, yet it fell victim to unethical behavior in part because its board of directors twice voted to suspend the code to allow the company's former CFO, Andrew Fastow, to launch business activities that created, for him, a conflict of interest. Ethics professionals warn against viewing educational programs as a once-and-done procedure. "Ethics training is perishable," Gilman says. "People forget." To deal with this problem, companies should schedule regular refresher courses for all employees.

FINDING HELP

While companies must enlist the cooperation of their own staff members to draft a code of ethics that will resonate with them, there's plenty of outside help available, too. Among the Big Four accounting firms, both Deloitte & Touche and PricewaterhouseCoopers offer ethics consulting services, says Gilman. So do some law firms and a number of nonprofit organizations and academic centers. Among the latter are Gilman's own Ethics

---

Resources

The following organizations can help accountants who are charged with developing, implementing or monitoring a corporation's code of ethics.

Ethics Officers Association
30 Church Street
Suite 331
Belmont, Massachusetts 02478
617-484-9400
www.eoa.org

Ethics Resource Center
1747 Pennsylvania Avenue, NW
Suite 400
Washington, D.C. 20006
202-737-2258
www.ethics.org

Institute for Global Ethics
P.O. Box 563
Camden, Maine 04843
207-236-6658
www.globalethics.com

Markkula Center for Applied Ethics
Santa Clara University
500 El Camino Real
Santa Clara, California 95053-0633
408-554-5319
www.scu.edu/ethics

Practicing Law Institute
810 Seventh Avenue
New York, New York 10019-5818
800-260-4PLI or 212-824-5710
www.pli.edu

Resource Center as well as the Ethics Officers Association in Belmont, Massachusetts; the Institute for Global Ethics in Camden, Maine; and the Markkula Center for Applied Ethics at Santa Clara University in California. (See box for information on how to contact these and other resources.)

While Sarbanes-Oxley specifically covers the CFO, the SEC has made it clear it's going to expect the entire organization to comply.

Elsewhere, the nonprofit Practicing Law Institute in New York City offers programs on ethics and corporate compliance several times a year, says McAvoy, and has published a series of books on the topic. All that said, Gilman cautions companies against off-loading too much responsibility to outside consultants. "Ethics are one of those things where you don't want someone doing an assessment and charging you a lot of money to tell you what you want to hear," he explains. The best ethics code is one drafted in-house.

Many companies that already have a code of ethics are unlikely to need a new one to respond to Sarbanes-Oxley, says attorney Tom Patton, a partner with Tighe Patton Armstrong Teasdale PLLC in Washington, D.C. This is especially true since the new law doesn't require a company to publish its set of guidelines but merely to confirm it has one. "The statute defines a code of ethics in very broad terms, so you have to make sure your existing code meets all of them; assuming it does, you probably don't need to develop a new one," he says.

Stephen Hill Jr., a partner with the Kansas City, Missouri, law firm Blackwell Sanders Peper Martin LLP, concurs but adds companies may still want to review their code point by point to make sure it covers all of the provisions in the new law and that they have a "full-blown compliance program in place." The proposed SEC regulations under Sarbanes-Oxley make it clear the code should promote "compliance with applicable government laws, rules and regulations."

At many companies, such reviews are already under way. "A number of companies are taking a hard look at their codes and making sure they're current and sharing them with their boards of directors," says Deloitte & Touche's McAvoy. "They're also taking a look at the financial reporting aspects and making sure they are as robust as they can be." Meanwhile, the Ethics Officers Association reports that about 100 companies have hired ethics officers through October of 2002 alone.

Hill says his firm is telling clients their entire organization, not just the CFO, must be prepared to deal with compliance issues. "Sarbanes-Oxley covers the CFO, but in its October 16 statement, the SEC makes it clear it's going to expect the entire organization to comply with the law," Hill says. By way of example, the proposed SEC regulations mandate that a company's code of ethics apply not only to senior financial executives but also to the "principal executive officer," even though that position was not specified in the act.

> ### Attorney Stephen Hill says most companies won't need new ethics codes but should review existing ones to make sure they cover all the new provisions.

According to the London-based Institute of Business Ethics (IBE) (**www.ibe.org.uk**) a code of ethics should include a preface, signed by the chairman or CEO, explaining what values are important to top management in conducting the business. It should then cover these key areas:

- The purpose of the business and its values.
- Employee relations including working conditions, recruiting, training, discrimination policies and use of company assets by employees.
- Customer relations guidelines.
- The importance of protecting the investment made by shareholders or other investors.
- Relationships with suppliers.
- How the company relates to society as well as to the wider business community.
- How the company will implement the code, including training.

The IBE also advises any company drafting a code to find a champion—hopefully the CEO—who is prepared to drive the introduction of a business ethics policy. Without this support, there is little chance the company will find the code a useful tool. The board of directors should also endorse the ethics policy.

WILL IT WORK?

Whether any of this will prevent unethical behavior is uncertain, although most experts say codes can make a difference when companies develop and implement them properly. "There's nothing we can do to prevent a crook from stealing if he or she wants to," says ethics committee member Wilgenbusch. "If people are greedy, a code won't prevent them from behaving unethically. But if the CEO gets the company's top 20 people in a room and says, 'We're going to adhere to both the spirit and letter of the law; we're going to play by the rules in every sense of the word and anybody who steps across that line of ethical behavior not only will be discharged immediately but prosecuted to the full extent of the law,' then you are going to avoid unethical behavior." That's a goal every accountant can endorse.

RANDY MYERS is a freelance financial writer who lives in Dover, Pennsylvania. His e-mail address is randy@randymyers.net.

From *Journal of Accountancy*, February 2003, pp. 28-33. © 2003 by the American Institute of Certified Public Accountants, Inc. Opinions of the authors are their own and do not necessarily reflect policies of the AICPA. Reprinted by permission.

Index

Index

Test Your Knowledge Form

We encourage you to photocopy and use this page as a tool to assess how the articles in *Annual Editions* expand on the information in your textbook. By reflecting on the articles you will gain enhanced text information. You can also access this useful form on a product's book support Web site at *http://www.dushkin.com/online/*.

NAME: DATE:

TITLE AND NUMBER OF ARTICLE:

BRIEFLY STATE THE MAIN IDEA OF THIS ARTICLE:

LIST THREE IMPORTANT FACTS THAT THE AUTHOR USES TO SUPPORT THE MAIN IDEA:

WHAT INFORMATION OR IDEAS DISCUSSED IN THIS ARTICLE ARE ALSO DISCUSSED IN YOUR TEXTBOOK OR OTHER READINGS THAT YOU HAVE DONE? LIST THE TEXTBOOK CHAPTERS AND PAGE NUMBERS:

LIST ANY EXAMPLES OF BIAS OR FAULTY REASONING THAT YOU FOUND IN THE ARTICLE:

LIST ANY NEW TERMS/CONCEPTS THAT WERE DISCUSSED IN THE ARTICLE, AND WRITE A SHORT DEFINITION:

We Want Your Advice

ANNUAL EDITIONS revisions depend on two major opinion sources: one is our Advisory Board, listed in the front of this volume, which works with us in scanning the thousands of articles published in the public press each year; the other is you—the person actually using the book. Please help us and the users of the next edition by completing the prepaid article rating form on this page and returning it to us. Thank you for your help!

ANNUAL EDITIONS: Business Ethics 05/06

ARTICLE RATING FORM

Here is an opportunity for you to have direct input into the next revision of this volume.
We would like you to rate each of the articles listed below, using the following scale:

1. **Excellent: should definitely be retained**
2. **Above average: should probably be retained**
3. **Below average: should probably be deleted**
4. **Poor: should definitely be deleted**

Your ratings will play a vital part in the next revision.
Please mail this prepaid form to us as soon as possible.
Thanks for your help!

RATING	ARTICLE	RATING	ARTICLE
	1. Thinking Ethically: A Framework for Moral Decision Making		36. Surviving in the Age of Rage
	2. Ethics: Time to Revisit the Basics		37. Managing for Organizational Integrity
	3. Ethics Can Be Gauged By Three Key Rules		38. Transparent Reporting?
	4. Why Good Leaders Do Bad Things		39. Using Conversation to Change the World
	5. Best Resources for Corporate Social Responsibility		40. Business Ethics in the Current Environment of Fraud and Corruption
	6. You've Got Mail…And The Boss Knows		41. Ethics for a Post-Enron America
	7. Up Against Wal-Mart		42. SOX Alone Won't Stop Fraud
	8. The Hidden Costs of Organizational Dishonesty		43. Are You Serious About Ethics?
	9. Corruption: Causes and Cures		44. "See No Evil, Hear No Evil, Speak No Evil"—Leaders Must Respond to Employee Concerns About Wrongdoing
	10. Crony Capitalism		45. Why Corporations Can't Control Chicanery
	11. Sexual Harassment and Retaliation: A Double-Edged Sword		46. Ensuring Ethical Effectiveness
	12. Harassment Grows More Complex		
	13. Attitudes Toward Affirmative Action		
	14. Where Are the Women?		
	15. "Rife with Discrimination"		
	16. Into Thin Air		
	17. A Hero—and a Smoking-Gun Letter		
	18. Hall Monitors in the Workplace: Encouraging Employee Whistleblowers		
	19. Academic Values and the Lure of Profit		
	20. Between Right and Right		
	21. The Padding That Hurts		
	22. Costco's Dilemma: Be Kind to Its Workers, or Wall Street?		
	23. The Parable of the Sadhu		
	24. Ethical Compass		
	25. Does It Pay To Be Good?		
	26. Trust in the Marketplace		
	27. Glass Breakers		
	28. Change of Heart		
	29. Privacy in the Age of Transparency		
	30. A Dose of Denial		
	31. Values in Tension: Ethics Away From Home		
	32. Mideast Businesswomen Fight for Respect		
	33. The Perils of Doing the Right Thing		
	34. A Matter of Trust		
	35. Diversity Training Ups Saks' Sales		

(Continued on next page)

BUSINESS REPLY MAIL
FIRST CLASS MAIL PERMIT NO. 551 DUBUQUE IA

POSTAGE WILL BE PAID BY ADDRESEE

McGraw-Hill/Dushkin
2460 KERPER BLVD
DUBUQUE, IA 52001-9902

NO POSTAGE
NECESSARY
IF MAILED
IN THE
UNITED STATES

ABOUT YOU

Name

Date

Are you a teacher? ❏   A student? ❏

Your school's name

Department

Address   City   State   Zip

School telephone #

YOUR COMMENTS ARE IMPORTANT TO US!

Please fill in the following information:
For which course did you use this book?

Did you use a text with this ANNUAL EDITION? ❏ yes ❏ no
What was the title of the text?

What are your general reactions to the *Annual Editions* concept?

Have you read any pertinent articles recently that you think should be included in the next edition? Explain.

Are there any articles that you feel should be replaced in the next edition? Why?

Are there any World Wide Web sites that you feel should be included in the next edition? Please annotate.

May we contact you for editorial input? ❏ yes ❏ no
May we quote your comments? ❏ yes ❏ no